SALT LAKE
PARK CIT
THE WASATCH
RANGE

MAYA SILVER

Contents

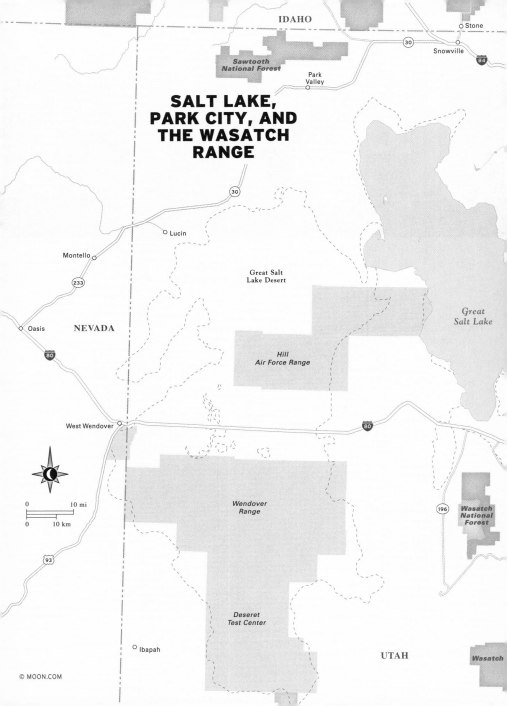

SALT LAKE, PARK CITY, AND THE WASATCH RANGE

IDAHO

Stone

Snowville

Sawtooth National Forest

Park Valley

Lucin

Montello

Great Salt Lake Desert

Great Salt Lake

NEVADA

Oasis

Hill Air Force Range

West Wendover

Wendover Range

Wasatch National Forest

0   10 mi
0   10 km

Deseret Test Center

Ibapah

UTAH

Wasatch

© MOON.COM

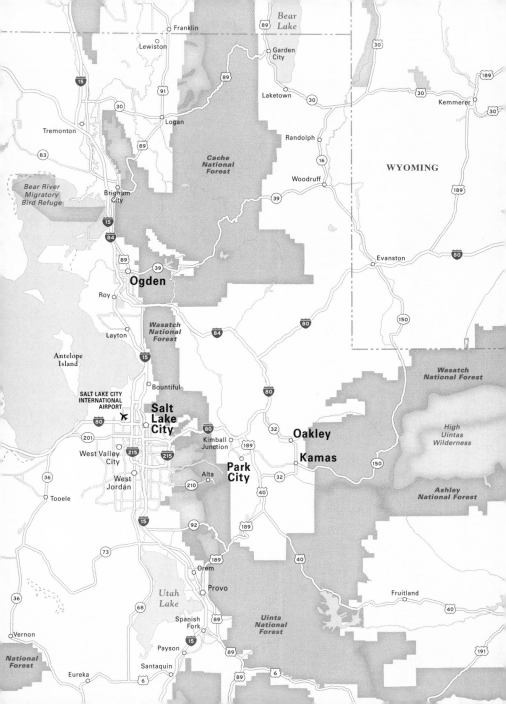

Salt Lake, Park City & the Wasatch Range

I n 1861, Mark Twain took a trip you might be about to embark on yourself. By stagecoach, he rode into Salt Lake City through the mountains where he saw "the most stupendous panorama of mountain peaks." With equal parts curiosity and fascination, he encountered Mormonism, speculating about polygamy and chatting up Governor Brigham Young. On horseback, he rode 17 miles from the city to "the American 'Dead Sea'"—the Great Salt Lake. After his sojourn in Utah, Twain summed up Salt Lake City and its mysterious Mormon ways as "a fairy-land" and the mountains ringing it, a "sublime spectacle."

Well over a century later, a similar trip awaits today's visitor to the Wasatch. The capital is still the best place in the world to learn about Mormonism, though religion is no longer the sole heartbeat of the city. Balanced by a strong LGBTQ+ community, growing ethnic populations, and defiant counterculture, Salt Lake City offers a lot more than the Mormon experience to the traveler, from funky boutiques to funky beers. And if you're curious about Mormonism as Twain was, or want to get in touch with your own religious roots, Temple Square and other historic sites offer a glimpse into the Church of Jesus Christ of Latter-day Saints.

Clockwise from top left: a mountain biker on the Glenwild trail system; frozen waterfalls en route to the summit of Mount Timpanogos; Seagull Monument on Temple Square; the Capitol Theatre in Salt Lake City; Silver Lake Trail at Deer Valley; Utah State Capitol building.

Culture aside, Salt Lake City is also base camp for a more modern stripe of adventure. Journeys to the capital's nearby natural wonders and adventures go a lot faster by car than horseback, so you can easily visit the Great Salt Lake on a half-day or day trip. Another popular excursion from the city is a venture into Big or Little Cottonwood Canyon, our capital's unofficial backyard.

Rising up around the city is the Wasatch Range of the Rocky Mountains. Salt Lake and the Ogden area fall into the Wasatch Front, on the western side of the mountains. On the eastern side of the range lies the Wasatch Back—Park City, Sundance, and a slew of small towns that make for quieter getaways.

From one of those towns—Kamas—the Uinta Mountains soar higher than any in the state, topping out well over 13,000 feet (3,962 m), and uniquely running east-west. Both the Wasatch and Uinta Mountains can be explored via the hundreds of miles of trails, or, come winter, by skiing at one of the Wasatch's 10 resorts, which are buried in upward of 500 inches (12.7 m) of legendary powder every winter.

Whether you bike, hike, ski, climb, or ride across these mountains, the sublime landscape of the Wasatch remains a wilderness that beckons the wild inside us all.

Clockwise from top left: panoramic view of Salt Lake City in evening; Lake Blanche; the Salt Lake Temple; the Egyptian Theatre in Park City.

8 TOP EXPERIENCES

1 Ski or ride legendary powder at one of **10 ski resorts** in the Wasatch (page 32).

2 Step into the shoes of an Olympian on the bobsled track at the **Utah Olympic Park** (page 112).

3 Hear the famed **Tabernacle Choir** sing in **Temple Square** (page 49).

4 Traverse a moon-like landscape and compose mind-bending photographs at the **Bonneville Salt Flats** (page 223).

>>>

5 Discover **Spiral Jetty,** the world's most famous land art, in the Great Salt Lake (page 211).

>>>

^^^
^^

6 Watch film premieres and catch sight of celebrities at the **Sundance Film Festival,** the country's largest independent film fest (pages 26, 75, and 134).

7 Get a taste of **local spirits and craft brews** (pages 70 and 196). You can even ride Town Lift from Park City Mountain to **High West Distillery & Saloon** for sips of award-winning bourbon (page 140).

>>>

The High West Mission

To make delicious whiskey, to share our love of whiskey with our customers, and to celebrate our home, the West

We sum up our mission into one phrase... "Because Whiskey Matters"

8 Summit **Mount Timpanogos** for sweeping views of the state (page 255).

Planning Your Trip

Where to Go

Salt Lake City

Some come just to tour, explore, and shop **Utah's capital.** For those who view Salt Lake City as merely base camp for adventure, it's still worth allocating at least half a day to check out the main attractions. **Family-friendly** activities also abound. The metropolitan Salt Lake City area spans many **distinct neighborhoods,** including the downtown, university campus, 9th and 9th, Sugar House, the Avenues, and Capitol Hill.

Park City

Like any place on the National Historic Register, **Park City** is a transportive experience. While the businesses lining **Main Street** are in fine shape, they are by and large **original structures,** rebuilt after the 1898 fire burned down much of **Old Town.** Most visit Park City with an objective in mind—such as **skiing, biking,** or attending the **Sundance Film Festival**—but nearly all take time to wander Main Street, window shopping and eventually grabbing, say, a bison burger at No Name Saloon & Grill.

Big and Little Cottonwood Canyons

Salt Lake City has two backyards: **Big Cottonwood Canyon** and **Little Cottonwood Canyon.** Up both lie **camping, hiking, climbing,** and, of course, **skiing.** There's **Alta** and **Snowbird,** which are connected, allowing you to ski both in one day. Head to **Solitude** if you're seeking what its name suggests. And **Brighton** is considered by more than a few a

the top of the Living Room Trail overlooking Salt Lake City

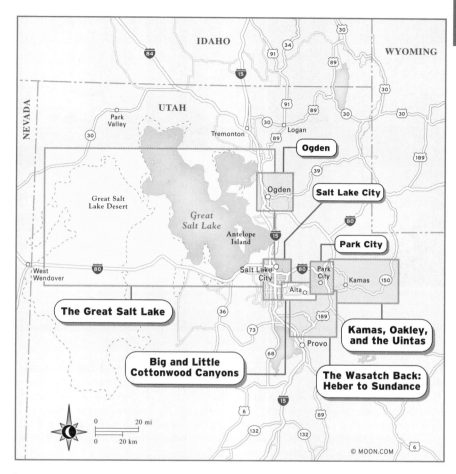

best-kept secret. Travel time from Salt Lake City can take anywhere from 30 minutes to several hours depending on your destination and weekend ski traffic.

Ogden

Once the bad boy of Utah, Ogden was home to brothels, moonshiners, and outlaws. Today, it's cleaned up its act, but is still a blast to visit. Ogden is also just a 30-minute drive to **skiing** at **Snowbasin, Powder Mountain,** or **Nordic Valley Ski Resort.** Along with nearby **Eden,** Ogden also has a handful of **distilleries** and **breweries** worth the trip here in their own right.

The Great Salt Lake

Utahns love to hate the **Great Salt Lake.** The place *is* a little weird. Optical illusions at the sprawling white **Bonneville Salt Flats.** The bird-lined land bridge to **Antelope Island.** And the brooding **Spiral Jetty** land art. Fair warning: There's also occasionally a rotten egg smell produced by algae blooms, and hatches of minuscule sand fleas (don't worry, they don't bite). But this

the Great Salt Lake

otherworldly landscape is definitely worth exploring.

The Wasatch Back: Heber to Sundance

Opposite Salt Lake City on the back side of the Wasatch Mountain Range lies Park City. But that's not the end of the story. On the backside are a string of **charming towns,** including family-friendly **Heber** and "Little Switzerland" (aka **Midway**), as well as **Sundance Mountain Resort.** The latter is a mandatory overnight stop for couples looking to escape it all, and also a great day trip for **scenic lift rides, hiking,** and tasty milkshakes. Just south of Sundance lies **Mount Timpanogos,** the most legendary peak in the Wasatch Range.

Kamas, Oakley, and the Uintas

The Uintas are the only range in the United States that runs east-west, rather than north-south. But the real reasons you should visit are the mind-blowing **panoramas** and bottomless **wilderness.** It would take a lifetime to really get to know the Uintas, but give it all the time you can spare for a **day hike** or **camping** experience under epic night skies. **Kamas** and **Oakley,** the unofficial **gateways** to the Uintas, offer fun post-hike refueling options.

When to Go

Deciding when to visit the Wasatch all depends on what you hope to do. If you want to **ski,** the time to go is obviously **winter.** But to beat the crowds and find great deals, skiing in **late fall** or **early spring** is another great option. Resorts tend to open around Thanksgiving, and while some close mid-April, others keep the lifts spinning until the snowpack will no longer suffice—through May some years, to the Fourth of July on others. Snowbird has the reputation for staying open the longest of any ski resort in the Wasatch.

You may also want to come in the **winter** just to behold the snow-covered mountains, not to mention that Danish feeling of *hygge* that comes with winter in the Wasatch—wood-burning fires, sleigh rides, and mugs of something strong. And it's not all about downhill skiing—**Nordic trails,** winter hiking with **snowshoes,** and **ice climbing** are just a few examples of other ways to explore outdoors in the cold. The one other consideration for a winter visit is whether you want to vie with **crowds.** Over Christmas, during the Sundance Film Festival (late Jan.-early Feb.), and on busy holiday weekends like Presidents' Day, lodging books up early and slopes can get dangerously crowded.

Summer is actually the **most popular time** to visit the Wasatch, providing ease of travel and **countless outdoor activities** (including mountain biking, golfing, hiking, and water sports, to name just a few) that are more accessible and less expensive than winter sports tend to be. Summer is also the season of **festivals,** and you'll often find parts of downtown Salt Lake and Park City's Main Street closed for events.

Fall is my favorite time in the Wasatch because it's a little **quieter** throughout the region and the cold air decks our hills in psychedelic shades of orange, red, and yellow. And while the days are shorter, we lose the oppressive midday heat that can be hard to stomach in the peak of summer. Generally, most of the summer activities continue on through autumn with **less crowded trails.** Our fall is short, however, with **foliage** usually peaking in September, and snow beginning to fall that same month or soon after.

Spring is perhaps the **riskiest time** to visit the Wasatch, because you never know what you're going to get. It's often a wet time of year, not a warm time of year, with snow pressing on through May or into June, and cold rain muddying up the trails everyone is so eager to get back on. That said, you'll find **great lodging and dining deals** during this time—just don't count on the ability to adventure outside.

Explore Salt Lake

Express Itinerary:
Salt Lake City and Park City

Taking a long weekend to discover the Wasatch? Check out the urban and alpine highlights alike on an express trip through the capital and the state's favorite ski town.

Day 1
Arrive in **Salt Lake City** early and plan a visit to **Temple Square** around one of the free daily performances of the **Tabernacle Choir.** Pick and choose how many museums, visitors centers (there are two), and other attractions you take in at **Temple Square,** depending on your appetite for Mormon history. For the full experience, get lunch at **The Lion House Pantry.** Go shopping and strolling around the **9th and 9th**

neighborhood, where you can look for souvenirs at **Cahoots** and get dinner at **Pago.** Head to one of the city's many **craft breweries** for a drink before calling it a night.

Day 2
In the morning, head straight to **Gourmandise** and order breakfast, plus a box of pastries (or even a cake, if you're feeling decadent) for later. Take the scenic route to Park City via Emigration Canyon—this is the way the Mormons headed into town over a century ago! Stop at one of the Foothills attractions, like the **Natural History Museum of Utah,** and consider a short hike along the **Bonneville**

Natural History Museum of Utah in Salt Lake City

No Name Saloon & Grill in Park City

Shoreline Trail, accessible behind the museum. Continue on through Emigration Canyon and stop for lunch at the iconic **Ruth's Diner.** Emigration Canyon will connect with East Canyon and take you straight to **Park City** via I-80. When you arrive in Park City, head to **Old Town** in the early evening to stroll up and down Main Street, get a drink at **No Name Saloon & Grill,** and grab dinner at **High West Distillery & Saloon.**

Day 3

Before breakfast, stroll around the **McPolin Farm** and get some impressive sunrise shots. Then head out for a **hike** at **Deer Valley** or at **Park City Mountain Resort,** before getting lunch at a base-area eatery like **The Farm** or the **Glitretind Restaurant.** If it's the off-season, head to Old Town again to eat before making the drive back to Salt Lake City. This is also a great time to pocket some souvenirs and check out some of Main Street's many art galleries.

Base Camp Salt Lake:
The Cottonwood Canyons

Whether you're headed to the Wasatch in summer or winter, make Salt Lake City your base camp for adventure in the city's unofficial backyard: the Cottonwood Canyons. Staying in the Sandy/Cottonwood Heights area, at the **Hansen House B&B,** for example, will position you closest to the canyons.

Skiing

Plenty of resort, sidecountry, and backcountry skiing awaits in both Cottonwood Canyons. Skiers and snowboarders who want to maximize time on the slopes may wish to lodge at the ski resorts, while others who want to plan a rest day in between or take advantage of the greater diversity of dining and lodging options in an urban area can consider Salt Lake City their base camp.

LITTLE COTTONWOOD

Unless you're a snowboarder, get a ticket transferrable between the canyon's adjacent resorts, **Alta** and **Snowbird,** and ski the best of both worlds. You hit Snowbird first on the drive up, so park and start from there. If you're a snowboarder, Alta only allows two planks, so just plan to ski Snowbird.

BIG COTTONWOOD

Brighton and Solitude are your two options in Big Cottonwood. **Solitude** skis like its name suggests—ditch the crowds and find quiet powder turns plus plenty of backcountry access. **Brighton** is beginner-friendly, family-friendly, low-key, and a park rat's paradise.

Summer Trails

If you're visiting Salt Lake City in the summer, take day trips into the Cottonwoods for first-rate hiking and rock climbing. Bear in mind that dogs are not allowed in either canyon.

LITTLE COTTONWOOD

Cecret Lake is a great jaunt if you've only got a couple hours to visit the Cottonwoods. It's also very accessible and makes for a nice sunrise/sunset hike. If you're looking for a longer excursion, consider summiting **Mount Pfeifferhorn,** the third-highest peak in the Wasatch.

BIG COTTONWOOD

One of the most popular hikes in Big Cottonwood Canyon is **Donut Falls,** which crescendos in a scramble over slick rock to view the waterfall that descends through a hole in a rock into a small watery cave (hence, the name). A somewhat less trafficked and arguably more scenic hike heads to **Lake Blanche.**

The Wasatch Back: Park City and Beyond

The Wasatch Back lies on the eastern side of the Wasatch Mountain Range. Park City is its most well-known town, but there are several other communities to discover in this region. As little as a 30-minute drive from the Salt Lake City International Airport, a long weekend getaway to the Wasatch Back can be filled with equal parts adventure and serenity.

Day 1

Arrive in **Park City** in the morning and go on a **hike** or **snowshoe** to work out your travel ya-yas. Head to the Kimball Junction area for lunch at **11Hauz** and then spend the afternoon at the Utah Olympic Park, where you can learn about Olympic history, take a tour, and get your adrenaline pumping on the tubing hill or bobsled track. Then check into your lodging and head to **Old Town** in the evening for strolling, shopping, and dinner at **Tupelo.**

Day 2

Get breakfast at **Windy Ridge Café** and stock up on baked goods and sweets (the makings of a decadent lunch on the go!) at **Windy Ridge Bakery** across the parking lot. Then head through Kamas into the **Uintas.** Drive to the summit of **Mirror Lake Scenic Byway** and get your scenic shots (the summit at Bald Mountain Pass is just under 30 miles/48 km from Kamas; the road closes at mile marker 14.6 from around November through May). On the way back down, stop for a **hike, cross-country ski,** or **snowshoe** at one of the many trailheads. Then head to **Midway** and get dinner at **Midway Mercantile** on Main Street before going back to Park City for the night.

Day 3

Spend the morning **hiking** in **Wasatch Mountain State Park,** doing some **Nordic skiing** at **Soldier Hollow,** or **golfing** at one of

Mirror Lake

Sundance Survival Tips

Utah's largest tourist-attracting event, the **Sundance Film Festival** is an annual international film festival spanning a little under a fortnight in winter. Pioneered by Robert Redford, Sundance draws celebrities and film industry members to Park City with a program that includes documentaries, international films, shorts, and all genres of other independent films. Many of the films are paired with panel discussions from cast and crew, and after-parties are held across town. The festival typically runs from late January to early February, with most of the excitement spanning the first weekend of the event.

If you come to Park City during the Sundance Film Festival, you should do so on purpose. Otherwise, this is not the best time to visit the area, since you'll find booked-out lodging, restaurants closed for private events, hiked-up prices, and a town so crowded you can scarcely get from point A to B.

If you will be in Park City during Sundance *for* Sundance, here are some tips to survive the film festival:

the Egyptian Theatre in Park City

- **Book lodging as early as possible** before it reaches capacity, which it most certainly will. I'm talking six months or more out! Staying in Salt Lake City or outlying areas are good alternatives, though you'll have to make the trek into Park City if you want to be in the thick of things.

- **All tickets and passes must be purchased in advance online,** then picked up at one of the main box offices in Park City (136 Heber Ave.), Salt Lake (Trolley Square, 602 S. 700 E.), or at Sundance Mountain Resort, regardless of which theater your screening will be held. Festival passes range around $300-4,000, while tickets are $25 and up.

- **Park City isn't the only place where you can catch screenings of Sundance films.** Theaters in Salt Lake City, Ogden, Sundance, and Kimball Junction also host the festival. You'll find securing tickets easier for theaters outside of Park City. And bigger cities like Salt Lake City or Ogden are better equipped to handle the rush.

- Another way to increase your chances of getting tickets is to **consider more untraditional show times,** from bright-and-early 8:30am shows to midnight screenings. The festival also runs about 10 days, so partaking in the second half of the festival is another strategy to beat the crowds.

- Renting a car may seem like the right choice until you're stuck in insane traffic for what amounts to hours on end. **Public transit and walking** are the most efficient way to get around Park City during the festival.

- **Don't expect to land a table at any restaurant in Old Town Park City without a serious wait.** Some restaurants close and others won't take reservations. Stave off a case of hunger by bringing snacks and eating opportunistically.

- **If you're in it for the experience and not the movies per se, take a deep breath,** pack the necessities (water, layers, portable phone charger) and embrace the delays, traffic, and general chaos as you play paparazzi on Park City's Main Street.

- **Rumor has it one of the best places to see celebrities is the grocery store.** Head to Fresh Market or Whole Foods if you're hoping to catch someone famous shopping for the necessities.

- **Embrace the madness!** Be flexible with your plans, be opportunistic, and enjoy the craziness that is Sundance.

the three courses in the area, followed by a soak in the **Homestead Crater.** An alternative plan with young kids: Head to **Heber** to ride the **Heber** **Valley Railroad.** Get lunch at **Back 40 Ranch House** in Heber before departing.

The Wasatch Front: Salt Lake City and Ogden

On the western side of the Wasatch Mountains lies the Wasatch Front, Salt Lake City, its many outlying areas, and Ogden to the north. This is by far the more urban side of the Wasatch, but just over a dozen miles east of Ogden, the towns of Eden and Huntsville offer skiing and a reprieve from the bustle.

Day 1
Start your day in **Salt Lake City** by heading to **Temple Square** in the morning. Tour the grounds, staying for a show from the **Tabernacle Choir.** In the afternoon, take a short hike on the **Bonneville Shoreline Trail** starting from the foothills of the city. Then get dinner at **Laziz Kitchen** and head downtown to **Bar-X** for drinks.

Day 2
Next, you'll head to **Ogden**—but plan to stay in Ogden Canyon or in **Eden** or **Huntsville,** where the accommodations are quainter. Head to **Snowbasin** to ski a half day or go for a **hike.** Then check into your lodging and drive into Ogden for beers at **Roosters B Street Brewery and Taproom** and dinner at **The Angry Goat.**

Day 3
Get breakfast and a cup of worldly coffee at the **Mad Moose Café** in Eden. Then spend a half day **skiing** at **Snowbasin** again, or head into Ogden and **hike** the **Bonneville Shoreline Trail.** Then return to downtown Ogden to stroll **Historic 25th Street** and discover the exhibits at **Union Station.** Get lunch at **Pig & a Jelly Jar** before hitting the road.

The Sundance Kid

Robert Redford fanatic? Indie film buff? Or just all-around lover of alpine beauty? Then this Park City and Sundance Mountain Resort itinerary is for you.

Day 1
On your way to **Old Town Park City** in the early afternoon, stop by the **Kimball Art Center,** the host of the town's annual arts festival, to check out the exhibits on display. Go **gallery-hopping** on Main Street, ogling paintings of cowboys and stunning wildlife photography. Don't forget to pause at the art **Banksy** left behind when he visited for the 2010 Sundance Film Festival at the corner of 4th and Main! Get drinks on the rooftop patio at **No Name Saloon & Grill.** Then head to **Grappa** for an early dinner before catching a show at the **Egyptian Theatre.**

Day 2
Leave Park City early and stop at **Dottie's Kolache Co.** in Heber for delectable filled pastries known as kolaches. Head to **Timpanogos Cave National Monument** for a tour of a cave with a romantic legend (book a tour time in advance). Then check into **Sundance Mountain**

Resort. Spend the afternoon strolling around the grounds. Just beyond the general store, walk through a hallway that serves as a mini exhibit of Sundance's past—you'll find historic photos of skiing at Sundance in the early 20th century, Robert Redford in his heyday, and legendary musical acts that have played the venue. Get dinner at **The Tree Room** and drinks at **The Owl Bar.**

Day 3
Enjoy breakfast at the **Foundry Grill**, then set out for a hike to **Stewart Falls.** Afterwards, grab a sandwich and giant cookie to-go at the **Sundance Deli** and take a scenic lift ride up to get as close to **Mount Timpanogos** as you can without putting in the 19-mile hike!

On the Spirited Trail

The makers of local libations carry on a strange tradition of drinking in Utah. Prior to Prohibition, the Latter-day Saints in the state did imbibe a spirit all their own: valley tan. They also drank their own sacramental wine in church ceremonies. Brigham Young was known to sip the valley tan, and Orrin Porter Rockwell, his personal bodyguard, even owned a brewery. One of the biggest breweries in the state back in the day was called Wagener Brewing, located in Emigration Canyon and owned by a German immigrant. But since Prohibition took hold of the nation, Utah has imposed strict alcohol legislation, and the days of semi-sanctioned Mormon imbibing are long gone.

There's nothing like a challenge to stoke the fires of creativity. Perhaps that's what you can chalk up the award-winning beers and spirits of Utah to. Do brewers, distillers, vintners, and mixologists in one of the driest states in the nation face an uphill battle? You bet. Do they let it deter them? Heck no.

Beer and Spirits
SALT LAKE CITY
Increasingly, Utah is home to some great breweries. In Salt Lake City, some of the best include recent Great American Beer Festival award-winners **Shades Brewing, TF Brewing,** and **Kiitos Brewing.** While its location in a mall

High West Distillery

Before you hit the spirited trail, know Utah's liquor laws and how to navigate them. Here are some of the key rules to keep in mind:

- **A dining or drinking establishment must be licensed as a restaurant or as a bar.** If the establishment is licensed as a bar, only adults (ages 21 and over) are allowed inside. The majority of breweries and distilleries in the state are licensed as such. If the establishment has a restaurant license, customers of all ages are allowed inside, but you must order food when you order a drink. Usually, a low-cost item like chips and salsa will be presented as an option.

- **The vast majority of liquor stores are owned by the state and closed on all holidays and Sundays,** with relatively limited hours (e.g., closing at 7pm). The other drawback is that the state liquor stores do not sell refrigerated product. So, you'll need to plan ahead if you're picking up a 12-pack or a bottle of champagne, for example. Pro tip: The one liquor store I've discovered in the Wasatch that is not state-owned is in Kamas, of all places, right by the grocery store as you pull into town. ICBs, here you come.

- The Department of Alcoholic Beverage Control (DABC) requires **all beers and beverages poured on draft or sold in grocery stores** to clock in **below 5 percent alcohol by volume** (that's 4 percent by weight). That means that if you visit a brewery, you can't try any full-strength versions of its brews on tap. Unless you're looking for a session experience, order that high-octane IPA by the bottle or can. Most breweries brew a compliant low-alcohol version and a full-strength version of their beers. Usually, this will be made clear on the menu.

- **Utah is the only state in the nation with a legal definition of a shot: 1.5 fluid ounces.** A cocktail can contain up to 1.5 fluid ounces of alcohol, as well as 1 ounce of a "flavoring agent," which cannot be the same as the 1.5-ounce shot. So, a 2.5-ounce pour of Maker's Mark neat: illegal. A 1.5-ounce pour of Maker's and 1-ounce pour of Vermouth: A-Okay. This makes a drink like a martini less than ideal to order in Utah.

- **Bars were once all required to have a "Zion Curtain" by the bar**—a physical barrier to hide the drink-mixing process from patrons. Zion Curtain laws have grown laxer, but you may still find one in some restaurants, since minors cannot sit within 10 feet of a bar without one.

- **It's illegal to host a happy hour** or offer any discounts or deals on alcoholic beverages. And set your alarms: Bars here must serve their last pour by 1am and close the doors at 2am.

- **Legally, you can't bring alcohol into or outside of the state.** If you're road-tripping in from Colorado, think twice before you illicitly import that growler of strong beer. And if you visit High West and want to purchase a bottle of bourbon to take home in your checked baggage, know that if you're caught, your booze will be confiscated.

These are the main highlights when it comes to imbibing in Utah. Be grateful! It wasn't always so "easy" to get a drink in the state. Laws have become progressively looser over time. Up until 2009, you had to be part of a private club to even order a drink in Utah, paying a membership fee on top of your drink!

inside Trolley Square is less than glamorous, **Desert Edge Brewery** is one of the oldest in the state and worth a visit. **Epic Brewing Company,** which shifted headquarters from Salt Lake to Denver, but still has a brewery here, is a go-to for experimental, bold styles.

PARK CITY

Wasatch Brew Pub became the first post-Prohibition brewery in Utah when it opened atop Main Street in Park City in 1988. It has since opened a location in Salt Lake City and merged with the award-winning Squatters Craft Beers,

It should come as no surprise that Utah is a family-friendly state—we've got the highest number of kids per capita in the nation. Activities abound throughout the Wasatch that are great for the whole family. Most ski resorts offer kids' lessons, bunny hills, and on-site childcare options. And with a little planning, our trails and campgrounds are great places for little ones to spend time in nature.

The one non-family-friendly aspect of Utah compared to other states, however, is that establishments licensed as bars are 21 and over only, which includes most of the state's breweries. Don't assume that a restaurant is family-friendly—call and ask if it allows minors before making plans.

Between the many attractions and outdoor activities, one more thing your kids will love is all the sweets. Plenty of edible rewards exist around the Wasatch, from ice cream shops to bakeries. The promise of an ice cream cone will work wonders in bribing your kids to power through a long hike!

George S. Eccles Dinosaur Park in Ogden

SALT LAKE CITY

Some of Salt Lake City's top kid-friendly attractions are **This Is The Place Park** and the **Hogle Zoo**, which are within walking distance of each other for a fully loaded day. The **Leonardo Museum** downtown is also filled with genius and creative exhibits that will appeal to kids of all ages—and parents, too.

PARK CITY

In Park City, one of the best places for kiddos is a **ski resort,** which offers bunny hills, kids' lessons, and s'mores in the winter. In the summer, Park City's base area offers a whole host of adventure activities, from the alpine slide to ziplining. A scenic summer chairlift ride and a little hiking is another option that's great for the whole family.

In Old Town Park City, kids of all ages will love the activities and look into the past at the **Park City Museum.** For older kids, **Park City Ghost Tours** offers an experience they're likely to talk about for days to come. In the Kimball Junction area, the **Utah Olympic Park** will inspire your kid to be an Olympian with obstacle courses, tubing, bobsled rides, and more fun experiences. And the **Swaner Preserve and EcoCenter** gets youth thinking about the local ecosystem and the characters inhabiting it.

OGDEN

Kids will have fun exploring **Fort Buenaventura State Park,** which has replicas of the 19th-century fort and cabins. Encounter life-size T. rexes and raptors at the **George S. Eccles Dinosaur Park.**

THE WASATCH BACK

Cap a day of skiing with a visit to the blinged-out frozen waterfalls of the **Midway Ice Castles,** a magical sight for young kids in particular. Over in Heber, a ride on the **Heber Valley Railroad** is a great year-round family experience, with rides themed according to the season.

OAKLEY, KAMAS, AND THE UINTAS

If you're on a ski vacation, take a break from the slopes and wow your kids with a guided **dogsledding** experience through the forest.

which also maintains breweries in both Park City and Salt Lake. All Wasatch and Squatters locations are licensed as restaurants and allow families, except in the bar areas. This brewing family jabs at the state with its notorious Polygamy Porter—the label is a must-see.

For **whiskey** lovers, a visit to Park City isn't complete without a stop at **High West Distillery.** Whether you visit the saloon in Old Town for one of the best Manhattans money can buy, trek over to the distillery in Wanship for a tour and brunch, or experience both locations, Utah's most beloved distillery is a mandatory stop.

OGDEN

The Ogden area is home to a couple of noteworthy local breweries, as well as an award-winning distillery. **Roosters B Street Brewery and Taproom** doesn't shy away from creative styles like a blackberry cream ale. And for small-batch Mexican beers to pair with your tacos, head to **Cerveza Zólupez Beer Co.** Head over to

Eden to sample **New World Distillery**'s award-winning Oomaw Gin, Oomaw Vodka, and delightful liqueurs.

FESTIVALS AND EVENTS

A couple of great places to sample a wider variety of Utah beers include the annual summer **Utah Beer Festival** in Salt Lake City, as well as the fall **Oktoberfest** at Snowbird Resort.

Wine

If it's **wine** you're looking for, prioritize restaurants with great wine lists rather than local vintners. Whether it's the terroir or the lack of deep-rooted winemaking experience, Wasatch-area wineries here are limited. Your best bets include **La Caille,** a restaurant in Sandy that creates a small private-label French wine from its own grapes, as well as the *Wine Spectator*-recognized **BTG Wine Bar** in Salt Lake City, with over 75 bottles served by the glass and wine-friendly small plates.

Get Outside!

Ski Utah

Winter is no time to hibernate or slow down in the Wasatch. The mountains are calling! Between our 10 ski resorts, ample backcountry terrain, and miles of groomed Nordic trails, the cold just calls for the right layers and a little ambition.

Which Resort Is Best for You?

With 10 great ski resorts to choose from in the Wasatch, where do you start? Here's a primer on how to pick the best resort for your ski vacation.

IF YOU GET BORED EASILY
With 7,300 acres, **Park City Mountain Resort** is the biggest in the Wasatch—and in the entire United States. From a kids' learning area and multiple terrain parks to traverse-accessed powder bowls, Park City also has a run for every skier/snowboarder.

IF YOU LOVE A LITTLE LUXURY
Ski with the stars on pristine groomed corduroy at **Deer Valley** in Park City, and enjoy an opulent après and lodging experience, to boot.

IF YOU WANT TO MASTER THE HALF-PIPE
You'll find the best terrain parks in the Wasatch at **Brighton** in Big Cottonwood Canyon—not to mention fast chairlifts and the best night-skiing experience.

skiing at Snowbasin

IF YOU'RE TRAVELING WITH A NORDIC SKIER

Also in Big Cottonwood Canyon, **Solitude Mountain Resort** offers a full Nordic Center, as well as a quieter skiing experience and plenty of lift-accessed backcountry terrain.

IF YOU'RE ALL ABOUT BIG EXPOSED LINES

Over in Little Cottonwood Canyon, **Snowbird** offers plenty of big mountain terrain, known for being the most extreme in the Wasatch and Utah in general. Even if you're not a pro, you can bask in that alpine feeling with a ride up the aerial tram.

IF YOU'RE LESS THAN ENTHUSED ABOUT SNOWBOARDERS

Just a tad farther down the road from Snowbird lies **Alta,** which bans snowboarders and lays claim to being the second-oldest ski resort in the country, after Sun Valley.

IF YOU WANT TO ESCAPE THE CROWDS

Head to the family-owned **Snowbasin** in Huntsville near Ogden for peace, quiet, and tasteful luxury.

IF YOU'RE READY TO GET OFF THE CARVED-UP SLOPE

At 8,464 acres, **Powder Mountain** actually has more skiable acreage than Park City, but the majority of its terrain is not lift-accessed. If you're ready to get farther afield by hiking or taking a cat, this resort in Eden near Ogden is your powdery dream come true.

IF YOU DON'T WANT TO FORK OVER A FORTUNE

Skiing is a notoriously pricey sport, but at **Nordic Valley Ski Resort,** you can get out for just $45 a day. Sure, the terrain is less sprawling than its Wasatch compatriots, but this little resort in Eden is great for beginners and families looking to get in a few turns.

IF YOU HATE THE CORPORATE FEEL

Escape to Robert Redford's authentic, independently owned **Sundance Mountain Resort,** where you can stay in a log cabin and drink hot toddies at The Owl Bar.

Backcountry

Some of the best backcountry terrain in the region lies in the **Cottonwood Canyons.** Of the two Cottonwood Canyons, Little Cottonwood is known for having more extreme terrain, but both have many lines featured in the famous backcountry guide *The Chuting Gallery* by Andrew McLean.

In the **Uintas,** more backcountry skiing awaits, from yurt trips to alpine-style climbs. Due to the main road through the area, Mirror Lake Scenic Byway, closing around mile marker 14.6 from November through May, some of the backcountry skiing is only accessible by snowmobile.

And at most of the ski resorts throughout the Wasatch, the versatile skier or splitboarder can find ample sidecountry terrain. Some of the best resorts for backcountry access include **Park City Mountain, Solitude, Alta,** and **Powder Mountain.**

More Snow Sports

Not keen on the idea of hurtling down a hill? Winter isn't only the season of skiing and snowboarding. The Wasatch offers incredible classic and skate **cross-country skiing** trails, from the **White Pine Nordic Center** in Park City to an Olympic course at the **Soldier Hollow Nordic Center** in Wasatch Mountain State Park, and both groomed and ungroomed trails in the **Uintas.** Many of these trails are also fair game for fat bikers and snowshoers. Other winter sports you can pursue in the region include **dogsledding** and **ice climbing.**

Hiking

The Wasatch isn't only about extreme sports. Northern Utah is also home to plenty of hiking trails that can be explored **nearly year-round.** And from mountain bikers and trail runners to horseback riders, trails tend to be **most crowded** in the **summer**—be sure to abide by local trail rules (e.g., biking-only trails) and respect other trail users. Many trails also close intermittently throughout the summer for races.

When the snow melts, most of the **ski areas** become **hot spots of hiking.** You'll find tons of trails for all ability levels at Park City Mountain, Deer Valley, and at the resorts in the Cottonwood Canyons, though you'll often be competing for trail space with mountain bikers. And in the Cottonwood Canyons, no dogs are allowed.

One place you'll hardly ever run into bikers? The **Uintas**—especially the parts that are designated wilderness areas, where bikers are prohibited.

Meanwhile, you can more or less hike right from the foothills of **Salt Lake City.** The trails in Salt Lake City are best in the **late fall** and **early spring,** but can feel pretty exposed and hot come summer.

Hiking Highlights
SALT LAKE CITY AND OGDEN
Following the original eastern shoreline of ancient Lake Bonneville, the relatively level **Bonneville Shoreline Trail** rings part of the capital and runs along the eastern foothills of the Ogden area—it actually travels over 100 miles (161 km) through northern Utah, stretching all the way from Provo into Idaho.

PARK CITY
With its rich flora and expansive views, the **Mid-Mountain Trail** (21.9 mi/35 km one-way, 8-10 hours, moderate) is beloved by all users, from

a fall hike in Park City

Climbing

Where there are mountains, there's rock. And where there's rock, there's climbing—sport, trad, bouldering, multi-pitch, and more.

COTTONWOOD CANYONS

Local climbers love the rock in the Cottonwood Canyons. Find quartzite walls in **Big Cottonwood Canyon**, and plenty of granite in **Little Cottonwood Canyon**. Little Cottonwood is the preferred local climbing spot of the two, and its exposed **Hellgate Cliffs** in particular will test your nerve and ability. You can also find bouldering in Little Cottonwood.

UINTA MOUNTAINS

In the Uintas lie a number of popular crags accessible via a short hike off the Mirror Lake Scenic Byway. The **Ruth's Lake** area, which encompasses several crags, is a local favorite. And about a mile (1.6 km) hike in, **Cliff Lake** is another great spot to go with a mix of trad and sport lines, as well as the possibility of top-roping.

canines to hikers and bikers to moose. The trail runs from Deer Valley to Pinebrook, west of Park City. Take advantage of the multiple entry/exit points to make your hike as short or as long as you'd like.

BIG COTTONWOOD CANYON

The mellow, short hike to **Donut Falls** (3 mi/4.8 km round-trip, 1.5 hours, easy) is rewarded with a beautiful waterfall that cascades through a doughnut-shaped hole in a shallow cave.

GREAT SALT LAKE

You can explore **Antelope Island**—and catch sight of the resident bison herds—by hiking around the various scenic stops along Antelope Island Road. The short jaunt to **Buffalo Point** (1 mi/1.6 km round-trip, 30 minutes, easy) makes for a great sunrise or sunset hike, with panoramic views of the island, the Great Salt Lake, and the Wasatch Range.

THE WASATCH BACK

While **Wasatch Mountain State Park** can be hiked year-round, trekking in fall is particularly glorious, with remarkable foliage and pleasant temperatures. The **Wasatch Over Wasatch (WOW) Trail** (9.4 mi/15.1 km one-way, 5-6 hours, strenuous) offers beautiful views all along the way as well as a heart-pumping workout.

THE UINTAS

Excellent for wildlife-spotting, the remote **Uinta Highline Trail** (95.7 miles/154 km, at least a week, extremely strenuous) is an epic traverse across the biggest mountains in Utah. Much of the trail lies above tree line, which makes for expansive views of the Uinta mountains, forest, lakes, and wildflower meadows.

Peak-Bagging

While Utah may not be filled with fourteeners—mountains at least 14,000 feet (4,267 m) high—like Colorado, there are plenty of tall peaks demanding to be summited, including a couple of thirteeners (3,962 m). The **safest** bet for a summit is **summertime** when mountains are mostly free of snow and avalanche danger. **Mild autumns** can also be a great time of year to bag peaks, since you'll find **less crowded** trails. Spring is usually a little too early for summit season, due to big mountain snowpacks. And while attaining summits and ski mountaineering expeditions are absolutely possible in the wintertime, they typically require some technical knowledge of how to get up and down as well as specialized equipment.

Before you summit, always **check the forecast** to ensure a thunderstorm doesn't lurk in the afternoon. Always bring plenty of water and food, sun protection, warm layers, and a rain shell.

Wasatch Mountains

You can summit a number of the peaks in the Wasatch with the help of a chairlift. Whether it's winter or summer, many chairlifts will take you to the tops of mountains, or close enough to finish the job with 20 minutes of hard work. Outside the resorts in the Cottonwood Canyons are many other summer summits that can be attained via popular trails, including **Kessler Peak** (10,403 ft/3,171 m) and **Mount Pfeifferhorn** (11,326 ft/3,452 m), the third-highest peak in the range.

Indisputably Utah's most famous peak, **Mount Timpanogos** (11,750 ft/3,581 m) is also a popular, non-technical summit. This is a full-day endeavor and one that many other locals and tourists undertake, so don't be surprised to find a crowded summit and plenty of people on the trail.

Uinta Mountains

The Uinta Mountains tower higher than the

There's no shortage of peaks to bag in the Wasatch.

Wasatch Range, and are home to the state's tallest mountain: **Kings Peak** (13,527 ft/4,123 m). While on a map, it might appear that you could summit Kings via Mirror Lake Byway coming from Kamas, you actually need to drive up into Wyoming to start. The nearly 30-mile (48-km) round-trip hike is non-technical and typically completed as an overnight trip. Don't let the Wyoming start deter you; Kings is still attainable as a two-day backpacking trip starting from Salt Lake City or the Wasatch Back.

Another popular summit in the Uintas is **Bald Mountain** (11,943 ft/3,640 m), which starts close to the summit of the Mirror Lake Byway. This short 4-mile (6.4 km) round-trip hike can easily be completed in a morning or afternoon, and takes you to sweeping views of the High Uintas. However, risks lurk at the top in the form of a narrow trail and big exposure that can become a hazard in the event of strong winds or lightning. Heed forecasts and the skies, and bring trekking poles if you're anything shy of surefooted.

Biking

Northern Utah is a cyclist's dream, whether it's a course across International Mountain Bike Association gold-rated trails in Park City, or road biking Emigration Canyon.

Mountain Biking

Lung-busting climbs. Tacky single-track. Flowy berms. Steep wood features. Playful rock gardens. **Park City**'s biking knows no limits. You can string together just about any ride you'd like on the hundreds of miles of trails here, from beginner loops to expert shuttles.

One of the classic rides is the **Wasatch Crest Trail**, which be ridden a variety of ways, shuttled or looped. As the name suggests, the trail travels a ridgeline in the Wasatch through quaking aspen

the Rail Trail in Park City

groves and fields of wildflowers. To complete this ride, you could weave in another Park City classic: the **Mid-Mountain Trail**, which traverses the Wasatch for over 20 miles (32 km) from Deer Valley to the neighborhood of Pinebrook, just west of Park City.

Speaking of **Deer Valley**, its lift-serviced downhill park is the best in Utah. **Snowbird** also offers lift-serviced downhill riding, but there's really only one trail down from the hair-raising summit: the **Big Mountain Trail**. This 10-plus miles (16-plus km) of single-track is a dream for advanced and expert riders, touring exposed switchbacks, tight berms, and fast straightaways through aspen groves.

Road Biking

Drive through any canyon or country road in Utah, and you're likely to vie for asphalt with spandex-clad cyclists pumping up serious elevation gain. Join the peloton with a bike tour of **Mirror Lake Scenic Byway** or **Emigration Canyon**—two classic rides in the Wasatch. For more of a gravel experience, consider riding the **Rail Trail** in Park City, a historic railroad line converted into a bike path that stretches from Park City to Echo Reservoir.

Get Out on the Water

Utah may be the second-driest state, but you can still find plenty of water in the form of reservoirs, lakes, and rivers. The reservoirs are usually strategically placed between more urban areas. Lakes are much smaller and are most often found in the high alpine. And rivers rage throughout the Wasatch, fed by melting snow and filled with trout for the catching.

Reservoirs

If you've got kids reluctant to vacation away from the beach, you can find a similar experience and activities at Utah's reservoirs. With sand, **rental boats, Jet Skiing,** and more, the **beach experience** is totally attainable in the Wasatch. The area's primary reservoirs include the **Jordanelle** between Park City and Kamas, **Deer Creek** between Heber and Sundance, **Rockport** between Oakley and Wanship, and **Pineview** in Ogden. Reservoirs are typically managed by Utah State Parks and charge day-use fees, and most also offer **camping** along the shore at an additional fee. Check with each individual reservoir for day-use fees and available boat/activity rentals.

Lakes

The biggest name in lakes in the Wasatch is the **Great Salt Lake,** which is the descendant of the much larger ancient Lake Bonneville. Today, the lake is known as the Dead Sea of the United States, with salty water that supports little in the way of marine life besides brine shrimp. While you might not want to jump in to partake in your usual lake activities, the Great Salt Lake is a special place to visit all the same, whether it's for **bird-watching, boating,** or a trip out to **Antelope Island.**

The most beautiful lakes in the Wasatch usually require a hike or at least a drive on rough 4WD roads. These are our **high alpine lakes,** found in the basins beneath peaks. The **Uintas** is home to over 1,000 lakes, many of which offer superb fishing. The most accessible is **Mirror Lake,** which you can actually drive right up to on a paved road. For that reason, it's also the most crowded. **Cliff Lake** requires a hike but offers a little more solitude. Here you can **fish, swim,** or **paddleboard,** if you're willing to hike in with the gear.

You can also find turquoise high alpine lakes

in the **Cottonwood Canyons. Lakes Blanche and Catherine** are a couple popular lakes within a half day's hiking distance. However, the lakes in the Cottonwoods do not permit any swimming or water sports since this area is a watershed for Salt Lake City.

Rivers

The two main rivers that run through the Wasatch are the **Provo** and the **Weber,** both of which originate in the Uinta Mountains and are fed by snowmelt. The Weber runs down to the Great Salt Lake, while the Provo empties into Utah Lake in Provo. Both rivers are great for **fly-fishing, tubing,** and **kayaking.** You can fish for a variety of trout in both rivers. To **float** or **boat** the Provo, a popular put-in spot lies on Highway 189 just minutes from Sundance. For the Weber, the go-to put-in is off I-84 about 30 miles (48 km) east of Ogden. Local gear rental shops and outfitters can help arrange shuttles.

Sleep Outside

While there are plenty of luxurious lodges, charming bed-and-breakfasts, and Airbnbs to find in the Wasatch, why not sleep in the outdoors if you're visiting in temperate weather? There's plenty of convenient car camping with all the amenities you could ask for alfresco, including both developed campgrounds and dispersed camping. And with ample wilderness and trails, there are even more backpacking destinations for those who wish to trade convenience for a little more solitude.

Car Camping

One of the most obvious places to camp in the area is at the local **reservoirs,** which double as state parks. You'll also find plenty

the view from atop Mount Timpanogos

of campgrounds in the **Uintas**, at **Wasatch Mountain State Park**, on **Antelope Island**, throughout the **Cottonwood Canyons**, and at the trailhead to summit **Mount Timpanogos**. All of these campgrounds require advance reservations and nightly fees. Many book up months in advance, so plan your trip ahead of time if possible.

When the campgrounds all book up—or if you want a little more peace and quiet— the Uintas is also home to around 300 free **dispersed campsites** reachable in a 4WD/ AWD vehicle. The best way to pursue a dispersed campsite is to stop at a ranger's office for a map and recommendations. Of course, you'll need a 4WD/AWD vehicle as well.

Backpacking

If you're willing to carry your sleep system, food, and other supplies on your back, then backpacking offers a great way to sleep beneath the stars minus everyone else who had the same idea as you. Backpackers can almost always find a patch of solitude out in the wilderness on foot.

The best place to backpack in the Wasatch is indisputably the **Uinta Mountains**, where miles and miles of trail can take you past mountain goat herds to the state's tallest summits beneath a vibrant Milky Way. Options in the Uintas abound. You can plan a mellow overnight that involves a mile (1.6 km) or less hike from the car. You might work a summit goal into your backpacking trip—say, **Kings Peak**, which offers great camping options off the trail. Or you can plan a backpacking epic on the **Uinta Highline Trail**, traversing nearly 100 miles (161 km) over the range's spine.

Salt Lake City

At the corner of 200 S. and 200 E. downtown,
you will find two murals that embody the sundry and sometimes at-
odds cultures of Salt Lake City. The first shows Ave Maria, pulling
back her green shawl to reveal a fiery sacred heart. In 2009, El Mac
and Retna—a widely known graffiti duo—sprayed this image onto the
historic Guthrie Bicycles building, one of the oldest bike shops in the
United States. The artists don't depict Mary as the fair-skinned, pure-
hearted virgin mama she's often cast as. Instead, she looks like a young
woman who could be of Latinx or Middle Eastern descent, with a facial
expression and body language that reads confidence and sagacity, with
a hint of "I-told-you-so" bite.

A few years after the Ave Maria mural came onto the scene, an

Highlights

Look for ★ to find recommended sights, activities, dining, and lodging.

★ **Discover LDS history** and the **Tabernacle Choir** at **Temple Square,** the heart of Salt Lake City (page 48).

★ **Explore This Is The Place Heritage Park,** a Mormon history theme park of sorts, and partake in the annual Pioneer Day celebration (page 57).

★ **Immerse yourself at the Natural History Museum of Utah,** where you can learn about the state's rich geologic history and Indigenous heritage (page 57).

★ **Hike or bike along the Bonneville Shoreline Trail,** following what was once the shore of the ancient predecessor to the Great Salt Lake (page 59).

★ **Bike up Emigration Canyon** and stop at the iconic Ruth's Diner for epic biscuits on a picturesque patio (page 60).

★ **Explore the craft brewery scene,** which serves up a growing list of award-winning microbrews (page 70).

★ **Experience Utah's vibrant multicultural community** through food, dance, and artwork at the annual **Living Traditions Festival** (page 76).

★ **Surrender to your sweet tooth** at one of the city's many bakeries, patisseries, and ice cream shops (page 81).

artist plastered an elk in a psychedelic landscape on the building next door, a gun shop called Gallenson's, established by a Russian immigrant in 1916. From afar, the two murals almost appear as one, with the Madonna rising from a wild landscape like a revisionist history from the organic chaos of the truth.

This confluence of religion, art, wildlife, powerful women, immigrants, guns, and bikes epitomizes the city of Salt Lake. Of course, as most people assume, Salt Lake City is Mormon. Not only is it the official headquarters of the religion, but parts of downtown are even owned by the Church of Jesus Christ of Latter-day Saints. Yet while Mormonism is foundational to the city, it's also a hub of immigration, home to an emerging art scene, base camp for outdoor enthusiasts, and one of the gayest cities in America.

Did I mention that these two murals appear just across the street from Beer Bar, the craft brew-focused spot owned by Ty Burrell of *Modern Family*? And that around the corner is Gourmandise, a bakery owned by a husband-and-wife team originally from South Africa that would bowl over Mary Berry? Both businesses represent two other cornerstones of Salt Lake City: artisan alcohol and sweets, the twin indulgences of our city. The former is a newer trend in Salt Lake City. As liquor laws loosen and the state becomes increasingly heterogenous, more and more microbreweries and distilleries have opened. Utah's sweet-toothed reputation, however, has been around for a while. Rumor has it, the prevalence of sweets in the state can be attributed to the fact that Mormons don't indulge in alcohol, and thus need another consumable guilty pleasure. The city is filled with places to enjoy pastries, cookies, doughnuts, ice cream, chocolate, and other confections.

The patchwork of cultures that is Salt Lake City means that its identity at times feels indeterminate, self-contradictory, and in flux.

The city has changed dramatically since it became the state capital in 1856, going from an agricultural Mormon settlement to a place where Mormons are now in the minority and LGBTQ+ residents are many. One minute, you're strolling through the immaculate grounds of Temple Square; the next, you're drinking martinis at The Copper Onion, only to impulse-buy an old Black Sabbath vinyl at The Heavy Metal Shop next door. That's all within a five-block radius downtown!

The upside of Salt Lake's composite identity is that you can experience the city in a variety of ways. Witness the city rising up together during Pride Fest, parades, and protests flooding the capitol building. Take a deep dive into Mormon history, from downtown up to the foothills. Explore the more marginal histories of Salt Lake, from the Indigenous people who've been here for thousands of years, to the vibrant immigrant communities and their amazing food. And when you've had your fill, escape to one of the city's backyards—from Park City to the Cottonwoods.

PLANNING YOUR TIME

Salt Lake City is small as far as state capitals go, and you can easily get to know it fairly well in a few days. If you want an in-depth exploration of the state's Mormon history, give yourself at least half a day to stroll through Temple Square and This Is The Place Park. For any of the museums, budget at least a few hours. And to explore a certain neighborhood—like Downtown or Sugar House—plan for about half a day as well.

If your main destination in Utah lies outside Salt Lake City, but you'd like to spend a little time in the city, consider spending a full day or two half days in the city on either end of your trip. Explore Temple Square and downtown, then head up into the foothills for a little perspective. From there, you can visit the Natural History Museum or Red Butte Garden, take a hike to get a bird's-eye view of

---

Salt Lake City

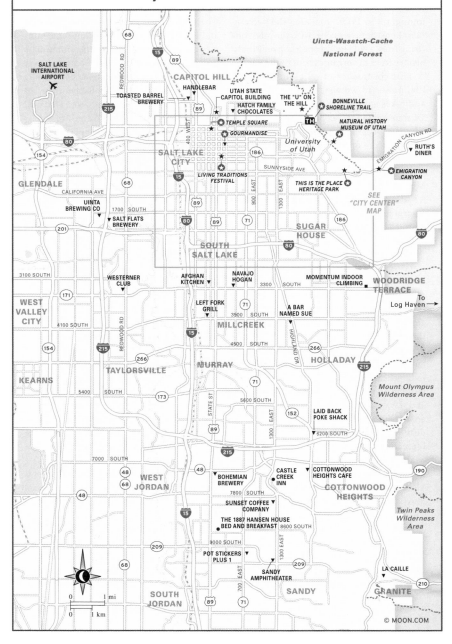

© MOON.COM

the city, and venture into Emigration Canyon to grab a bite at Ruth's Diner.

To spend a few days in the city, string together an itinerary suited to your interests. Tap into the left and right sides of your brain at The Leonardo Museum, then peer into an eccentric sculptor's mind at Gilgal Sculpture Garden. Eat your way through the city, then keep up your appetite with a short hike right from the foothills or the capitol. Or plan an aggressive tour of craft breweries in Salt Lake. If you're in it for the Mormon history, consider staying downtown. If you'd like a quieter place to spend the night, head to The Avenues or Capitol Hill.

If you only want to spend a half day or so in the city, I recommend strolling around downtown to get a sense of Salt Lake, popping into Temple Square, and then getting some food or a beer in one of the other neighborhoods that sound appealing to you, like Sugar House or 9th and 9th.

ORIENTATION

Salt Lake City is a very manageable city to explore. It's reasonable to expect that you could get a decent sense of the city and its prominent neighborhoods in just a day or two. Walkability, bikeability, ample parking, and the TRAX light rail also help make Salt Lake easy to navigate.

Generally speaking, Salt Lake City can be divided into about seven neighborhoods, including downtown. There are also many bedroom communities surrounding Salt Lake that might be considered part of the Greater Salt Lake area. Most of what I discuss in this chapter lies in Salt Lake City proper, though I do include a few sights and dining options in the adjacent cities of Sandy and Cottonwood Heights, which lie south of the city. If you plan to visit the Cottonwood Canyons, you'll pass through one of these two communities on the way from Salt Lake.

Downtown

The nucleus of the city is its most Mormon area. This is where the official world headquarters of the Church of Jesus Christ of Latter-day Saints is located, also known as Temple Square. The church also extends its influence at City Creek, an outdoor shopping mall owned by the church with a similar immaculate feel to the Temple grounds. While City Creek and Temple Square are among the most prominent landmarks downtown, you'll also find high-rise office buildings, the convention center, and the

view of downtown Salt Lake City from trails in the Foothills

Decoding Addresses

One thing you'll immediately notice about Salt Lake is that it's **constructed on a grid,** with each street denoting the distance and direction from the Mormon Temple. For example, 100 S. is one block south of Temple Square, while 200 E. runs two blocks east of Temple Square. So, the address 209 E. 500 S. would be located on the fifth block south of Temple Square, just slightly past its intersection with 200 E. This is how most of the cities and towns in northern Utah are plotted as well, with all streets oriented around the downtown Mormon Temple. Minor streets are often the exceptions to this rule. In addition, some of the numbered streets have been assigned secondary names. For example, 500 S. is also Cesar Chavez Boulevard, while 900 S. doubles as Harvey Milk Boulevard. If you're a left-brain thinker, this grid system makes the city fabulously easy to navigate. But if you're a right-brain thinker like me, you can't remember which street a certain restaurant is located on for the life of you.

street sign using the grid system

Gallivan Center, where food trucks dock on Thursdays.

Downtown might be Mormon-dominated, but it is cut with decidedly non-Mormon enterprises—namely, bars. All of the city's major hotels and some great restaurants can also be found downtown.

Central City

There's no clear distinction where downtown ends and Central City begins, but you may be able to sense it. Just southeast of downtown, buildings grow a little farther apart and more homes and parks begin to pop up amid businesses. The vibe will feel a little less manicured and a little more organic. Along University Boulevard (400s), you'll find a mix of strip malls, tasty fast-casual finds, a Trader Joe's, and some dives. Central City is also home to the restaurants and retail of historic Trolley Square, as well as the enormous Liberty Park, and the Tracy Aviary that lies within it. Central City is also a great place to discover a few funky boutiques and some great food. Wide streets and bike lanes make much of Central City very bikeable as well.

The Avenues

If "The Avenues" sound a little high and mighty to you, you're not totally off the mark. Located on a hill northeast of downtown, this neighborhood is known as one of the nicest places to live in Salt Lake. This is because of its historic and stately housing stock, in addition to its position slightly above the city, where the inversion causing poor air quality is not quite as bad as in, say, low-lying South Salt Lake. The northern part of The Avenues also backs up to open space and hiking and biking trails, making it an even more appealing place to live. While the neighborhood leans residential, you'll also find quieter places to lodge—think bed-and-breakfasts in historic Victorians—plus a few good cafés.

Capitol Hill

As the name implies, this neighborhood is home to Utah's state capitol, site of politics and protests alike. Once known as Arsenal Hill, this land was the site of explosives manufacturing until the city donated it to the state to serve as the location for the capitol. As downtown slopes north into the foothills of the Wasatch, the capitol building and grounds rise over the city. Capitol Hill sits so close to the foothills that you can even go for a short hike directly from the capitol for views of the city. In character, Capitol Hill is similar to The Avenues: historic buildings, ample trees, and charm. Thanks to fruit trees planted along streets by Mormon settlers, the western part of Capitol Hill is known as the Marmalade District. These early inhabitants used to produce and sell jam (or marmalade) made from these trees, and the name stuck. Marmalade also has a strong LGBTQ+ community, and was even once home to a gay club called JAM.

9th and 9th

Coffee shops that take themselves seriously (in a good way), an eclectic mix of restaurants, funky boutiques—this is what defines the small 9th and 9th district. Named for the confluence of E. 900 S. (Harvey Milk Boulevard) and S. 900 E., this very walkable neighborhood is known for being equal parts hip and pleasant. It lies just southeast of Central City and also includes residential areas.

Sugar House

In addition to planting fruit trees in what's now the Marmalade District, the Mormon settlers also grew sugar beets southeast of downtown. What's now known as Sugar House is a far cry from a religious agricultural outpost. Just south of Central City, Sugar House is considered by most to be a quirky, liberal place to shop, eat, and live. Discover breweries, restaurants, fun shops, and an eponymous park. Believe it or not, this 110-acre public park with trails and a big pond used to be the site of the state prison, but you won't see much in the way of a relic of that history here.

Foothills

East of downtown and Central City, the Foothills are dominated by the University of Utah campus and the student housing surrounding it. You may also hear this neighborhood referred to as the University area.

However, there are other players in the Foothills, namely several sights worth the uphill trek. South of campus, where Emigration Canyon runs into the city, lies the Hogle Zoo and This Is The Place Park, a heritage site of the Latter-day Saints. This is also your entry point into Emigration Canyon, where you can find the historic Ruth's Diner, squeeze in a quick road biking ride, or take a more scenic route toward Park City. On the eastern end of the Foothills area, you'll find the Natural History Museum, as well as Red Butte Garden and its amphitheater, a popular outdoor concert venue. And if you head up past the museums, office buildings, and campus squares into the foothills of the Wasatch itself, you'll find the Bonneville Shoreline Trail and other hiking and biking paths that lead you to vistas of the city.

Ballpark/Granary District

The area surrounding Smith's Ballpark, where the Minor League Baseball team the Salt Lake Bees play, is known as the Ballpark neighborhood. Previously more of an industrial area home to the city's flour mills and silos, this section of the city is also referred to as Granary Row or the Granary District. While restaurants and retail are sparser in this area, there are some gems to be discovered, accessible by the TRAX light rail.

South of the Center

The areas of South Salt Lake, Millcreek, Holladay, and everything else south of the central core are categorized here as South of the Center. Go south for fabulous ethnic eats and some entertainment options in the city.

Sandy/Cottonwood Heights

Venture 13 miles (20.9 km) southeast of Salt Lake City toward the Wasatch Mountains and you'll encounter the adjacent communities of Sandy and Cottonwood Heights. Both were settled shortly after Salt Lake City as farming communities. Today, they exist as bedroom communities of the capital and entryways to the Cottonwood Canyons. In light of their location between Salt Lake City and the Cottonwoods, they can make for convenient places to stop en route to and from Salt Lake and Big and Little Cottonwood Canyons.

West of the Center

Glendale, West Valley City, and other areas farther west of downtown are where you'll find a handful of Salt Lake's breweries and more fine ethnic food.

Sights

DOWNTOWN

★ Temple Square

Just like Arches and Zion National Parks and Utah's ski resorts, **Temple Square** (between North Temple, West Temple, South Temple, and N. State St., www.templesquare.com, 9am-6pm daily, free) draws millions of visitors every year. The headquarters for the Church of Jesus Christ of Latter-day Saints (LDS) is the heart of the city—all of the streets are named for their distance from the temple. It's also located right smack in the middle of downtown. Today, the original 19th-century temple is joined by a dome-shaped concert hall, library, museum, and many other buildings filling a four-acre religious complex, adorned with impeccably manicured grounds, colorful flowers, and very friendly people.

If you're a member of this Church, then Temple Square is probably already at the top of the list for your visit. If you're not, however, you might still consider a visit to the headquarters of a religion with 15 million followers worldwide. For one, it's a historical and cultural look into the religion, as well as into the state as a whole. Exploring Temple Square will also help you better understand the influence of this Church on the culture of Utah, which you'll encounter throughout your visit to the Wasatch—from the logic behind the street naming and the celebration of multiculturalism, to the drink menu at every restaurant.

The Church provides **free daily tours** of Temple Square at regular intervals starting at the west side of the Conference Center. You can also book your own free private tour

or tour a specific attraction on-site, such as the Beehive House or the gardens (www.templesquare.com/tour).

Currently, Temple Square is undergoing a renovation that will conclude in 2024. Some buildings may be partially or fully closed during this period.

THE SALT LAKE TEMPLE

While Latter-day Saints can explore the inside of the **Salt Lake Temple,** non-believers are not allowed beyond the fence surrounding it. But anyone can walk the perimeter of the towering temple of quartzite and—if you're there on a weekend—witness wedding party after wedding party posing for photographs outside. This is just one of many excellent people-watching opportunities at Temple Square—count the different languages you hear spoken from visitors worldwide!

The first stone of white was laid in 1853, and some four decades later, the 210-foot (64-m) Latter-day Saints temple, the largest in the world, was complete. The church is crowned by a golden statue of the angel Moroni—the LDS believe that he delivered the source material for the Book of Mormon to Joseph Smith, the founder of Mormonism, and will blow his trumpet to signal the return of Christ. The Salt Lake Temple does not hold regular services and is only open to church members for "sacred rites," such as marriages. While anyone who is not a member of the Church is not permitted to visit, nonmembers may check out a to-scale replica of the temple in the South Visitors' Center.

VISITORS CENTERS

The **South Visitors' Center** (50 W. South Temple, 801/240-2534, 9am-9pm daily) gives you a peek into the history of both the religion as well as the construction of the Salt Lake Temple.

The **North Visitors' Center** (50 W. North Temple, 801/240-4872, 9am-9pm daily) offers a somewhat more spiritual experience, with a galactic rotunda and a giant statue of Christ. Here you'll also find exhibits on the roles of family and altruism in the Church.

CHURCH HISTORY MUSEUM

Dive deeper into Latter-day Saints history with a visit to the **Church History Museum** (45 N. West Temple, 801/240-3310, 9am-9pm Mon.-Fri., 10am-6pm Sat., free), which stores church records from 1830 on, including books, photographs, audiovisual archives, and Church artifacts, like the design plans for churches and a pair of Brigham Young's sunglasses.

BRIGHAM YOUNG'S HISTORIC HOMES

The **Beehive House** (67 E. South Temple, 801/240-2681, 10am-6pm Mon.-Sat., free), one of the former homes of Mormon leader Brigham Young, derives its name from a beehive sculpture that sits on top of the house—a symbol of the hard, hive-like work of the Latter-day Saint pioneers in turning a salty desert into a fruitful, thriving home (and the reason why Utah is nicknamed "The Beehive State"). In this 1854-built Greek Revival home, you can also view the former belongings of Young and take a free 30-minute tour anytime between 10am and 5pm. You might find it on the large side for a single-family home in the 19th century, but as a polygamist with 55 wives, Young had a larger-than-average family. He lived in the Beehive House until he passed away in 1877, and the adobe-sandstone structure was restored in the mid-20th century and staged with period decor.

In 1856, just a couple of years after the Beehive House was built, another even larger home was built to accommodate Young and his growing family: **The Lion House,** named for the statue of a lion at the entryway. This veritable mansion made from sandstone stands just a couple doors down from the Beehive House, and once housed over 70 of Young's family members. It now houses a series of private-event rental rooms as well as a restaurant open to the public and known as **The Lion House Pantry** (63 E. South Temple, 801/539-3257, 11am-8pm Mon.-Sat.).

TOP EXPERIENCE

THE TABERNACLE

A must on any Temple Square tour should be a visit to the **Tabernacle**—home to the legendary **Tabernacle Choir at Temple Square,** formerly known as the Mormon Tabernacle Choir (and still known colloquially as MoTab). The Tabernacle was completed in 1875, but Brigham Young had integrated music into the Church far earlier than that. He brought along musicians in some of the first groups of pioneers to travel to Utah, and staged a small choir performance within the first few weeks of arriving. And it was Young who is said to have conceived of the Tabernacle's unique design, which he envisioned after beholding a hollow, cracked eggshell.

Today, the Grammy- and Emmy-decorated choir sings inside what is considered one of the most acoustically impeccable buildings in the world. Built from 1863 to 1875 and renovated in 2007, the choir hall is equipped with an 11,623-pipe organ capped by a domed roof enclosed in steel. There are free daily performances (noon Mon.-Sat., 9:30am and 2pm Sun.), as well as more elaborate scheduled choir events like the three-day Christmas concerts that sell out each year.

FAMILY HISTORY LIBRARY

Though the **Family History Library** (35 N. West Temple, 801/240-6996, www.familysearch.org/locations/saltlakecity-library, 8am-9pm Mon.-Fri., 9am-5pm Sat., 1pm-5pm Sun., free) is located within

City Center

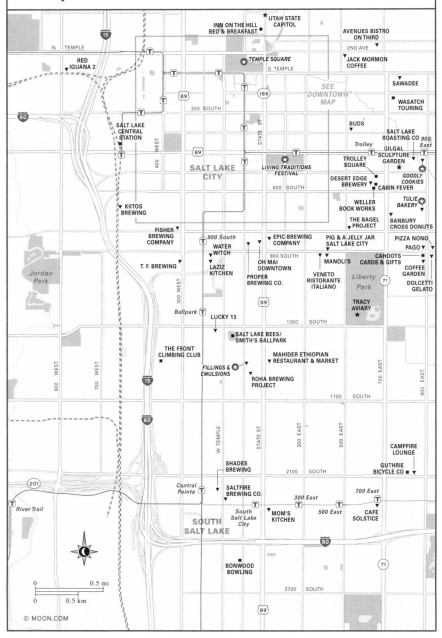

INN ON THE HILL
BED & BREAKFAST ●
UTAH STATE
CAPITOL ★

AVENUES BISTRO
ON THIRD ▼
2ND AVE ▼

RED
IGUANA 2 ▼

N TEMPLE

TEMPLE SQUARE ✦
S TEMPLE

JACK MORMON
COFFEE ▼

SAWADEE ▼

SEE
"DOWNTOWN"
MAP

WASATCH
TOURING ■

200 SOUTH

STATE ST

BUDS ▼

SALT LAKE
ROASTING CO ▼ 900
East

Trolley

SALT LAKE
CENTRAL
STATION

SALT LAKE
CITY ✦

LIVING TRADITIONS
FESTIVAL ✦

600 SOUTH

GILGAL
SCULPTURE
GARDEN ★

TROLLEY
SQUARE

DESERT EDGE
BREWERY ▼■
CABIN FEVER

GOODLY
COOKIES

TULIE
BAKERY ✦

WELLER
BOOK WORKS

THE BAGEL
PROJECT ▼■

BANBURY
CROSS DONUTS

KIITOS
BREWING

FISHER ▼
BREWING
COMPANY

900 South

EPIC BREWING
COMPANY ▼

WATER ▼
WITCH ▼

T. F. BREWING

LAZIZ
KITCHEN ▼

OH MAI
DOWNTOWN ▼

900 SOUTH

PROPER
BREWING CO. ▼

PIG & A JELLY JAR
SALT LAKE CITY

MANOLI'S ▼

VENETO
RISTORANTE
ITALIANO

PIZZA NONO ▼
PAGO ▼

CAHOOTS
CARDS & GIFTS ■

COFFEE
GARDEN ▼

DOLCETTI
GELATO ▼

Liberty
Park 71

TRACY
AVIARY ★

Ballpark

LUCKY 13 ▼

1300 SOUTH

SALT LAKE BEES/
SMITH'S BALLPARK ■

THE FRONT
CLIMBING CLUB ■

FILLINGS & ✦
EMULSIONS

MAHIDER ETHIOPIAN
RESTAURANT & MARKET ▼

ROHA BREWING
PROJECT ■

1700 SOUTH

CAMPFIRE
LOUNGE ▼

SHADES
BREWING ▼

2100 SOUTH

GUTHRIE
BICYCLE CO ■ ▼

Central
Pointe

SALTFIRE
BREWING CO. ▼

300 East

700 East

South
Salt Lake
City

MOM'S
KITCHEN ▼

500 East

CAFE
SOLSTICE ▼

SOUTH
SALT LAKE

BONWOOD
BOWLING ■

2700 SOUTH

0   0.5 mi
0   0.5 km

© MOON.COM

River Trail

Jordan
Park

© MOON.COM

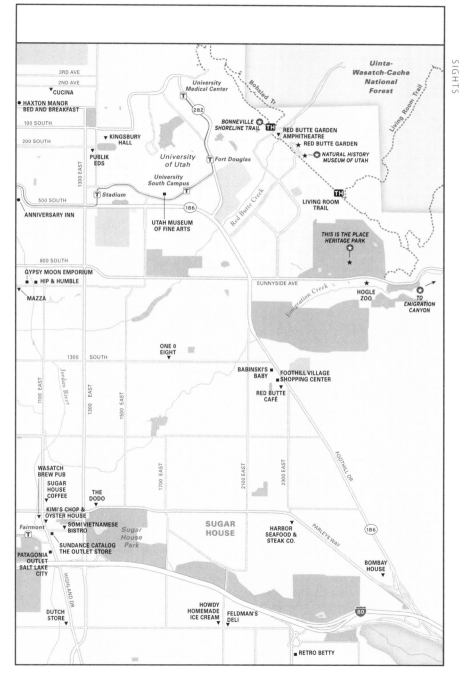

Downtown

NORTH TEMPLE STATION
300 WEST
North Temple Bridge
3RD AVE
ELLERBECK MANSION BED & BREAKFAST
2ND AVE
N TEMPLE
CHURCH HISTORY MUSEUM
SALT LAKE TEMPLE
TEMPLE SQUARE
STATE ST
1ST AVE
A ST
B ST
C ST
50 NORTH
FAMILY HISTORY LIBRARY
THE TABERNACLE
THE LION HOUSE
BEEHIVE HOUSE
PUNCH BOWL SOCIAL
Arena
S TEMPLE
S TEMPLE
SALT LAKE CITY
UTAH JAZZ/ VIVINT SMART HOME ARENA
Temple Square
CITY CREEK CENTER
SOUTH VISITORS' CENTER
THE COMPLEX
ABRAVANEL HALL
City Center
HARMONS GROCERY- CITY CREEK
DISCOVERY GATEWAY CHILDREN'S MUSEUM
100 SOUTH
VISIT SALT LAKE
LAST COURSE
ECCLES THEATER
PRETTY BIRD CHICKEN
EVA'S BAKERY
BOURBON HOUSE
400 EAST
Old Greek Town
CLARK PLANETARIUM
Planetarium
W TEMPLE
CAPITOL THEATRE
MAIN ST
BAR-X
500 WEST
CAMPOS COFFEE ROASTERY & KITCHEN
200 SOUTH
KIMPTON HOTEL MONACO SALT LAKE CITY
BAMBARA
ESTE PIZZERIA
GOURMANDISE
THE ROSE ESTABLISHMENT
ZEST KITCHEN & BAR
THE DAILY
GALLIVAN CENTER ICE SKATING
THE COPPER ONION
CURRENT FISH AND OYSTER
BRUGES WAFFLES & FRITES
TONY CAPUTO'S MARKET & DELI
THE PEERY HOTEL
Gallivan Plaza
ALAMEXO
RIO GRANDE ST
LAAN NA THAI
Pioneer Park
WHITE HORSE SPIRITS & KITCHEN
CHEERS TO YOU
300 SOUTH
TAVERNACLE SOCIAL CLUB
VALTER'S OSTERIA
TAKASHI
THE REST
THE HEAVY METAL SHOP
BODEGA
Liberty
400 SOUTH
BTG WINE BAR
THE GREEN PIG PUB
Washington Square
Liberty Square
500 WEST
400 WEST
AREA 51
200 WEST
Courthouse
LIVING TRADITIONS FESTIVAL
THE LEONARDO
500 SOUTH
THE LITTLE AMERICA HOTEL- SALT LAKE CITY
300 WEST
CANYON SPORTS
GRAND AMERICA HOTEL
STATE ST
LES MADELEINES
300 EAST
600 SOUTH
600 SOUTH
R&R BBQ
THE STATE ROOM
200 EAST
700 SOUTH
W TEMPLE
MAIN ST

0   250 yds
0   250 m

© MOON.COM

Temple Square and is owned by the Latter-day Saints Church, it's a terrific resource for all. A family-oriented religion, Mormonism has a natural interest in preserving family records. According to LDS belief, families can be joined together for eternity through the performance of sacred sealing services in the temple. Proxy rites can also be performed for the dead. The ancestors on whose behalf the services are performed are believed to have a choice of accepting or rejecting these rites.

As the largest genealogical record-keeper in the world, the Family History Library is a must for anyone exploring their ancestry. With data on over three billion of our collective ancestors, 600,000 books, and 1.4 million microfilm rolls of archived material to peruse, you're bound to find something about someone to whom you're related. Staff and volunteers are on-site to help you with your search. While you rustle around your family tree, send your kids over to a children's area to keep them entertained.

1: the Salt Lake Temple 2: Utah State Capitol with the Joseph Smith Memorial Building's beehive roof in foreground 3: the Tabernacle on Temple Square

MORE AT TEMPLE SQUARE

While the buildings and attractions listed above are the primary highlights of a Temple Square visit, there are several other buildings you can tour. The **Conference Center** (60 W. North Temple, 801/240-0075, 10am-8pm daily) is a massive auditorium that holds 21,000 and hosts the semiannual conferences of the church, broadcasted in dozens of languages around the world.

Originally a hotel, the **Joseph Smith Memorial Building** (15 E. South Temple, 801/531-1000, 9am-9pm daily) today serves as a hub of dining and entertainment at Temple Square. Inside this ornate and stately building you'll find several restaurants open to the public as well as the Legacy Theater, which screens free short films about the Church of Jesus Christ of Latter-day Saints—topics range from Joseph Smith to reenactments of the Book of Mormon—10am-6pm daily.

At the **Assembly Center** (50 W. South Temple, 801/240-4872, 9am-9pm daily), built from the same granite as the Salt Lake Temple, the church holds various events, lectures, and concerts, including free performances on Friday and Saturday nights.

Several organizations within the Church have their home in the **Relief Society Building** (76 N. Main St., 801/240-4450), constructed in 1956. This serves as the world headquarters for the Primary organization for kids, the Young Women organization, and the Relief Society, which is for all adult women in the church. You'll find artifacts and paintings on display here, which you can observe during one of the free 30-minute tours available 9am-4:30pm on weekdays.

Finally, right across from the Salt Lake Temple sits the 28-floor **Church Office Building** (50 E. North Temple, 801/240-1000, 9am-4pm Mon.-Fri.), a brutalist structure finished in 1972, which, as the name suggests, houses church offices. If you want to check out views of everything from the Great Salt Lake to the neighboring mountain ranges from the 26th-floor observation deck, schedule a free tour (contact COBhosting@ldschurch.org).

Aside from the buildings, the grounds of Temple Square are great for people-watching and observing the various memorials and statues paying homage to the Church's historic leaders and to the pioneers who braved their way across the country to Utah. One particularly noteworthy sculpture is the **Base and Meridian** (0 W. South Temple). Located at the southeast corner of Temple Square, this plaque marks the origin point of Salt Lake City's entire grid system—point zero East, zero South, zero West, and Zero North.

Clark Planetarium

Step into the shoes of a synesthetic and watch a spectacular cosmic light show synced with Led Zeppelin songs in the **Clark Planetarium** (110 S. 400 W., 385/468-7827, https://slco.org/clark-planetarium, 10:30am-7pm Sun.-Wed., 10:30am-10pm Thurs., 10:30am-11pm Fri.-Sat., free exhibits, IMAX tickets range $5-9). This is perhaps one of the most appealing adult offerings at the planetarium, but family-friendly activities and shows are as plentiful as the stars in the night sky. Catch exhibits on space weather and solar flares, or head to the dome-shaped IMAX theater to behold the wonder of Earth and beyond, from the speed of light to volcanoes.

The Leonardo

We have art museums, and we have science museums. Why can't we have one place to explore the curiosities of both the left *and* right sides of our brains? That's the thinking behind **The Leonardo** (209 E. 500 S., 801/531-9800, www.theleonardo.org, 10am-5pm daily, $12.95 adults, $8.95 children), a downtown museum inspired by the dualities of Leonardo da Vinci. With exhibits exploring everything from the magic of flight to existentialism, the curation here manages to appeal to kids and adults alike. For a more hands-on experience, artists and non-artists are welcome to visit Leonardo's Studio for fine-arts projects. To get in touch with the left side of your brain, visit the Laboratory, where you can find live demonstrations of scientific principles. And bring it all home at Leonardo's Workshop, which lets you design, engineer, and build, just as the Renaissance man himself once did.

Discovery Gateway Children's Museum

If you're traveling with little ones, the **Discovery Gateway Children's Museum** (444 W. 100 S., 801/456-5437, www.discoverygateway.org, 10am-6pm Mon.-Thurs., 10am-7pm Fri.-Sat., noon-6pm Sun., $12.50 pp) is a great hands-on experience well suited for ages 2 to around 10 years old. Especially on rainy or cold days, this is a great place to let your kids run free for an afternoon. A few unique exhibits include a climbing area centered around honeybees (real, live ones in a hive!), a giant foam-block building area, and a sensory room. For babies, there are also a couple of suitable play areas, as well as a nursing area for mothers. The museum is located in the Gateway center, so there are plenty of dining options nearby.

CAPITOL HILL
Utah State Capitol

It took Utah two decades after officially becoming the 45th state in 1896 to construct a capitol building on what was once known as Arsenal Hill, named for the weaponry originally stored there. Following a significant renovation, the capitol now contains two legislative chambers and the state supreme court, as well as other offices. A visit to the **Utah Capitol** (350 State St., 801/538-1800, https://utahstatecapitol.utah.gov, 7am-8pm Mon.-Thurs., 7am-6pm Fri., 8am-6pm Sat.-Sun.) will expose you to more than just politics, however. This is also a great place to find Western artwork and to peek into the state's history. You can take an hour-long tour (meet at the front desk by the east doors on the first floor, every hour on the hour 9am-4pm Mon.-Fri., ages 10 and over, free), or explore the capitol yourself with the help of a self-guided tour brochure at the visitors center. While you won't be able to take a tour on weekends, you might be privy to one of the frequent protests

and demonstrations that march from downtown up to Capitol Hill to flood its halls.

CENTRAL CITY
Gilgal Sculpture Garden

Take a turn down a random alley in a quiet residential neighborhood and discover some of the strangest sculptures in Salt Lake City—or just about anywhere, really. **Gilgal Sculpture Garden** (749 E. 500 S., 801/972-7860, http://gilgalgarden.org, 8am-8pm daily Apr.-Sept., 9am-5pm daily Oct.-Mar., free) was the passion project of mason and Latter-day Saints bishop Thomas Battersby Child Jr., who worked on the 12 sculptures and 70 stone engravings from 1945 right up until his dying day in 1963. The small garden takes its name from a biblical site where Israelites camped, likely translated from a Hebrew word for "circle of stones." You'll find everything from a quartzite Sphinx to a face and body parts strewn across moss-covered stone (a giant in the biblical King Nebuchadnezzar's dream). While many of the Gilgal carvings are religiously inspired, the garden has an eclectic vibe that will appeal to the religious, the spiritual, and the agnostic alike. Gilgal is an easy stop to make if you're already in the Central City area shopping at the nearby Trolley Square or Trader Joe's. Visit for the sake of your own youthfulness—as Child once said, the gardens were designed to help "keep one's mind young."

Tracy Aviary

The Great Salt Lake and its Antelope Island are not the only places to spy birds in Utah. The nation's oldest and biggest independent aviary is located right in Liberty Park near downtown Salt Lake. For over 80 years, the **Tracy Aviary** (589 1300 S., 801/596-8500, https://tracyaviary.org, 9am-5pm daily, open until 8pm Mon. June-Aug., $11.95 adults, $7.95 children) has been a home and conservation advocate for birds of Utah, the Amazon, Chile, and many more places. In closely replicated habitats, you can spy bald eagles, over 30 birds from South America, and Andy the Andean

Condor. You can also have nose-to-beak experiences with the more-convivial feathered friends, and watch bird trainers work with everything from pelicans to Chilean flamingos. And don't miss the 360-degree head rotations happening in the Owl Forest.

FOOTHILLS

Drive up Sunnyside Boulevard from Foothill Drive past the University of Utah and various office buildings, and you'll find yourself in a veritable playground of fun, educational activities for kids and adults alike. Within a short walking distance of one another—no more than a mile (1.6 km)—are the Natural History Museum of Utah, Hogle Zoo, Red Butte Garden, and This Is The Place Park, all just steps below the Bonneville Shoreline Trail ringing the northeastern part of Salt Lake City. Continue on Sunnyside to head into Emigration Canyon—a popular road bike ride—home to the popular Ruth's Diner, which makes a nice complement to any of the above activities.

★ This Is The Place Heritage Park

Loaded with history and attractions, This Is The Place Heritage Park (2601 Sunnyside Ave. S., 801/582-1847, www.thisistheplace.org, 10am-5pm daily, $13.95 adults, $9.95 children) draws families in search of fun activities as well as visitors seeking to explore the Latter-day Saints heritage in Utah. It came into being as a site of importance on July 24, 1847, when Brigham Young and his caravan of followers emerged from Emigration Canyon and declared, "This is the right place. Drive on." The location became This Is The Place Park, and the day eventually became Pioneer Day, a celebratory state holiday. Today, the park is sort of like a Latter-day Saints theme park. For families of all faiths, it's a great place to let your kids get their ya-yas out. But you can also relive Utah's past here. In Heritage Village, you'll find over 50 replicas of historic buildings and relocated historic buildings alive with historical reenactors, including Brigham Young's barn, a shaving parlor, and pioneer cabins. There's also a Native American village and trains that chug around the park. For the little ones, there's a petting zoo, a water park, and treats like ice cream.

★ Natural History Museum of Utah

As a D.C. native, I have high standards when it comes to natural history museums, and Utah's more than exceeds my expectations. In a building designed to reflect the landscape surrounding it, the Natural History Museum of Utah (301 Wakara Way, 801/581-4303, https://nhmu.utah.edu, 10am-5pm daily, open until 9pm Wed., $14.95 adults, $9.95 children, $5 after 5pm Wed) curates innovative and culturally intelligent exhibits on everything from Utah topography to the first people to inhabit the Great Basin of Utah (spoiler alert: it wasn't the Latter-day Saints). Aside from the excellent special exhibitions, be sure to discover the permanent multisensory exploration of the Great Salt Lake, as well as the top-floor hall of Native Voices, which lets local Indigenous tribes speak for themselves. Designed together with local tribes like the Paiute and Navajo, this exhibit tells stories of the first people here through photos, artwork, and audiovisual recordings. Best of all, you can head right onto the Bonneville Shoreline Trail behind the museum to discover the landscape you just learned about. Before your visit, check the events calendar; the museum often hosts events ranging from speakers and nature walks, to bluegrass and barbecue festivals on summer evenings.

Red Butte Garden

While Red Butte Garden (300 Wakara Way, 801/585-0556, www.redbuttegarden.org, 9am-5pm daily Jan.-Mar. and Oct.-Dec., 9am-7:30pm daily Apr. and Sept., 9am-9pm daily May-Aug., $14 adults, $7 children) may

1: This Is The Place Park 2: Mormon Battalion Monument at the Utah State Capitol 3: Gilgal Sculpture Garden

be better known to some as an outdoor concert venue, it is first and foremost a botanical garden—the biggest in the Rocky Mountain West. Find everything from daffodils to conifers across these 100 acres of gardens and trails owned by the University of Utah. Walking the gardens is made even more pleasant by poems on display beside many of the exhibits. The spring is a particularly glorious time to visit, when half a million flowers are in bloom. Aside from the regular outdoor summer concerts, Red Butte Garden hosts several other events, from yoga and art exhibits to programs revolving around the birds who visit the gardens.

Hogle Zoo

Explore many a landscape and species at the **Hogle Zoo** (2600 Sunnyside Ave. S., 801/584-1700, www.hoglezoo.org, 9am-6pm daily Mar.-Oct., 10am-5pm daily Nov.-Feb., $18.95 adults, $14.95 children May-Sept., $16.95 adults, $12.95 children Oct.-Apr.), just across the road from This Is The Place Park. From the African Savanna and the big cat-filled Asian Highlands, to the watery world of sea lions, polar bears, and otters, this is in the upper echelon of zoos in the world, and does make an effort to support endangered species

outside its gates. This inherently kid-friendly destination is made all the more so with daily bird shows, the Creekside playground area for kids, and the Lighthouse Point Splash Zone.

The "U" on the Hill

As you drive into Salt Lake City, you may notice a big, white letter "U" on a hill above the city. If you're a resident of the Southwest, the sight of a letter on a hill might be familiar. But if you're traveling from elsewhere, you might be wondering why the landscape has been labeled with a letter. Of the 400-some hillside letters out West, the 100-foot-tall (30-m) "U" is one of the first, built by students above the University of Utah campus in 1909. While you may prefer to behold the "U" on Mount Van Cott from afar, you can actually hike up to the thing and take a seat on an old sofa some college students placed in its shadow. To get to the "U," which sits somewhat awkwardly above an affluent neighborhood, put "Block U" into Google Maps, or navigate to the end of New Bedford Drive, accessed via Popperton Park Way. From here you'll find a rec path leading to the "Block U," as the university has trademarked it. Whether you regard hillside letters as graffiti or historic monuments, getting up close and personal with these massive

Red Butte Garden

letters is an interesting experience. Plus, you can behold the entire city below, not to mention the Wasatch and Oquirrh Mountains.

University of Utah Campus

Wherever you are in the Foothills, you'll probably pass by or through the **University of Utah** (www.utah.edu) campus. Originally founded by Mormon pioneers in 1847 as the University of Deseret, today the institution is known for being far more secular than its religious counterpart in Provo, Brigham Young University. There are a few historical and entertainment attractions on campus for the non-academic visitor. **Kingsbury Hall** (1395 Presidents' Circle, 801/481-7100, https://kingsburyhall.utah.edu) often hosts speakers, comedic acts, film festivals, and concerts. Discover everything from local artists and ancient mummies to exhibits on Spiral Jetty at the **Utah Museum of Fine Arts** (410 Campus Center Dr., 801/581-7332, https://umfa.utah.edu, 10am-5pm Tues.-Sat., open until 9pm Wed., $15.95). The **South Physics Observatory** (115 S. 1500 E., 801/581-6901) is open to the public on clear Wednesday evenings (7pm-11pm) for star parties. During college football season, you can catch the Utes playing at **Rice-Eccles Stadium** (451 S. 1400 E., 801/581-5445, https://stadium.utah.edu). And war buffs may want to pay a visit to the Fort Douglas area of campus, where you'll find the **Fort Douglas Military Museum** (32 Potter St., 801/581-1251, www.fortdouglas.org, noon-5pm Tues.-Sat., free). There is also a large medical campus toward the northeast end of the university campus.

Recreation and Activities

Not only is Salt Lake City close to many recreational opportunities, but you can even access trails right from the city.

HIKING AND BIKING
The Living Room Trail

Whoever cut in **The Living Room Trail** (2.7 mi/4.3 km round-trip, 1,000 ft/305 m elevation gain, moderate) must have been impatient. This classic Salt Lake City hike, in the Foothills just minutes from downtown, doesn't bother with switchbacks, instead choosing to march more or less straight up toward its destination, which is an outcropping of slabs and boulders naturally arranged in such a way that they resemble living room furniture. Take a seat on the sofa and spread out your sandwich on the rock table beside you, then take in the views, which include the city and the Wasatch and Oquirrh Mountains. Due to the steep trail, budget 1-2 hours depending on your pace. This trail is dog-friendly and does tend to draw quite a bit of traffic. While there are several different starting points, the most common trailhead starts off a small road behind office buildings (383 Colorow Rd.).

★ Bonneville Shoreline Trail

Named for the ancient massive lake that gave way to the modern Great Salt Lake, the **Bonneville Shoreline Trail** (www.bonnevilleshorelinetrail.org) follows the original eastern shoreline of Lake Bonneville. While this dirt trail travels over 100 miles (161 km) through northern Utah, the section outlining the northeastern edge of Salt Lake City spans 13.5 miles (21.7 km), with over a dozen trailheads and several other intersecting trails. This means you can make your Bonneville Shoreline Trail experience as short or long as you please. Most of the trail runs relatively level without the dramatic elevation gain characteristic of some other trails that climb into the mountains. Popular trailheads include the City Creek Trailhead (intersection of City Creek Canyon Rd. and Bonneville Dr.), the Avenues Trailhead (off Popperton Park

Rd. in the Avenues), and the Red Butte Creek Trailhead (right behind Red Butte Garden).

Locals love to hike, run, and bike along the BST, which intersects with numerous other trails, including the Living Room Trail and **Bobsled** (1.5 mi/2.4 km one-way, 20 minutes, 880 ft/268 m elevation loss, difficult), a popular downhill mountain biking trail. With little shade, the BST is not ideal for midday summer pursuits, but as a result of this exposure, it can often be hiked year-round.

Eventually, if fundraising and planning goes as planned, the Bonneville Shoreline Trail will be expanded to cover some 280 miles (450 km) from just south of Provo to the Idaho border.

★ Emigration Canyon

Arguably the most popular road bike ride in Salt Lake City is the climb up **Emigration Canyon** (16 mi/26 km round-trip, 1.5-2.5 hours depending on pace, 1,350 ft/411 m elevation gain, difficult). Many begin this out-and-back ride from Rotary Park in the Foothills, but it could easily be started from the University of Utah campus or any point within the city. The smooth road navigates its way east of Salt Lake up a curvy road through residential neighborhoods to the top of Little Mountain Summit, where you can behold Little Dell and East Dell Reservoirs—a glorious sight during fall foliage. A very popular post-ride stop is **Ruth's Diner** (4610 Emigration Canyon Rd., Salt Lake City, 801/582-5807, https://ruthsdiner.com, 8am-9pm Sun.-Thurs., 8am-10pm Fri.-Sat.), a locally beloved and bustling restaurant. Due to the exposure and steep climb, this ride is best done at sunrise or sunset in the summer, or in the autumn.

EQUIPMENT RENTALS AND TOURS

There are numerous places right in Salt Lake City where you can buy, rent, or demo the gear you need to explore the Wasatch. If you're heading to the ski resorts, you might wonder why you would bother to procure your gear in the city, when you can just as easily rent from a base area shop. The answer is that not only will you find cheaper prices, but you'll also experience shorter lines, meaning more time on the hill, less time sizing your boots. Unless you're only renting ski or snowboard gear for a day, it makes sense to rent in Salt Lake City.

If you're renting a mountain bike, keep in mind that you'll need a way to transport your bike to the trails. Be sure that your vehicle has enough trunk space to accommodate a bike or is equipped with a bike rack.

Downtown

Canyon Sports (517 S. 200 W., 801/322-4220, www.canyonsports.com, 10am-6pm daily, extended hours during the ski season Nov.-Apr.) has been in the business of outfitting adventures for over 25 years. This downtown rental shop offers year-round rentals, including ski gear (starting at $48 per day), mountain bikes (starting at $55 per day), tents, and paddleboards (starting at $30 per day). You can also purchase discount ski lift tickets to resorts in the Cottonwood Canyons, as well as get your own gear tuned and repaired.

The Avenues

The story of **Wasatch Touring** (702 E. 100 S., 801/359-9361, www.wasatchtouring.com, 9am-7pm Mon.-Sat., mountain bikes start at $50 per day, touring skis start at $45 per day for skis and boots) starts in 1968, when the future owners took a ski trip to Utah and got blissfully socked in by a fierce winter storm at Alta ski area. Four years later, they decided to move to Salt Lake City and open a backcountry specialty ski rental shop, the first of its kind in the city, specializing in renting backcountry touring equipment. Wasatch Touring sells, demos, and rents equipment for skiing, biking, water sports, and more.

Foothills

Since 1972, **Sports Den** (1350 Foothill Dr.,

1: The Living Room Trail 2: a stretch of the Bonneville Shoreline Trail

Renting vs. Demoing Gear

If you're wondering what the difference is between renting and demoing gear—whether for biking or skiing—it boils down to intention and quality. A gear shop's rental stock is usually a little beat up and older, especially at the end of a season, but will do the trick if you just want to get out. For this reason, rentals are less expensive. The idea behind demoing gear is that the user is usually looking to buy and wants to try out some of the latest models before committing to a purchase. Demo stock is thus usually newer and higher quality—and more expensive.

801/582-5611, www.sportsden.com, 10am-8pm Mon.-Fri., 10am-6pm Sat., 10am-5pm Sun., mountain bikes starting at $70 per day, ski rentals starting at $20 per day) has been helping people get out on bikes and skis in the Wasatch at competitive prices. With gear for sale, rent, and demo—as well as tuning and repair services—Sports Den is a great one-stop-shop for all skiing and biking adventures. The shop also vends discounted tickets to nearby ski resorts, including Deer Valley, Snowbasin, Alta, and Snowbird.

Sugar House

If you like your bike rentals with a side of history, head straight to **Guthrie Bicycle Co.** (803 E. 2100 S., 801/484-0404, www.guthriebike.com, 9:30am-7pm Mon.-Fri., 9:30am-6pm Sat., rentals $75 per day, demos $150 per day). This local shop got its start in 1888 when a pair of local brothers started building bikes in Salt Lake City. And for the past five generations, the shop has been owned and operated by the same family. If you're looking to rent or demo a bike, this is the best place to do so, since it specializes in bikes and bikes only. Road, mountain, cruiser, electric, and children's bikes are available here from brands like Santa Cruz, Trek, Electra, and Zerode.

PARKS
Central City
LIBERTY PARK
At the 80-acre **Liberty Park** (600 E. 900 S., bounded by 900 S., 700 E., 1300 S., and 500 E., 8am-11pm daily), you can easily while away a whole day and evening. At this vast,

grass-filled park, you can jog around a 1.5-mile (2.4 km) path, where the miles will click by thanks to superb people-watching. Throw around some balls at the volleyball, tennis, or basketball courts. Take the kiddos to the playground and then have a picnic in one of the gazebos. Take a seat on a bench overlooking the pond. Take a nap beneath the shade of one of many cottonwood trees. Visit the Tracy Aviary, a bird sanctuary within the park's limits. And wind it all down with a game of horseshoes.

Sugar House
SUGAR HOUSE PARK
At 110 acres, **Sugar House Park** (1330 E. 2100 S., bounded by 1300 E., 2100 S., 1700 E., and I-80 to the south, 801/467-1721, www.sugarhousepark.org, 7am-10pm daily summer, 7am-9pm daily winter) is the largest in the city. With mountain views, plenty of trees, a large bird-filled pond, and rolling green grass, it's also one of the most pleasant. You'd never guess this was the former site of the state prison (now demolished)! Aside from the agreeable setting, amenities include a nearly 2-mile (3.2-km) jogging path and several pavilions.

ICE SKATING
Downtown
Gallivan Center Ice Skating (50 E. 200 S., 801/535-6117, http://thegallivancenter.com/ice-skating, 4pm-9pm Mon.-Thurs., noon-midnight Fri.-Sat., noon-7pm Sun. mid-Nov.-mid-Feb., $9 adults, $8 children for admission and rentals) is a great activity for a winter afternoon in Salt Lake City, with pleasant music,

lit trees, colorful ice, and a concession booth vending hot chocolate, cappuccinos, churros, and more snacks. If you skate on Tuesdays and Thursdays, you'll only pay $5.

CLIMBING
Ballpark/Granary District
If I had to spend a whole day inside in Utah, it would be at **The Front Climbing Club** (1470 S. 400 W., 801/466-7625, https://frontslc.com, 6am-11pm Mon.-Fri., 9am-10pm Sat.-Sun., day pass $25). A colorful purveyor of great tunes and a hub for community, The Front is the place to be, located on the edge of the Ballpark neighborhood. In addition to excellent lead, top-rope, and bouldering options, there are good vibes to be found here. If you're heading to The Front solo but not into bouldering, take advantage of the two auto-belay stations, where you can bust out a 5.8, 5.10, or 5.12 all by your lonesome. If you're heading here to escape bad weather without sitting around, in addition to climbing, you can work out at the gym, squeeze in a yoga class, or hang out at the second-floor café, which serves light fare, kombucha, wine, and beer. This is especially important because The Front, like many climbing gyms, is located in the middle of nowhere.

South of the Center
Located in Millcreek, **Momentum Indoor Climbing** (3173 E. 3300 S., 801/906-2132, www.momentumclimbing.com/millcreek, 6am-11pm Mon.-Fri., 10am-11pm Sat., 10am-6pm Sun., day pass $20) offers some of the best indoor climbing in Utah in an unassuming strip mall. With 100-plus top-rope climbs, plenty of lead opportunities, bouldering, concrete cracks, and even a 50-foot (15-m) arch that evokes our state's red rock climbing to the south, you'll never get bored at Momentum. Here you can also use the gym, take a yoga class, and busy your little ones in a kids' climbing area or with the on-site daycare service. There are also a couple of other Momentum locations in the Salt Lake area.

BOWLING
South of the Center
Whether you're looking for a family-friendly activity or just a fun way to pass a winter's night, **Bonwood Bowling** (2500 S. Main St., South Salt Lake, 801/487-7758, www. bonwoodbowl.com, 9am-midnight Sun.-Thurs., 9am-1am Fri.-Sat., starting at $6 for two games and shoes) is your answer. Affordably priced and time-tested (since 1957), this 42-lane alley is a hit with locals, leagues (50 and counting!), and visitors alike. One unique league that plays here revolves around heavy metal. To get your metalhead on, check out "SLC Metal Bowling League" on Facebook. Complement your experience with snacks, beer, and wine from the on-site café and Trophy Room Lounge.

SPECTATOR SPORTS
Basketball
What's a team called the "Jazz" doing in Salt Lake City, which isn't exactly known for the genre of music? The NBA team actually started in New Orleans and moved to Salt Lake City in 1979, hence the name. Today, the **Utah Jazz** play at the **Vivint Smart Home Arena** (301 S. Temple, 801/325-2000, www. nba.com/jazz, Oct.-Apr., tickets start at $19) downtown.

Baseball
Team quirks, better seats, cheaper tickets—these are just a few reasons to catch a Minor League Baseball game. All summer long, the **Salt Lake Bees** swing bats over at **Smith's Ballpark** (77 W. 1300 S., 801/350-6900, www. milb.com/salt-lake, Apr.-Sept., tickets start at $10), located south of downtown. If you upgrade your ticket and shell out $25, you can sit in the Ford Zone, which includes a lawn seat and all-you-can-consume popcorn, nachos, hot dogs, churros, and soda. Or save your appetite for a burger over at **Lucky 13** (135 W. 1300 S., 801/487-4418, www.lucky13slc.com, 11am-2am daily), a popular sports bar and restaurant located nearby.

Shopping

Alfresco shopping centers, a historic train depot filled with shops, walkable neighborhoods sporting spunky boutiques—these are a few of the shopping experiences that await in Salt Lake.

DOWNTOWN
City Creek Center
Shop in the open air amid flowing water and aquatic plants at the retail pride of downtown, **City Creek Center** (50 Main St., 801/521-2012, https://shopcitycreekcenter.com, 10am-9pm Mon.-Thurs., 10am-9:30pm Fri.-Sat., first two hours of parking free). You'll find a mix of department stores like Nordstrom and Macy's, apparel shops ranging from Lululemon to Anthropologie, an Apple store, and more. At this LEED Silver-certified shopping center, you'll also find dozens of dining options, mostly fast-casual chains, including CoreLife Eatery, Rocky Mountain Chocolate Factory, Taste of Red Iguana, and Tibet Bowl & Sushi. While a creek does run through this outdoor shopping center as the name suggests, unfortunately it's an artificial one fed by a faucet. While there is an actual City Creek that originates in a canyon of the same name, it's been routed underground.

The Gateway
Located in the historic Union Pacific train depot, **The Gateway** (400 W. 100 S., 801/456-0000, http://shopthegateway.com, 10am-9pm Mon.-Sat., noon-6pm Sun.) is neither a shopping center nor a mall, but more of a plaza filled with shops, museums, entertainment, and a couple of unique places to drink: daytime (La Barba Coffee) or nighttime (Seabird Bar). In the educational world, explore the cosmos at the Clark Planetarium, and send the kids to the Discovery Gateway Children's Museum. For entertainment, head to Dave & Buster's, laugh it up at a comedy club, or check out the new Punch Bowl Social, which is, in a nutshell, a gaming emporium with great food and punch. The latter concept—born in Denver and quickly spreading across the country—blends playful, from-scratch food and entertainment, from bowling and arcade games to karaoke. The Gateway also frequently hosts events like concerts, Wednesday night outdoor film screenings, Sunday yoga, and art strolls.

Other Downtown Shopping
Tucked away on a small side street off State Street, **The Heavy Metal Shop** (63 Exchange Pl., 801/467-7071, www.heavymetalshop.com, noon-6pm Mon.-Sat.) has been "peddlin' evil" in Salt Lake City since 1987. The shop is scarcely large enough for half a dozen customers, with every inch of real estate dominated by metal vinyls. The shop is owned by local legend Kevin Kirt, who sort of resembles the title character of *Wayne's World,* gracefully aged. If you don't own a record player, make your souvenir selection "The Heavy Metal Shop" shirt—a timeless tee that has been worn by the likes of Alice Cooper.

9TH AND 9TH
If you like your shopping experience to be less mall-like and more organic, the 9th (900 E.) and 9th (900 S., also known as Harvey Milk Boulevard) neighborhood, just upstream of downtown, is a mecca for quirky boutiques that you could easily spend a whole day browsing. This family-friendly neighborhood is very walkable, sports a touch of funk, and also hosts great dining.

One unique store is the **Gypsy Moon Emporium** (1011 E. 900 S., 801/521-9100, www.gypsymoonemporium.com, 10:30am-5pm Mon.-Fri.), which has been carrying ancient and present-day relics of Celtic culture

1

2

3

since 1986 in a charming Victorian cottage. For gag gifts, Utah paraphernalia, and other unique souvenirs, head to **Cahoots** (878 E. 900 S., 801/538-0606, www.cahootssaltlake. com, 10am-9pm daily). And if it's women's clothing you're looking for, shop the racks of casual, on-trend apparel at **Hip & Humble** (1043 E. 900 S., 801/467-3130, https://hipandhumble.com, 10am-7pm Mon.-Sat., noon-5pm Sun.), which also carries select home decor, gifts, and dish towels with attitude.

CENTRAL CITY

Though it might technically be defined as a mall, **Trolley Square** (602 E. 500 S., 801/521-9877, www.trolleysquare.com, 10am-9pm Mon.-Sat., noon-5pm Sun.) is delightful as far as shopping centers go. Originally built in 1908 as a series of barns to store streetcars, Trolley Square also celebrates the heritage of the Salt Lake Rail Company at the **Trolley History Museum** (5pm-9pm Thurs.-Fri., free). The part-outdoor/part-indoor shopping center is home to a yoga studio, a coffee shop, Whole Foods, and a host of other chains and independently owned businesses. If you're searching for souvenirs and gifts to bring back to your home fries, stop by **Cabin Fever** (552 S. 602 E., 801/363-0828, www. cabinfevercards.com, 10am-9pm Mon.-Sat., noon-5pm Sun.), which is several decades deep in the eclectic gift game, not to mention a wide collection of greeting cards. Pair your shopping experience with an ale at **Desert Edge Pub & Brewery** (273 Trolley Square, 801/521-8917, https://desertedgebrewery.com, 11am-10pm Mon.-Wed., 11am-11pm Thurs.-Fri., 11:30am-11pm Sat., noon-10pm Sun.), or a very Instagrammable "composed" ice cream cone (a scoop of soft serve, dipped in chocolate and decorated with toppings) from the **Normal Ice Cream** truck parked inside Trolley Square (385/800-1367, www.normal. club, noon-10pm Mon.-Sat., noon-8pm Sun.).

One locally beloved, historic shop at Trolley Square is **Weller Book Works** (607 Trolley Square, 801/328-2586, www.wellerbookworks.

com, 11am-8pm Mon.-Thurs., 10am-9pm Fri.-Sat., noon-5pm Sun.), which has been helping Salt Lake discover great reads since 1929. Established by Gustav Weller, a German immigrant and Mormon convert, the shop originally specialized in Mormon reading and went by the name Zion's Bookstore. Today, this two-floor book shop serves up a well-balanced mix of new, used, and rare books. There's even a New West section to highlight local writers speaking to Western history and culture.

FOOTHILLS

Just a few blocks off one of the first I-80 West exits into Salt Lake City lies the **Foothill Village Shopping Center** (1400 Foothill Dr., 385/232-5527, www.foothillvillage.com, 9am-8pm Mon.-Sat.). Find a mix of fitness centers, retail shops, chain dining, and a grocery store. If you're seeking equipment for outdoor adventures, stop by **Sports Den** (1350 Foothill Dr., 801/582-5611, www.sportsden. com). For an uber-fancy baby and kids' shop experience, visit **Babinski's** (1324 Foothill Dr., 801/583-2229, https://babinskis.com), where you can invest in high-dollar albeit very high-quality apparel, toys, tech, and more—the perfect pre-baby shower stop. If you're looking for a place to eat, **Red Butte Café** (1414 Foothill Dr., 801/581-9498, https:// theredbuttecafe.com) offers a solid lunch menu, plus a very tempting array of cakes and pies you'd be remiss to skip.

SUGAR HOUSE

The Sundance Catalog got its start when former guests of Robert Redford's Sundance Resort would ask the staff where they could find products from the Sundance general store closer to home. Thus, a mail-order catalog was born in 1989. The catalog still exists and has branched out to a handful of Sundance stores scattered around the Southwest, Midwest, and Southeast, as well as Salt Lake City's own **Sundance Outlet** (Sugar House Shopping Center, 2201 Highland Dr., 801/487-3400, www.sundancecatalog.com, 10am-8pm

Mon.-Sat., noon-5pm Sun.). The inventory spans men's and women's clothing, jewelry, decor, and other knickknacks, all inspired by the refined Southwestern aesthetic of the Sundance Resort.

What do you do when you're dying to buy a new ski jacket or high-quality fleece from "Patagucci"—as Patagonia is jokingly dubbed for its steep prices—but don't want to shell out? Head to the **Patagonia Outlet** (2292 Highland Dr., 801/466-2226, www.patagonia. com, 10am-7pm Mon.-Fri., 10am-6pm Sat., 11am-6pm Sun.), where you'll find a mix of current and past-season styles on sale and clearance. This store also serves as a local community hub for everything from environmental speakers to yoga, so check the events calendar before you go.

Throw it back to the 1950s and 1960s at **Retro Betty** (2821 S. 2300 E., 801/467-2222, www.retrobettyslc.com, 10am-6pm Mon., 10am-7pm Tues.-Sat.), about a mile (1.6 km) southeast of Sugar House. Whether you're just reviving your wardrobe or shopping for a costume, discover vintage threads like a red polka dot mermaid skirt, bowler shirt, or white dress bedecked with bright red cherries. You can also go retro with funky socks, stationery, gifts, and accessories.

WEST OF THE CENTER

The **Native American Trading Post** (3971 S. Redwood Dr., 801/952-0184, 10am-7pm Mon.-Sat., 10am-6pm Sun.) got its start as a flea market in 1987, before expanding to the large brick-and-mortar it is today. While it's not Indigenous-owned, the Trading Post does support Indigenous artists and artisans, selling everything from rugs and herbs to flour for fry bread. The Trading Post has come to serve as an unofficial hub of all things Native American in Salt Lake—the majority of the customers are Native American, a bulletin posts upcoming community events, and the store supports causes like the Adopt-a-Native-Elder program.

Entertainment and Events

While Salt Lake City is not a destination for its nightlife, it does offer an unexpected hodgepodge of places to drink and dance. But you may have to call it a night a little earlier than you're used to—last call in Utah is 1am, and bars must close by 2am.

NIGHTLIFE
Downtown

Bar-X (161 E. 200 S., 385/259-0905, www. beerbarslc.com, noon-close daily) traces its roots back to the year Prohibition was repealed: 1933. In 2010, the bar got new life thanks to Ty Burrell—the nerdy dad in *Modern Family*—who purchased it with his brother and another partner. Burrell and company have transformed this historic bar into a locally beloved hangout, with dim lighting, a backlit bar, and a mean list of cocktails. The more casual connected concept **Beer Bar** (161 E. 200 S., 385/259-0905, www.beerbarslc.com, noon-close daily) is a destination for beer lovers and also serves a food menu originally conceived by local celebrity chef Viet Pham. At this industrial space with wood community tables, you'll find elevated pub food from local purveyors like Vosen's Bakery and Salt & Smoke Meats.

You might call Salt Lake City a nightclub desert. There ain't much, but if it's a nightclub you want, a nightclub you shall get at **Area 51** (451 S. 400 W., 801/534-0819, www.area51slc. com, 9pm-2am Wed.-Sat., $5-7 cover). Waltz on over to one of its two floors, seven dance areas, and three bars, each specializing in a different theme or event, depending on the evening. Thursday is '80s night, Saturday is by request only—whether that's a specific song or just a decade—and every night is karaoke night at Area 51.

Prefer to dance to the tune of live dueling pianos? Go shake it at the **Tavernacle Social Club** (201 E. 300 S., 801/519-8900, www.tavernacle.com, 8pm-1am Sun.-Thurs., 5pm-1am Fri.-Sat.). This bar places special emphasis on special events, so if you're celebrating a birthday, anniversary, or other occasion and enjoy being serenaded by a large crowd of strangers, be sure to let the Tavernacle know. Karaoke also takes the stage Sunday, Monday, and Tuesday nights. If you're hungry, grab some pub fare at the bar's Steyk Center restaurant next door.

BTG Wine Bar (404 S. West Temple, 801/359-2814, http://btgwinebar.com, 5pm-midnight daily) specializes in wine, with over 75 bottles available by the glass, and also serves cocktails, beer, and a small menu of plates like prosciutto-wrapped dates or dark chocolate cake. Recognized by *Wine Spectator* magazine, BTG offers both domestic and international wines. BTG also serves a full menu of Italian fare from Caffe Molise, located in the same historic Eagle building, constructed in 1916. The vibe here is sophisticated and sultry, with high-backed black leather booths, black-stained wood floors, walls decked in emerald, and red accents. Check the events calendar to see if any wine pairing dinners coincide with your trip.

In Utah, drinking in a secretive location just feels right. Given the state's maze of alcohol legislation and taboos, a tucked-away speakeasy like **Bourbon House** (19 E. 200 S., 801/746-1005, www.bourbonhouseslc.com, 11am-1am daily) is the perfect place to sip something strong. The massive cocktail list includes a whole section devoted to Manhattans alone (10, count 'em). Another excellent choice is the house mint julep. Sip it over conversation or while watching the game—Bourbon House manages to maintain its speakeasy vibe while also acting as a sports bar with eight flatscreens.

Have a beer where it seems probable that everyone could know your name at **Cheers to You** (315 S. Main St., 801/575-6400, 11am-1am daily). Inspired by the 1980s-era sitcom, this local dive bar offers very affordable drinks in a warm, homey setting. Slide into a red booth and ask if Bob, the New Jersey owner, is around! Watch the big game while playing one of your own at the pool table. Come on a Monday, or come on Christmas—Cheers to You is open every single day of the year.

If there's a football or baseball game on

Bar-X and Beer Bar

that you're hoping to catch with fellow fans, head straight to **The Green Pig Pub** (31 E. 400 S., 801/532-7441, http://thegreenpigpub. com, 11am-1am daily), a Salt Lake City institution. Sports aside, this neighborhood bar has a rooftop patio that's been voted best in the city and has a lively program with something going on most every night of the week. Open blues jam on Mondays, trivia night on Wednesdays, acoustic Thursdays, breakfast buffet on Sundays—the Green Pig never slows its roll. One more thing to love: This pub prioritizes sustainability, sourcing planet-friendly materials and including a large vegetarian/vegan section on its pub fare menu. Impossible Burger, anyone?

Capitol Hill

Mustaches, bicycles, and beer. That's the triumvirate of inspiration at **HandleBar** (751 N. 300 W., 801/953-0588, www.handlebarslc. com, 11am-1am daily). In a small, circular space adorned with bike parts and filled with mustachioed individuals, you can sample one of 20 beers and one cider on draft. Or drink a cocktail like the Bee-Have with local Beehive Gin, elderflower liqueur, muddled lime, and soda. Pair it with elevated pub food, like burnt ends or roasted cauliflower with a choice of eight different sauces.

Sugar House

There are two reasons to visit **Campfire Lounge** (837 E. 2100 S., 801/467-3325, www. campfirelounge.com, 5pm-1am Mon.-Thurs., 4pm-1am Fri., 11am-1am Sat.-Sun.). The first is the vibe, which feels like a friend's patio, complete with strung lighting, sports games playing on the televisions inside, and dogs leashed on the patio (Campfire is pooch-friendly). The second is a dish: the tater tot nachos. This craving-satisfying, generously sized platter comes in many stripes. Go basic with the Tot-chos, a take on traditional nachos involving salsa, guacamole, and bacon. Or go crazy with the vegetarian Buffa-tots: tater tots tossed in buffalo sauce. However you top 'em,

these tots will be even more tempting after a drink or two, so think twice before you share.

Ballpark/Granary District

Water Witch (163 W. 900 S., 801/462-0967, http://waterwitchbar.com, noon-2am Tues.-Sun.) has a few tricks up its sleeve when it comes to the craft cocktail. So many tricks, in fact, that it changes its drink menu weekly, posting it online in the form of a photograph of a black-and-white letter board hung on the Water Witch walls. The walls, by the way, are a shade of green that match the emerald skin of that Wicked Witch of the West. Bewitching as the bar's drinks may be, when it comes down to it, Water Witch is a humble neighborhood bar that decorates its space with local materials and art.

South of the Center

Johnny Cash fans, unite, at **A Bar Named Sue** (3928 Highland Dr., 801/274-5578, www. abarnamedsue.net, 11am-1am daily). Sports bar, pool hall, purveyor of songs like "A Boy Named Sue" and other hits from Johnny himself, this bar may be a few miles south of downtown and off the beaten path, but it will feel just like home. You'll also find a game room plus live music on Friday and Saturday nights.

West of the Center

Throw on your cowboy boots and two-step over to **The Westerner Club** (3360 S. Redwood Rd., West Valley City, 801/972-5447, www.westernerslc.com, 6pm-2am Wed.-Sat.), a true Salt Lake City classic. Since 1962, this country dance hall has been teaching locals to dance and hosting big names in country, from Brad Paisley to the Dixie Chicks. Located about 15 minutes southwest of downtown, the Westerner has live music every weekend, plus free mechanical bull rides. If you're looking for dancing lessons, get instruction in line dancing on Wednesday and Friday nights, and couples dance coaching on Thursday nights (8pm-9:30pm).

★ CRAFT BREWERIES

A decade or so ago, the craft brewery scene in Salt Lake was, well, a little lonely. Today, more and more breweries are opening around the city and showing up on the shelves of local liquor stores. My refrain when it comes to alcohol in this guide has been a friendly reminder to stay aware of the drinking laws. While many feel that draft is the tastiest way to experience beer, bear in mind that in Utah, draft beer also means reduced alcohol-content beer, topping out at 4 percent alcohol. Most breweries will note this on their menu, and refer to their full-strength bottled or canned line as "full-strength" or "high point."

If you find it funny that many breweries advertise the fact that they sell cold beer as if it were a commodity, know that this is because Utah liquor stores are generally prohibited from selling cold beer. So, if you need a six-pack to bring to a picnic or hike right away, your best bet is to pick it up at the brewery rather than one of the state-owned and -run liquor stores.

Downtown

Of all the breweries in Utah, **Epic Brewing Company** (825 State St., 801/906-0123, www.epicbrewing.com, 11am-9pm Mon.-Thurs., 10am-11pm Fri.-Sat., 11am-7pm Sun.) is probably the highest profile, particularly among beer aficionados. Epic got its start in 1992—the early days of Utah brewing—and went on to re-headquarter its operation to Denver, where it is less limited by arcane alcohol laws. With exposed brick and a social vibe, the Epic Utah taproom serves its many award-winning classic and experimental styles. Celebrate the state you're visiting with a pick from its Utah series (gotta love that Spiral Jetty IPA), or get funky with its wilder brews like the Sour Apple Saison.

Find a well-rounded beer list plus a few experimental styles for good measure at **Proper Brewing Co.** (857 Main St., 801/953-1707, www.properbrewingco.com, 11am-1am

Mon.-Fri., 10am-1am Sat.-Sun.), which almost has more of a wine bar than brewery vibe. The flagship ale doesn't over-index on hops or malt, striking a careful balance among ingredients to yield a sweet bread-crust flavor with a measured hit of bitterness. More outside-the-box brews include a gose with coriander and an herbed gruit. Proper offers nightly deals—like $6 PB&Js (Proper Beer and a shot of Jameson)—and also hosts events including beer-pairing dinners and karaoke. The brewery also serves incredible burgers, which you can find just one door down at the more casual **Proper Burger Co.** (857 Main St., 801/953-1707, www.properburgerslc.com, 11am-10pm Sun.-Thurs., 11am-11pm Fri.-Sat.).

Located on the outskirts of downtown, **Kiitos Brewing** (608 W. 700 S., 801/215-9165, kiitosbrewing.com, 11am-11pm Mon.-Thurs., 11am-midnight Fri.-Sat., 11am-10pm Sun.) brews the basics, with some sassier seasonals. With bar-top seating and strung lighting, this Finnish-inspired brewery also has sustainability on the mind, with a cutting-edge water- and energy-efficient brewing system and a can-only operation. Especially in summer, the beers here lean fruity in the vein of the Blackberry Sour, Grapefruit Hard Seltzer, and Fruit Milkshake Ale made with mango and guava. Kiitos doesn't have its own kitchen, but does serve Mexican dishes from local Rico Foods.

Central City

Desert Edge Pub & Brewery (273 Trolley Square, 801/521-8917, https://desertedgebrewery.com, 11am-10pm Mon.-Wed., 11am-11pm Thurs.-Fri., 11:30am-11pm Sat., noon-10pm Sun.) got its start pouring Coors for local college students. In 1995 the bar decided to get into the beer biz, and quickly began picking up medals, including a Great American Beer Fest Gold for its Happy Valley Hefeweizen. As a draft-only operation, Desert Edge is a little nimbler when it comes to its beer list, frequently introducing new seasonals. But at this pub-style brewery, you can always count on a pilsner, a pale ale, a dry

Irish stout on nitro, and that award-winning hefeweizen on tap. Sip your pick guilt-free, knowing that Desert Edge is 100 percent wind-powered and reuses its water and spent grain. The food is also solid, with a daily pasta salad featuring from-scratch pasta, plus select cakes and pies from nearby Red Butte Café.

Capitol Hill

While some breweries might be more about the beer-food nexus or the good times shared over a pitcher, **Toasted Barrel Brewery** (412 W. 600 N., 801/657-6942, www.toastedbarrelbrewery.com, 4pm-8pm Thurs.-Sat.) is unequivocally about the beer and the beer only. That rings true right when you walk into the taproom, which is a simple space of weathered wood, subdued lighting, and backless barstools. Toasted Barrel specializes, unsurprisingly, in barrel-aged beers, as well as sours, mixed fermentation methods, and other wild brews like the Belgian White IPA or the Black Currant Sour. If the tasting room experience sounds a little too austere for you, you can also find Toasted Barrel's beers on tap in restaurants around town.

Prefer your fermented beverage brewed with apples rather than malt? **Mountain West Hard Cider** (425 N. 400 W., 801/935-4147, https://mountainwestcider.com, 11am-9pm Mon.-Thurs., 11am-10pm Fri.-Sat., 11am-7pm Sun.) is your answer in Salt Lake. This cidery has won awards for its cider, which does everything but follow the rules. There's the classic Ruby Hard Cider, but Mountain West also makes a session cider, a hopped-up cider, and even a prickly pear cider with a citrusy finish that goes down easy on a summer day. At this intimate cidery with red barstools, you can sip a flight of cider before you commit, or test out one of the cider cocktails.

Sugar House

When **Wasatch Brew Pub** (2110 Highland Dr., 801/783-1127, www.wasatchbeers.com, 11am-midnight Mon.-Fri., 10am-midnight Sat.-Sun.) opened in Park City in 1986, it became the first brewpub in the state. Later, it opened up shop in Salt Lake City and merged with Squatters Craft Beers. As one of the powerhouses of brewing in the state, Wasatch Brew Pub is known for its award-winning lineup of beers, as well as spunky seasonals. The SLC pub has a modern industrial feel with drop-down lighting, and local favorites include the Polygamy Nitro Porter and the Ghostrider IPA. The pub fare gets the job done, and the weekend brunch menu is a great excuse to drink a beer before the clock strikes noon.

Ballpark/Granary District

The 1980s and 1990s might sound ancient when it comes to beer in Utah, but the truth is the state has a longer, more veiled history with malty beverages. Proof lies in **A. Fisher Brewing** (320 W. 800 S., 801/487-2337, www.fisherbeer.com, 11am-11pm Mon.-Wed., 11am-midnight Thurs., 11am-1am Fri.-Sat., 11am-10pm Sun.), which was originally established in Salt Lake back in 1884. Those were the days when the Mormon pioneers of yore actually drank beer (shh, don't tell that to the church!). What was once a massive operation with regional distribution shut its doors during Prohibition, but reopened in 1934. Soon after, it was sold. But recently, Tom Fisher, great-great-grandson of original owner Albert Fisher, revived his family's brewery as an employee-owned concept. Fisher Brewing as we know it today isn't bottling yet, but you can sample one of the dozen beers on tap—including the flagship American pilsner—or one of the 10 seasonals at the cozy yet classic tasting room, which hosts a rotating cast of local food trucks.

TF Brewing (936 S. 300 W., 385/270-5972, www.tfbrewing.com, noon-11pm Mon.-Thurs., noon-midnight Fri.-Sat., noon-10pm Sun.) pays homage to the German style of beermaking: long, slow processes using only the best ingredients. TF brews classics like Schwarzbiers and exercises a little more creative muscle with brews like the Coconut Guava Berliner. Enjoy your Deutschland pint on the homey, convivial patio with fire pits

and strung lighting, paired with the house charcuterie board or a dish from the rotating lineup of food trucks.

RoHa Brewing Project (30 Kensington Ave. S., 385/227-8982, www.rohabrewing. com, 11am-8pm Mon.-Wed., 11am-10pm Thurs.-Sat.) is the brainchild of buddies Rob Phillips (the "Ro") and Chris Haas (the "Ha"), the latter an award-winning brewmaster in his own right prior to partnering on this cans-only concept. RoHa is one of the newer breweries in the Salt Lake scene, but has already fermented some local favorites like the Back Porch Pale Ale and the Thursday IPA, named for the thirstiest day of the week.

South of the Center

Imbibe on the fringe of society at **SaltFire Brewing** (2199 S. West Temple, South Salt Lake, 385/955-0504, www.saltfirebrewing. com, 3pm-8pm Mon.-Thurs., 11am-11pm Fri.-Sat., 11am-8pm Sun.). The brewers here describe themselves as "zymotic transcendentalists working on the edges of the event horizon." Translation: SaltFire ferments beer for the community without harming nature during what are beginning to feel like apocalyptic times. This idiosyncratic brewery also focuses on craft, not trend, to produce small-batch beers like a lemon-ginger saison or a dirty chai stout. It fosters community through events like its Sunday morning yoga sessions. And its labels reflect the chaos of the times with a frenetic font and design reminiscent of Dogfish Head Brewery's aesthetic.

Shades Brewing (154 W. Utopia Ave., South Salt Lake, 435/200-3009, www. shadesofpale.com, 3pm-10pm Tues.-Thurs., 3pm-midnight Fri., noon-midnight Sat.) is all about variations on the ale, from pales to IPAs. In a space that feels like your friend's garage, the brewery doesn't veer too far off the beaten track with its standard lineup, but lets its creative genius reign with special releases like sours aged in, say, tequila barrels.

If you're stopping by, Shades can be a bit hard to find; look for the red door by the loading dock. Shades serves burritos and also allows you to bring your own food or order delivery right to the brewery.

If your general stance on beer is, "Why mess with tradition?", go enjoy the centuries-old European lagering legacy at **Bohemian Brewery** (94 Fort Union Blvd., Midvale, 801/566-5474, www.bohemianbrewery.com, 11am-11pm Mon.-Fri., 10am-11pm Sat., 10am-10pm Sun.), about 20 minutes due south of downtown. The Bohemian Lager is a classic that pairs beautifully with the old-world dishes served here, including Bohemian goulash and pierogies. The vibe is cabin in the Alps, decked out with artwork, taxidermied animals, and old scooters. Come fall, look for the seasonal Oktoberfest, one of the best in the city.

West of the Center

In tribute to the Bonneville Salt Flats International Speedway, **Salt Flats Brewing** (2020 Industrial Circle, Unit B, 801/828-3469, https://saltflatsbeer.com, 11:30am-3pm Mon.-Fri.) makes beer for people who race, watch races, and generally enjoy going fast. Because driving and beer go together like hops and malt, right? Well, perhaps not quite, but the beer is just fine and the tasting room a sight to see, with red leather booths and racing paraphernalia to ogle as you sip. Just a couple miles southwest of downtown, Salt Flats Brewing specializes in session beers that you could theoretically swill several of without passing out on a hot day on the speedway.

Poll the locals for beer recommendations, and many will point you to the 100 percent wind- and solar-powered **Uinta Brewing** (1722 S. Fremont Dr., 801/467-0228, www. uintabrewing.com, 11am-9pm Tues.-Sat.). It's a little out of the way (about 15 minutes from downtown) but more than worth the trip. Uinta—pronounced "you-IN-tah" and named for the mountain range—is a hopped-up institution founded in 1993 in what had been a car mechanic's garage. One of the most popular

1: Uinta Brewing 2: Metallica playing at the Vivint Smart Home Arena

picks is the Cutthroat Pale Ale (Uinta's first release) and the Hop Nosh IPA, including its tangerine and grapefruit variations. More exploratory styles include the Baba Black lager, a coffee pilsner, and a cucumber saison aged in gin barrels. While you're there, grab a burger made from cows fed Uinta Brewing's spent grain, or pulled jackfruit tacos.

THEATERS
Downtown
All three of the downtown theaters listed below are part of the Salt Lake County Arts & Culture organization (www. saltlakecountyarts.org).

Home of the Utah Symphony, Abravanel Hall (123 W. South Temple, 385/468-1010) is considered a world-class example of acoustic excellence. It takes its architectural cues from some of the greatest concert halls in the world, with a rectangular shape, absence of right angles, and sound lock corridors leading from the entrance to the hall itself. Not only is this the site of instrumental gold, but it's the site of literal gold—12,000 square feet (1,115 sq m) of 24-karat leaf hand-brushed onto the stairways and other parts of the interior. In addition to symphony performances, Abravanel Hall also occasionally hosts other musical acts.

The George S. and Dolores Dore Eccles Theater (131 Main St., 385/468-1010) is the hub of Broadway musicals in the city, including *The Book of Mormon,* a local favorite! The Eccles Theater also hosts comedians, community events, concerts, and black box theater.

The most historic downtown venue for the performing arts, the Capitol Theatre (50 W. 200 S., 801/355-2787) was built in 1913 and renovated in 2019. This grandparent of theaters in Salt Lake is home to Ballet West and the Utah Opera, and also hosts other acts, including concerts and dance performances.

Foothills
Kingsbury Hall (1395 Presidents' Circle, 801/481-7100, https://kingsburyhall.utah.edu) is the University of Utah's historic concert hall and event center. The hall opened in 1930 and

has hosted legendary speakers and artists, from Eleanor Roosevelt to Alvin Ailey. Today, its stage doesn't confine itself to one genre of the arts or type of act. The Utah Symphony, the Utah Opera, Ballet West, outdoor film festivals, political speakers, stand-up comics, TEDx events, and more have all taken Kingsbury's stage.

CONCERT VENUES
Downtown
With a capacity of 18,300, the Vivint Smart Home Arena (301 S. Temple, 801/325-2000, www.vivintarena.com) is by far the biggest concert and sports venue in Salt Lake City. Vivint is also home to the Utah Jazz basketball team, and hosts some of the biggest musical acts that come to Utah, from Elton John to Metallica. Vivint also hosts kid-friendly shows like Disney on Ice, the Harlem Globetrotters, and hockey games. Located on the northwestern outskirts of downtown, this nearly four-acre arena is just a few minutes from dining and hotels. And you won't find your usual stadium fare here. Instead enjoy custom menus from local favorites like R&R BBQ.

As its name suggests, The Complex (536 W. 100 S., 801/528-9197, www.thecomplexslc. com) is a few concepts in one. The biggest is Rockwell, which can accommodate 2,500 and has some of the most dazzling lighting effects of all the venues. The Grand is the second largest, hosting 850 people. Vertigo is the 21-and-over-only concept, usually reserved for nightclub-style dance parties. Finally, Papa Wolf's is really more of a lounge than a venue, where the cool kids can hang out during the show. The Complex typically hosts touring live music, but occasionally puts on other types of shows, from boxing to film screenings.

A local favorite music venue, The State Room (638 State St., 801/596-3560, https:// thestateroompresents.com) can hold 299 and draws everything from hip-hop and indie acts to folk. Once a children's theater, this slate-gray, graffiti-adorned brick building also holds one of the more intimate stages in the city, especially if you manage to work your way through the open dance floor toward the singers on the stage.

Foothills

On a warm summer night, the place to be is **Red Butte Garden** (300 Wakara Way, 801/585-0556, www.redbuttegarden.org/concerts), watching a concert and enjoying the somewhat rare opportunity in Utah to BYOB. This outdoor amphitheater draws big-name acts, from Bela Fleck & the Flecktones to the Steve Miller Band. The seating is all outdoors on a sloping green, and—except for a small amount of reserved seating—is all first-come, first-served and rain or shine. The most seasoned Red Butte Garden attendees come well-prepared, with cozy chairs, picnic materials, rainwear, and coolers full of beer. While snacks and non-alcoholic beverages are sold on-site, the best move is definitely to haul in your own goods. If a show is sold out, you can hike up the Living Room Trail behind the venue and enjoy the music from the hills of Salt Lake (bring a headlamp for the hike down).

Sandy/Cottonwood Heights

The **Sandy Amphitheatre** (1245 E. 9400 S., Sandy, 801/568-6097, www.sandyamp.com) brings in live music, especially older, more timeless acts, as well as performances of musical soundtracks like *Mamma Mia!* One of the biggest draws of the Sandy Amphitheater is its location. Set against the backdrop of the Wasatch Mountains near the Cottonwood Canyons, this outdoor venue offers a laid-back yet intimate concert experience in an unparalleled setting. The amphitheater holds 2,000 theater seats and 750 unreserved spots on the lawn.

FESTIVALS AND EVENTS
Pioneer Day

On July 24, 1847, the Mormon pioneers marched through Emigration Canyon into what is now Salt Lake City and never looked back. A decade later, after they'd gotten their feet under them, the Mormons celebrated their arrival in their forever home. Ever since, July 24 has been known as **Pioneer Day,** an official state holiday. Many workplaces and businesses shut down, and members of the Church of Jesus Christ of Latter-day Saints take to the streets of their respective cities and towns in Utah to display their exuberance. The annual Days of 47 Parade (http://daysof47.com) kicks off from the intersection of South Temple and State Street downtown at 9am and travels to Liberty Park. And at This Is The Place Heritage Park, a rip-roaring day of family fun and sugar ensues, involving a parade, a Candy Cannon, a bird show, a watermelon-eating contest, and Brigham's doughnuts in the Social Hall!

Meanwhile, the rest of the state has established its own way to celebrate July 24: Pie & Beer Day. While many breweries, bakeries, and others offer deals involving this combo, the unofficial host is Beer Bar downtown (www.beerbarslc.com), which bills its celebration as "literally the nation's largest assemblage of pie and beer." We're talking 26 types of beer and 7,000 pieces of pie.

TOP EXPERIENCE

Sundance Film Festival

While many pigeonhole **Sundance** (www.sundance.org) as an elitist and inaccessible Park City event, the annual winter film fest actually takes over the theaters of other areas. In Salt Lake City, five theaters transform into Sundance venues come the end of January: the **Broadway Centre Cinema** (111 E. Broadway), the **Grand Theatre** at the Salt Lake Community College (1575 S. State St.), the **Rose Wagner Performing Arts Center** (138 W. 300 S.), the **Library Theatre** (210 E. 400 S.), and the **Tower Theatre** (876 E. 900 S.). Sundance also operates a box office inside **Trolley Square** (602 S. 700 E.), where you can purchase and pick up tickets, and hosts festival lounges with live music and performances at a rotating lineup of local bars.

Utah Beer Festival

As if to disprove our state's reputation that it legally can't hold its alcohol, Utah has been hosting a **beer festival** (Utah State Fairpark, 155 N. 1000 W., https://utahbeerfestival.com, mid-Aug., admission ranges from $5 for non-drinker Designated Driver admission to $50 for a VIP experience with early admission and lounge access) of relatively epic proportions since 2009. This weekend-long, 21-and-over event pours over 200 varieties of full-strength beer and cider for sampling from national, regional, and local breweries you love (like Uinta) and those you've never heard of (like Mountain West Hard Cider). Food carts and trucks keep everyone sated and grounded, while a full stage of live music keeps things festive. A ticket grants you admission, a sampling mug, and a wristband, which you can preload online or at the entrance with credits for samples.

★ Living Traditions Festival

From the Native Americans who predated the Mormon pioneers by millennia, to the ethnic communities who make Salt Lake City the unique place it is today, the **Living Traditions Festival** (Library Square and Salt Lake City and County Building, http:// livingtraditionsfestival.com, mid-May) celebrates the customs of all who call Utah home. Since 1986, this annual three-day festival with free admission has been bringing Utahns together over fine arts, crafts, dance, music, food, and kids' activities from over 90 different cultures. Watch live performances on four stages, take a workshop on Bollywood dancing, or learn to play the digeridoo. The Food Market unites over a dozen cuisines from Ghana, Cambodia, Pakistan, and many more countries. If you miss the May fest, from July through early September, Living Traditions hosts a free concert series on Monday evenings (7pm-9pm) in Liberty Park.

Native American Celebration Powwow & Festival

Since 1993, local tribes have gathered to celebrate and showcase their cultures on July 24 in Liberty Park. The **Native American Celebration Powwow & Festival** (801/688-9297, $5) features music, fine arts, and dancers moving to the beats of a drum circle. Over 65,000 people come to this event to explore arts and crafts booths, tribal food, and more. Kid-friendly activities are also available. This event takes place on Pioneer Day at noon after the downtown parade. After hours of

Pride Fest

Pacific Heritage Festival

The Pacific diaspora in Utah is strong, evidenced by Polynesian food, a school dedicated to connecting kids with their Pacific heritage, and the ghost town of Iosepa, built and inhabited by Hawai'ians for some three decades as a Pacific outpost in Utah. In 2012, Governor Gary Herbert even declared August to be Utah Pacific Islander Heritage Month. Every summer, Pacific Islanders in Utah and those interested in learning more about their cultures come together with visual, performing, and culinary arts to explore Polynesian, Micronesian, and Melanesian cultures. The weekend-long **Pacific Heritage Festival** (801/793-4639, https://pik2ar.org) kicks off Pacific Island Heritage Month with films from the Pacific Islands, over a dozen cultural stations, storytelling and other performances, and Pacific fare.

Pride Fest

Many are surprised to learn that Salt Lake City was once dubbed the Gayest City in America by the magazine *The Advocate* (2012). And since 1974, Utahns have been celebrating their pride. Today, **Pride Fest** (Washington Square Park, www.utahpridecenter.org) takes place in early June and is 35,000 people strong (and counting). Pride Fest involves marches, spiritual services, rallies, entertainment, and, of course, the parade itself. Leading up to the official Pride weekend is a whole month of events designed to empower and give voice to the LGBTQ+ population.

Bee Fest

This free annual event celebrates bees and other pollinators through workshops, a market, entertainment, and more. Hosted by local nonprofit magazine *CATALYST*, the one-day **Bee Fest** (Green Team Farm, 622 W. 100 S., https://catalystmagazine.net/slcbeefest, mid-June) gives you the opportunity to stock up on plants for your garden, get gardening expertise from the pros, learn how to host and catch your own bees, and hear poetry about the birds and the bees. You can also enjoy treats baked with honey and take a tour of the urban garden that hosts the event to the tune of a harp.

Food

There are some great eats to be found in Salt Lake City—and at a more reasonable bang for your buck than what you might find in San Francisco, New York, or other U.S. food destinations. What does Utah do particularly well in the kitchen? In short, spice and sweets. By spice, I mean ethnic foods. There are some great international eats and markets to discover throughout the city, and especially in South Salt Lake and at Food Truck Thursday at the Gallivan Center. You can find everything from Middle Eastern cuisine and Pacific Island dishes to Peruvian food prepared by second- or third-generation Americans, immigrants, and refugees who have made Salt Lake City their home. And when it comes to sweets, you'll have plenty of bakeries, creameries, and other sugar-vending shops throughout the city to choose from.

DOWNTOWN
Cafés and Breakfast

Craving edibles of the French kind? **Les Madeleines** (216 E. 500 S., 801/355-2294, https://lesmadeleines.com, 8am-4pm Tues.-Thurs., 8am-5:30pm Fri.-Sat., pastries $2.25 and up) is your answer. Owner Romina Rasmussen makes impossibly flaky, crisp *kouign-amann,* colorful macarons, and many more tempting baked goods. She also makes a mean lunch sandwich or salad, serving all of it

Spice Kitchen Incubator

In light of Utah's conservative reputation, it comes as a surprise to some that the state is welcoming to immigrants. This is largely thanks to the fact that the members of the Latter-day Saints Church view themselves as refugees, who were pushed westward due to religious discrimination. The upshot of this past is that the state is welcoming to immigrants, refugees facing religious persecution in particular. In response to the wave of states banning the resettlement of refugees from Muslim-majority countries in 2016, former governor Gary Herbert stated that Utahns know what it was like to be persecuted because of religion, adding, "When people come to Utah, we welcome them. We need to have a tall fence, but we also need to have a wide gate."

One of many aspects of a city with a "wide gate" is food. In honor of this near universal truth, the **Spice Kitchen Incubator** (https://spicekitchenincubator. org) came onto the Salt Lake scene in 2013 with the goal of helping refugees, immigrants, and people of low income set up shop in the food business. Spice Kitchen has

Moroccan cuisine by Zahara Kitchen

helped some 30 catering companies, food trucks, and even brick-and-mortar businesses launch, with cuisines running the gamut from Venezuelan and Somalian to Iraqi.

Craving some exciting new eats? Find Spice Kitchen at various farmers markets around town, or order dinner ($10) from a rotating Spice Kitchen business by noon on the Tuesday prior and pick it up to enjoy on Thursday. You can also check out the Spice-launched chefs online and discover where and when you can find their food around the city.

in a low-key, brightly lit café just a few blocks off the bustle of downtown proper.

Owned by the same talented team behind The Copper Onion, **The Daily** (222 S. Main, Ste. 140, 385/322-1270, www.thedailyslc.com, 7am-5pm Mon.-Fri., 8am-3pm Sat.-Sun., $7-13) is anything but quotidian. It's the only place in the city where you can get your caffeine fix with the award-winning Stumptown Coffee. With your cup of strong Joe, enjoy a breakfast sandwich on homemade sourdough, dig into a cheddar-mustard scone, or buckle to temptation and have a cookie for breakfast.

Like your cafés with a touch of hipster flair? Head to **The Rose Establishment** (235 S. 400 W., 801/208-5569, www.theroseestb. com, 7am-6pm daily, $7-11), where the Portlandia panache comes through strong. Located in a historic brick meatpacking building, The Rose has filled its space with subway

tile, drop lighting, and plenty of plants. On the menu, this translates to savory porridges, avocado tartine, and a menu of brilliant seasonal drinks, like Melon Milk Tea with fresh honeydew and sage.

The fact that **Tony Caputo's Market & Deli** (314 W. 300 S., 801/531-8669, https:// caputos.com, 9am-7pm Mon.-Sat., 10am-5pm Sun., sandwiches $9) has a cheese cave should be enough to persuade most foodies to pick up fodder for a picnic here. This family-owned market also serves Italian deli-style sandwiches perfect to enjoy in the café-style seating area or take on a day trip, and stocks a charcuterie selection to pair with that cheese. Everything you find here is inspired by the Caputo family's Italian heritage and their frequent trips back to the Boot. Warning to chocolate lovers: You will probably end up spending more than you'd like on cacao-based products, since this market carries over 400 bars. Look for several other Caputo's locations across the city.

American

Chef Ryan Lowder grew up in Utah, but he's no homebody. He's lived and cooked everywhere from Portland to Colombia. But luckily for Utahns, he came home and opened up ★ **The Copper Onion** (111 E. 300 S., Ste. 170, 801/355-3282, http://thecopperonion.com, 11:30am-3pm and 5pm-10pm Mon.-Thurs., 11:30am-3pm and 5pm-11pm Fri., 10:30am-3pm and 5pm-11pm Sat., 10:30am-3pm and 5pm-10pm Sun., $14-32). The concept defies labeling, but might basically be described as globetrotting cuisine for the modern locavore. Cases in point: spicy braised octopus, house-made pastas, patatas bravas, saag paneer, and an outstanding, affordably priced burger with duck fat aioli. Lowder also owns the small plates-oriented Copper Common next door, as well as a couple other concepts in the area.

In an industrial space with lofty ceilings and a simple color scheme, **Current Fish & Oyster** (279 E. 300 S., 801/326-3474, www.currentfishandoyster.com, 11am-10pm Mon.-Fri., 4pm-10pm Sat., 5pm-10pm Sun., $19-38) serves sustainable, American seafood from both coasts. Purists will love the oysters, green lip mussels, and ceviche, while others may gravitate toward creations like a fish stew flavored with coconut, lemongrass, and serrano. The menu also offers turf and vegetarian options, and a dessert list you won't want to miss with picks like guava cheesecake and a gelato parfait.

Proper Burger Co. (857 S. Main St., 801/953-1707, www.properburgerslc.com, 11am-10pm Sun.-Thurs., 11am-11pm Fri.-Sat., $4.49-9.99) serves some of the best burgers in the city. In the same building, Proper brews beers that pair beautifully with everything that comes off the flat top. Burgers run the gamut from the no-frills Plain Jane (lettuce, tomato, ketchup) to outside-the-box toppings like beer-cheese rarebit sauce, kale pesto, and kimchee. Vegan burgers are also on offer. If you come for weekend brunch, you can experience the oxymoron of a beef patty served up on a vegan doughnut, or spring for the Benedict Burger.

Bambara (202 Main St., 801/363-5454, https://bambara-slc.com, 7am-10am, 11:30am-2:30pm, and 5:30pm-10pm Mon.-Fri., 8am-2pm and 5:30pm-10pm Sat.-Sun., $28-48) is hotel dining at its finest. Located inside the Hotel Monaco, Bambara gets it right on all levels, including decor, service, and, of course, food. Marble, arched windows, brass here and there—it's all a little lavish, but in a good way. The food is, too, with acclaimed chef Nathan Powers putting on a show of cookery from an open kitchen. The menu is aggressively New American, showcasing local ingredients and adeptly blending traditions from different regions. The chef is even bold enough to throw in a sake-and ginger-flavored risotto on the sides list. Vegans, vegetarians, and the gluten-free don't get short shrift here either. If you're just coming to drink, head to the more intimate bar space known as **The Vault** (11:30am-close daily) for cocktails in a space that feels like a bank because it once was.

Vegans, vegetarians, and the gluten-free unite at **zest kitchen & bar** (275 S. 200 W., 801/433-0589, www.zestslc.com, 11am-9:30pm Mon.-Thurs., 11am-10:30pm Fri., 10am-10:30pm Sat., 10am-9:30pm Sun., $15-16). Zoodles, cashews masquerading as cheese, a chocolate beet cake—the usual suspects of healthy eats are all here. But what's a little more unexpected is how zest skillfully translates the principles of health and organic foods to the bar. In addition to kombucha and a long tea list, zest serves 100 percent organic wines and cocktails made from fresh-pressed juices and local spirits.

Owned by local celeb chef Viet Pham—a winner of *Iron Chef America*—**Pretty Bird** (146 Regent St., www.prettybirdchicken.com, 11am-3:30pm and 5pm-9pm Mon.-Sat., $9.50-15) keeps things simple with Nashville-style hot chicken. There are only a few choices to make, and you can't go wrong. Sandwich or plate? Make it a combo with some cider slaw? Add PBR, soda, or canned rosé? One more thing: How much spice can you handle on that bird?

There's not really a rhyme or a reason to how **Bodega** and **The Rest** (331 Main St., 801/532-4042, https://bodegaslc.com, 5pm-1am Tues.-Sat., $19-39) do things. At Bodega, you'll find turquoise salon waiting-room chairs, neon lighting galore, and a vibe of dive bar meets Brooklyn slice shop. The menu is a mix of simple bar food, from tacos to breakfast sandwiches. Or, you can head downstairs to the speakeasy known as The Rest, for which, somewhat counterintuitively, you can actually make reservations online (not required, but highly recommended on weekends). At The Rest, the divey slice shop gives way to a late 19th-century intellectual's crypt, filled with books and faded photographs where vinyl spins quietly in the background. Tacos give way to a rotating and extensive menu of hipster-esque dishes like beer can chicken and beignets.

Behind the bar at **White Horse Spirits & Kitchen** (325 S. Main, 801/363-0137, www. whitehorseslc.com, 11am-1am daily, $18-28) is a wall of spirits stacked ceiling-high. Aside from the prominent display of booze, White Horse strikes a similar speakeasy tone as its sister concept Bourbon House a couple blocks away, with brick walls, dim lighting, and high-backed leather booths. The spirited wall here includes massive collections of whiskey and rum, six absinthes, and 35 aperitifs and digestifs. Not on full display is Utah's largest collection of draft ciders: 10, all full-strength. While White Horse is a great place to get a drink, the food is just as good, with a lively American brasserie menu filled with dishes like oysters Rockefeller and steak Lyonnaise.

After sweeping state competitions and vying for smoky glory in national and international barbecue battles, twin brothers Rod and Roger opened **R&R BBQ** (307 W. 600 S., 801/364-0443, https://randrbbq.com,

11am-9pm Mon.-Fri., 11am-10pm Sat., $9-16). Testament to their barbecue's success are the eight always busy locations across the state, including this one. The menu keeps it simple with pulled pork, ribs, brisket, and other meats with your usual lineup of sides, including hush puppies. You can also shake it up with the Caveman Burger, topped with smoked sausage, pulled pork, cheese, and fried jalapeños.

Originally a one-off concept in Denver, **Punch Bowl Social** (6 N. Rio Grande St., 801/948-2989, https://punchbowlsocial.com, 11am-midnight Mon.-Fri., 10am-1am Sat., 10am-midnight Sun., $11.75-17.24, 21+ only) has spread its playful wings across the country, from D.C. and Chicago to Salt Lake City. Located in the Gateway center, Punch Bowl Social manages to succeed in being three things: a bar, a great restaurant, and a game emporium with everything from bowling to karaoke and antique arcade games. The menu is anything but what you'd expect at a glorified bowling alley. Keep it real with the Superfood Grain Bowl or share the nachos, which come topped with all manner of unconventional ingredients (think poblanos and squash). Of course, Punch Bowl Social serves several takes on punch, as well as other craft cocktails and fabulous desserts.

Eat lunch or an early dinner inside the former home of Brigham Young at **The Lion House Pantry** (63 E. South Temple, 801/539-3257, www.templesquare.com, 11am-8pm Mon.-Sat.). The dishes are simple but tasty, perhaps much like the dishes that one of Young's 50-some wives might have cooked him in this very building back in the pioneer days. The setting is equally homey, with round wooden tables clustered together in what feels like, well, the unfettered dining room of a 19th-century pioneer. You'll feel right at home as you dig into chicken meatloaf with a buttery Lion House roll. Top it all off with an ice cream cone courtesy of the Brigham Young University's legendary creamery, which churns an unreal number of flavors over in Provo.

☆ Sweet Tooth Satisfaction

The sweet-toothed visitor to Salt Lake may be delighted to know that the sugar content of Salt Lake City is staggering. As the theory goes, because members of the Latter-day Saints Church cannot imbibe alcohol, coffee, and other hot drinks, their primary indulgence is sugar.

Instead of starting the day with coffee, many spring for not just a can of soda, but a **soda mixer.** These soda mocktails—one or more sodas mixed with Torani syrups—are readily available throughout Salt Lake City, often from the convenience of a drive-thru.

Sugar also comes in the form of baked goods and ice cream. For classic French pastries, you can head to **Les Madeleines** (216 E. 500 S., 801/355-2294, https://lesmadeleines.com, 8am-4pm Tues.-Thurs., 8am-5:30pm Fri.-Sat., pastries $2.25 and up) downtown or **Tulie Bakery** (863 E. 700 S., 801/883-9741, www.tuliebakery.com, 7:30am-6pm Mon.-Fri., 8am-5pm Sat.-Sun., pastries starting at $4) in Central City. If it's more elaborate patisserie that speaks to you—think elaborate cakes and petit four à la *The Great British Bake Off*—ogle the display at

Goodly Cookies

Gourmandise (250 S. 300 E., 801/328-3330, www.gourmandisethebakery.com, 7am-10pm Mon.-Thurs., 7am-11pm Sat.-Sun., pastries starting at $2.95) or venture a little farther from downtown to the celebrity chef-owned **Fillings & Emulsions** (1475 Main St., 385/229-4228, 8am-6pm Tues.-Fri., 9am-7pm Sat., pastries starting at $2) in the Ballpark District. One of my favorite places in town to get a sugar high is Central City's **Goodly Cookies** (432 S. 900 E., 385/743-0022, https://goodlycookies.com, 11am-11pm Mon.-Thurs., 11am-1am Fri.-Sat., cookies starting at $3.50), which bakes up colossal cookies and donates 1 percent of every sale to cancer research. You'll also find chocolatiers, gelaterias, and more places to load up on sweets.

Ethnic Eats

Owned and operated by a Bruges transplant, **Bruges Waffles & Frites** (336 W. 300 S., E. Broadway, 801/363-4444, www.brugeswaffles.com, 9am-9pm Mon.-Thurs., 9am-10pm Fri.-Sat., 9am-2pm Sun., $5-15) went from a Belgian waffle cart peddling around Main Street to a local multi-location waffle empire, and for good reason. Start simple with the Liège waffle, made with a family recipe, and then get crazy, adding on everything from fresh fruit and chocolate to bacon. You can also enjoy other Belgian dishes like frites and Flemish stew.

If, when you crave Thai food, you don't just mean pad Thai, then venture to **Laan Na Thai** (336 W. 300 S., 801/363-2717, 11am-9pm Mon.-Fri., noon-9pm Sat., $8.49-10.49) for

authentic dishes from owner Yupin Chareon's homeland. Yupin and her husband moved to the United States in 2004 in the hopes of creating a better life for their daughter. After working at another now-closed Thai restaurant, Yupin worked with Spice Kitchen Incubator to open her own restaurant. At Laan Na, she prepares soulful, spicy dishes like Kuay Tean, a soup with oxtail and handmade noodles, or Nam Tok, a salad with sticky rice and flank steak, tossed in a citrusy-spicy sauce. And if it is pad Thai you want, you'll find that on the menu, too.

One of the most popular Vietnamese spots in the city is **Oh Mai Vietnamese Sandwiches** (850 State St., 801/575-8888, www.ohmaisandwich.com, 11am-9pm Mon.-Sat., $4.98-7.98). Find a dozen banh mi varieties, including variations involving brisket, short ribs, sardines, eggs, and vegetables. Pho does the trick in the winter, and if you're a "bun" buff, get the Honey Glazed Pork atop a pile of chilled rice vermicelli.

Ask just about anyone in Salt Lake City where to find the best sushi and Japanese cuisine, and there's a good chance they'll send you to Takashi (18 W. Market St., 801/519-9595, 11:30am-2pm and 5:30pm-10pm Mon.-Thurs., 11:30am-2pm and 5:30pm-11pm Fri., 5:30pm-11pm Sat., rolls $7-14). In an elegant dim space lit with paper lanterns, Takashi serves Japanese-style surf and turf in the form of nigiri, sashimi, rolls, and entrées like chicken yakitori or flank steak with Asian pesto. Dishes are well matched in the drink department, with a rotating menu of cocktails that are as cleverly named as they are conceived. Takashi is a great spot to splurge on lunch, or head out on a date come evening.

If you like dinner laced with spice and tequila, head to Alamexo (268 S. State St., 801/779-4747, www.alamexo.com, 11:30am-9pm Mon.-Tues., 11:30am-10pm Wed.-Fri., 3pm-10pm Sat., 3pm-9pm Sun., $19-30). This is one of those restaurants where you can easily eat dinner and hang out for drinks afterward without a change of venue. Servers deliver the Latin dishes here with a touch of drama, from guacamole assembled tableside, to tacos al carbon that show up in a sizzling cast-iron skillet with a tray of garnishes for you to decorate your order. Be sure to get an order of plantains with queso fresco, too. The tequila list is fantastic, and the cocktails inventive.

Italian and Pizza

In a narrow spot on Main Street, Este's Pizza (156 E. 200 S., 801/363-2366, www.estepizzaco.com, 11am-10pm Mon.-Thurs, 11am-11pm Fri., noon-11pm Sat., 4pm-9pm Sun., $20-25 for a large pizza) transports pizza-lovers to a low-key pizza parlor in Brooklyn, from its subway-inspired sign to its big, thin-crust slices that just about demand to be folded over. Supreme pies, vegan options,

lasagna pizza with ricotta and meatballs—you really can't go wrong.

One of the best places for high-end Italian cuisine in Utah is ★ Valter's Osteria (173 Broadway, 801/521-4563, https://valtersosteria.com, 5:30pm-10pm Mon.-Sat., $28-38). Locally beloved as a special-occasion spot, Valter's transports you to an agricultural villa in the hills above Florence. You know the menu is legit when you can scarcely understand the names of the dishes—they're all in Italian. But fret not, the English descriptions will clear things up. Settle in for the typical Italian dining experience of an antipasto, from-scratch pasta, a big Piedmontese steak, and, of course, many glasses of wine from the Italian-dominated list.

Coffee Shops

Utah is lucky to be blessed with two locations of the Australian-born Campos Coffee Roastery & Kitchen (228 S. Edison St., 801/953-1512, https://us.camposcoffee.com, 7am-5pm Sun.-Wed., 7am-10pm Thurs.-Sat., $9-14.50). While Campos vends its beans all over and operates around half a dozen locations in Australia, the two Utah cafés are the only locations in the United States as I write. This specialty coffee company has one location in downtown Salt Lake and another in Park City. Campos sources all of its beans sustainably and funds a community project in every region from which it sources beans, like a school in Ethiopia. You'll discover standard and unexpected coffee orders alike here, including a flat white, an ever-changing signature coffee drink, and a flight of espressos. The food menu is a delightful mix of brunch and food that appeals all day long: avocado toast, a chicken tabouleh wrap, a burger that can be made Impossible, and a meat pie—Vegemite and all.

Bakeries and Ice Cream Shops

Stray a few blocks from downtown and

1: Mazza, a Middle Eastern restaurant 2: fancy cakes at Gourmandise Bakery

all of a sudden, you'll find yourself at the most charming and brilliant French patisserie and café in the city: the legendary ★ **Gourmandise** (250 S. 300 E., 801/328-3330, www.gourmandisethebakery.com, 7am-10pm Mon.-Thurs., 7am-11pm Sat.-Sun., pastries starting at $2.95). Everything from the service and the sign outside to the classic, well-stocked pastry case screams yesteryear. This dose of nostalgia is what you need—almost as much as a raspberry-pistachio tartlette. The sheer scope of baked goods available on a daily basis is truly staggering. Come for the sweets, but stay for lunch. Gourmandise serves a lovely breakfast and lunch menu, like an avocado toast piled high with heirloom tomatoes and micro-greens, drizzled with olive oil.

In a bright blue building that might as well be on Paris's Rue du Bac, **Eva's Bakery** (155 Main St., 801/355-3942, www.evasbakeryslc.com, 7am-6pm Mon.-Sat., 9am-3pm Sun., $9-11) is a boulangerie that pays tribute to the owner's grandma. Using only organic local flour, Eva's bakes up croissants, breads, and more, and also serves a French-leaning breakfast and lunch with dishes like vegetable quiche, French onion soup, and a variety of Boulange croques, including one topped with shiitakes and sun-dried tomatoes.

Grocery Stores

One of my favorite places to go when traveling is the local grocery store. The selection, design, and vibes can tell you a lot about a place. Plus, it's a more affordable way to eat than dining out for every single meal. Whether you're just picking up snacks for your hotel room or food for day trips from Salt Lake City, the place to do it is **Harmons Grocers** (135 E. 100 S., 801/428-0366, www.harmonsgrocery.com, 6am-11pm daily). Once just a fruit stand, Harmons is now a local chain known for a pleasant shopping experience, a strong selection of niche international items, and its in-house prepared foods, specifically baked goods. Don't miss the cakes or the Beehive Rolls, which will make every dinner that

much better. Harmons also has several other locations throughout the Salt Lake area.

9TH AND 9TH

American

You know a restaurant isn't fibbing about farm-to-table when it actually grows its own food like **Pago** (878 S. 900 E., 801/532-0777, www.pagoslc.com, 5pm-9pm Mon.-Thurs., 5pm-10pm Fri., 10:30am-2:30pm and 5pm-10pm Sat., 10:30am-2:30pm and 5pm-9pm Sun., $19-32) does. In addition to the micro-farm that provides food to the kitchen, the chefs here create their New American dishes with local meat, cheese, and more produce from nearby producers like Clifford Family Farm and Beehive Cheese. With just 17 tables inside and out, Pago is small, and so are many of its dishes—from daily crudos to daily soup—so sharing several small plates is a great strategy here.

Pizza and Italian

Pizza Nono (925 E. 900 S., 385/444-3530, www.pizzanono-slc.com, 11:30am-9pm Mon.-Thurs., 11:30am-10pm Fri.-Sat., pizzas $11-13) is a big yes-yes. Inspired by Brooklyn pizzerias, Pizza Nono puts out artisan Neapolitan pies made with high-quality ingredients and baked in a wood-fired pizza oven. The menu is small, which makes decisions easy. Choose from just a handful of pizzas—plus a pizza of the week—a couple of salads, and a seasonal side. A local fave is the Beehive with tomato, mozzarella, calabrese sausage, pickled jalapeño, and a drizzle of honey.

Ethnic Eats

When I first moved to Salt Lake and asked around about where to eat, top of the list was always **Mazza** (912 E. 900 S., 801/521-4572, www.mazzacafe.com, 11am-3pm and 5pm-10pm Mon.-Sat., $19-25). A wide-ranging, Lebanese-influenced menu covers all the bases: hummus the way it ought to be prepared, kebabs made with lamb and chicken, flatbreads, *mujaddara* (lentils and rice), vegan pumpkin *kibbeh*—the list goes on. Mazza is also a great place to drink, with a huge selection of Middle Eastern beers and wines, as well as a cocktail list sporting Middle Eastern flavors like rose water, orange zest, and arak.

Coffee Shops

The Coffee Garden (878 E. 900 S., 801/355-3425, 6am-11pm Mon.-Thurs., 6am-midnight Fri.-Sat.) is always abuzz—with people, a massive menu of drinks, and treats that you may inadvertently end up grabbing while in line. Indeed, the house-made pastries, cookies, lemon danishes, and macarons will call your name from the moment you step in. With community tables, tucked-away booths, and a small patio, there are seating options for all occasions. Enjoy the decor, which ranges from shelves of colorful books and vintage kitchen equipment to local art hanging on the brick interior walls.

Bakeries and Ice Cream Shops

Dolcetti Gelato (902 E. 900 S., 801/485-3254, https://dolcettigelato.com, 11am-11pm Mon.-Sat., 11am-10pm Sun., scoops starting at $4.25) is a father-daughter gelato shop that lays claim to being the first gelato shop in the state. The gelato flavors change daily, and the 150-strong flavor arsenal covers a mix of classics like stracciatella and unusual flavors like sticky rice and mango chili. If you're dairy-free, try one of the fruity sorbettos on offer. Dolcetti also serves house-made macarons, tea, and espresso drinks.

CENTRAL CITY

Cafés and Breakfast

Vegan sandwich lovers unite at **Buds** (509 E. 300 S. #4001, no phone, www.budsslc.com, 11am-5pm Mon.-Sat., $6.50-7). The Pesto Sub, the Cheesesteak, the Barbacoa Burrito—it's all 100 percent vegan and made in-house. Continue the veg-a-thon with a zucchini chocolate chip cookie.

A proper Southern brunch is served all day at **Pig & a Jelly Jar** (401 E. 900 S., 385/202-7366, www.pigandajellyjar.com, 7:30am-3:30pm Mon.-Wed., 7:30am-9pm Thurs.-Sun.,

$8-13). This café with a touch of funk puts out indulgent dishes like fried chicken and Belgian waffles, fried green tomatoes, and beignets with blueberry-lavender jam. That jam and others like it, by the way, are available in a jar as the restaurant's name suggests. Pair your order with one of the three beer cocktails on the menu, like a Bloody Mary with Uinta Brewing's Lime Pilsner, or an OJ & IPA.

Baking legit bagels outside the strip of East Coast from New York to DC is indeed a project. As far west as Utah, it's a situation. But the **Bagel Project** (779 S. 500 E., 801/906-0698, www.bagelproject.com, 6:30am-2pm Mon.-Fri., 7:30am-2pm Sat.-Sun., $14 per dozen) has succeeded in rising to this yeasty challenge, which is why it has opened up a second, more lunch-oriented shop downtown called Bagels and Greens. The bagels (and bialys) are exactly what an East Coaster craves: chewy with that delicately crisp exterior. The bagel sandwiches shirk tradition with combinations like the Poblano Picasso with a pumpkin seed-poblano spread, tomato, arugula, cilantro, and Manchego cheese.

Ethnic Eats

Greek diners and restaurants pop up all over the city, but one of the best options is **Manoli's** (402 E. Harvey Milk Blvd. #2, 801/532-3760, www.manolison9th.com, 5pm-10pm Tues.-Fri., 10am-2:30pm and 5pm-10pm Sat.-Sun., entrées $16-19). Inside a modern dining room, you'll find provocative interpretations of Greek cuisine, like halloumi with sweet potatoes, tahini, and sumac, or a Utah elk chop with savory rice pudding and poppy seeds. Plenty of mezze, or small plates, make this a great place to share a few dishes, too, over cocktails or shots of, say, ouzo.

Italian and Pizza

Behind **Veneto Ristorante** (370 E. 900 S., 801/359-0708, https://venetoslc.com, 5:30pm-10pm daily, $39-75) is a love story between a local Utahn and a man from Verona—yes, that's *Romeo & Juliet*'s Verona. Today, Amy and Marco bring a taste of Northern Italy, from Venice to Verona, to Salt Lake City at one of the most romantic restaurants in the city. Dine in an old-world setting established by European decor and furnishings on house-made pastas and the pièce de résistance: the Bistecca Piemontese Frollata, aged for over three months. Veneto doesn't accept tips, but if you do leave a gratuity, it will be donated to the Danielle Byron Henry Migraine Foundation.

Coffee Shops

Hate pretentious coffee shops? Then you'll love **The Salt Lake Roasting Co.** (820 E. 400 S., 801/363-7572, www.roasting.com, 6:30am-9pm Mon.-Sat.), which welcomes students parking it for the caffeine and Wi-Fi, to-go orders, and ladies and gentlemen who lunch alike. This roastery and café keeps it simple and accommodates questions about coffee terminology, roast types, and more with grace. And as a souvenir, take home one of its dozens of bagged beans and blends sourced from around the world and roasted in Utah.

Bakeries and Ice Cream Shops

Tulie Bakery (863 E. 700 S., 801/883-9741, www.tuliebakery.com, 7:30am-6pm Mon.-Fri., 8am-5pm Sat.-Sun., pastries starting at $4) produces a wide array of pastries, sweets, and hot beverages from its simple café in a quiet part of town. Discover Danishes, *pain au jambon,* quiches, tarts, cakes, bags of cookies, and cartoonishly large biscotti. Tulie also offers a diverse coffee and tea menu and has another location where you can enjoy its baked goods.

Salt Lake City may not be a great spot for late-night eats, but thanks to ★ **Goodly Cookies** (432 S. 900 E., 385/743-0022, https://goodlycookies.com, 11am-11pm Mon.-Thurs., 11am-1am Fri.-Sat., cookies starting at $3.50), it's a fine place for late-night cookie cravings. Goodly is also—in my opinion—the creator of the best cookie in Salt Lake City, if you like your cookies chewy. Modeled after the massive chocolate chip cookies from Levain Bakery in New York, the Goodly cookie often towers upwards of two inches and comes in flavors like Oh Sweet Lemon and Big CinnaJon, with bursts of crisp cinnamon flavor. Goodly delivers cookies around the city and also operates out of its brick-and-mortar shop, where you can get ice cream cookie sandwiches. Eat your cookie in good conscience—1 percent of every cookie sale is donated to Utah's Huntsman Cancer Institute.

Banbury Cross Doughnuts (705 S. 700 E., 801/537-1433, 5am-5pm Mon.-Sat., 6am-1pm Sun., doughnuts starting at $1) doesn't make a fuss over its doughnuts—no outside-the-box fillings, no savory leanings with bacon bits, and forget the cameos from clever toppings like Fruit Loops. Every day, Banbury churns out a wide selection of classic doughnut flavors, from your basic glazed and old-fashioned cake doughnuts, to pink-frosted with sprinkles. Beyond doughnuts, the bakery also offers pastries such as cinnamon rolls and apple fritters. You can even stock up for your adventures around or near the city by swinging through the drive-thru.

THE AVENUES
American

The cornerstone of **Avenues Bistro on Third** (564 E. 3rd Ave., 801/831-5409, www.facebook.com/avenuesbistroonthird.com, 10am-3pm and 5pm-10pm Tues.-Sun., $10-22) is its backyard urban garden, which grows cucumbers, tomatoes, and other veggies and herbs for the restaurant kitchen. This self-reliant eatery also raises chickens and operates an apiary. When the weather's nice, you can dine on the patio right in the garden on a simple menu of sandwiches, salads, and entrées featuring a protein such as trout.

By day, **Cucina** (1026 2nd Ave., 801/322-3055, www.cucinawinebar.com, 7am-9pm Mon.-Thurs., 7am-10pm Fri., 8am-10pm Sat., 8am-9pm Sun., sandwiches $8.50, dinner $25-35) is a coffee shop and café with deli sandwiches and pastries to enjoy on the quiet patio in a residential neighborhood. By evening, Cucina transforms into a wine bar with over 100 bottles on the list, 60 of which are available by the glass. If you have trouble choosing, order a flight of six. For dinner, find Italian-inspired dishes that pair well with wine, like osso bucco, pumpkin risotto, or the house-made pasta of the day.

Ethnic Eats

In a bright space in a strip mall, **Sawadee Thai** (754 E. South Temple, 801/328-8424, www.sawadee1.com, 11am-3pm and 5pm-9:30pm Mon.-Thurs., 11am-3pm and 5pm-10pm Fri.-Sat., $11-21) serves all of your favorite Thai dishes and then some. Especially on a cold winter day, you can't go wrong with a Thai curry. Or veer a little more unconventional with a dish like the honey-ginger duck with mashed sweet potatoes. Sawadee also serves a large vegetarian menu, as well as beer and wine.

Coffee Shops

Particular about your roast? At **Jack Mormon Coffee Co.** (82 E St E., 801/359-2979, https://jackmormoncoffee.com, 8am-6pm Mon.-Sat.), you can pick out your beans, tell the baristas exactly how you want them roasted, and leave with a bag of your own custom roast just half an hour later. With over 60 single-estate, organic beans to choose from—not to mention cold brew on nitro—Jack Mormon coffee is truly a mecca for coffee lovers. Wondering about the name? Jack Mormon is the term for someone who was raised Mormon, but left the church—and, in this case, decided to take up a coffee habit.

Bakeries and Ice Cream Shops

Four generations back, Grandma Hatch started dipping confections in chocolate. Today, her descendants run **Hatch Family Chocolates** (376 8th Ave., 801/532-4912, www.hatchfamilychocolates.com, 11am-10pm Mon.-Thurs., 11am-11pm Fri.-Sat.), which hand-dips a traditional lineup of confections in milk and dark chocolate. Peanut butter truffle, raspberry cream, and salted caramel are just a few varieties you might find in your box. Hatch also serves caramel-chocolate apples and homemade ice cream.

FOOTHILLS
Cafés and Breakfast

For half a century, a hole-in-the-wall known as Big Ed's cured the hangovers of University of Utah students. When it closed its doors in 2017, the folks behind Publik Coffee, a local roastery with cafés around the city, swooped in to open **Publik Ed's** (210 University St. E., 385/549-1928, https://publikcoffee.com, 8am-8pm Mon.-Sat., $7-8.50) the next year. The new concept blends the greasy-spoon elements of Big Ed's and the coffee and finesse of the Publik concepts to make for a café that's equally up for the tough job of hangover-curing. Dig into a simple, delightful burger topped with special sauce and American cheese, or enjoy a tribute to an Ed's menu item known as the Gawdawful: tater tots topped with chili, pickled onions, cheese, and a couple of eggs. Healthier fare also exists, like salads and a portobello sandwich on a waffle.

Red Butte Cafe (1414 Foothill Dr., 801/581-9498, https://theredbuttecafe.com, 11:30am-9pm Mon.-Thurs., 11:30am-10pm Fri.-Sat., 11am-8:30pm Sun., $11.50-13.50) is a local's spot inside the Foothills Shopping Center, occasionally stumbled upon by visitors. If you're in the area, stop for a Southwest-inspired sandwich or the daily pasta salad, and don't miss a pick from the award-winning bakery. The cakes, pies, and cookies will start luring you in from their prominent position behind a glass pastry case the moment you open the door.

American

From the former chef of High West Saloon in Park City, **One 0 Eight** (1709 E. 1300 S., 801/906-8101, 5pm-9pm Tues.-Thurs., 5pm-10pm Fri., 9:30am-3pm and 5pm-10pm Sat., 9:30am-3pm and 5pm-8:30pm Sun., $13-38) takes over where several other failed concepts in this space left off. The concept is an elevated neighborhood joint with affordable orders like wood-fired barbecue brisket pizza or herbed corn chowder, as well as higher-end dishes like the fresh fish of the day. Watch it all come together in the open kitchen, and don't miss one of the Utah-inspired cocktails like the Emigration Gimlet.

The surf and turf at **Harbor Seafood & Steak** (2302 Parleys Way, 801/466-9827, www.harborslc.com, 5pm-9:30pm Mon.-Thurs., 5pm-10pm Fri.-Sat., 10am-2pm and 5pm-8:30pm Sun., $43-62) go from "dock to table" in this dimly lit neighborhood restaurant with a great cocktail list. You'll find simply prepared wild-caught seafood and wagyu several ways on the menu. Where the chefs really shine here is the sides, sauces, and compound butters, which are many and anything but run-of-the-mill.

Ethnic Eats

It's basically an undisputed fact that **Bombay House** (2731 Parleys Way, 801/581-0222, https://bombayhouse.com, 4pm-10pm Mon.-Sat., $12-18) has been serving the best Indian food in Utah since 1993. Many of the dishes and breads here are prepared inside a clay oven heated with coal, known as a tandoor, which imparts a subtle smoky flavor. The award-winning kitchen produces flatbreads that go beyond your standard naan, and it serves up the Indian dishes you know and love (think curries and masalas) as well as those you've never heard of, like onion *bhaji*, India's answer to onion rings. Don't skip over the beverage list, which, in addition to beer and wine, carries refreshing *lassis* and Indian tea.

SUGAR HOUSE
Cafés and Breakfast

In a colorful, sunny space that sort of makes you feel like you're in Costa Rica, **Café Solstice** (673 Simpson Ave. S., 801/487-0980, www.facebook.com/cafesolstice, 10am-7pm Mon.-Sat., 10am-5pm Sun., $7-8.75) offers light fare, baked goods, and standout smoothies (think mango basil). But the real reason to visit? The array of hot and cool caffeinated beverages. In addition to locally roasted coffee and organic loose-leaf teas, Solstice serves

unique drinks like a yerba mate latte, a matcha granita, and a Mayan cacao mocha you won't want to miss.

American

Kimi's Chop & Oyster House (2155 S. Highland Dr., 801/946-2079, http://kimishouse.com, 11:30am-9pm Mon.-Thurs., 11:30am-9:30pm Fri., 4pm-9:30pm Sat., $21-50) is really two concepts: the restaurant and the 21-and-over Oyster Bar Lounge, which drives a hard bargain with $5 martinis, wine, and champagne. Wherever you sit, the setting is palatial and modern, and the seafood, delicious. Go raw with the seafood bar, where you'll find fresh oysters and daily ceviche and tartare. Share a medley of seafood-oriented tapas like spicy calamari or coconut shrimp cakes. And if you've had your fill of fish when it comes time for the main event, dig into something meatier, from Swedish meatballs and fried chicken to a big rib eye.

The Dodo (1355 E. 2100 S., 801/486-2473, www.thedodorestaurant.com, 11am-11pm Mon.-Fri., 9am-11pm Sat., 9am-10pm Sun., $13-20) is something of a local institution. A popular lunch spot, it's also well-known for the litany of pies and cakes it has been baking up since the 1980s. Longtime pastry chef Ramon puts out a dozen desserts a day, half of which never change (like the Toll House Pie), leaving the remainder to rotate between treats like Black Forest cake and seasonals like pumpkin pie. Whichever dessert you land on, never skip the whipped cream, which The Dodo makes from scratch and even sells by the container to-go. Aside from desserts, The Dodo serves an American grill menu of salads, sandwiches, and entrées like quiche or cajun chicken alfredo.

Ethnic Eats

The Old Dutch Store (2696 Highland Dr., 801/467-5052, www.olddutchstore.com, 10am-6pm Mon.-Fri., 9am-5pm Sat., $6.45-6.95) is a specialty food shop and deli that pays homage to a broader region than its name suggests. Scandinavia, Norway, Dutch

Indonesia—there are delicious finds like stroopwaffles and shrimp chips from all over. But wander to the back of the hodgepodge of worldly foods, and you'll find the sandwich side of the business. Build your own or get one of the geographically themed specialties, like the Broodje Met Kaas with cheese, margarine, pickles, and lettuce on a croissant.

In a bright space with light wood and lime-green walls, **SOMI Vietnamese Bistro** (1215 E. Wilmington Ave. #100, 385/322-1158, 11am-9pm Mon.-Thurs., 11am-10pm Fri.-Sat., noon-8pm Sun., $10-45) adeptly prepares Vietnamese and Chinese classics like pho, rice plates, and a chicken vermicelli with chile-lime vinaigrette ($13). Among the chef specialties are a whole ginger-flavored branzino ($29) and a Peking duck ($45). Don't skip the daily house-made organic ice cream served with fresh berries.

You'll find everything you could possibly want from an East Coast Jewish deli at **Feldman's Deli** (2005 E. 2700 S., 801/906-0369, www.feldmansdeli.com, 8am-10:30am and 11am-3pm Tues.-Wed., 8am-10:30am, 11am-3pm, and 5:30pm-8:30pm Thurs.-Sat., $11-23), though at a higher cost than you might find in, say, a strip mall in New Jersey. I'm willing to pay the upcharge to anyone willing to re-create my childhood favorites and import ingredients like Taylor ham all the way to Utah. Owner Michael Feldman serves up matzah ball soup, potato latkes, bagels, and more, all made with love in the farthest reaches of the diaspora. Located just south of I-80 and Sugar House Park, Feldman's also hosts events like singer-songwriters and Old Jews Telling Jokes.

Coffee Shops

A hub of the neighborhood, **Sugar House Coffee** (2011 S. 1100 E., 801/883-8867, https://sugarhousecoffee.com, 6am-midnight Mon.-Fri., 7am-midnight Sat., 7am-11pm Sun., $3.50-5) is where everyone goes to caffeinate, get a little work done, and catch up with friends. This café serves all the coffee drinks you'd expect, with locally roasted Rimini

Coffee plus teas, smoothies, local kombucha, fresh-pressed juices, and a luxurious turmeric-ginger golden milk. There are a number of affordable café-style items to sate your appetite, including panini, quiche, oatmeal, and fudgy espresso brownies. You'll often stumble on live music here in the evenings, and can count on jazz on Thursday nights. On the second Friday of every month, Sugar House Coffee gives its walls over to art during the neighborhood Art Walk.

Bakeries and Ice Cream Shops

Howdy Homemade Ice Cream (2670 S. 2000 E., 801/410-4302, www.howdyslc.com, noon-9pm Mon.-Sat., $3.50 for single scoop) makes dozens of tempting flavors from scratch every day, including a line of flavors infused with soda. The crowning jewel of the latter collection is Dr. Pepper chocolate chip. If you're more of a traditionalist, you'll also find strawberry, raspberry Oreo, and coffee chip made with Publik Coffee. Located just south of Sugar House below I-80, Howdy is also an ice cream shop with a mission, providing job opportunities for people with disabilities.

BALLPARK/GRANARY DISTRICT
American

The main draw at ★ **Lucky 13** (135 W. 1300 S., 801/487-4418, www.lucky13slc.com, 11am-2am daily, $7-21) is the burger, which has reaped many a local award. There's a burger order for everyone, from the Nut Butter Burger, made with peanut butter, to the Fungus Amongus with red wine-sautéed mushrooms, garlic, and Swiss (my favorite). The order for the brave is the foot-tall, 28-ounce Lucky 13 Challenge Burger, which many have attempted and few have finished. Beef aside, Lucky 13 is also a popular sports bar, located within walking distance of Smith's Ballpark.

Ethnic Eats

If you're craving Middle Eastern cuisine,

Food Trucks

Like most cities across America, Salt Lake has been swept up in the food truck craze. While a total truck count is anyone's guess, new trucks appear on the streets, while others transition to brick-and-mortar concepts or disappear altogether. And like with most food truck scenes, Salt Lake's lets ethnic cooking shine, offering a more affordable, low-investment way for talented chefs to get food out to the public.

If you're hunting for mobile dining, one good place to check is the **University of Utah** campus near the Marriott Library (295 S. Campus Dr.) and the Ray Olpin Student Union (200 S., Central Campus Dr.) around lunchtime. Not on campus? Head to the Gallivan Center for **Food Truck Thursday** (www.facebook.com/FoodTruckThursdays), wherein different vendors line up on Gallivan Avenue just off East Broadway 11am-2pm on Thursdays year-round. If you're really motivated, drive 15 minutes south of Salt Lake to **The Hub Food Truck Park** (982 S. Jordan Pkwy., South Jordan, https://thefoodtruckleague.com/thehub, 11am-2pm Tues.-Sat., 5pm-9pm Wed. and Sat.). The Hub offers indoor seating and posts a daily truck schedule to its site daily. And for several years now, food trucks and local breweries have been vying for the favor of the public and critics in an annual **Food Truck and Brewery Battle,** held in early August at the Gateway plaza (100 S. Rio Grande St.).You'll also find food trucks visiting local breweries, at many outdoor events, and parked in random vacant lots or along streets here and there throughout the city. Here are a few local favorites.

The Blue Bird Stand (385/743-0616, www.facebook.com/navajofoodstandnslc, $7-9) offers a taste of Navajo cooking. You can find Blue Bird at the Native American Trading Post, at Indigenous events around the city, and at other festivals. On the menu: Navajo tacos, frybread, blue corn mush, hominy stew, a Navajo burger, and many more Navajo dishes.

CupBop (801/849-1289, www.facebook.com/cupbop, $7.50-8.50) is a longtime locally beloved Korean barbecue joint in a bright yellow truck. A classic order is the KKO-KKO BOP, with Korean barbecue chicken over rice, lettuce, and noodles.

Soul of Salt Lake (801/716-1767, $8.50) brings a taste of soul food to the city with simple, delicious renditions of all the classics: fried chicken, cornbread, mac and cheese, collard greens, and more.

Black's Sliders (979/549-1449, www.blackssliders.com, $4 per slider) makes "farm-to-truck" sliders from locally sourced hormone-free, antibiotic-free meat. The truck also puts out vegan sliders. Check its Twitter or Instagram pages to find Black's around the city.

The Salty Pineapple (385/319-6664, https://the-saltypineapple.com, $9-10) serves Hawai'ian barbecue in a blue truck decked out in pink flowers. Good bets: the kalua pig bowl or the pineapple barbecue tofu plate. Get it with Polynesian macaroni salad and a fresh young coconut.

Hayat's Grill (385/495-1894, www.facebook.com/hayatgrill, $10-11) serves the cuisine of Afghanistan like spiced fried chicken and *bolani,* a thin dough stuffed with seasoned potatoes, fried in a pan, and served with a cilantro-pepper chutney that packs heat. Hayat Stoman, the man behind the truck, is a refugee who got his start thanks to the Spice Kitchen Incubator and was voted one of the best new trucks on the scene in 2019.

Boba Shack (518/400-2622, www.facebook.com/bobashack, starting at $4.39) is at the ready to refresh you in a blue-and-white trailer serving boba-infused smoothies in over a dozen flavors, from mango to taro.

Amkha Misky (801/691-4412, www.facebook.com/amkhamisky, $9-11) brings a taste of Peru to Utah in a bright red truck. You really can't beat a $3 empanada. Another must-try is the supremely creamy Queen's Avocado, stuffed with a chicken or vegetable salad over lettuce. Polish it all off with an Inca Kola!

World Dog (801/831-2078, www.worlddogslc.com, $3-5) is a longtime local favorite serving up globetrotting hot dogs, sausages, and tofu dogs. Go barbecue-style with The Memphis, or veg out with The Malibu, a tofu dog topped with sprouts, avocado, and vinaigrette.

★ **Laziz Kitchen** (912 Jefferson St. W., 801/441-1228, www.lazizkitchen.com, 11am-3pm and 5pm-10pm Tues.-Sun., $9-28), located on the edge of downtown, is one of the best places in the city to go. Owned by a refugee of the Lebanese-Israeli conflict, Laziz serves food that leans Lebanese, but also travels around other Middle Eastern countries. The talented chefs at Laziz offer traditionally crafted dips, mezze, and other dishes, and put a Lebanese spin on American dishes like burgers.

Some of the best Ethiopian food in the city can be found in a strip mall at **Mahider Ethiopian Restaurant & Market** (1465 State St. #7, 801/975-1111, www.mahiderethiopian.com, 11am-3pm and 5pm-10pm Tues.-Sat., noon-3pm and 5pm-10pm Sun., $6-13). While the interior is nothing to write home about—think lights a little too bright and a dining room that looks more like a retail space—the service is great and the food delicious. If you'd like a full discovery of Ethiopian cuisine, order the Taste of Mahider, which showcases smaller portions of several dishes, all served on a large tray. All orders come with spongy, tangy *injera* flatbread, which you'll use to sop up the stews—standard utensils are by request only. Mahider also offers an Ethiopian Coffee Ceremony and serves Ethiopian beers and *tej,* a honey wine made with raw honey and hops.

Bakeries and Ice Cream Shops

If you're a patisserie person, a requisite destination is ★ **Fillings & Emulsions** (1475 Main St., 385/229-4228, 8am-6pm Tues.-Fri., 9am-7pm Sat., pastries starting at $2). Located in the Ballpark District just south of downtown, Fillings & Emulsions is owned by celebrity chef Adalberto Diaz, who has been decorated with many an award and has frequently appeared in baking competitions on the Food Network. Diaz's signature bake is the macaron, which comes in a delightful rainbow of colors, as well as stuffed with ice cream if you please. But that's just one of many things to sample from the pastry case, from Cuban meat pies and vibrant *petits gâteaux* to tarts and cheesecakes.

SOUTH OF THE CENTER
Diners

A few miles south of downtown, **Left Fork Grill** (68 W. 3900 S., 801/266-4322, http://leftforkgrill.com, 6am-3pm Mon.-Tues., 6am-8pm Wed.-Thurs., 6am-8:30pm Fri.-Sat., 7am-3pm Sun., $10.99-17.99) may be a little out of the way, but is a must for diner connoisseurs. If nothing else, come for the pies, which regulars often order before their lunch. There's even a pie shelf available at each booth where you can place your slice to ogle as you diligently eat your savory order first. In the fall, get a slice of apple pie baked in a cheddar crust. Or try one of the owner's personal favorites: raspberry cream. Crust aficionados will delight in the well-browned, crisp pastry shell, which the pastry chef attributes to lard and a glass pie dish.

Ethnic Eats

The stretch of State Street south of downtown is known for two things: car dealerships and some of the best hole-in-the-wall dining in Salt Lake. If you think you have a high spice tolerance, ask for a 10 out of 10 on the ★ **Mom's Kitchen** (2233 State St., South Salt Lake, 801/486-0092, www.momskitchensaltlakecity.com, 11:30am-10pm Mon.-Sat., noon-9pm Sun., $7.99-14.99) heat scale, and then talk to me. This Taiwanese and Chinese restaurant serves no-frills, traditional dishes that will warm you up from the inside out, starting with the tongue. But don't sweat: You can always ask for a 1 on that heat scale and emerge satisfied and unscathed from dishes like Mom's dumplings.

The family-owned and -operated **Navajo Hogan** (447 E. 3300 S., South Salt Lake, 801/466-2860, www.navajohogan.biz, 11am-3pm and 5pm-6:30pm Tues.-Fri., 11am-5pm Sat., $5.89-6.75) serves popular Indigenous cuisine off the beaten path. The house specialty is a Navajo taco—homemade frybread slathered with chili and decorated with cheddar, lettuce, tomatoes, onions, and salsa. You can also enjoy frybread à la carte or try other dishes like mutton stew.

Another great South Salt Lake pick is **Afghan Kitchen** (3142 Main St., South Salt Lake, 385/229-4155, https://afghan-kitchen.com, noon-9pm Tues.-Fri., 1pm-9pm Sat.-Sun., $14-23), which was opened by two immigrant families in 2014. If you're new to Afghan food, know that you won't find very spicy dishes, but rich flavors you've perhaps yet to experience in dishes like pumpkin turnovers, beef dumplings, and slow-cooked rice and meat entrées. Afghan Kitchen is vegetarian-friendly and also serves several refreshing yogurt drinks.

About 20 minutes south of downtown in Holladay, **Laid Back Poke Shack** (6213 Highland Dr., Holladay, 801/635-8190, www.laidbackpokeshack.com, 11am-8pm Mon.-Sat., $7-14.50) lets you build your own poke bowls from the bottom up with sustainably sourced fish from the Honolulu Fish Auction, seaweed salad, and saucy kalua pig, among other ingredients. This is one of the best places in Utah to get a taste of the cuisine of the Pacific Islands, which have a large presence in Salt Lake.

SANDY/COTTONWOOD HEIGHTS
Cafés and Breakfast

Cottonwood Heights Cafe (7146 Highland Dr., Cottonwood Heights, 801/947-0760, 7am-2:30pm daily, $5-10) is not a fancy breakfast or brunch place, but it serves a solid breakfast and a lunch that leans heavy. Cuisine-wise, Cottonwood Heights Cafe falls into that niche category of Greek American diner, with gyro meat and Mediterranean flavors making appearances. Choose from the large omelet menu, or dig into a short stack of blueberry pancakes.

Ethnic Eats

La Caille (9565 Wasatch Blvd., Sandy, 801/942-1751, www.lacaille.com, 5pm-9pm Mon.-Fri., 10am-2pm and 5pm-9pm Sat.,

10am-3pm and 4pm-8pm Sun., $36-68) is a slice of the French countryside in the mouth of Little Cottonwood Canyon. On over 20 acres, La Caille grows its own grapes, produces its own small Chateau La Caille wine label, and runs an award-winning French restaurant. La Caille also offers limited lodging options, if this French retreat sounds so good you'd like to spend more than a meal there. The classic French menu draws on produce from its own garden to drum up dishes like grilled quail, escargot, and duck risotto. And the vibe from the moment you drive up the cobblestone drive is quintessential French vineyard, with a country cottage draped in greenery and flowers that looks like it belongs in the Bordeaux countryside, 18th-century decor within, and peacocks strutting around the grounds.

Potstickers Plus 1 (9197 S. 700 E., Sandy, 801/987-8620, www.potstickersplus1.com, 11am-9:30pm Mon.-Sat., 4pm-9pm Sun., three potstickers starting at $3.89) serves potstickers hand-built from the wrapper up. Established and run by a former scientist, Potstickers Plus 1 has an attention to detail and process that comes through in the flawlessness of the dumplings—whether pork or vegan—and the brilliant filling combinations. And solo diners are more than welcome; the "Plus 1" in the restaurant name refers to the other dishes you'll find here, like slow-cooked lamb ribs.

Coffee Shops

Sunset Coffee Co (7978 S. 1300 E., Sandy, 801/233-9151, www.mysunsetcoffee.com, 6am-1am Mon.-Sat., 7am-1am Sun.) handily one-ups Starbucks with extravagant sweet coffee beverages that you may want to photograph before you sip. Check the chalkboard menu for the daily specials named for celebrities real and fictional, like Marilyn Monroe and Voldemort. And you can always keep it real with a simple drip coffee.

1: pie shelf at Left Fork Grill **2:** killer Mexican food at Red Iguana

WEST OF THE CENTER
Ethnic Eats

As far as Mexican food goes in Salt Lake City, **Red Iguana** (736 W. North Temple, 801/322-1489, www.rediguana.com, 11am-10pm Mon.-Thurs., 11am-11pm Fri., 10am-11pm Sat., 10am-9pm Sun., $10-18) is the unequivocal favorite. Since the mid-1980s, the Cardenas family has been sharing their award-winning Mexican dishes with the city. The must-try menu item is one of the several rich moles, along with a margarita or other cocktail, made with fresh-squeezed juices and ingredients. A testament to the restaurant's popularity? In spite of its sizable space, it opened a second successful location—**Red Iguana 2** (866 W. South Temple, 801/214-6050)—just two blocks from the first.

GREATER SALT LAKE CITY
Diners

Utah's oldest continually operated restaurant, ★ **Ruth's Diner** (4610 Emigration Canyon Rd., Salt Lake City, 801/582-5807, https://ruthsdiner.com, 8am-9pm Sun.-Thurs., 8am-10pm Fri.-Sat., $10-22) is the type of place to plan a day around. The namesake of this local institution originally opened her diner downtown in 1930 and then relocated it in 1949 to a trolley car that sits toward the Salt Lake City end of Emigration Canyon. Only about 2 miles (3.2 km) east of the Foothills, Ruth's kicks typical diner fare up a notch. Be sure to try the house-smoked salmon that appears in a few dishes, and indulge in the chocolate malt pudding. Bear in mind that whatever your entrée order is, it will come with a massive, pillowy biscuit. Buffer your trip to Ruth's with a road bike ride through Emigration Canyon—or at least a scenic drive. Once you arrive, expect a wait, unless you've visited at an odd hour. But there's no shortage of lovely patio seating and complimentary coffee to tide you over.

American

Log Haven (6451 Millcreek Canyon Rd., 801/272-8255, www.log-haven.com, 5:30pm-9pm daily, $27-49.50) is a romantic retreat with a fine steak-house menu. Tucked away on 40 quiet acres in Millcreek Canyon about 30 minutes southeast of downtown, the restaurant is located in a log cabin on steroids, initially constructed in 1920 as a private getaway. The property fell into disrepair, but was revived and opened as a restaurant in 1984. Amid the waterfalls and wildflowers of the Wasatch National Forest, Log Haven serves elegant dishes like mussels with saffron aioli, a corn and enoki mushroom risotto, and a pepper-seared fillet with aged gouda.

Accommodations

Salt Lake City offers a modest mix of luxury, boutique, and budget lodging options. If you're looking for world-class, premium hotels, don't stay in Salt Lake—head to Park City, where the crème of the lodging crop lies. If you're willing to settle for run-of-the-mill luxury, look on the bright side: You won't be paying exorbitant prices! The major hotels lie in the downtown area, with a few smaller inns sprinkled around other neighborhoods like the Avenues.

Strange yet true, Salt Lake City unofficially specializes in themed lodging. You'll find three different inns or bed-and-breakfasts where each room takes its cues from a different destination, character, or sentiment.

DOWNTOWN

The name of the ★ **Grand America Hotel** (555 S. Main St., 800/304-8696, www.grandamerica.com, starting at $259) doesn't

1: Grand America Hotel 2: Ellerbeck Mansion B&B
3: Inn on the Hill Bed & Breakfast

lie. Think marble, gold accents, and the sort of ornate, baroque design found in that final scene of *2001: A Space Odyssey*. Even the humblest rooms feel luxurious, as they should in a AAA Five-Diamond hotel—the only one in Salt Lake City. The good news is, this is Salt Lake City, and even the nicest hotel in town doesn't come with an outlandish price tag. And don't let the lavishness fool you; the Grand America is also family-friendly. You can request a crib in your room or book a babysitter right at the hotel. Polish off the fancy experience with afternoon tea or cocktails to the tune of live jazz (7pm-10pm Fri.-Sat.). Though it's downtown, the Grand America is on a slightly quieter block, but still very close to dining and nightlife.

If you're all about luxury hotels, another great option is the **Kimpton Hotel Monaco** (15 W. 200 S., 801/595-0000, www.monaco-saltlakecity.com, starting at $307). The Monaco has a sleeker, more modern interpretation of luxury than the Grand America. It's also a little more in the thick of things than its primary competitor, right by the Gallivan Center, across from the Capitol Theatre, and close to plenty of dining options, including a fabulous one right inside its walls: Bambara.

For lodging that doubles as museum, spend a night at **The Peery Hotel** (110 W. Broadway, 801/521-4300, www.peeryhotel.com, starting at $179). Not only is the building historic (established in 1910), but inside you'll find a motley mix of art and vintage furnishings everywhere from the lobby to the guest rooms and the dining room. While the art and decor within this independently owned boutique hotel spans decades, the overarching aesthetic is art deco. The Peery is located downtown close to dining and museums like The Leonardo.

Strike a compromise between luxury and affordability at the **Little America Hotel** (500 Main St., 801/596-5700, https://saltlake.littleamerica.com, starting at $189), part of a western chain that includes the more opulent Grand America, which lies just across Main Street. Little America is huge, with 850 rooms

ranging from huge tower suites with views to smaller one-bed quarters. It rocks the same baroque style as sister hotel Grand America, but more subdued. Amenities include a fitness center, a giant indoor/outdoor pool, and an array of dining options.

For an inexpensive lodging option downtown, consider the **Metropolitan Inn** (524 S. West Temple, 801/531-7100, www.metropolitaninn.com, starting at $58). It may be free of frills, but the Metropolitan is conveniently located downtown, keeps clean rooms with Tempur-pedic mattresses, and includes continental breakfast. In addition to the 60 rooms, there's one suite that offers a little more space (sleeps four).

If you want to be as close to Temple Square as possible, the **Salt Lake Plaza Hotel** (122 W. South Temple, 801/521-0130, www.plaza-hotel.com, starting at $80) is right next door. Of course, even if proximity to Temple Square isn't your priority, this hotel is also right smack in the middle of downtown and within steps of a TRAX light rail station. This affordable hotel has 150 rooms appointed with bright, modern furnishings, and all beds have high-end mattresses.

Located on the eastern outskirts of downtown, **The Carlton Hotel** (140 E. South Temple, 801/355-3418, https://carltonsaltlakecity.com, starting at $99) was built in the 1920s and honors its heritage in building design and decor. While there are many lodging options in historic inns or bed-and-breakfasts in other neighborhoods, The Carlton is one of few in the downtown area. You can enjoy a complimentary continental breakfast, but you might consider a 10-minute walk to the nearby Gourmandise bakery for morning pastries or brunch instead. The lobby also serves hot tea and cookies every day.

If you prefer the familiarity and reputation of a larger national hotel chain, the **Hilton Salt Lake City** (255 S. West Temple, 801/328-2000, www.hilton.com, starting at $113) is a great option. Conveniently located downtown, this 18-floor tower is close to everything from

Temple Square to restaurants and TRAX. The hotel is also kid- and dog-friendly and has an award-winning steak house located on the main floor. Amenities include an indoor pool and, for the warmer months, an outdoor hot tub and sundeck.

Another well-rated national chain in the downtown area is the **AC Hotel by Marriott** (225 W. 200 S., 385/722-9600, www.marriott.com, starting at $136). Located across from the Salt Palace Convention Center, the AC features European-inspired chic design with rooms beholding cityscapes and alpine landscapes alike. While there are many dining options nearby, the hotel also has a breakfast bar as well as a lounge that serves drinks and tapas.

CAPITOL HILL

One of the lone lodging options in the Capitol Hill neighborhood is the ★ **Inn on the Hill Bed & Breakfast** (225 N. State St, 801/328-1466, https://inn-on-the-hill.com, starting at $145). Originally a home built in 1906 in the Renaissance Revival style, the building was converted into a bed-and-breakfast in the late 1990s and does indeed sit on a hill. While dimensions, bed size, and decor vary depending on whether you're staying in a premier room, an executive room, or a luxury room, they're all beautifully appointed with elegant early 20th-century finishings and named for a place in Utah, like Saltair or Zion. For a real special occasion, book the two-story, separate Carriage House, which includes a kitchenette.

CENTRAL CITY

If you love theme parks—or themed anything—then you'll probably geek out on a stay at the ★ **Anniversary Inn** (460 S. 1000 E., 801/363-4900, www.anniversaryinn.com, starting at $169). Each of the 36 rooms here has a unique theme, often locally inspired, which is implemented with impressive accuracy. Your room may transport you to a railroad car of the Wild West, a gondola in Venice, or an Egyptian catacomb—does it get any more romantic than that? It does

indeed if you book the romantic getaway special that includes dinner ($350). A stay includes complimentary breakfast, as well as a bottle of non-alcoholic sparkling cider. The Anniversary Inn also has a location in the Lower Avenues neighborhood.

THE AVENUES

If you like the idea of staying in a more residential part of town with a collegiate vibe, consider the **Ellerbeck Mansion B&B** (140 N. B St. E., 801/699-0480, www.ellerbeckbedandbreakfast.com, starting at $117). This historic inn boasts the design and trappings of the late 19th century, when it was built. The decor is stately, but not overdone, with each of the nine rooms bearing unique decorations and antique touches, like stained-glass windows, throughout. The breakfast part of the deal is no granola or over-easy situation. Wake up hungry for a fluffy frittata or French toast stuffed with Nutella.

Go full-on Victorian at the small, elegant **Haxton Manor** (943 E. South Temple, 801/363-4646, www.haxtonmanor.com, starting at $120). While the house has been renovated, it stays true to its 1906 pioneer roots in style and service. The Victorian charm remains, but the inconveniences of a Victorian manor (think erratic room temperature and walls and floors that are anything but sound barriers) have been thankfully addressed. The Haxton has just four rooms and three suites, and serves a complimentary breakfast. There are plenty of quiet nooks within the house where you can unwind, like a big, cozy chair in the Boar's Head Pub common room.

SANDY/COTTONWOOD HEIGHTS

If you want to stay as close to the skiing and trails in the Cottonwood Canyons as possible, but with the conveniences of an urban area, consider lodging in Sandy or Cottonwood Heights, which lie southeast of the city.

Hansen House B&B (8586 S. 150 E., Sandy, 801/562-2198, http://hansenhouse.

com, starting at $89) may very well be the oldest place to bed down in Salt Lake. This house was built in 1887 by a former mayor of the town of Sandy. The innkeepers have taken care to preserve the period vibe of this home, outfitting it with decor, furniture, and even kitchenware that recalls the Victorian era. You can spend the afternoon reading in the library, play the grand piano in the parlor, or enjoy drinks in the garden. The six rooms here are each decorated according to themes ranging from mountain man Paul Bunyan to an English fox hunt.

Another themed lodging option for your consideration is the **Castle Creek Inn** (7391 Creek Rd., Cottonwood Heights, 801/567-9437, www.castlecreekbb.com, starting at $149). The name doesn't lie; the exterior is designed to resemble a castle, and all 10 rooms are themed around a place or a story where castles tower high. Think *Romeo & Juliet* or the verdant hills of Scotland. The themes here are not over the top, but the amenities are. Indulge in the all-night snack bar or unwind in the two-person outdoor hot tub surrounded by trees and rocks.

Information and Services

TOURIST INFORMATION
Located downtown right by the Salt Palace Convention Center, the Salt Lake City Visitors Center, known as **Visit Salt Lake** (90 S. West Temple, 801/534-4900, www.visitsaltlake. com, 9am-5pm daily), can recommend specific itineraries or activities and provide maps and brochures.

EMERGENCY SERVICES
Salt Lake is home to several major hospitals with 24-hour emergency rooms. The **University of Utah Hospital** (50 N. Medical

Dr., 801/581-2121, https://healthcare.utah.edu) is a very reputable hospital in the Foothills area. Just a couple minutes down the road, **Primary Children's Hospital** (100 Mario Capecchi Dr., 801/662-1000) offers great pediatric care. **Salt Lake Regional Medical Center** (1050 E. South Temple, 801/350-4111, https://saltlakeregional.org) is another hospital option close to downtown. There are also several 24-hour pharmacies near downtown, including a **CVS** in Sugar House (1269 E. 2100 S., 801/486-0695).

Getting There and Around

GETTING THERE
Air
Modern and easy to navigate, **Salt Lake City International Airport** (SLC; 776 N. Terminal Dr., 801/575-2400, www.slcairport. com) lies just a short 15-minute drive from downtown Salt Lake. The airport lies less than 7 miles (11.3 km) west of downtown via I-80. Travel from the airport to the city or other regional destinations by renting a car, calling a taxi or rideshare, or taking the TRAX light rail's Green line (www.rideuta.com) outside Terminal 1.

Train
Amtrak runs trains into Salt Lake City to the downtown **Salt Lake Central Station** (340 S. 600 W., www.amtrak.com). It takes about 15 hours from Denver ($84 one-way) and 31 hours from Los Angeles ($162 one-way). This is a scenic albeit slow way to travel to Salt Lake.

Long-Distance Bus

A long-distance bus is a faster ground transportation method to Salt Lake City than the train. **Greyhound** (www.greyhound. com) runs bus service to the **Salt Lake Intermodal Transit Center** (300 S. 600 W., 801/355-9579) in downtown Salt Lake City. It takes about 10 hours from Denver ($90 one-way) and 15 hours from Los Angeles ($140 one-way).

Car

If you're on a road trip, you'll most likely arrive in Salt Lake City via **I-15,** which runs north-south through the city, or **I-80,** which runs east-west through the city, unless you're taking back roads. Traffic on I-80 usually doesn't get too congested, but I-15 can become quite backed up with the inevitable accident during rush hour on weekdays. Traffic can also be bad exiting the city on Friday afternoons and entering on Sundays as people head off on weekend road trips into the mountains. Winter weather exacerbates traffic.

GETTING AROUND
Train

The **TRAX light rail** (www.rideuta.com, trains come every 15 minutes during peak times daily, $2.50 one-way) covers most of the city, is easy to use, and is affordable. The Green line begins at the Salt Lake City International Airport and runs through downtown all the way to the industrial areas of West Valley City. The Red line originates at the University of Utah in the Foothills neighborhood and travels southwest. The Blue line runs from downtown to Draper. Most lines run from around 5:30am or 6am until around midnight. You can buy one-way or round-trip tickets, or day passes for about $5 that give you unlimited access to both the TRAX light rail and local Utah Transportation Authority buses. Day passes are available in five-packs online or can be purchased at stations individually.

Local Bus

To complement the light rail lines, the **Utah Transportation Authority** (www.rideuta. com) also operates over 100 bus routes (www. rideuta.com, $2.50 one-way) throughout Salt Lake and its surrounding counties. Find schedules and routes online.

Bicycle

The **Salt Lake City Transportation Division** runs a helpful online resource (www.bikeslc.com) with routes, maps, bike parking areas, and other information. You can also pick up a bike throughout the downtown area through **Green Bike SLC Bikeshare** (https://greenbikeslc.org).

If you're planning to bike between the downtown areas and the Foothills or Avenues, plan to power through some hills that, combined with the altitude, may knock the wind out of you.

Taxi/Rideshare

The only safe bet for finding a taxi in Salt Lake is the downtown area. But throughout Salt Lake City's major neighborhoods, it's very easy to call a Lyft or Uber. Do not rely on taxis or rideshares to get to and from a trailhead or ski resort, however, because finding a ride home may be difficult or impossible. A couple of 24-hour cab services in the area include **City Cab Co.** (801/363-5550, www. citycabut.com) and **Ute Cab** (801/359-7788, http://utecabco.com).

Car

The usual litany of car rental companies is available at the Salt Lake City International Airport as well as downtown. You'll save a few bucks by renting in town rather than at the airport, but the convenience may well be worth the money, especially in inclement weather. If you're driving in the winter, be sure to request 4WD/AWD as well as snow tires. If you're visiting in the summer and plan to do a little off-roading, you may also want to request 4WD/AWD as well as a high-clearance vehicle. One highly rated local company that specializes in 4WD/AWD and more mountain-ready vehicles is **Rugged Rental & Sales** (2740 W. California Ave. #2, 801/977-9111, www.ruggedrental.com, $46-52 per day depending on vehicle).

If you're heading downtown, there are few areas where you'll end up circling blocks searching for parking spaces, except during major festivals or events. Generally, there is plenty of parking to be found in shopping center garages, lots, and on the street. Between 8am and 8pm on weekdays, you'll have to pay for most spots and max out at two hours. On Saturdays, parking is typically free but time-restricted, and on Sundays, you can park for free and for as long as you like in most spots. The **Park SLC** app (www.parkingslc.com; available for Apple and Android) makes paying for spaces a lot faster. Beyond downtown, street parking is generally free, though it can be restricted to residential only in certain neighborhoods.

Park City

Among ski towns, Park City is one of those lucky few that manages to strike a balance between convenience and adventure. Many of the best ski towns out West tend to lie hours from a major airport. Park City, however, is less than 45 minutes from Salt Lake City International Airport and the state capital.

The town of Park City is also anomalous in that it's not Mormon-dominated like much of the state of Utah. You could travel to Park City and hardly notice the influence of the Church of Jesus Christ of Latter-day Saints, aside from its modest real estate on Main Street and the modest pour you'll receive if you order, say, a High West bourbon on the rocks (more on that later).

Like many places with properties on the National Historic Register,

Highlights

Look for ★ to find recommended sights, activities, dining, and lodging.

★ **Go for a gallery stroll** on Old Town's historic Main Street to check out Wild West history and art (page 110).

★ **Discover the legacy of the 2002 Olympics**—and experience it for yourself—at the **Utah Olympic Park** (page 112).

★ **Hike, run, or bike** on the never-ending **Mid-Mountain Trail** that runs from Deer Valley well past Park City (pages 115 and 119). (And beware of moose!)

★ **Bike the Rail Trail**—former Union Pacific railroad tracks turned iconic rec path—from Park City to Echo Reservoir (page 117).

★ **Ski at Park City Mountain Resort,** the largest ski resort in the United States, where there's a run for everyone (page 120).

★ **Carve corduroy groomers** and pamper yourself at luxurious **Deer Valley Resort** (page 122).

★ **Listen to live music** at the **free outdoor summer concerts** held around the Park City area (page 132).

★ **Catch a show** at the historic **Egyptian Theatre,** one of the predominant theaters of the Sundance Film Festival (page 133).

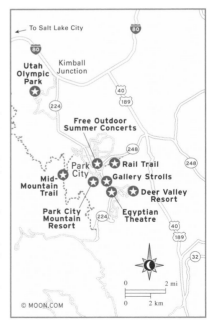

Park City stays in touch with its history, which began with the discovery of silver in the fall of 1868. The first mine in Park City was established soon after, and growth escalated. As more mines opened, people poured into the area to find work and homestead. In 1872 the town was officially dubbed "Parley's Park City," after Parley P. Pratt, an early LDS leader and explorer (the name was later shortened to just "Park City" in the early 1900s). By 1898 the population had peaked at nearly 10,000 people; today, there are some 8,300 residents in the area.

One more landmark in the town's history: the Great Fire of 1898 that raged through town, destroying most of its buildings. Yet like a phoenix, the town emerged stronger. Within two years, it had rebuilt, swapping flammable wood for brick. As a result, most of the quaint historic buildings on Main Street date back to the turn of the 20th century, aside from a few facades and structures from earlier days that managed to survive the flames. A few mine closures and economic depressions later, a mining company—of all parties!—established the first ski area in 1963: Treasure Mountain Resort, which is now part of Park City Mountain Resort.

In the town's 2014 General Plan, it reflected that Park City ". . . has constantly reinvented itself." Nothing could be truer of Park City. Born as a boom-bust mining settlement, Park City rose to the challenge of becoming a stop on the Union Pacific Railroad, before transforming into a ski town. Park City's story doesn't stop there; it turned itself into an Olympic venue and international skiing destination—not to mention a westward hub of the arts. Indeed, Park City is a master of reinvention, and only time will tell what paths the town will travel next.

Any of Park City's many pasts and identities can be experienced by the visitor. From the annual Miner's Day Parade and the Utah Olympic Park to the annual Sundance Film Festival, the past is as electric here as the present.

PLANNING YOUR TIME

For some, Park City is the one and only destination in Utah. If you only want to spend time in Park City, you can go straight from the Salt Lake City International Airport to the mountains, without ever setting foot in Salt Lake City. For others, Park City is on the agenda as an afternoon excursion or day trip during a Salt Lake-focused vacation. Some may simply pass through Park City en route to the Uinta Mountains, Sundance Mountain Resort, or other destinations.

If your time frame is on the lower side (a day or less), you may decide to focus on getting a sense of the town and its history. Head to Old Town and stroll around Main Street, where you can window shop, peruse local history at the Park City Museum, and grab lunch. Come summer, you can also ride the Town Lift right from Main Street up the mountain to take in epic panoramas. You could also come to Park City just for the day to ski or get in a mountain bike ride, skipping the historical and cultural offerings.

For a long weekend spent in Park City, pick both a primary and a secondary activity. In the winter, for many this may be skiing and snowboarding, which constitute the draw for the bulk of seasonal tourists. Among several days of skiing, it's nice to plan one other activity (like dogsledding) or a half-day trip (to Midway in the Greater Wasatch Back, for example) from Park City to give your legs a rest or in case the snow isn't great. The secondary activity could also be something less adventurous and more illuminating (a visit to the Kimball Art Center) or relaxing (a splurge treatment at one of Deer Valley's high-end spas).

Summertime activities are more divergent. Some visitors come to clock miles on Park City's gold-rated mountain bike trail system,

Previous: Old Town Park City; the Mid-Mountain Trail running through Park City Mountain Resort; statues of ski jumper Alf Engen and ski industry pioneer Joe Quinney at the Utah Olympic Park.

Park City Area

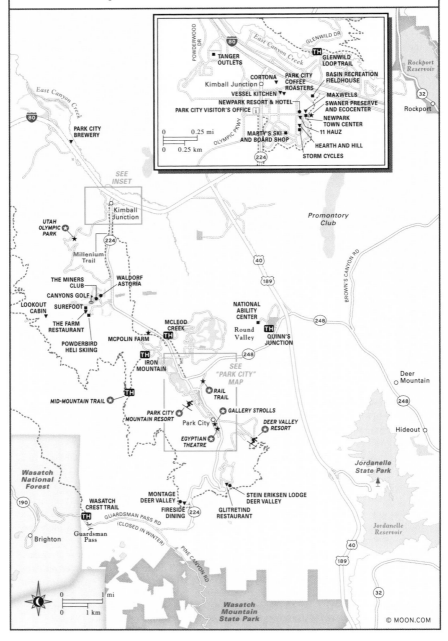

INSET:
POWDERWOOD DR
East Canyon Creek
GLENWILD DR
80
TANGER OUTLETS
GLENWILD LOOP TRAIL
CORTONA
Kimball Junction
PARK CITY COFFEE ROASTERS
BASIN RECREATION FIELDHOUSE
VESSEL KITCHEN
MAXWELLS
NEWPARK RESORT & HOTEL
SWANER PRESERVE AND ECOCENTER
PARK CITY VISITOR'S OFFICE
NEWPARK TOWN CENTER
MARTY'S SKI AND BOARD SHOP
11 HAUZ
HEARTH AND HILL
STORM CYCLES
OLYMPIC PKWY
224

0   0.25 mi
0   0.25 km

East Canyon Creek
80
PARK CITY BREWERY

SEE INSET

Kimball Junction

UTAH OLYMPIC PARK
224
Millenium Trail

Promontory Club

40

189

THE MINERS CLUB
WALDORF ASTORIA
CANYONS GOLF
LOOKOUT CABIN
SUREFOOT
THE FARM RESTAURANT
POWDERBIRD HELI SKIING
MCPOLIN FARM
MCLEOD CREEK TH
IRON MOUNTAIN TH

NATIONAL ABILITY CENTER
Round Valley
QUINN'S JUNCTION TH
248

BROWN'S CANYON RD

Deer Mountain
248
Hideout

SEE "PARK CITY" MAP
248

MID-MOUNTAIN TRAIL TH
RAIL TRAIL
PARK CITY MOUNTAIN RESORT
Park City
GALLERY STROLLS
DEER VALLEY RESORT
EGYPTIAN THEATRE

Jordanelle State Park

Wasatch National Forest
190
WASATCH CREST TRAIL
GUARDSMAN PASS RD (CLOSED IN WINTER)
TH
Guardsman Pass
Brighton
MONTAGE DEER VALLEY
FIRESIDE DINING
224
STEIN ERIKSEN LODGE DEER VALLEY
GLITRETIND RESTAURANT
PINE CANYON RD

Jordanelle Reservoir
40
189

0   1 mi
0   1 km

Wasatch Mountain State Park

32

Rockport Reservoir
32
Rockport

© MOON.COM

while others plan to explore the area at a more leisurely pace through hiking, scenic lift rides, and perhaps a day on the Jordanelle Reservoir. Long weekend trips might be dominated by one big hike or bike ride, complemented by another outdoor excursion on the water, for example.

For itineraries spanning a week or longer, no matter the season, multiple activities can be packed into a Park City visit. The diversity of offerings in the area is a huge perk for couples with distinct interests, or families with kids who want to dip their toes in a little bit of everything. If someone gets bored in Park City, the culprit is likely the person, not the place!

One thing that might legitimately get in your way of a good time? Crowds and weather. If you happen to plan your trip to Park City during a peak season, or during one of its notoriously bustling weekends, you may find yourself sitting in the traffic you sought to escape, or unable to secure a dinner reservation. Generally speaking, summer (June-August) and winter (December-March) are peak seasons, and tourism traffic spikes on the weekends. Holidays draw even more traffic. Some of the busiest times on the slopes include Christmas, New Year's, Martin Luther King's Day weekend, and President's Day weekend. In the summer, you'll battle crowds during the July Fourth and Labor Day weekends. Other extremely busy times to visit Park City? Festivals, in particular, the Sundance Film Festival, which runs about two weeks late January-early February. While you may be planning a trip during this time because you want to spend a holiday in Park City or attend Sundance, if that's not your goal, you might consider visiting at a quieter time.

Another obstacle to a visit to Park City could be winter weather. While a snowstorm rarely shuts down Park City, it can make getting around difficult, or skiing near impossible with small children. This obstacle is somewhat out of the hands of wintertime visitors. The best recommendation here is to embrace the weather as best you can, which is why I include indoor activities—and a tip to always spring for a rental car with AWD/4WD.

ORIENTATION

Park City is the most prominent town in the Wasatch Back, which refers to the town's location on the backside of the Wasatch Mountains. Conversely, Salt Lake City lies west of Park City along the front of the Wasatch range. Park City is about 30 minutes

the Orange Bubble Express chairlift at Park City Mountain Resort

Town Lift

Park City's Town Lift

Town Lift provides a way to ride directly from the slopes of **Park City Mountain Resort** (https://parkcitymountain.com) into Old Town Park City. This essentially means the town of Park City itself is ski-in/ski-out, a unique amenity for a ski town if there ever was one. Town Lift loads from Town Lift Plaza off Main Street, just past the intersection with 9th Street. You can also ski right back into town—whether it's for lunch or drinks in town, or just on your way back home at the end of the day—via a few different blue runs. A popular move is to ski down to High West Distillery for lunch, then hop back on Town Lift for a couple more hours of afternoon turns. To ride Town Lift, you will need a ski pass or lift ticket for Park City Mountain Resort, which you can purchase online or at the base areas (Park City Mountain Village or Canyons Village).

from Salt Lake and a good 45 minutes from the Big and Little Cottonwood Canyons; as the crow flies, however, Park City is only a few miles from Solitude and Brighton in Big Cottonwood Canyon, and just a little farther than that to Snowbird and Alta. Guardsman Pass more efficiently connects the dots between these destinations than I-80, but remains closed in the winter.

The town of Park City sits within Summit County, though a broad swath of the county is colloquially referred to as Park City. Technically, "Park City Proper" consists of a smaller area commonly called **Old Town,** so named because it was the first hub in the area to be developed. Old Town consists of the area's historic district and the classic Main Street—complete with colorful late

19th-century Western architecture and, of course, a saloon. Old Town is also directly connected to the skiing at Park City Mountain via the Town Lift.

While the **Prospector** and **Kimball Junction** areas are technically not in Park City, they're often referred to as such. Kimball Junction is located about 12 miles (19.3 km), or 20 minutes by car, north of Old Town Park City. If you're coming from Salt Lake City, you'll pass through Kimball Junction on your way into town. Prospector lies only about a mile (1.6 km) north of Old Town. In these two peripheral areas, you'll find a number of sights and recreational opportunities, as well as more affordable and prolific dining, shopping, and lodging options. Park City, Prospector, Kimball Junction, and Park City Mountain

Park City

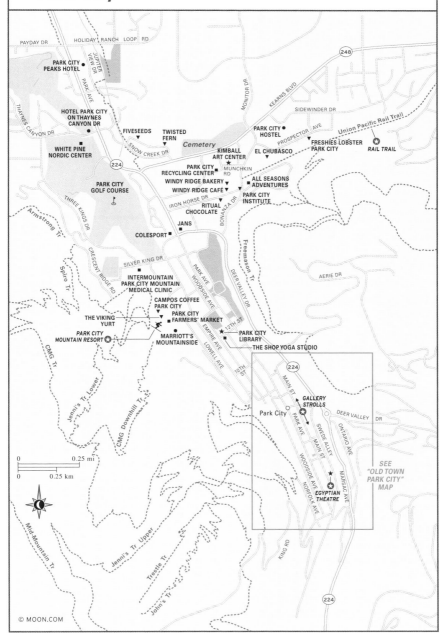

PAYDAY DR
HOLIDAY RANCH LOOP RD
248
PARK CITY PEAKS HOTEL
JUPITER VIEW DR
PARK AVE
MONITOR DR
KEARNS BLVD
SIDEWINDER DR
THAYNES CANYON DR
HOTEL PARK CITY ON THAYNES CANYON DR
FIVE5EEDS
TWISTED FERN
Cemetery
SNOW CREEK DR
PROSPECTOR AVE
PARK CITY HOSTEL
Union Pacific Rail Trail
FRESHIES LOBSTER PARK CITY
RAIL TRAIL
WHITE PINE NORDIC CENTER
224
KIMBALL ART CENTER
EL CHUBASCO
PARK CITY RECYCLING CENTER
MUNCHKIN RD
PARK CITY GOLF COURSE
WINDY RIDGE BAKERY
WINDY RIDGE CAFÉ
ALL SEASONS ADVENTURES
THREE KINGS DR
IRON HORSE DR
BONANZA DR
PARK CITY INSTITUTE
RITUAL CHOCOLATE
Armstrong Tr
JANS
COLESPORT
Freemason Tr
DEER VALLEY DR
AERIE DR
CRESCENT RIDGE RD
SILVER KING DR
Spiro Tr
INTERMOUNTAIN PARK CITY MOUNTAIN MEDICAL CLINIC
PARK AVE
WOODSIDE AVE
CMG Tr
CAMPOS COFFEE PARK CITY
THE VIKING YURT
PARK CITY FARMERS' MARKET
12TH ST
PARK CITY MOUNTAIN RESORT
MARRIOTT'S MOUNTAINSIDE
EMPIRE AVE
LOWELL AVE
PARK CITY LIBRARY
THE SHOP YOGA STUDIO
10TH ST
Jenni's Tr. Lower
CMG Downhill Tr.
224
MAIN ST
GALLERY STROLLS
Park City
PARK AVE
SWEDE ALLEY
MAIN ST
DEER VALLEY DR
ONTARIO AVE
0   0.25 mi
0   0.25 km
WOODSIDE AVE
NORFOLK AVE
MARSAC AVE
EGYPTIAN THEATRE
SEE "OLD TOWN PARK CITY" MAP
Mid Mountain Tr.
Jenni's Tr Upper
Trestle Tr.
John's Tr.
KING RD
224

© MOON.COM

Resort all lie off Highway 224, which is the main artery through town.

Park City's two **ski resorts,** Deer Valley and Park City Mountain, both offer their own collection of lodging, dining, and retail. Some dining options are actually on-mountain (lift-accessed), but most are clustered around the resort base areas. **Park City Mountain** starts north of Old Town and continues adjacent to it. It has two base areas: The **Canyons Village** begins a few miles north of Old Town just off Highway 224, while **Park City Mountain Village** is located just steps from Old Town. As a Vail-owned resort, Park City Mountain may give off a faux Little Switzerland/Disneyland vibe characteristic of its resort portfolio—for a more authentic Park City experience, after skiing, head to Old Town rather than sticking around the base areas for après or dinner. **Deer Valley** spans the mountains south of Old Town. It has three primary resort areas: **Snow Park,** the main base area and the closest to Old Town, which is 1-2 miles (1.6-3.2 km) away depending on specific location; the mid-mountain **Silver Lake Village;** and **Empire Pass,** which snakes its way above the ski area and ultimately turns into Guardsman Pass.

Sights

Sightseeing is not the reason why most people come to Park City—that would be outdoor adventures—but while you're here, there are some great landmarks and activities to discover. These are mostly museums, galleries, and historic sites, many of which offer lenses into Park City's past. For families in particular, these places of interest may come in handy to break up a ski vacation, give the kids a break from hiking, or fill in rainy days.

OLD TOWN PARK CITY
Park City Museum
You could spend a whole day enjoying all there is to offer on Park City's historic Main Street, in no small part due to the **Park City Museum** (528 Main St., 435/649-7457, https:// parkcityhistory.org, 10am-7pm Mon.-Sat., noon-6pm Sun., $12 adults, $5 children). A portion of the museum, including its Main Street facade and the entrance-area gift shop, is located inside the old City Hall, built in 1885. The building, like many in Park City, was mostly destroyed in the 1898 Great Fire, then rebuilt. Today, history has replaced politics within the building's brick walls. Permanent and temporary exhibits within cover everything from the pioneers who settled the town to Park City's silver mining days

to its transformation into a ski town for the wealthy and occasionally famous. This story is told through original artifacts, replicas, and interactive, kid-friendly displays. Don't miss unique historical sights like the "skier subway," a 1960s-era rebuilt mine car that carried skiers up the mountain, or the town's historic stone jailhouse, which was located in the basement of the original City Hall. The museum also arranges 75-minute walking tours of Old Town ($7 pp) that highlight points of historical interest along Main Street.

Main Street Art Galleries
Interspersed with the saloons, restaurants, and outdoor apparel stores along Main Street are **art galleries.** While collections vary, the overriding themes are, unsurprisingly, mountains, local wildlife, and ranching. Another recurring subject? The McPolin Farm, an iconic sight just north of town that's been rendered by many a local artist in every medium imaginable. Given the preference for local subject matter, a tour of Old Town's art galleries is not only artistic exploration, but a historical, cultural, and ecological tour de Park City. **Gallery MAR** (436 Main St., 435/649-3001, www.gallerymar.com, 10am-9pm daily), for example, hangs oil paintings

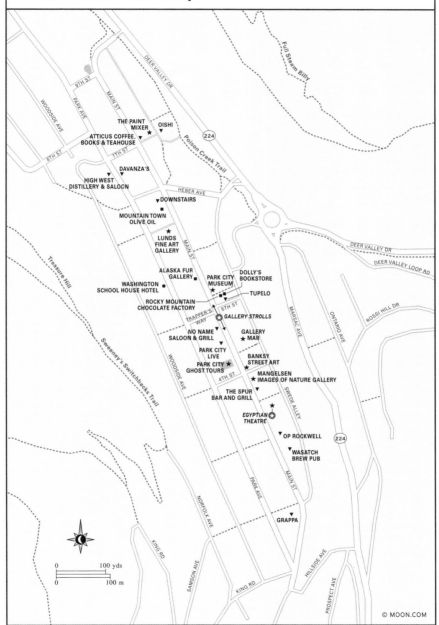

Old Town Park City

9TH ST
DEER VALLEY DR
Full Steam Billy
WOODSIDE AVE
PARK AVE
MAIN ST
224
Poison Creek Trail
8TH ST
7TH ST

THE PAINT MIXER
OISHI
ATTICUS COFFEE, BOOKS & TEAHOUSE

DAVANZA'S
HIGH WEST DISTILLERY & SALOON

HEBER AVE

DOWNSTAIRS

MOUNTAIN TOWN OLIVE OIL

DEER VALLEY DR
DEER VALLEY LOOP RD

LUNDS FINE ART GALLERY

MAIN ST

Treasure Hill

ALASKA FUR GALLERY
WASHINGTON SCHOOL HOUSE HOTEL
PARK CITY MUSEUM
DOLLY'S BOOKSTORE

TUPELO

ROCKY MOUNTAIN CHOCOLATE FACTORY
5TH ST
TRAPPER'S WAY
GALLERY STROLLS

MARSAC AVE
ONTARIO AVE
ROSSI HILL DR

NO NAME SALOON & GRILL
GALLERY MAR

Sweeney's Switchbacks Trail
WOODSIDE AVE
PARK CITY LIVE
BANKSY STREET ART
PARK CITY GHOST TOURS
4TH ST
MANGELSEN IMAGES OF NATURE GALLERY

THE SPUR BAR AND GRILL

SWEDE ALLEY

EGYPTIAN THEATRE

OP ROCKWELL
224

WASATCH BREW PUB

PARK AVE
MAIN ST

0   100 yds
0   100 m

NORFOLK AVE
KING RD

GRAPPA

SAMSON AVE
KING RD
HILLSIDE AVE
PROSPECT AVE

© MOON.COM

of hulking bears and romping pooches (Park City's a big dog town). If you're a nature photography fan, then you probably know the name Thomas D. Mangelsen and will want to stop by **MANGELSEN Images of Nature Gallery** (365 Main St., 435/649-7598, www.mangelsen.com/park-city, 10am-10pm daily), where magnificent photos of moose and bears chomping down on thrashing salmon await. For paintings that will remind you of the sights and sounds of Park City, head to the **Lunds Fine Art Gallery** (591 Main St., 435/655-4349, https://lundsfineart.gallery, 10am-9pm daily), showcasing the paintings of Alan Lund, depicting everything from aspen groves in autumn to that beloved and bucolic McPolin Farm.

★ GALLERY STROLLS

During the final Friday of every month, the Park City Gallery Association hosts a **Last Friday Gallery Stroll** (https://parkcitygalleryassociation.com, 6pm-9pm Fri.). During this free, rain-or-shine event, visitors can tour 18 participating galleries, which will have new art on display as well as light refreshments, which sometimes include wine. This makes for a great pre- or post-dinner way to get to know Main Street—and a few galleries that lie beyond the bounds of Old Town—and discover Park City-based or -inspired artists. If you partake in the gallery stroll during winter months or in inclement weather, wear layers and sturdy footwear.

Banksy Street Art

Among Park City's many celebrity visitors past, perhaps the most notorious is street artist Banksy, who showed up in town for a screening of *Exit Through the Gift Shop,* a documentary about him and other graffiti artists, during the 2010 Sundance Film Festival. Needless to say, he left his mark—as many as 10 marks, actually, according to some sources. Yet all but two have been vandalized or deliberately removed. The easiest **Banksy Street Art** to behold can be found at 402 Main Street by the Java Cow coffee and ice cream shop.

Here, Banksy depicted in black ink a man with a camera filming a flower with petals of pink—the only color in the image. This local artistic asset has been framed in wood and covered in glass for protection, so it's relatively easy to spot as you walk along Main Street.

Park City Library

There are a lot of reasons to stop by the **Park City Library** (1255 Park Ave., 435/615-5600, https://parkcitylibrary.org, 10am-9pm Mon.-Thurs., 10am-6pm Fri.-Sat., 1pm-5pm Sun.) in Old Town. The first is history. The library has been more or less operational since 1888, though it has had a few different homes over the years. Today, it's located inside a stately historic building originally constructed in 1928 to house the high school. The second reason to visit is for the sake of your kids. If you've got little ones under six, there's a sizable children's play area, guinea pigs, and programming for babies and toddlers, from story time to sing-a-longs with a ukulele. While you're at the library, grab a hot chocolate and a latte on the first floor at **Lucky Ones** coffee shop, which is staffed by and supports developmentally disabled adults. Another reason to visit the library lies on the building's fourth and highest floor: the **Jim Santy Auditorium,** home of the Park City Film Series, as well as a Sundance Film Festival venue.

McPolin Farm

In 1886 the **McPolin Farm** (3000 Hwy. 224, free to visit) was established as a homestead that eventually became a dairy farm, which operated until the middle of the 20th century. The site—which includes a 1922-built barn, several historic outbuildings, and the surrounding acreage—is now owned by the town of Park City, open to the public, free to visit, and located just a couple miles north of Old Town. Park on the side of the road across Highway 224, then stroll on the

1: sights along a Main Street gallery stroll
2: Banksy's most prominent artwork in Park City

1

2

paved Barn Trail through a tunnel that leads to and around the barn. While the inside of the barn is closed except for special events, other buildings on-site are partially open so you can at least peek in. Plaques around the site offer more information about the farm and its history, but you can also download an app on your phone to guide you on a walking tour (search for "Utah Heritage Walks"). The combination of the historic buildings, pastoral landscape, and alpine backdrop makes the McPolin Farm a perennial favorite for photo shoots, so come with your camera at the ready if you're always looking for photo ops. The barn also hosts events throughout the year, like a fall scarecrow festival and a summer fundraising party. The barn doesn't have its own website, but you can find information on the Town of Park City website (www.parkcity.org), or on the McPolin Farm's Facebook page.

Park City Ghost Tours

One of my favorite ways to learn about a city's past is to take a ghost tour. Sounds hokey, but these tours offer a great way to discover regional mythology and historical tales. So, if you're a history buff with a soft spot for ghost stories, add a tour with **Park City Ghost Tours** (435/615-7673, www.parkcityghosttours.com, 7pm nightly Nov.-Apr., 8pm nightly May-Oct., $20 adults, $10 children, reservations required 24 hours in advance—if less than 24 hours, call and inquire) to your schedule. Run by a pair of retired history teachers, this 75-minute walking tour reveals local paranormal research and escorts you inside allegedly haunted historic buildings. Tours depart by a bronze miner statue at 415 Main Street.

PROSPECTOR
Kimball Art Center

The unofficial headquarters of the fine arts in the Park City area is the **Kimball Art Center** (1401 Kearns Blvd., 435/649-8882, https://kimballartcenter.org, 10am-5pm Mon.-Fri., noon-5pm Sat.-Sun., admission free, class/

event prices vary), which features temporary exhibits (often by local artists) in a variety of mediums, from paintings and photography to sculpture. Peruse one of the free rotating exhibitions, attend an evening art talk, or enroll in a one-time class, which range in topic from open painting studios to pottery. Kids will find plenty of opportunities here, too, like Friday Artful Afternoons ($25 pp), 2.5-hour classes that let kids unleash their creative spirit by producing crayon art or making dreamcatchers, for example. Toddlers, meanwhile, can join a free recurring story time art program. In early August, the Kimball Art Center also hosts a massive art festival on Main Street, with even more class offerings, auctions, street stands, and more.

KIMBALL JUNCTION

★ Utah Olympic Park

The 2002 Winter Olympics left an indelible mark on Salt Lake, Park City, and surrounding areas. The Olympic legacy includes training facilities and venues that have been partially converted into museums and recreational amenities. In Park City's case, this means the **Utah Olympic Park** (3419 Olympic Pkwy., 435/658-4200, https://utaholympiclegacy.com, 9am-6pm daily, admission to grounds and museums free, venue tours $12 adults, $7 youth and seniors, other activity/event pricing varies).

Year-round, the Utah Olympic Park is a fun place to visit, whether to learn more about the Olympics or get an adrenaline rush, Olympian-style. The park is a sight seen by all who exit I-80 from Salt Lake City in the form of two massive ski jumps careening down the hills directly to the east, green in the summer, snow-covered come winter. These jumps are used throughout the year for everything from ski jump lessons and a giant tubing hill to an uphill grunt for the annual Red Bull 400 race.

You might catch athletes training at the facility, such as ski jumpers practicing their aerial jumps in the summer. For a more in-depth experience, take a one-hour **tour** (11am, 1pm, and 3pm daily) that takes you to the top of the jumps and shares more stories about the Olympic history here. The park also houses a museum dedicated to the 2002 games, adventure courses, and a **bobsled track,** where you can do a run with a professional pilot who takes you for a lap around the track at 125 mph for 90 seconds ($125 pp).

The other museum located within the Utah Olympic Park is the **Alf Engen Ski Museum** (3419 Olympic Pkwy., 435/658-4240, https://engenmuseum.org, 9am-6pm daily, free). Named for Norwegian American Olympic ski jumper and ski resort entrepreneur Alf Engen, who landed in Utah in the early 1930s, the museum displays throwbacks to ski fashion over the years, vintage ski photos, a ski jump simulator, and more.

Swaner Preserve and EcoCenter

Tucked behind the retail jungle of Kimball Junction lies an oft-overlooked landscape in the Wasatch Back: wetlands. Dedicated to preserving and educating visitors about the 1,200 acres of wetlands under its charge, the **Swaner Preserve and EcoCenter** (1258 Center Dr., 435/649-1767, www.swanerecocenter.org, 10am-4pm Wed.-Sun., free access to the preserve, pricing varies for exhibits/activities) offers rotating exhibits (on everything from snakes to defensive posturing in the animal kingdom), winter snowshoe tours, a summer geocaching experience, and even an ecosystem-themed **climbing wall** (1pm-3pm Sat.-Sun., $14 adults, $10 children). The preserve itself is accessed through the EcoCenter during its regular operating hours—stop by the front desk to get a key to open any of the access gates to trails, including the **Wetland Discovery Trail** (0.32 mi/0.5 km, self-guided and guided tours available), a dirt path enriched with information about Swaner and its history. Though the trail is built on a raised old railroad bed, it can get muddy in the spring and early summer, so wear appropriate footwear. If you're lucky while you're out on the wetlands, you'll catch sight of an elk or one of the 90 species of visiting birds, like a sandhill crane ducking its long bluish neck into the grasses in search of insects.

aerial ski jump training pool at the Utah Olympic Park

Recreation and Activities

The arts, shopping—even dining—all play second fiddle to outdoor adventures in Park City. The reason we're almost all here—whether to live or visit—is the wild and beautiful setting. The saying "there's something for everyone" is a cliché but does hold true for the area. Crush moguls or take a spin around the cross-country track. Pump out a mountain bike ride, or take the kids on a hike on 400-plus miles (645-plus km) of trail. Rent a pontoon and cruise around the Jordanelle Reservoir, taking dips to cool off. Take a leisurely tour of the rec path that stretches from Kimball Junction to Old Town on an electric bike. The name of the game is the outdoors, and the way to play is up to you.

BIKING

Whether you're a pro coming to Park City with your own bike and a trail you've been dreaming of, or someone who hasn't been on a bike in years, there's a path forward in Park City. Single-track lovers will likely want to hop on the miles of trails hidden beneath snow in the winter around the area's ski resorts: Deer Valley and Park City Mountain. Downhillers may decide to pay for lift rides up so they can focus on the descent. In the winter, diehard cyclists may opt to take to the snowpacked trails of Round Valley on fat bikes instead of hitting the resort. And road riders can crank out miles on the Rail Trail or on a scenic trip to Kamas and back. More casual cyclists may decide to cruise on a townie or a rentable electric bike along the rec path that connects Old Town and its many outlying areas.

Mountain Biking

Park City boasts the first mountain biking trail system in the country rated gold by the International Mountain Bike Association. While Park City might not be home to the hardest riding around, it does boast miles upon miles of impeccably marked single-track

for all ability levels. Few rides require toughing it out on ranch roads or asphalt to meet riding objectives, and almost all include views worth stopping for. For detailed, downloadable maps of most of these trails that will help you craft your route, check out the **Mountain Trails Foundation** (https://mountaintrails.org).

WASATCH CREST TRAIL

This International Mountain Bike Association "epic" ride travels the spine of the Wasatch Mountains, with Salt Lake on one side and Park City on the other. The **Wasatch Crest Trail** (12.5 mi/20.1 km one-way, though often ridden with a shuttle, 2-3 hours depending on pace, about 1,080 ft/329 m elevation gain, strenuous) climbs steep single-track and dirt roads to cash in on panoramic views of turquoise lakes and exhilarating downhill. Depending on snowpack and weather, the Wasatch Crest is usually ready to ride in full by late June or early July and stays rideable through September.

The route described here (22.4 mi/36 km one-way, 5-6 hours) presumes that you've booked a shuttle to pick you up at the Salt Lake City end (**Big Rack Shuttle Co.,** 801/882-7225, https://bigrackshuttle.com, $12; pick-up in Millcreek on odd days only). From the Park City Mountain Village, ride Armstrong up to the Mid-Mountain Trail. When you connect with Pinecone Trail, the real climb begins. Put your head down until you top out on Scott's Hill, a popular spot to snack and selfie. Next up: a mix of meandering single-track through wildflowers and short-burst climbs on the Wasatch Crest proper. Finally, descend Millcreek Big Water Trail to where your shuttle awaits. This ride can also be done as an out and back (25 mi/40 km, 6-8 hours depending on pace) from the trailhead off Guardsman Pass or from the Millcreek Big Water Trailhead about 20 miles

(32 km) southeast of downtown Salt Lake City. Plan ahead and pack layers and fuel.

★ THE MID-MOUNTAIN TRAIL

If long, flowy rides are your thing, traverse the **Mid-Mountain Trail** (21.9 mi/35 km one-way, 3-5 hours depending on pace, about 1,800 ft/549 m elevation gain, moderate), which runs all the way from Deer Valley to Pinebrook, just west of Park City. Snowpack and weather pending, the single-track Mid-Mountain Trail is usually rideable by mid- or late June, and can be ridden through September or even mid-October. This is a superb tour of Wasatch riding, weaving through aspens, conifer forests, and fields of summer wildflowers; crossing through two ski resorts; and beholding gorgeous views of the surrounding area. While you can start at Silver Lake Village in Deer Valley, there are numerous entry points where you can hop on or off if you don't feel like riding the whole thing. Whether ascending or descending, the grade of the Mid-Mountain is fairly mild. Craft however small or large a taste of the Mid-Mountain as you want! This is a popular multiuse trail, so respect the rules of the trail and watch out for hikers, runners, and moose.

LIFT-SERVICED DOWNHILL BIKING AT DEER VALLEY

In the winter, Deer Valley might not have the most edgy, extreme reputation among Utah's many ski resorts (Snowbird holds that honor), but come summer, the **Deer Valley lift-serviced downhill biking** (www.deervalley.com, 10am-5pm daily mid-June-Sept., $25-48 depending on age, day of week, and time of day) is not for the faint of steep pitches and colossal rock gardens. But with 70-some miles (113 km) of trail, there really is single-track for everyone. There are beginner and intermediate trails, but Deer Valley tends to draw talented riders seeking expert terrain. Deer Valley also offers trails for uphill riding, but pay close attention to whether a trail is marked downhill-only, or risk being ambushed. Duration is totally up to

the rider—you could take just one lap for the thrill of it, or play all day on this lift-accessed terrain. In addition, while the lifts only run mid-June-September for downhill riders, bikers can tackle the trails before or after these time frames; they'll just have to work for the descents.

GLENWILD LOOP TRAIL

One of the best early-season mountain bike trail systems in the Park City area, the **Glenwild Trails** (25-plus mi/40-plus km, moderate) are mostly exposed and south-facing, meaning they dry out faster than most other single-track in the area, occasionally as early as April or May. So named for the residential development and country club/private golf course that lie above the trails, Glenwild may not be the most "out there" or epic riding in the Park City area, but still offers beautiful lookouts, aspen groves, and flowy single-track. Go-getters can ride **Flying Dog** (17-mi/27-km loop, 3-5 hours depending on pace, about 1,900 ft/579 m elevation gain, strenuous), the longest loop in this trail system, but it's not as prime for early/late season riding as some of the shorter loops that stick to the sunny sagebrush. While there are a few possible starting points, the most popular has the same starting point as the Glenwild Loop Trail: Spring Creek Trailhead (1303 Pheasant Way), right in Kimball Junction.

One of my favorites here is the **Glenwild Loop Trail** (6-mi/9.7-km loop, 1-1.5 hours depending on pace, about 800 ft/244 m elevation gain, moderate), which I like to call the lunchtime loop because at about an hour in riding time, it's perfect as a lunch or otherwise short ride. Start at the Spring Creek Trailhead, where you can use the restrooms, fill up your hydration pack, and even tune your bike at a mini mechanic station. This loop can be ridden either way, but I prefer to start by cranking out a climb on relatively mellow switchbacks. This is the trailhead on the right side of Glenwild Drive just before the Glenwild arch. Follow the switchbacks up and stay on the Glenwild Loop Trail, rather

than veering off on Blackhawk or any other side trails. Toward the top of the switchbacks, you'll see a bench, just past which you'll have the choice to stay straight or hang a left onto the final switchback in this section. If you were to stay straight, you'd be following the Flying Dog path. Hang a left, cross the road, and keep ascending—you're about halfway up at this point! When the trail tops out on a dirt road, turn left and you'll find the continuation of the trail at the end of the road, just past another bench. From here on out, it's pretty much all downhill, with a few fun rock gardens to keep you on your toes—nothing an intermediate rider can't handle.

Road Biking

There are many road biking opportunities surrounding Park City, but not much within the town limits itself. That said, on just about any road shoulder in the summer, you'll find spandex-clad riders everywhere from country roads to rec paths and highways. And you're likely to come across the most dedicated riders pedaling the asphalt just about any time of year, snow or shine. Due to a high concentration of competitive athletes in the Park City area—Olympians included—many bikers are training for competitive events, so they need to get in miles, wherever, whenever. This is something that not only the prospective cyclist should keep in mind, but also drivers road-tripping to Park City or planning to rent a car to explore the area. It's good to be aware that you're likely to pass riders on most roads in the summer, so avoid speeding, stay on the lookout, and give wide berth when you pass.

★ RAIL TRAIL

The Trans-Pacific Railroad charted its line through Park City in the 1870s, which was good news for the coal mines in need of more efficient ways to transport product. The line was decommissioned in the 1980s, and the

track was transformed into the **Rail Trail** (27.7 mi/44.6 km one-way, 3-5 hours depending on pace, about 1,500 ft/457 m elevation gain from Echo to Park City and loss in the opposite direction, moderate). Alternating between dirt and paved asphalt, the trail stretches from Park City to the little town of Echo. The Rail Trail is often rideable for most of the year, but you'll need a fat bike in the winter, and in the spring the dirt sections can get muddy and rutted out. The ride offers a scenic potpourri of local landscapes, from ranch lands and mountains to red rock toward the end. Unless you're in the mood to ride 50-plus miles (81-plus km), park a car beforehand at Echo Reservoir, then head back to the first Park City trailhead (at the intersection of Kearns Boulevard and Iron Horse Drive) to start the ride. If you want just a taste of the trail, there are numerous entry/exit points every couple miles or so. For a detailed, downloadable map, visit **Mountain Trails Foundation** (https://mountaintrails.org).

MILLENNIUM TRAIL AND MCLEOD CREEK TRAIL

There are a number of variously named rec paths that connect the area known as Kimball Junction to Old Town Park City where you can walk, run, or bike, with dogs and children in trailers in tow if desired. The main takeaway is that yes, if you like, you can bike on mellow paved paths all the way from one end of the area to the other, and yes, there are paved paths for year-round running/leisurely walking. The trails are clearly marked. Two of the main segments of the stretch following Highway 224 from Kimball Junction to Old Town Park City are the **Millennium Trail** and the **McLeod Creek Trail** (together about 6 mi/9.7 km one-way, 40 minutes, about 500 ft/152 m elevation change, easy). While the Millennium Trail actually starts to the west in the outlying area of Summit Park, you can easily pick it up in Kimball Junction from the Basin Recreation Fieldhouse (1743 Redstone Ave.), the Kimball Junction Transit Center, or at the junction of Highway 224 and Olympic

---

1: descending the Wasatch Crest Trail **2:** riding an extended version of the Glenwild Loop **3:** lift-serviced downhill biking

Parkway. The Millennium Trail ends at the intersection of Highway 224 and Silver Springs Drive, at which point you can cross the highway and jump on McLeod Creek Trail to continue toward Old Town. Along the way, the paved path has numerous intersection points that allow you to explore surrounding neighborhoods if you want to extend your excursion. The trails also intersect with numerous points of interest (including the historic McPolin Farm), as well as with other trails, including the Rail Trail. While the trails run along the highway, you'll also be pedaling alongside the Wasatch Mountains.

BROWN'S CANYON LOOP
The **Brown's Canyon Loop** (approx. 30-mi/48-km loop, 3-5 hours depending on pace, about 2,100 ft/640 m elevation gain, strenuous) takes you from Park City to Kamas and back, offering alpine and pastoral views alike. A popular place to start is at the Quinn's Junction dog park near the intersection of Highways 40 and 248. (You can park there, but if you're carless, you can also bike from wherever you're staying or renting a bike—it will just add a few miles.) From there, head east on Highway 248 toward Kamas. This stretch of Highway 248 is very popular with road bikers and has been a part of the Tour de Utah route. While it is heavily trafficked, the shoulder is mostly quite wide and the ride beholds beautiful views of Mount Timpanogos and the Jordanelle Reservoir, which you'll pass on the right. When you descend into Kamas, hang a left on Main Street. After the one-minute ride through Kamas (blink and you'll miss it!), the road turns into Highway 32 and passes through several small ranching towns, including Oakley. Be sure to stay on Highway 32—sometimes you have to veer slightly left or right to follow this country road. If you're on a leisurely time frame and wish to stop, there are a few restaurant options in Kamas, as well as the Road Island Diner in Oakley. Once you reach Peoa, turn left on Browns Canyon Road, which parallels Highway 248 through scenic, open ranch lands. Bike along the winding road until you intersect with Highway 248 again, where you'll hang a right for a short climb back to the parking lot.

HIKING
Most of the trails that can be mountain biked in Park City can also be hiked, though a few bike-only exceptions exist, mostly within the resort area trails. This means two things: There are hundreds of miles of well-marked

countryside near Brown's Canyon Loop

trails that can be hiked, and you should also watch out for mountain bikers! Technically hikers have the right of way on all multiuse trails, but occasionally you'll encounter an unaware or ill-mannered rider who won't pull over for you. Of course, if you find it easy to duck off the trail to make way for a rider, you're more than welcome to do so.

Also be cognizant of trail conditions—avoid hiking or running on a muddy trail, which can cause damage. Generally, this means waiting for the snow to melt after winter and for the ground to dry (which may happen anytime between March and June, depending on the year), as well as avoiding trails after rain. Generally, trails at lower elevations stay dry through October or November, while trails at higher elevations around the ski resorts may close a month or two earlier.

Hikes in Park City range from short jaunts and loops with scenic stops to long treks that could max out a day. Of course, any of the trails that can be hiked are also prime for trail running, and often host races and even ultra-marathons throughout the summer months. For detailed, downloadable maps of these trails, visit the **Mountain Trails Foundation** (https://mountaintrails.org).

★ The Mid-Mountain Trail

With its rich flora and expansive views, the **Mid-Mountain Trail** (21.9 mi/35 km one-way, 8-10 hours depending on pace, about 1,800 ft/549 m elevation gain, moderate) is beloved by all users, from canines and trail-runners to serious bikers and hikers to moose. Yes, moose—look out for them on the trail, and never try to get them to move out of your way. The Mid-Mountain Trail runs all the way from Deer Valley to Pinebrook, which lies west of Park City. You can catch the trail at its starting point from just behind the Goldener Hirsch Inn at Deer Valley's Silver Lake Village, or via numerous other access trails beginning at the bases of both ski resorts. You can hike the whole thing (if you arrange a ride at one end, or take the Routes 7 and 6 Park City Transit buses back to your

starting point), or take advantage of the multiple entry/exit points to make your hike as short (think a couple of miles) or as long (up to 22 mi/35 km) as you'd like. This trail is highly trafficked on summer weekend days, so if you're looking to shirk the crowds, visit during unconventional days or hours. In terms of season, the Mid-Mountain Trail typically sees the snow melt and its dirt dry sometime in June, and stays passable through early fall, depending on the year.

Silver Lake Trail

Silver Lake Trail at Deer Valley (4 mi/6.4 km round-trip, 2 hours, about 1,300 ft/396 m elevation gain, strenuous) is easily accessed from the resort's base area and makes for a great, scenic jaunt any time of day. One of the best things about hiking this trail is that it's hiking only—meaning, no bikes to watch out for. The trail begins by the Sterling Express chairlift in an aspen grove, which will be all the more magical when the leaves blush orange or red come fall. The trail winds its way up to the top of Bald Mountain, where you can behold the Jordanelle Reservoir from up high. You can go down the same way you came, or turn it into a loop by hopping on Ontario Trail, which will add about a mile (1.6 km) and 20-30 minutes to your trip and take you back to the base. Another option is to buy a single lift ticket ($12 weekdays, $14 weekends) and ride the chairlift up if you're strapped on time.

Iron Mountain

One local trail that gets slightly less traffic than others is **Iron Mountain** (4 mi/6.4 km round-trip, 2 hours, approx. 900 ft/274 m elevation gain, strenuous), which begins at the end of a residential cul-de-sac right off Highway 224, just 10 minutes north of Old Town. Another upside is this trail's efficiency. You'll get a great workout in just a few miles, rewarded with a sweeping view of the Park City area. Due to its steep pitch, it also isn't bikeable, which means no riders to battle with over trail real estate. Expect the climb to the top of Iron Mountain to result in sweat and possibly tears if you're out of shape, so take breaks and keep in mind the reward of a beautiful lookout! This trail is also a good option on hot, sunny days, since most of it is forested.

To get to the trailhead from Old Town, drive north on Highway 224, turn left on Payday Drive, right on Iron Canyon Drive, right on Iron Mountain Drive, then right on Iron Canyon Court. Follow it just a few hundred feet until it dead-ends in a cul-de-sac, where you'll likely see other cars parked along the street. You'll find the trailhead at the end of Iron Canyon Court.

Keep an eye out for a mild-mannered neighborhood dog known to appear toward the beginning of the trail and escort hikers to the top and back down again.

SKIING AND SNOWBOARDING

For many, skiing or snowboarding is the beginning and end of a Park City trip. As home to two resorts (including the biggest resort in North America), Park City is the dream destination of many skiers, domestic and international alike. What type of skiing *doesn't* Park City offer? That family-owned, unique character you'll find at smaller, locally owned resorts in Utah like Sundance or Snowbasin. The story of skiing in Park City stretches back to the 1920s and 1930s, and actually begins with the sport of ski jumping, pioneered by local record-setting Norwegian ski jumper Alf Engen. By 1963, Park City had its first official ski resort, dubbed Treasure Mountain, and, along with it, exponential growth. The 2002 Olympics also played an instrumental role in putting Park City on the map as an international snow-sports destination. Another noteworthy event in the growth of the local ski industry came in 2014-2015, when Vail bought and merged Park City Mountain and Canyons Resorts, in effect creating the largest ski resort in North America. For those seeking a more bespoke ski experience, there are a number of excellent local guiding and outfitting services that can make you feel like an extra in a James Bond ski chase scene, as you

drop out of a helicopter into the mountains while a hawk soars by.

Ski Areas

Park City is home to two ski resorts and close to many more. Both resorts have colorful histories involving a whole host of different owners, operations, closures, re-openings, and names. One resort is Deer Valley, a legendary destination for skiers (no snowboarders allowed!) with a ritzy reputation, known for its impeccable grooming. The other is Park City Mountain, which, until 2015, was two separate resorts, and is now the largest ski resort in North America.

★ PARK CITY MOUNTAIN RESORT

If bigger is better in your book, then ski **Park City Mountain Resort** (435/649-8111, https://parkcitymountain.com, 7,300+ acres, 9am-4pm daily mid-Nov.-early Apr., tickets starting at $169 adults), which spans an area stretching from about 5 miles (8 km) northwest of Old Town clear through historic Main Street. You'll be hard-pressed to ride every lift, let alone turn down all 330-plus runs in a weekend. If you're a snowboarder who wants to ride in Park City, this is also your only option.

Park City Mountain has **two base areas,** and essentially two mountains, that pre-2015 were distinct: **Park City Mountain Village** and **Canyons Village.** Since Vail bought and merged these mountains with the Quicksilver Gondola, it committed itself to rebranding with the motto: "There is only one." But really there are two—two base areas, two main parking lots, two mountains (divided by a valley), and even two sets of ski patrollers. Luckily, you only need one expensive lift ticket to access these dual mountain amenities!

In terms of difficulty, if you're used to East Coast skiing, know that ski run ratings tend to be a little less generous out West, so you may be alarmed at the pitch of a blue. Advanced skiers will find plenty of challenging terrain, but the most expert skiers may come up short after a few hours searching for cliffs to huck

Year-Round Recreation at Park City's Ski Resorts

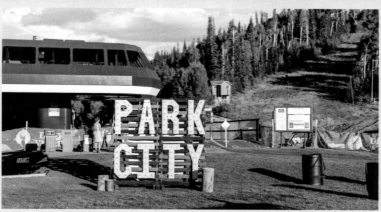

summer at Deer Valley

While we tend to think of ski areas as squarely within the domain of winter, it's worth noting that there are near-year-round reasons to visit. Spring skiing in April is a great chance to work on your goggle tan and enjoy bluebird days at on-mountain yurts or base area patios. After the resorts close, there is a bit of a lull during "mud season" (as it's known in ski towns) as the snow melts, revealing mud that must dry. When all the snow finally does run off and the dirt dries, vast networks of hiking and biking trails surface. Come summer, the chairlifts start spinning again for both scenic rides and lift-serviced downhill mountain biking. Live music plays and base area activities—like ziplining tours—attract youth and families. So, aside from the early spring mud season and the very last days of autumn when the resorts are busy making snow if the skies aren't, consider both Deer Valley and Park City Mountain multi-season destinations.

In the summer, both base areas of **Park City Mountain** turn into outdoor adventure parks, with ziplining, a thrilling alpine slide, and many more activities. You can also take scenic lift rides late May-September (day-pass pricing starts at $25 adults). An adventure pass ($52-85 depending on your height) includes all the base area activities, from the alpine slide to a mountain coaster (à la carte pricing is available for these activities, starting at around $12 children), as well as lift rides. Hiking and biking (as long as you're not riding the lift up) are free.

In **Deer Valley,** the lifts start spinning for summer daily in mid-June-August, and continue on weekends only through September (10am-5pm, starting at $12 adults for a single ride and $22 adults for a day pass). On Tuesday evenings in July and August, you can also take a Twilight ride (4pm-8pm, $25 pp). Deer Valley doesn't operate a full-on kid-oriented outdoor adventure arena like Park City Mountain, but you can find a quieter place to explore here in summer, whether that's on a hike, mountain bike ride, or just a scenic lap on the chairlift.

or slope angles to scare them. First-timers will enjoy the **Treasure Mountain Family** Area on the Park City side, where mellow bunny slopes await. Park rats should head to the half-pipes and jumps off the **Payday Lift.** Expert skiers should concentrate their turns near **Jupiter Peak** on the Park City side, or around **9990 Lift,** which crowns the Canyons area and lets you traverse for a few minutes to savor the steep pow runs known as the **Red**

Pine Chutes. Those who are in it more for the on-mountain beverages than the turns will want to check out the Viking Yurt on the Park City side, or Lookout Cabin many runs to the west over by the Orange Bubble Express chairlift on the Canyons side.

★ DEER VALLEY RESORT

Located less than 2 miles (3.2 km) southeast and uphill of Old Town, **Deer Valley Resort** (435/649-1000, www.deervalley.com, 2,026 acres, 9am-4pm daily early Dec.-early Apr., tickets starting at $169 adults) is known for three things: (1) luxury, (2) incredible corduroy (a nickname for groomed runs), and (3) no snowboarders allowed. Luxury, meaning you can have your boots and skis delivered to you right at the lift, eliminating the awkward hustle with skis tenuously resting on your shoulder. Luxury *also* meaning the highest-end accommodations, restaurants, and spas in the Park City area. Ready to drop a grand on one of the best hotel rooms you've ever stayed in?

We're not sure what makes the groomed runs here so fabulous, except perhaps, talented groomers with painstaking attention to detail—and a lack of snowboarders flattening out the lines. Deer Valley often ranks top of the list when it comes to corduroy, so unless it's a powder day, enjoy carving your way down the resort's famous groomers.

Deer Valley is basically comprised of just over 100 runs spread across four mountains. The one closest to the base area—and the most mellow—is **Bald Eagle Mountain.** From there, you can head looker's left to **Bald Mountain,** looker's right to **Flagstaff Mountain,** and even farther right to **Empire Mountain,** which peaks out highest at 9,570 feet (2,917 m). All but Empire Mountain have green runs to the bottom of the lift, meaning if your party is comprised of skiers with different ability levels, you can at least all ride most of the lifts up together. Beginners may want to hang out around Bald Eagle Mountain, where easy terrain abounds. Flagstaff is great for cruising down blue groomers, and kids will love the "woop-de-doos," as a former Deer Valley employee puts it, on the green Ontario run off Flagstaff.

Glade skiers will enjoy exploring the abundant forested terrain of Deer Valley, and should make sure to hit the **Triangle Trees** off Bald Mountain. Experts will want to stick to the Empire area and anything off the **Mayflower Lift** on Bald Mountain, where you'll find exposed rocks and even a few cliffs.

a ski patroller at Deer Valley

Since developers recently purchased 2,300 acres of skiable terrain, Deer Valley will soon dramatically expand. The New York-based developers are planning to develop 900 acres of that terrain into Mayflower Mountain Resort, which will be annexed to Deer Valley. The rest of the space will be devoted largely to lodging and residential development. Timelines and details are still up in the air, but when complete, there will essentially be a new town called "Mayflower" east of Deer Valley, and a third more terrain to ski.

So, groomers, trees . . . what else does Deer Valley specialize in? Après. Well, and lunch. Reward your turns with the best of the best, from legendary turkey chili at Deer Valley Grocery Café to an epic Bloody Mary and full-on skier's buffet at the Glitretind that may change your status from "stoked" to "food comatose."

Backcountry Skiing

If you'd rather ditch the lift lines and manifest powder by skiing the backcountry, there are a few options, though the best backcountry skiing is accessed from the resorts themselves. This is in part due to the fact that most of the mountains in Park City are within the bounds of the mammoth Park City Mountain or neighboring Deer Valley, leaving little unspoken-for terrain to access. If you'd rather go farther afield, consider hiring a local guide and outfitting service—perhaps one equipped with snowmobiles, a snowcat, or even a helicopter—to take you from Park City to nearby backcountry terrain.

However you decide to venture into the backcountry, **safety** is a key consideration. Always travel with a partner. Never go into the backcountry if you're uneducated about snow safety and rescue. If you're not knowledgeable about avalanche safety, the best bet is to go with a guided service. Before heading out, check avalanche conditions at the **Utah Avalanche Center** (www. utahavalanchecenter.org). Before you drop in to any line, assess the snowpack to ensure you're not dropping in to a high-risk line. And always carry a shovel, beacon, and probe—the trio of snow safety gear that will save the life of anyone unfortunate enough to be caught in an avalanche. People die every year in Utah due to avalanches—you don't want your name added to this list.

RESORT-ACCESSED BACKCOUNTRY

One of the easiest ways to access the backcountry is to check out the **resort-accessed backcountry**—the term for terrain that lies adjacent to ski areas, but out of bounds. While Deer Valley doesn't offer any backcountry access, **Park City Mountain** offers numerous access gates, more so on the Canyons side than the Park City side. One of the best options is accessible from the top of the 9990 chairlift, where you'll see a gate in front of you as soon as you step off the lift. From here, you can do a short hike carrying your skis just to get a little untouched powder, or skin farther afield, even up to the Wasatch Crest.

Remember that once you cross that line between resort and backcountry, the terrain is not controlled for avalanches by the resort, and your life becomes your own responsibility. The same rules stated above apply (though you may notice that many skiers and snowboarders do not heed them, assuming that their risk is somehow mitigated by proximity to the resort): Ensure you're educated, go with a partner, check avalanche conditions, assess snowpack, and carry a shovel, beacon, and probe.

Nordic Skiing

If skinny skis are more your pace, try **Nordic skiing**—or "nordorking," as some jokingly dub it. There are two types of Nordic skiing: classic and skate. The former is much simpler to master, and more or less consists of shuffling your skis forward on a track. The latter is what you'll see spandex-clad Olympians doing at breakneck speeds. While the pros make it look simple, skate-skiing is challenging from both a technical and endurance standpoint. While an athletic individual can generally get away with classic cross-country skiing for the first time sans instruction, most anyone who's never skate-skied before will want to sign up for a lesson before hitting the track.

Park City offers many different areas to Nordic ski, from designated Nordic-only trails to multiuse free winter trails.

WHITE PINE NORDIC CENTER

If you're renting gear and looking for impeccably groomed trails, head to the **White Pine Nordic Center** (1541 Thaynes Canyon Dr., 435/649-6249, https://whitepinetouring.com, 9am-6pm daily Thanksgiving-Mar., $20 rentals, $18 day pass, $80 private lessons), which offers everything from rentals and groomed trails, to lessons and guides who can take you farther afield for your cross-country skiing adventures. As essentially the hub of cross-country skiing in the Park City area, White Pine is also a great place to start for beginners who need an all-inclusive experience (i.e., rentals, lessons, and groomed trails). Yet beginners and experts alike will enjoy its 20-plus kilometers (12-plus mi) of perfectly groomed Nordic track. Located less than a mile (1.6 km) north of Old Town Park City, White Pine also outfits other experiences, from fat biking and snowshoeing to yurt camping.

ROUND VALLEY

If you're a pro cross-country skier (classic or skate), then you may prefer to bring your own gear or rent gear from a shop in Old Town or Kimball, rather than book a fully outfitted experience. Many options abound in the area, but perhaps the second most popular Nordic destination after White Pine Nordic Center is **Round Valley,** a 1,400-acre expanse of open space between Kimball Junction and Old Town. Groomed for both classic and skate skiing, this trail system is free to use and can be accessed via many different points. One of the most popular places to park and access the trails is **Quinn's Junction Trailhead** (84098 Gillmor Way). Another great, quieter place to start is the **Highland Trailhead** (plug that name into Google Maps and you'll be led right to the parking lot), which lies off U.S. 40 just a few miles shy of Kimball Junction. The **Mountain Trails Foundation** (https://mountaintrails.org) offers excellent downloadable maps of all Park City-area trail systems, including Round Valley winter trails. The biggest downside of Round Valley is that, unlike White Pine Nordic Center, this is a multiuse trail system. You'll find dogs cavorting alongside snowshoers, fat bikers, and hikers, all of which damage Nordic grooming.

skiing the sidecountry at Park City Mountain

Snowshoeing
GUARDSMAN PASS

Up in the mountains lies a magical mountain road that connects Deer Valley with Big Cottonwood Canyon: Guardsman Pass. In the summer, this is an alternative route to I-80 to access Solitude, Brighton, and the other gems of Little Cottonwood Canyon from the Park City area. While in the summer, Guardsman Pass offers a scenic drive, hiking, and abundant wildflowers, the pass closes in the winter and becomes a snowmobiling route and a beautiful place for a winter hike on snowshoes. From Park City, head south on Deer Valley Drive; at the traffic circle, exit onto Marsac Avenue. After 3.5 miles (5.6 km) winding past mammoth homes and hotels you'll encounter another traffic circle; take the third exit on to Highway 224, which will turn into Guardsman Pass. Just before the road turns to snow, there's a little parking area on your left. Snowshoe up the road about 1.5 miles (2.4 km) until it ends in a snowbank. From here, you can explore the powdery hills with views of Little Cottonwood Canyon, the Wasatch Mountains, and Park City. This is also a popular snowmobiling spot, so you'll likely see rows of parked snowmobiles and encounter a few snowmobilers on your outing.

BOATING AND FISHING

If some of the lakes in the West look a little strange, it's because many of them aren't lakes at all, but reservoirs, built throughout the 20th century to store water and generate electricity. (The *real* lakes you'll probably have to work for; they lie high in the alpine and are usually not so massive.) On the downside, these reservoirs destroy the ecosystems of the terrain they engulf, as well as the ecosystems of the rivers that once flowed through them. This makes life pretty difficult for the trout and salmon that once called rivers home, and now their populations are often managed by fisheries.

On the other hand, reservoirs serve as relatively clean energy sources (compared to fossil fuels, anyway), and vital contingency plans against drought, which is pervasive throughout much of the Southwest, including Utah, the second driest state in the nation after Nevada. And though they might be environmentally or ethically complicated, reservoirs also happen to be a lot of fun. Most of these reservoirs—and there are several throughout the Wasatch—have docks, manmade beaches, and marinas where you can rent boats of all manner. Many of these reservoirs also have fish, including kokanee salmon and several

Jordanelle Reservoir

species of trout, which can be caught from the shore or on a boat.

Jordanelle Reservoir

The closest body of water to Park City is the **Jordanelle Reservoir,** which is fed by the Provo River. **Jordanelle State Park** (515 UT-319, Heber City, 435/649-9540, https://stateparks.utah.gov/jordanelle, 6am-10pm daily, day-use fee $10-15 depending on entry point), which encompasses the reservoir, lies just 10 miles (16.1 km) southeast of the heart of Park City and has three entry points. **Hailstone** (off U.S. 189 between Park City and Heber) is the most developed entry point with a boat ramp and docks, RV and tent camping, the closest thing to a beach, and even reservable cabins and cabanas. **Ross Creek** (off Highway 248 between Kamas and Park City) offers access to 3 miles (4.8 km) of trails and a nonmotorized boat ramp. Finally, **Rock Cliff** (off Highway 32 between Kamas and Heber) holds a quieter experience with a nonmotorized boat ramp, some 20 miles (32 km) of trails, tent camping, and a nature center. If you're looking to rent water-sports equipment, your best bet will be found at Hailstone, where the **Jordanelle Marina** (515 State Rd. 319, Heber City, 435/615-7397, www.jordanellerentals.com, 8am-6pm daily in summer—specific opening/closing dates depend on weather every year) is located. There you can rent pontoon boats, Jet Skis, kayaks, stand-up paddleboards, and life vests, as well as purchase fishing bait and other supplies. During busy summer weekends, the marina does run out of equipment, so consider booking well in advance of your trip.

GOLF

Why golfing always seems to go hand-in-hand with skiing is anyone's guess, but where you find skiing, you're likely to find at least a golf course or two nearby. Park City has several golf courses, but many are private (meaning you need to be a member, know a member, or at least feign interest in becoming a member). The golfing season here is not very long since

winter (and lingering snow) can stretch from September through May some years. One of the best things about golfing in Park City is the gorgeous mountain backdrop, making for awe-inspiring sunsets if you're out in the evening.

Park City Golf Course

Park City Golf Course (1541 Thaynes Canyon Dr., 435/615-5800, www.parkcity.org, 7am-7pm daily mid-Apr.-early Nov., 18 holes $80 pp Memorial Day-Sept., $65 pp off-season) is owned by the Town of Park City and thus sports fewer frills than your average country club or private course; it's also less expensive, making it the perfect choice for those looking just to golf, rather than for a golfing *experience*. Reservations can be made up to eight days in advance.

Canyons Golf Course

Catering to the ski-golf trend, Park City Mountain Resort recently opened its own **Canyons Golf Course** (3720 N. Sundial Ct., 435/615-4728, 7am-8pm daily late May-Oct., starting at $95 for 18 holes during peak season). This par 70 course features seriously dynamic topography, with some 550 feet (168 m) of elevation gain across the terrain, and mountain views to boot. The course features a mix of bluegrass, bentgrass, and native grasses.

FITNESS FACILITIES

During a summer visit, if the weather's inclement, one of the best places to get in a workout and let your kids get their ya-yas out is the **Basin Recreation Fieldhouse** (1388 Center Dr., 435/655-0999, www.basinrecreation.org, 5:30am-10pm Mon.-Fri., 7am-9pm Sat.-Sun., $10 adults, $6 children) in Kimball Junction. Downstairs is a huge AstroTurf field where kids can run around, as well as an outdoor heated pool. Upstairs, you'll find the gym and an indoor track. Basin Rec also offers fitness classes, as well as an outdoor splash-pad play area for kids.

Opened in 1997, **The Shop Yoga Studio**

(1167 Woodside Ave., 435/649-9339, www. parkcityyoga.com, hours vary) offers a wide variety of yoga classes, with a focus on Anusara yoga, in a serene space with an adjacent garden. There are no set fees for classes— every class is offered for a voluntary donation, though The Shop recommends somewhere between $7 and $20. Class times vary, but you can usually count on a morning, midday, and evening classes, all with different themes ranging from vinyasa to creative flow.

GEAR RENTALS AND SERVICES

There is no shortage of places to rent gear in Park City, whether it's a full skiing setup for everyone in your family, cross-country ski gear, snowshoes, or a mountain bike. You'll find clusters of rental shops around the ski resorts' base areas in particular. However, the best deals usually lie a little farther from the resorts. If you're going for one day only, opt for convenience and rent from the mostly resort-owned rental shops at the base areas. If you're coming for a few days, it's worth getting your gear elsewhere.

Come summer, there are many places that rent out bike gear for road and trails alike. Many local bike rental shops partner with manufacturers to sponsor demo days (usually on weekends), where you can try out bikes for free, usually with a limited time frame (1-3 hours). If you happen upon a demo day, lucky you! Hop on that free bike and ride. Most rental shops also offer demos of their equipment anytime, which can be a good option if you're considering a purchase. While demo pricing is usually comparable to rental pricing, if you demo and decide to buy, the cost of your demo will usually be applied toward your purchase. Of course, if you didn't road-trip to Park City, then you'll also have to pay the cost of shipping the gear back home.

At first glance, you may mistake **ColeSport** (1615 Park Ave., 435/649-4800, www.colesport.com, 8am-9pm daily) for a big chain, because its branding is so sharp, its service so dialed, and its inventory so

expansive. ColeSport *is* a chain, but only a local one (with four locations) that dates back to the early 1970s in Park City. Owned by the Coles, a husband-and-wife team, ColeSport carries all the seasonal gear you need to get out and explore the area, and rents out skis, snowboards, and a wide variety of Giant bikes as well (ski packages starting at $23.20 per day, snowboard packages starting at $31.20 per day, bike rentals starting at $40 per day).

One of the more comprehensive gear rental services in the Park City area, **Jans** (1600 Park Ave., 435/649-4949, www.jans.com, 8am-7pm daily) has been a local institution since 1980, with satellite locations at both the Park City Mountain (2250 Deer Valley Dr., 435/649-8770, 8am-6pm daily) and Deer Valley (Silver Lake Lodge, 7600 Royal St., 435/645-6720, 9am-4pm daily) base areas. This gear and rental shop goes beyond resort skiing and riding setups (ski and snowboard packages starting at $29 per day) to offer equipment for Nordic skiing (full setup $25 per day), backcountry skiing (full setup $45 per day), snowshoeing ($18 per day), mountain and road cycling (starting at $48 per day), fly fishing (full setup $60 per day), and even outerwear (snow jackets and pants $25 per day each). Jans also offers or partners with local outfitters to provide guiding services for most of these activities.

White Pine Touring (https:// whitepinetouring.com) has a winter-oriented gear shop and outfitting service at the **White Pine Nordic Center** (1541 Thaynes Canyon Dr., 435/649-6249, 9am-6pm daily Thanksgiving-Mar.) as well as a location in the Prospector area (1790 Bonanza Dr., 435/649-8710, 9am-6pm daily). White Pine rents out gear for cross-country skiing (full setup $25 per day), snowshoeing ($18 per day), backcountry skiing (full setup $45 per day), and fat biking ($48 per day). In the Uinta Mountains, this shop also operates a backcountry ski-access yurt, which you can reserve by the night. If you need a guide to go with the gear, White Pine also offers private and group Nordic skiing lessons, as well as guided Nordic skiing, backcountry skiing, and fat biking (pricing varies depending on timing and group size).

In Kimball Junction, **Marty's Ski and Board Shop** (1635 W. Redstone Center Dr., Ste. 105, 435/575-7669, www.martysboardshop.com, 8am-8pm daily approx. Thanksgiving-mid-Apr., 11am-7pm daily the rest of the year, ski/snowboard rental packages start at $26 per day) rents out skis, poles, packages, and everything in between. Owned by a local snowboarder and skier named Chip, Marty's also sells gear and offers tuning services. If you opt to demo skis or a board and end up falling in love with the equipment, you can apply the cost of demoing to the gear purchase.

Skiing for the first time in a while and your feet hurt? Don't suffer in silence! While no one will claim that ski boots are downright cozy, they shouldn't put you in a state of unbearable physical pain. The pros at **Surefoot** (multiple locations, 435/649-6536, www.surefoot.com, hours vary) can address your boot woes and fix 'em. Magicians they are not, but they have tricks up their sleeves like custom boot liners and tailored performance insoles, and they can also equip you with heated boot liners that will help your boots mold to your feet, rather than stiffly encase them. Note that this is not a gear rental shop, but a boot shop that also offers customization and special fitting services for boots you already own. If you're skiing Park City Mountain, there's a convenient location in the Canyons Village within eyeshot of the lifts (4000 Canyons Resort Dr., 435/649-0065, 8am-6pm daily approx. Thanksgiving-mid-Apr.).

As Park City's only year-round bike shop, it's safe to say that **Storm Cycles** (1764 Uinta Way C1, 435/200-9210, https://stormcycles.net, 10am-6pm Mon.-Sat.) is cycle-obsessed. The service staff are very patient and approachable—no need to worry about whether you're familiar with hydraulic brakes, dropper seats, one-bys, or other biking jargon. Storm Cycles also doesn't stop at road and mountain biking; they dole out fat bikes in

the winter and electric bikes year-round. Like with skis, demo your bike, and if you decide to buy, Storm Cycles will knock off your demo fee from the purchase price (mountain bike demos $114 per day, e-bike demos $140 per day).

GUIDE SERVICES

If in addition to gear, you're also seeking a local guide to introduce you to a new sport or take you farther afield, there are many adept outfitters at the ready. Backcountry skiing, multiday backpacking trips, rock climbing, dogsledding, tours de local single-track—if there's an experience you can dream up, there's probably a guide at the ready. If you have very specific requirements or interests that don't seem to be addressed on an outfitter's website, give them a call before assuming they're not willing to customize a trip or experience to your desires.

If you'd like to try backcountry skiing, but the idea of sweating for your turns is less than appealing, consider letting a snowmobile or a snowcat do the work for you. That's the idea behind **Park City Powder Cats** (1000 Peaks Ranch, The Uinta Mountains, 435/649-6596, https://pccats.com, $599 pp), which grants you exclusive access to 43,000 acres in the High Uintas Wilderness area. All the elevation gain is achieved via snowcats during full-day excursions that cover intermediate to advanced terrain across four consecutive bowls: M&M, No Name, 4 Eagle, and Giant Steps. Powder, views, unforgettable skiing—you'll get it all.

Helicopter skiing may seem like one of those James Bond-esque, bucket list experiences that you'll probably never attain. But for a little over a grand, you can budget a day of heli-skiing right from Park City. **Powderbird** (801/742-2800, www.powderbird.com, starting at $1,260 pp) offers access to over 80,000 acres of skiing in both Park City and Little Cottonwood Canyon (specifically, around Snowbird Ski Resort). In Park City, Powderbird will pick you up from the Westgate Hotel, by the Canyons Village, and transport you to fathoms of untouched powder. Splurge, tick this item off your bucket list, and indulge in your best ski day ever.

If the idea of "earning your turns" is actually appealing, but you lack avalanche knowledge and safety gear, book a private backcountry tour with **Inspired Summit Adventures** (435/640-4421, www.inspiredsummit.com, starting at $400 pp for human-powered backcountry ski trips). Tours can be customized to your fitness and skiing ability level. Inspired Summit Adventures also guides hut trips (skiing from hut to hut with overnight stays), mountain biking, rock climbing, backpacking, and more, so consider them for your year-round recreation needs.

If I haven't covered an activity you're interested in finding a guide for yet, peruse the diverse offerings from **All Seasons Adventures** (1555 Lower Iron Horse Loop Rd., 435/649-9619, https://allseasonsadventures.com, 8am-6pm daily). Fly fishing, dogsledding, trap shooting (that's shooting clay pigeons, in lay terms)—it's all on the menu here. Prices vary widely depending on what type of adventure you book, time of year, and how many people are in your party. Individuals and groups both small and large can all be accommodated.

If you or a travel companion has a physical disability, the **National Ability Center** (1000 Ability Way, 435/649-3991, https://discovernac.org, 9am-5pm Mon.-Fri., 10am-4pm Sat.) can help you get out and explore. Specializing in adaptive recreation, the National Ability Center offers programs that run the gamut from skiing and rock climbing to water sports. You can book solo one-off adventures or group/family outings; scholarships and payment plans are available. While you can reserve lessons online, the best way for a prospective visitor to get started is to get in touch with the National Ability Center staff and see what options are most suitable for your party's needs and availability.

Do you have a soft spot for unconventional yoga pairings? You know, yoga at a brewery, or yoga with goats? Then check out the possibilities over at **Park City**

Yoga Adventures (415/695-4502, www.parkcityyogaadventures.com, prices start at $150 per yogi but vary depending on adventure and party size). This unique yoga outfitting service takes you to scenic locations in nature to practice unconventional yoga. You can snowshoe to a private cabin for a yoga session, or practice using silks to stretch it out at a pastoral ranch. Bend into asanas in an aspen forest, or tackle tree pose on a stand-up paddleboard in a crater. Since you'll probably be telling all your yogis back home about your epic yoga adventure, it's a nice perk that your yoga guide will also snap dozens of photos of you during the practice and share them with you for free.

SPAS

With the highest-end hotels, it makes sense that Deer Valley is also home to some of Park City's most luxurious spas.

The five-star **Spa at Stein Eriksen Lodge** (7700 Stein Way, 435/649-3700, www.steinlodge.com, 8am-8pm daily) is a European-style experience complete with a sauna, steam room, and a vast menu of treatments. Massages run the gamut from Thai and Himalayan hot stone to prenatal and one that incorporates CBD oils. You can also opt for one of the many facial offerings, a manicure and pedicure, or a body treatment.

At the **Remède Spa at the St. Regis Deer Valley** (2300 Deer Valley Dr., 435/940-5830, www.marriott.com, 10am-8pm daily), a reflecting pool and staircase set an elegant yet tranquil mood, while the spa therapists specialize in customizing treatments—from massage to facials—to the individual with the Remède's own collection of products.

The **Spa Montage Deer Valley** (9100 Marsac Ave., 435/604-1400, www.montagehotels.com/deervalley, 9am-6pm daily) offers a menu drawing on native Utah ingredients. The Mountain Stone Massage, for example, makes use of basalt rock from the volcanic area around Capitol Reef National Park. Other local ingredients include lavender, salt, honey, and aspen bark.

ART CLASSES

A rainy afternoon and you're cooped up in your hotel room? Get creative at **The Paint Mixer** (738 Main St., 435/604-0820, https://thepaintmixer.com, hours vary, $35-45 adults, $30 children), owned by a Park City native who graduated from the Art Institute of Chicago. A teacher leads the class in creating a rendition of a painting. If you're feeling creatively challenged, the bar serving alcoholic drinks may help you channel your inner Van Gogh. Of course, it's Utah, so at classes where alcohol is served, participants must be ages 21 and over, even if they're not imbibing. Typically, classes run two hours, and sessions staged earlier in the day do not serve alcohol and are open to minors and adults alike. Painting subject matter varies from class to class, and tends to be locally themed (think alpine landscapes and wildlife).

Shopping and Entertainment

SHOPPING

Approximately nobody comes to Park City just for the shopping, but it's here if you want it, whether you're looking to while away some downtime between activities or forgot to pack a few key items. In Old Town, you'll find more recreational shopping—pricier and locally oriented boutiques and shops. More affordable options lie outside Park City proper; closer to Kimball Junction, you'll find big box retail and outlets for necessity purchases.

Historic Main Street Boutiques

Upscale boutiques line Park City's historic Main Street. From high-end outerwear and local artisan products, to tchotchkes revolving around local themes like cowboys, Native Americans, and moose, you can easily spend a couple hours ducking in and out of Old Town shops.

You'll find luxury ski threads at **Gorsuch** (355 Main St., 435/731-8051, www.gorsuch.com/park-city-stores, 10am-9pm daily)—$1,000 ski bibs, anyone? This Park City-founded brand hangs its cashmere hat on high-end ski outerwear and ski mountain lifestyle attire for men and women, with some decor peppered in.

On Main Street, you'll also find fun novelty items, like the hard-to-miss fur-lined male thong (which somehow has yet to be defaced by PETA) in the storefront window of the **Alaska Fur Gallery** (537 Main St., 435/649-1241, https://sitkafurgallery.com, 10am-8pm daily), which carries mostly fur and leather apparel (men's, women's, and children's), as well as fur throws and mounts.

To read up on outdoor adventures, ski town history, or issues of the West, check out the independently owned **Dolly's Bookstore** (510 Main St., 435/649-8062, www.dollysbookstore.com, 10am-9pm Sun.-Thurs., 10am-10pm Fri.-Sat.), which offers a smart collection of books, including those on local topics or by local authors, as well as a great selection for the youngest readers. Dolly's is serendipitously co-located with a **Rocky Mountain Chocolate Factory** (510 Main St., 435/649-0997, www.rmcf.com, 10am-10pm daily), a chain sweets shop throughout the West with candied apples, ice cream, and other confections.

Got a hankering for high-end Western wear, such as Frye boots? Head to **Burns Cowboy Shop** (363 Main St., 800/453-1281, 10am-8pm daily). The prices may exceed your budget, but you'll have fun posing with that cowboy hat in the mirror.

Mountain Town Olive Oil Co. (613 Main St., 435/649-1400, www.mountaintownoliveoil.com, 10am-6pm daily) offers bottles of luxurious extra virgin olive oil, syrup-thick flavored balsamic vinegars, spice blends, and other treats for the culinarian in your life, and can ship whatever you buy.

Newpark Town Center

Searching for a strip mall where you can feed two birds with one scone? Head to **Newpark Town Center** in Kimball Junction. There you'll find a ski/snowboard shop, a bike shop, T.J. Maxx, Bed, Bath & Beyond, Best Buy, and just about all the other big box retail you could ever want (okay, with the exception of Walmart, which lies just across Highway 224).

Tanger Outlets

Got a grumpy teenager who just wants to seek fulfillment through shopping? **Tanger Outlets** (6699 N. Landmark Dr., 435/645-7078, www.tangeroutlet.com/parkcity, hours vary seasonally but are usually 10am-7pm daily) offers trendy retail in a sprawling outdoor mall in Kimball Junction. Think J. Crew, Express, and Old Navy. It's easy to park in the lot and travel from store to store on foot under mostly sheltered walkways.

Park City Farmers Market

During the summer, the **Park City Farmers Market** (Park City Mountain Village, 1315 Lowell Ave., 435/671-1455, https://parkcityfarmersmarket.com, noon-5pm Wed June-Oct.) takes place on Wednesday afternoons at the base of Park City Mountain. It's a fun scene, though it can be quite hot as a midday event during the peak of summer. Occasionally, live music plays, while offerings range from fresh produce and local meats to baked goods from local purveyors, like jalapeño-cheddar bread from Volker's Bakery and pies from Auntie Em's. This is a nice way to stock up on ingredients for a picnic (or dinner, if your accommodation has a kitchen). It's also a great place to find locally crafted gifts to bring home.

ENTERTAINMENT AND EVENTS

Park City does have a nightlife, though it's not as diverse and extensive as what you'd find

in a bigger city. A few bars and venues clustered around Old Town host DJs, local music, and occasionally big-name acts. There are also dive bars, cocktail lounges, and saloons to while away evenings here.

Keep in mind that bars in Utah must close up shop by 2am, so you'll find next to no options past that hour. If you're the type of person who likes to get dressed up for a night on the town, also remember that this mountain town can't accommodate the same footwear and apparel as some places in the winter. You'll likely need shoes that can handle snow and ice on steep sidewalks, and layers for frigid evening temps. Should your goal be to tie one on, refer to the Spirited Trail section earlier in this book to order adult beverages like a local.

For a full listing of **local events**—from concerts and festivals to classes and public speakers—there are a number of great resources to check out in advance of your trip. The **Park City Visitors Bureau** maintains an online event calendar (www.visitparkcity.com/events), and the local *Park City Magazine* also has a very detailed online calendar (www.parkcitymag.com/events). Local nonprofit **Mountain Town Music** hosts many of Park City's concerts and lists most of them on its website as well (https://mountaintownmusic.org).

Nightlife

If you're looking for the most nightclub-esque experience possible in Park City, head down the stairs to **Downstairs** (625 Main St., 435/226-5340, www.downstairspc.com, hours and cover charge vary). While it may not be quite up to par for those used to frequenting big-city nightclubs in places like L.A. or Manhattan, Downstairs does a good job for a small mountain town, with great DJ sets, top-notch VIP table service, and a posh atmosphere set by leather barstools and dim, colorful lighting. The energy within depends on the hour and the act, which can range from DJs to big-name bands.

Interested in paying homage to the

☆ Free Outdoor Summer Concerts

Locals joke that just about any evening of the week during the summer, you can find live music playing for free outside somewhere in Park City. Indeed, free outdoor summer concerts are fixtures of the Park City area from around late June or early July through mid-August or even September, depending on the location and the year (schedules and offerings tend to vary from summer to summer). Shows are usually held in the early evening and last for a few hours, and most are held rain or shine.

Genres of music vary from concert to concert, but common categories include country, folk, singer-songwriter, blues, soul, rock, bluegrass, and honky-tonk. The vibe is BYO and casual. Families, couples, and solo riders with pups in tow all flock to grassy fields and hills to catch the tunes, usually with a cooler in tow. What's in the coolers? Some venues allow you to bring your own alcohol, some look the other way, and others restrict it vehemently. Usually, beer and wine are available for purchase on-site, along with snacks from a food truck. Check the individual venue regulations for info on dogs and booze, as these rules can change any summer.

Other must-bring items for the outdoor summer concert-goer include a hat/sunscreen for sunny afternoon concerts, a raincoat or layer for chillier evenings, and a camp chair or blanket to perch on.

Mountain Town Music (https://mountaintownmusic.org) is the organization behind some of these concerts, and also provides a calendar of most of these shows online. Artists are usually discoverable on Spotify, but not big enough to drive high-dollar ticket sales. Occasionally, a small dance party will break out near the stage, but mostly the music serves as a nice backdrop to conversation and relaxation. Here are a few of the most popular outdoor concert series and how to attend:

- **Tuesdays or Wednesdays—Grand Valley Bank Community Series at Deer Valley** (www.deervalley.com): Mid-June-mid-August, Deer Valley hosts a free outdoor summer concert series at its breathtaking Snow Park Amphitheater venue. All seating is on the lawn, where you can set up your own chair and picnic. The day of the week has varied from year to year. The resort also hosts a ticketed annual summer music festival (https://deervalleymusicfestival.org) with bigger-name headliners—from Michael Franti to Lukas Nelson—playing with the Utah Symphony.

- **Thursdays—DeJoria Center at High Star Ranch** (970 UT-32, Kamas, 435/783-3113, www.dejoriacenter.com): The DeJoria Center is a big venue in a small town, and while it hosts bigger acts for a fee, it also offers free summer concerts late June-mid-August in its pleasant yard. There's plenty of room for kids to run free, as well as a food truck that serves booze and food. Bringing your own alcohol to this event is strictly prohibited.

- **Fridays—Peoa's Woodenshoe Park** (4558 Woodenshoe Ln., Peoa): In June and July, this small stage attracts fun acts to the quaint unincorporated town of Peoa, which lies about 15 miles (24 km) northeast of Old Town near Kamas. Food is usually served, and a more intimate, neighborly atmosphere prevails here than at some of the bigger concerts.

- **Saturdays—Park City Summer Concert Series** (https://parkcitymountain.com): In July and August, set up your chairs and blankets on the green at Canyons Village of Park City Mountain (4000 Canyons Resort Dr.). A giant sandpit keeps kids entertained, while beverages from the Umbrella Bar satisfy adults. After the show, there are many dining options in the vicinity.

- **Sundays—Park Silly Market** (https://parksillysundaymarket.com): On most Sundays early June-late September, Park Cityites come together in Old Town for an open-air celebration of food, light day drinking, local crafts, and, of course, live music. This event hosts two stages on Main Street, one at the intersection with 9th Street and one at the intersection with 5th Street. Acts take turns gracing all event-goers with tunes.

"Destroying Angel of Mormondom" while sipping an old-fashioned? Head to **O.P. Rockwell** (280 Main St., 435/565-4486, www. oprockwell.com, 5pm-1am Thurs.-Sat.), a concert venue and cocktail lounge named for Orrin Porter Rockwell, personal bodyguard and assassin of Joseph Smith, the founder of Mormonism. According to legend, Rockwell enjoyed his whiskey back in the day, when at least some Mormons distilled and drank the spirit. While the stage at O.P. Rockwell draws plenty of regional acts, it also attracts the occasional big name, like Neil Diamond. As a subterranean bar with dim lighting and Western decor like portraits of its mustachioed namesake, O.P. Rockwell successfully transports imbibers back to a speakeasy in the Wild West of yore.

There are not many places where you can find a great burger, a cocktail made with a specialty house whiskey, and live music every single night. **The Spur Bar and Grill** (352 Main St., 435/615-1618, www.thespurbarandgrill. com, 10am-1am daily) is one of these precious commodities, and more than worth your patronage if any of the above appeals to you. Perhaps a little unexpectedly, The Spur also makes a top-notch pizza, baked in a brick oven. And if you count yourself part of the world's whiskey militia, be sure to order a pour of the Spur Whiskey, made exclusively for the bar by local Alpine Distillery. Sit back and enjoy to the tune of whoever has the stage, from a bluegrass band to folk and even dueling pianos.

The grandfather of beers in the greater Wasatch, **Wasatch Brew Pub** (250 Main St., 435/649-0900, www.wasatchbeers.com, 11am-10pm Mon.-Fri., 10am-10pm Sat.-Sun.) is a time-tested brewery that has spread from a humble start in Park City to a multiple-location brewery with award-winning beer. One local favorite is the Polygamy Porter, which pokes fun at the polygamous tendencies of the fringe Mormons who appear on shows like *Three Wives One Husband*. For a rowdier atmosphere, get beers in the downstairs or second-floor bars. The rest of the space is dedicated to dining, serving pub fare that's a little lacking—stick to the pints.

Concert and Film Venues
★ **THE EGYPTIAN THEATRE**

Mandatory backdrop for Sundance selfies, hub of year-round entertainment, and historic Park City icon—this is **The Egyptian Theatre** (328 Main St., 435/649-9371, https:// egyptiantheatrecompany.org, box office

PARK CITY

SHOPPING AND ENTERTAINMENT

Wasatch Brew Pub

opens 9am daily until 7pm non-show days and 8:30pm show days). Its story dates to the late 19th century with what was then called the Park City Opera House. After the Great Fire of 1898 destroyed most of Old Town, including the opera house, the theater was rebuilt a year later and dubbed the Dewey. Drama struck once more in 1916, when the roof collapsed under heavy snow. A decade later, the theater reopened with a new name inspired by the dawn of Egypt-o-mania following the unearthing of King Tut's tomb. Even the theater's interior took cues from the growing obsession with all things ancient Egypt, from scarabs to hieroglyphic designs. Today, the Egyptian serves as one of the predominant theaters of the Sundance Film Festival, as well as a venue for acts ranging from stand-up comedy and classic rock concerts to theater like the annual performance of *Thriller* every fall. For reduced ticket pricing, catch a Thursday night show or a matinee rather than a weekend evening performance.

PARK CITY LIVE

The biggest music venue in town, **Park City Live** (427 Main St., 435/649-9123, https://parkcitylive.net, 8pm-2am daily, ticket prices range $5-100+ depending on the act) takes up significant real estate on Main Street. Show frequency depends on time of year. During the busy ski or summer season, the venue may stage several shows a week, while during the off-season (spring and fall), expect far fewer acts. Tickets often sell out, so check the schedule in advance and buy early if you're sure you want to go. Music genres range from hip-hop to rock and indie folk, with past acts including Dave Grohl, Ludacris, and The Shins.

PARK CITY FILM SERIES

On the fourth and highest floor of the **Park City Library** (1255 Park Ave., 435/615-5600) is the Jim Santy Auditorium, which hosts the **Park City Film Series** (https://parkcityfilm.org). This theater is a Sundance Film Festival venue, and also hosts year-round screenings of Sundance films, documentaries, and even

children's movies timed around school vacations like spring break. Sometimes screenings are free, but if not, tickets are affordably priced at just $8, with senior and student discounts. And you can always count on fresh-popped popcorn (bring your own bowl if you can to save money!).

PARK CITY INSTITUTE

The **Park City Institute** (www.parkcityinstitute.org) hosts theater, dance, concerts, and more mostly at the **Eccles Center** (1750 Kearns Blvd., 435/655-3114), a large, auditorium-style building right by the Park City High School in the Prospector area. The Eccles Center also serves as a premier Sundance Film Festival venue. The Park City Institute is also responsible for the summertime Big Stars, Bright Nights Concert Series, which has been held at both Deer Valley's Snow Park Amphitheater outdoors as well as the Eccles Center. On select evenings in July and August, the concert series cuts across genres and has drawn bigger acts including Taj Mahal, Willie Nelson, and Etta James (tickets start at $49).

Festivals

TOP EXPERIENCE

SUNDANCE FILM FESTIVAL

The **Sundance Film Festival** (www.sundance.org) is an annual international film festival pioneered by Robert Redford, and is also Utah's largest tourist-attracting event. Since its debut in 1981, Sundance (née the US Film & Video Festival) has drawn swarms of celebs and film industry members to Park City every winter. The festival runs for just under a fortnight stretching from late January to early February, with most of the excitement and visitors spanning the first weekend of the event. Sundance is most commonly

1: the Egyptian Theatre **2:** Kimball Arts Festival on Main Street **3:** downtown during the Sundance Film Festival

associated with the town of Park City, and while it is headquartered there, screenings also take place across Salt Lake City theaters, as well as at Robert Redford's own Sundance Resort between Heber and Provo. The most popular theater, however, remains the historic Egyptian Theatre on Main Street.

The program includes a mix of documentaries, international films, shorts, and all genres of other independent films, from drama to horror. Sundance also dips into multimedia art, showcasing the "New Frontier" of digital, 3D, VR, AR, and other cutting-edge technology, as it relates to storytelling. Many of the films are also paired with panel discussions from cast and crew, as well as after-parties across town.

Speaking of town, just about all of Old Town metamorphoses into Sundance mode during the first weekend of the fest and beyond. A good number of bars and restaurants close for private Sundance events, while other retail stores literally gut their inventory to rent out their space to pop-up experiences hosted by Sundance filmmakers or sponsors. The remaining places that are open to the public will have long lines or waitlists.

For these reasons, Sundance is a love-it-and/or-hate-it experience for many locals and tourists alike. Unless you're visiting specifically for the film fest, the weeks it spans are not the best time to come to Park City, which sees ever-larger crowds, restaurant closures for private parties, and jacked-up pricing for everything from a hotel room to a hamburger. It's worth noting that Sundance *is* generally a good time to ski Park City Mountain and Deer Valley since screens, not slopes, occupy most everyone in town.

DEER VALLEY SUMMER MUSIC FESTIVAL

One of the premier musical events in Park City is the annual **Deer Valley Summer Music Festival** (https://deervalleymusicfestival.org, general admission tickets on the lawn start at $36, reserved seating starts at $59), which runs early July-mid-August. Primarily held at the

outdoor Snow Park Amphitheater, the festival features several concerts a week (usually Fri. and Sat. evenings and 1-2 weekday evenings), most of which include the Utah Symphony accompanied by another act, which tend to be bigger names like The Beach Boys or the Preservation Hall Jazz Band. The Utah Symphony also plays a few solo themed nights, featuring the scores from Harry Potter or the music of John Denver.

KIMBALL ARTS FESTIVAL

One of many summer events to shut down Old Town Park City, the **Kimball Arts Festival** (parkcitykimballartsfestival.org) stages an artistic weekend-long takeover of historic downtown and its surroundings every year in early August. A fundraiser for the Kimball Art Center, this festival celebrates the arts in many ways. The main draw is artist booths set up along Main Street, wherein some 50,000 people come to stroll through the impromptu outdoor gallery, talk to artists about their work, and buy. If you're looking for some new art, you can usually negotiate pricing with the artist. The Main Street scene also features art classes right on Main Street, live music, food trucks, face painting, and other artsy kids' activities.

PARK SILLY SUNDAY MARKET

The **Park Silly Sunday Market** (https://parksillysundaymarket.com, 10am-5pm Sun. early June-late Sept.) is a weekly fixture of Old Town come summer. Stretching across most of Main Street, the market allows local vendors to sell their crafts, apparel, specialty foods, and other goods. Nonprofits also table at this event, like the ever popular Nuzzles & Co., which lures passersby to play with puppies, and would-be dog owners to consider adoption. At the downhill end of Main Street lies a small concert stage and a cluster of food trucks and tents. The event is free to attend and always absolutely packed, so be prepared to walk slowly amid a large crowd. Also

1: Autumn Aloft 2: Park Silly Sunday Market

remember that this is not a farmers market, so you'll mostly find only prepared foods at Park Silly.

MINER'S DAY CELEBRATION

Relics of the mining days in Park City can be easy to miss. There are a few old mine building ruins around the ski resorts, some history at the Park City Museum, and, every Labor Day weekend, **Miner's Day** (https://parkcityminersday.org). This unique one-day festival takes over Main Street in Park City with celebrations that hark back to the town's silver mining heritage. The event kicks off with the Running of the Balls, wherein thousands of balls, each "adopted" by someone, are released down Main Street. In this fundraiser for the local Rotary club, the first few of the 10,000-some golf balls set free to reach the bottom of Main Street win prizes. Then mid-morning, the Miner's Day Parade, complete with a marching band and mining-themed floats, takes over Old Town. This festival also includes other activities, from games to a 5K run with dogs.

AUTUMN ALOFT

Every year, locals and visitors alike gather during a fall weekend in mid-September to watch pro hot ballooners launch into the morning mist during **Autumn Aloft** (www.autumnaloft.com). While it might sound like a take-it-or-leave-it experience for all but photographers and diehard balloonists, a sky filled with boldly hued balloons, framed by the town's notoriously beautiful fall foliage is one worth beholding. The festival usually features two daytime launches (occurring between 8am and 10am depending on weather conditions), for which parking can be a challenge. If you can, bike or take public transit to the North 40 Fields, about 3 miles (4.8 km) north of Old Town, where the launches take place (2530 Kearns Blvd., Park City). Another popular spot is from atop the "PC" Hill (a large hill embellished with the big white letters "PC") behind the Park City High School (2780 Kearns Blvd., 2.5 mi/4 km round-trip, 1-1.5 hours depending on pace, 475 ft/145 m elevation gain). There's a small dirt lot by the trailhead, though you could also park at the high school or bike to the trailhead as well. There is also an evening celebration on the Saturday night of the festival that illuminates Main Street with candlelight and the flame-topped baskets of the hot air balloons. Keep in mind that this event is not rain or shine, wind or calm—weather must cooperate for the event to take place, so it may be canceled at the last possible minute.

Food

The rule of thumb for eating in Park City is generally thus: The farther you veer from Main Street, the less expensive your meal will be. Indeed, as is true in many locales, the best and least expensive food is often found in strip malls. To eat well in Park City, be discerning, and weed out the overpriced and over-hyped. If you're a carnivore, consider wild game, which always seems to make appearances on the menus of the West, where chefs know how to source and prepare it. Burgers also abound, and there are a few in town that hold special places in my memory, especially after chilly ski days or long bike rides. Believe it or not, Park City is also home to the world's best lobster roll, according to judges in Maine. No fact-checking fail here. The key takeaway from that fact is the affirmative answer to a question I'm often asked: "Can you really get decent sushi or seafood in landlocked Utah?" Otherwise, expect a potpourri of "new American" cuisine and various ethnic menus.

OLD TOWN PARK CITY

If, like me, you secretly always wish you were dining in a candlelit trattoria in Tuscany, hike (or drive) to the top of Main Street and head to **Grappa** (151 Main St., 435/645-0636, www.grapparestaurant.com, 5pm-9pm Sun.-Thurs., 5pm-10pm Fri.-Sat., $30-50). If it's peak season, make a reservation, because this restaurant is no well-kept secret. Named for the robust clear brandy that Italians tend to present after a meal, Grappa was the first restaurant in the Bill White Restaurant Group, which has grown to include seven concepts plus a farm focused on local food. The name of the game here is old: Bill White's oldest restaurant (1992), a century-plus-old building, a time-weathered Italian vibe. The osso bucco with polenta and kale is a must-try dish and likely the only of its kind in Park City. Non-negotiable (if you're a spirited drinker): a post-meal order of grappa.

Like most of the best food in Park City, at ★ **Tupelo** (508 Main St., 435/615-7700, https://tupeloparkcity.com, 5pm-10pm Mon.-Fri., 11am-2pm and 5pm-10pm Sat.-Sun., $36-50) it's made by a transplant—Chef Matt Harris—who is re-creating his home cuisine. In this case, it's Southern cuisine and it's the real deal. Tupelo also manages to do Southern without weighing you down. If you can, visit for brunch, when a Bloody Mary bar awaits, with so many sauces and garnishes that you'll probably end up overflowing your glass like I did. This simply means that you must order at least two so you can try all the garnish and sauce combinations you please. A requisite order: the biscuits. Flaky, buttery, reasonably sized sponges for whatever precious sauce or dressing remains on your plate. The sweet potato, a true tour de spud, makes for a great appetizer split between two or even three people.

Ever since my first bite of the burger at ★ **High West Distillery & Saloon** (703 Park Ave., 435/649-8300, www.highwest.com/saloon, 11am-10pm daily, $18-45, 21+ only), I haven't been able to put it out of my mind. It also happens to be one of the most affordable items on the menu and comes with a hefty side of fries. Particularly memorable is the sweet-savory onion-bacon jam. You also can't go wrong with pickle-brined

chicken wings or seared shishitos with two dipping sauces. You'll enjoy it all in a space that feels like a Wild West saloon gone fancy, with beautiful wood walls and flooring, a reclaimed wood bar, and dozens of candles lining the walls, with the distillery's blue vodka bottles adding a pop of color. Smart drink orders include a High West sampler, a neat pour of bourbon, or a whiskey cocktail that will go down dangerously easy. As one of the most popular places in Old Town to eat and drink, High West is often booked for private events or just very crowded. Go at odd times (think lunch, weekday dinner, off-season, etc.). The saloon doesn't take reservations, so expect to wait. High West is also the only ski-in/ski-out distillery in the world—ski straight to the saloon and enjoy lunch or a drink mid-ski day before hopping back on Town Lift!

The other burger worth your time in Park City lies inside **No Name Saloon & Grill** (447 Main St., 435/649-6667, www.nonamesaloon.com, 10am-2am daily, $11.50-16.50, 21+ only), a veritable museum inside an old firehouse. Good luck finding an unadorned patch of wall in this favorite local haunt. Vintage skis, a motorcycle, a taxidermy buffalo head, firefighting paraphernalia—it's all part of the No Name decor. While some of the food is *meh,* the signature buffalo burger is the bomb. If the weather's not inclement, head upstairs to the rooftop patio, where you'll find graffiti-laden toilets à la Marcel Duchamp, heat lamps for the cold, and great views of Main Street.

I have a theory that the barometer of good sushi is a bad website, maybe because it indicates that all hands on deck are dedicated to fish procurement and the art of sushi, not web design! I know there are many exceptions to that rule, but I can promise you that **Oishi Sushi Bar** (710 Main St., 435/640-2997, https://oishisushiandgrill.com, 5pm-9:30pm daily, rolls $11-19) fits this criteria, and feels authentic. So does the space—dimly lit and intimate with a fire pit outside. Don't miss the unique house Oishi Roll with salmon, lemon, and steamed asparagus topped with tuna and spicy mayo.

High West Distillery

These days, **High West** (www.highwest.com) is in good company as a Utah distillery, with more local spirits popping up all the time everywhere from Salt Lake City to the little town of Eden and Moab to the south. But when it opened in 2006, High West was the very first legal distillery to operate in the state since 1870. That's a long dry spell, but High West was worth the wait.

What began as a husband-and-wife-owned venture with one still in an old horse stable just off Park City's Main Street has become an operation spanning two properties with distribution across all 50 states. Many of its bottles have swept up awards, and the name now holds recognition throughout the country. In 2015, the *Whiskey Advocate* even named High West "Distiller of the Year." A year later, High West had enjoyed so much success that it sold to Constellation Brands for $160 million, though the original owners and staff remain heavily involved.

One of High West's most popular bottles is the American Prairie Bourbon, which is as great in an old-fashioned as it is neat or on the rocks. As if you needed another reason to drink this bourbon, 10 percent of every sale goes to protect an actual American prairie up in Montana: the biggest wildlife reserve in the continental United States. Another must-try bottle is the Rendezvous Rye, great for sipping. Keep in mind that the Campfire Whiskey—a fiery blend of Scotch, bourbon, *and* rye—is not for the faint of tongue. High West also distills vodka and bottles barrel-aged cocktails, as well as a host of specialty spirits only available during certain times of year.

Perhaps the most storied of High West's run-of-show, however, is the Valley Tan, which is made in the fashion of the Mormons pre-strict alcohol restrictions. On the label is O. P. Rockwell, Joseph Smith's right-hand man and assassin (as well as the inspiration and namesake for a cocktail lounge in Old Town). Legend has it that Rockwell enjoyed many a pour of Valley Tan, which is the actual name of whiskey distilled by Mormons back in the mid-19th century. Of the spirit, wrote Mark Twain, "Tradition says it is made of fire and brimstone. If I remember rightly, no public drinking saloons were allowed in the kingdom by Brigham Young, and no private drinking permitted among the faithful, except they confined themselves to Valley Tan."

How you enjoy High West on your trip to Park City is up to you. The **saloon in Old Town**—the distillery's original location—is conveniently located and perfect for everything from an après whiskey cocktail to dinner. The **High West Distillery & Saloon** (703 Park Ave., 435/649-8300, www.highwest.com/saloon, 11am-10pm daily, $18-45, 21+ only) is one of the first restaurants to fill up during busy times of the year, so be prepared for a long wait, since it doesn't take reservations.

Since 1979, family-owned **Davanza's** (690 Park Ave., 435/649-2222, www.davanzas.com, 11am-9pm daily, large pizzas start at $14.49) has been whistling the same tune: good pizza and good beer at a good price in a laid-back atmosphere—all accessible from Park City Mountain's Town Lift! Davanza's also offers some great deals—hungry skiers can grab two slices and a soda for just $7.99. The pizza may not blow you away, but it gets the job done, with a satisfying cracker-thin crust to boot.

Bookstores and coffee shops are well-matched concepts, and this is exactly the beat at **Atticus Coffee and Teahouse** (739 Main St., 435/214-7241, www.atticustea.com, hours vary seasonally, $7-12), toward the bottom of Main Street. Find a new book to read, order one of the 40 teas on offer, then settle into a cozy armchair as you watch the snow fall outside. Better yet, order a Magical CBD Matcha, mixed with 20 mg of CBD oil, which is alleged to treat everything from pain and insomnia to anxiety. You can also opt to add a dose of CBD to any beverage on the menu for just $4. While CBD won't give you the munchies like its THC counterpart, you will find plenty of tempting food to eat here, from smoothies to sandwiches. Atticus is also a great place to

During the ski season (late Nov.-mid-Apr.), you can even ski straight to the saloon for lunch or an après cocktail in your ski boots. On the far western edge of Park City Mountain Resort, take the blue Quit 'n Time or Creole runs all the way to the bottom to ski into High West. If you plan to head back to the slopes afterward, you can ride the Town Lift back up.

If you're a big whiskey drinker and have a little more time, make the trip to the **distillery in Wanship,** about 30 minutes north of Park City proper. At the **High West Distillery** (27649 Old Lincoln Hwy., Wanship, 435/649-8300, general store, kitchen, and tasting room open 11am-5pm Wed.-Sun.), you can take a free tour (book in advance by phone) and behold a massive 1,600-gallon copper still. The tours last about an hour and are available Wednesday-Sunday (11am, noon, 1pm, 2pm, and 3pm), with a 5pm tour available on Thursday evening.

High West Distillery collection

In Utah, alcohol-related tours cannot include tastings, so unfortunately, you'll have to wait to whet your appetite for whiskey until after the tour. Pair your tour with a flight of your own design in the tasting room, the decadent Sunday brunch buffet (10:45am-2pm, by reservation only), or dinner at the Thursday night Supper Club (6pm-9pm, by reservation only). If the weather is good, go straight to the patio where the views are as breathtaking as a pour of the Campfire whiskey. There you can enjoy a flight of whiskeys and Sunday brunch. The property is also a beautiful place to stroll around, high up in the Wasatch Back hills.

Your last stop up in Wanship should be the general store (11am-5pm Wed.-Sun.), where you can stock up on a small bottle to polish off during the rest of your stay—bear in mind that it's illegal to ship alcohol out of Utah or to pack it in your checked luggage. Other covetable items include hand-blown drinking glasses and whiskey-scented candles, which you most certainly can bring home with you.

find gifts, from books and house-mixed teas to CBD tea, tinctures, and honey.

A local's favorite on the outskirts of Old Town on the way to Deer Valley Resort, **Deer Valley Grocery Café** (Deer Valley Plaza, 1375 Deer Valley Dr., 435/615-2400, www. deervalley.com, 7:30am-6pm daily, $9.50-14.25) offers a low-key dining option with plenty of to-go options as well. You'll find a typical café menu of coffee and espresso drinks, soups, salads, and sandwiches for breakfast and lunch, along with vegan options. The standout order is the turkey chili, which is also available as a take-home chili

kit so you can re-create the experience back at home or gift it to a friend. Deer Valley Grocery Café also operates a full-on bakery that puts out fresh bread, pastries, and desserts on a daily basis. For that reason, add something sweet to your order, like a giant cookie or slice of carrot cake.

PROSPECTOR

How did a Utah lobstah shop earn the title of "World's Best Lobster Roll"? Head to **Freshie's Lobster Co.** (1897 Prospector Ave., 435/631-9861, www.freshieslobsterco. com, 11am-8pm daily, $6-26) to taste the answer to that question. Owned by New England natives, Freshies competed in Maine's inaugural 2017 lobster roll festival and reeled in the highest of honors. Originally a food truck, Freshies now has locations in Park City and Salt Lake. This landlocked anomaly imports fresh lobster straight from Maine, and serves big chunks of it tossed in mayo in a buttered hot dog bun. The lobster rolls are $12-26, depending on size—spendy, but totally worth it. The larger takeaway from the Freshies story? Excellent seafood is in fact possible in Utah. Frozen on-site and flown here in often less than 24 hours, great fish is not hard to find.

Eating on a budget in Park City can present its challenges. That's one reason to head to **El Chubasco** (1890 Bonanza Dr., Ste. 115, 435/645-9114, www.elchubascomexicangrill. com, 11am-8:30pm Sun.-Thurs., 11am-9pm Fri.-Sat., $4.75-10.95), but others include the laid-back vibe and extensive salsa bar. Then there's the fact that El Chubasco has swept the award for Park City's Best Mexican Restaurant year after year since 2013. Yup, forgo the pricier Mexican joints in the area, and head to an unassuming strip mall for your street taco fix from chef Yuliana Cortez of the Michoacán area of Mexico. Savor the chiles rellenos or a gigantic burrito, then adorn your order with a few of the 20-plus salsas available at the salsa bar.

Australian café culture has staked its claim in Park City at ★ **Five5eeds** (1600 Snow Creek Dr., 435/901-8242, www.five5eeds. com, 7:30am-3pm daily, $9.50-14.50), a breakfast and lunch spot easily overlooked in the Snow Creek shopping center. The menu leans healthy, but not in a way that feels ascetic. It's more that every dish manages to incorporate fresh ingredients and at least a vegetable here and there. Go full wholesome with the PC Superfood Grain Salad, or strike a balance with the pulled pork Benedict that laces its hollandaise with apple cider vinegar and serves Granny Smith apples on the side. Light or a tad heavier, every dish here is prepared beautifully and with some unique flourishes.

The coffee is also spot-on; try the "Aussie-style" cold brew on nitro.

Despite the fact that **Twisted Fern** (1300 Snow Creek Dr., 435/731-8238, www. twistedfern.com, 5pm-9:30pm Mon.-Tues., 11:30am-9:30pm Wed.-Sun., $15-30) is located in a strip mall (the Snow Creek shopping center), inside it feels like a friend's dining room, or maybe the world's smallest wedding dinner. In other words, with simple design and a subtle hand with lighting and music, the interior feels more residential than commercial. The menu refuses to bow to trends, throwing together an unexpected mix of dishes that range from an open-faced short rib sandwich to a root vegetable cassoulet. One more thing to love is that chef/owner/dad Adam Ross doesn't underestimate young palates: His kids' menu is filled with items like seared trout and cauliflower grits; mac and cheese, of course, makes the menu, but is accompanied by a salad.

I'm a sucker for a good pastry case, which is why I can't go to ★ **Windy Ridge Bakery** (1750 Iron Horse Dr., 435/647-2906, www. windyridgebakery.com, 8am-4pm Sun., 8am-6pm Mon.-Fri.) without coming home with one (or three) too many baked goods. From cakes and mile-high pies to lemon bars and cookies, the pastry case at Windy Ridge Bakery is hard to resist, with colorful pastries, towering pies, and tempting petit four. The bakery is strictly to-go, but is not strictly sweets, with takeout quiches, lasagna, and more at the ready for easy dinners with flavors and technique superior to those that most home cooks can conjure up. Across the parking lot from the bakery is the **Windy Ridge Café** (1250 Iron Horse Dr., 435/647-0880, www.windyridgecafe.com, 11am-9pm Mon.-Fri., 8am-9pm Sat.-Sun.), where a strong selection of soups, salads, and sandwiches awaits, plus desserts brought to you by the bakery arm of the concept. The space itself is charming with colorful walls, natural light, vintage posters, and quirky furnishings.

1: pizza at Tupelo **2:** pulled pork Benedict at Five5eeds **3:** pies at Windy Ridge Bakery

Ritual Chocolate Cafe (1105 Iron Horse Dr., 435/200-8475, www.ritualchocolate.com, 7am-6pm Mon.-Sat., 8am-5pm Sun.) is a lovely café and worthy destination, but by no means the only place where you can find award-winning Ritual chocolate. Originally established in Denver, Ritual relocated to Park City, Utah, in 2015 and has spread its cacao love everywhere from Whole Foods to many a local coffee shop where its bars can be found. But if you head to this café in the Iron Mountain area or the **satellite café at Whole Foods** in Kimball Junction (6598 N. Landmark Dr., 8am-7pm Mon.-Sat.), you can order one of the signature luscious sipping chocolates, which will temporarily seduce you away from coffee as your hot beverage of choice. Like a good mole, a strong sipping chocolate illuminates cacao's ability to swing both ways (savory and sweet, that is). Made with ethically sourced cacao, Ritual Chocolate bars also make great gifts for the people back home; strong picks are the Mid-Mountain (named for the local trail) and the minty Ski Dreams, though the lineup is ever changing.

MOUNTAIN DINING
Park City Mountain

How do you know that **The Viking Yurt** (435/615-9878, www.vikingyurt.com, lunch served approx. 11:30am-3pm, dinners meet at 6pm and end by 10pm, lunch $11-13, dinner $182 pp), up on the Park City side of Park City Mountain, is no tourist trap? Because it's owned by actual Vikings. Okay, not Vikings, but a native Norwegian and his wife (a local) who also lived in Scandinavia for enough years to earn her chops as honorary modern Viking. Vik and Joy Ger run an homage to the cuisine of Norway and its surroundings every ski season, housed in a cozy yurt. By day, the yurt serves lunch, glogg, and giant cookies to hungry skiers. Snap a photo by the giant heart sculpture just outside, inspired by one the Gers encountered in the Alps. Come night, a sled transports diners up the mountain to the yurt, where a multicourse dinner awaits, to the tune of live piano. The menu

can vary from year to year and night to night, but generally includes Scandinavian dishes like braised red meat, lingonberry sauce, and cheeses. The whole experience is a splurge, but well worth it.

One of the hardships of being a skier who likes to indulge in Utah is that only a handful of on-mountain bars and restaurants serve liquor. A beer will do now and then, but many of us crave Bloody Marys and Irish coffees on cold days in between laps on the mountain. If you're in that same spirited boat, ski over to **Lookout Cabin** (435/615-2892, 11:30am-3:30pm daily during ski season, $19-30), which is one of the only places on-mountain that serves a full beverage menu, as well as great food to boot, out of an open kitchen in the center of the dining room. An easy way to access Lookout is by riding up the Orange Bubble Express from the Canyons Village, then staying skier's right until you run into the cabin on your right. The Shortcut Lift will also take you there. While Lookout's food and drinks (like most on-mountain dining options) are pretty pricey, the eponymous "lookout" over a forested gully, the fabulous Bloody, and the soul-warming soup are well worth the price. The rest of the menu offers modern American fare with some Southwestern flavors. The biggest downside of a visit to Lookout Cabin is that you'll find it hard to tighten up your boots and get back out there.

If a barn was converted into a cocktail lounge, it might resemble **The Farm** (Canyons Village, 4000 Canyons Resort Dr., 435/615-8080, https://parkcitymountain.com, 11:30am-10pm daily, $23-44), located in the Canyons Village. This Park City Mountain-owned restaurant offers lunch, an après-ski menu, and dinner. In the summer, it boasts a great patio and is located right by the free Canyons Village outdoor concert area. While the menu changes seasonally, the focus is upscale New American cuisine. You'll find a mix of cheese and charcuterie boards, salads, soups, and surf and turf. The après-ski menu shines in particular with a bison chili garnished with local cheddar, and the cleverly named and extremely satisfying Yard Sale—a sloppy joe topped with coleslaw and crispy onions on a brioche bun that will fill the giant sandwich-sized hole in any skier's or rider's stomach after a big pow day.

Campos Roastery & Café (1385 Lowell Ave., 435/731-8377, https://us.camposcoffee. com, 7am-5pm daily, $9-14), in Canyons Village, is exactly what it sounds like: a great place to pick up coffee and a light breakfast or lunch. The café actually got its start in Australia, where you'll find independently owned locations all across the country. In 2016, just before the annual Sundance Film Festival, it made its American debut right here in Park City, and opened a Salt Lake City location a couple years later. If you haven't tried a flat white before, now's the time. This Australian coffee drink is like a latte, but with a higher proportion of coffee to milk—think a happy milk medium between a cappuccino and a latte. If you decide you're a fan of their roasts, you can order more of their coffee online when you get back home. As for food, the menu is a mix of toasts, Benedicts, and salads. If you're a Vegemite fan, consider the meat pie, which features this legendary British spread along with braised short ribs, or the Full Aussie, a breakfast sandwich with eggs, bacon, roasted tomato, baked beans, mushrooms, and, of course, Vegemite.

Deer Valley

If you want a traditional spot to celebrate, splurge, or otherwise be romantic, turn to the old-world-style **Glitretind Restaurant** (Stein Eriksen Lodge, 7700 Stein Way, 435/645-6455, www.steinlodge.com/ glitretind, 7am-10pm daily, $28-58) in Deer Valley. And if, like many Europeans, you consider good food integral to the skiing experience, then step off the slopes for the Skier's Buffet (11:30am-2:45pm Mon.-Sat., $44 pp). This lunchtime spread will more than refuel you for afternoon skiing with salads, charcuterie, cheeses, seafood, hot dishes, carving stations, and the Stein's wild game chili. If you're really going all out, select from the

over 20 desserts prepared by the in-house pastry chef. The Glitretind dinner menu features aesthetic, edgy salads, entrées revolving around local proteins, and always-elevated options for pescatarians and vegetarians, like hazelnuts and farro risotto with goat cheese and a turmeric-beet sauce. Want to get a sense of the Glitretind vibe without dishing out? Head to the adjoining **Troll Hallen Lounge** (10am-midnight daily) to grab a beer and one of the more modestly priced bar snacks like a Bavarian pretzel ($6).

If a little dated, **Fireside Dining** (Empire Canyon Lodge, 9200 Marsac Ave., Ste. 306, 435/645-6632, www.deervalley.com, 5:45pm-9pm Wed.-Sat., $75 adults, not including beverages) is a unique culinary experience where the name says it all. Most everything is cooked and served fireside. Dinner consists of five stations situated beside fireplaces, with culinary cues taken from Switzerland. The first station is the star: raclette, the semi-hard Swiss cheese, melted over the fire and pulled onto warm plates in a tempting puddle. The cheese plate can then be adorned with a variety of charcuterie, mustards, olives, and a must-try strawberry chutney. The next course consists of soups and salads, a welcome interlude between heavier courses. The next two stations are meats, roasted over the fire and served with sauces and accompaniments like rösti and pappardelle. Finally, dessert is a buffet of fruit, cookies, and other sweets that can be dipped into warm caramel or chocolate fondue. As a disclaimer, the cooking here is uneven, as it is at many buffets. Some dishes are spectacular, while others can be lacking. Splurge on Fireside for the experience, and be discerning as you plot your course through fire.

KIMBALL JUNCTION

As a D.C. native, I do hurt for a few of the foods I grew up with back East, like the New York slice. **Maxwell's** (1456 Newpark Blvd., 435/647-0304, www.maxwellsece.com, 11am-midnight Mon.-Fri., 10am-midnight Sat.-Sun., $21-24) comes awfully close, dishing

out creative pies and surprisingly delightful salads. Featured on *Diners, Drive-Ins & Dives,* Maxwell's bills itself as an outpost of East Coast cuisine. The inside is unglamorous and often frequented by families (read: uneaten crusts discarded on the floor and maybe a little raucous at times), but still manages to pull off a fun sports bar-cum-pizza joint vibe. This is also one of the few places where you can usually manage to grab a large table for a big group within a reasonable amount of time, even on the busiest of Park City ski weekends. Don't miss the Fat Kid pie, with puddles of ricotta, pepperoni, and spinach.

It makes sense that within relatively close proximity to Park City's bobsledding track (up at the Utah Olympic Park) lies Jamaican food worth writing to Kingston about. **11Hauz** (1241 Center Dr. L140, 435/200-8972, https://11hauz.com, 11:30am-9pm Mon.-Thurs., 11:30am-10pm Fri.-Sat., $11-20) is a relatively new addition to the Kimball Junction shopping complex, and still lies under the radar of many Park Cityites. Inspired by her grandma Florence's recipes, Sheron Grant opened 11Hauz with her husband Errol and daughters Nyesha, Tanisha, and Anita. The inside is authentic and quaint, with colorful walls, rustic wood tables, and, of course, reggae on the stereo. As enjoyable as the food are the menu subheadings: Finga Tings, Green Tings, and Full Yuh Belly. Don't miss the jerk wings with a mango-pineapple chutney, the coconut-cream Rasta Pasta, or the weekend special: goat, made with an Indo-Jamaican spice mix.

If you like restaurants that play hard to get and for good reason, consider ★ **Cortona** (1612 W. Ute Blvd. #112, 435/608-1373, www.cortonaparkcity.com, 5pm-9pm Tues.-Sat., $17.95-29.95), which serves the best Italian food in all of Park City. During the day, one might assume that Cortona is permanently shuttered; with little signage and blinds drawn closed, it lays low in its humble space in a strip mall in the northwestern corner of Kimball Junction. But when the clock strikes 5pm, the place comes alive as locals flock to the warm, trattoria-esque space decorated with paintings of pastoral Italy brushed right onto the flaxen walls in true Tuscan style. With a capacity of about 40 people, reservations made by phone are absolutely requisite. If lasagna is your thing, you also need to state that you'd like an order of it when making your reservation. In similar fashion, the posted menu is liable to change at any time since all pastas are made fresh every single day, and there's always a pasta *del giorno.*

One of the newer additions to Kimball Junction dining is **Hearth and Hill** (1153 Center Dr., 435/200-8840, https://hearth-hill.com, 11:30am-10pm daily, $12-35), a local couple's dream realized. This is a welcome addition to Kimball, with a more upscale, modern feel than any of its area competitors. A big space with high ceilings, a lively bar area, and live music in the evenings, Hearth and Hill is as good for a couple of cocktails as it is for a large group celebration. While the menu modus operandi of "something for everyone" can result in diluted quality, it is nice to have a place where most in your party can be happy, and where the vibe is jovial and facilitates conversation. This is that place. What you lose in truly exquisite food, you gain in relatively affordable, agreeable food and environment alike. The food, to be more specific, is Asian fusion in some places, new American in others. You'll find everything from ramen and gyoza to flatbread and well-composed salads. For dessert, don't miss the nacho waffles sundae.

In the land of fast-casual concepts around the Kimball Junction area, **Vessel Kitchen** (1784 Uinta Way, Ste. 1E, 435/200-8864, www.vesselkitchen.com, 11am-9pm daily, $10-14) reigns supreme. The menu leans Mediterranean, and the falafel is tops. For those who love to customize every detail of a meal, go at it and mix together the proteins and sides that call your name, from

1: fire pit on the deck at Park City Mountain's Lookout Cabin **2:** jerk chicken wings at 11Hauz in Kimball Junction **3:** raclette melting by the fire at Deer Valley's Fireside Dining

roasted chicken to macaroni and cheese. The Mediterranean bowl offers a nice medley of elements, from roasted cauliflower and hummus to falafel. Another bonus here is kombucha on tap, in three rotating flavors, like tangerine ginger.

Everything you could want in a coffee shop exists at ★ **Park City Coffee Roasters** (1764 Uinta Way, 435/647-9097, www.pcroaster.com, 6am-6pm daily), in a lively corner of Kimball Junction. The house-roasted coffee makes for tasty lattes sipped in sturdy ceramic mugs at the window bar seating, and said sturdy mugs plus bags of their coffee make great souvenirs and gifts to tow back home. I challenge you not to succumb to one of the baked goods on display, from berry scones and colossal biscotti to cinnamon buns so large, a stranger in line once asked if I'd be willing to eat half of his. If you need to squeeze a little work into your vacation, there's a quieter room beyond the main entrance, as well as a closed-off room reservable for meetings, but usually used by people who've come to type rather than chat.

Accommodations

The driving questions for where to stay in Park City are (1) How much do you want to spend? and (2) What are your priorities? If you live in a city and this is your one chance to get into the mountains, you may decide that views and alpine setting are king. If you're on a strict budget, consider the Park City Hostel or lodging farther from skiing and Old Town. Another option is to go budget for the majority of your stay, and splurge on just one or two nights at one of the luxury hotels in Deer Valley. If skiing is your priority, it may be worth it to stay somewhere that's ski-in/ski-out. And if you have a big group and don't want to dine out all the time, consider booking an Airbnb/VRBO.

OLD TOWN PARK CITY
$100-200

The name says it all. **Marriott's MountainSide** (1305 Lowell Ave., 435/940-2000, www.marriott.com, starting at $118), located in Old Town Park City, is indeed ski-in/ski-out from Park City Mountain. Depending on whether you visit during a quieter time of year or the height of ski season, you may pay for your proximity to Old Town, but it's well worth it if you're looking for a hassle-free experience. And if you like the idea of an Airbnb (e.g., homey feel, group accommodations, a kitchen to reduce dining out), but also enjoy the amenities and standardization of a hotel experience, the MountainSide strikes the perfect balance. Guest rooms offer kitchenettes and sofa beds so you won't feel cooped up. Villas range from one to two bedrooms and feature kitchens, soaking tubs, and washers/dryers. Some of the choice amenities include a heated outdoor pool, a theater that kids will love, and free parking (a serious commodity in the Old Town area).

$200-300

Treasure Mountain Inn (255 Main St., 435/655-4501, www.treasuremountainn.com, starting at $209) is located right at the top of historic Main Street. When it first opened back in 1963, its name paid homage to the current name of the ski resort. History is indeed the heartbeat here, with historic photos filling the hallways and antique decor. Amenities include a small eco-friendly hot tub, a fitness room, and a courtyard. With a refined mountain lodge feel and 46 uniquely decorated rooms, Treasure Mountain Inn defines itself as a condominium hotel. This basically means the 46 rooms are a little larger than your typical accommodations and include kitchenettes or full kitchens, ranging from junior suites to two-bedroom condos.

The inn is also an environmentally friendly choice, with recycling, organic food, water conservation practices, wind energy, and carbon footprint offsets.

Over $500

As the name suggests, the ★ **Washington School House Hotel** (543 Park Ave., 435/649-3800, https://washingtonschoolhouse.com, starting at $605) is set inside a historic 19th-century school that managed to mostly survive the Great Fire of 1898. Now a historic landmark in Park City, the Washington is also one of the most elegantly appointed places to stay in Old Town, if not in the whole Park City area. Twelve unique rooms range from the 16-Foot Ceiling Room ($605) with windows taller than you, oak barnwood floors, and a marble bathroom, to a penthouse suite with crystal chandeliers ($1,405). The overarching vibe is bed-and-breakfast meets modern art gallery, with a mix of vintage finishes, a white-dominated color scheme, and an eclectic mix of art. As the hotel itself points out, the biggest issue with a stay here is that you'll be hard-pressed to ever leave the property for the many outdoor amenities that await in the surrounding mountains, especially with the in-house chef who serves complimentary organic breakfasts and après-ski snacks in the ski lounge. The Washington School House is truly an education in attention to detail and elegance.

PROSPECTOR

Under $100

The least expensive lodging option in Park City (aside from a friend's couch) is undoubtedly the **Park City Hostel** (1781 Sidewinder Dr., 435/731-8811, https://parkcityhostel.com), established in 2016. For those with hostel horror stories from Europe (or who have seen the actual horror movie *Hostel*), banish all preconceptions about this relatively cheap form of accommodation. The Park City Hostel will undoubtedly be one of the swankiest hostels you've ever stayed at, complete with regionally inspired mountain decor within. The lovely common area includes a large kitchen, pool table, and library as well as a rooftop patio. Located right in Prospector Square, the hostel is close to everything from ski rental shops to restaurants, and it's accessible by public transit and the Rail Trail. Prices vary seasonally but typically start at $40 for a six-bed dorm room (mixed gender or female-only available) and $100 for a private room. All rooms have shared hallway bathrooms. A bonus for those traveling solo or looking for new friends: the Park City Hostel hosts recurring weekly events, like bar crawls and group ski outings.

$200-300

Park City Peaks Hotel (2346 Park Ave., 435/649-5000, www.parkcitypeaks.com, $250 for king room) is about as affordable as lodging gets this close to the ski resorts and Old Town. Peaks is a fine option, especially considering the convenience of its co-location with Christy Sports, where you can rent all the ski and snowboard gear necessary for the slopes. With mid-century modern decor and contemporary artwork and photography on the walls, Peaks is also a nice option for those who don't love the rustic mountain lodge feel so prevalent in the Park City area. Spacious rooms sport streamlined, chic design with high-end bathroom finishes and artistic touches throughout, like turquoise lamps and colorful artwork. The Peaks Hotel is also on the bus route, as well as near the shops and dining of the Prospector area. But you don't have to venture far to eat; Peaks offers its own dining options. The Mercato Cafe serves a casual breakfast, while Versante Hearth + Bar is an Italian restaurant serving wood-fired pizzas.

Over $500

If you're more into Nordic than alpine when it comes to skiing, consider a stay at the **Hotel Park City** (2001 Park Ave., 435/940-5000, www.hotelparkcity.com, $950-1,200), which is co-located with the White Pine Nordic Center and backs miles of groomed cross-country trails. Similarly, in the summertime, if you're a golfer, consider this hotel's proximity to the Park City Golf Course. One could easily enjoy a vacation within the bounds of this hotel's property considering it also houses Bandannas Grill (for breakfast and lunch), as well as Ruth's Chris Steakhouse. Skate-ski, spa, eat, sleep, repeat, all in one place. Convenience may be king here, but the rooms are no slouch, with alpine design touches and amenities like jetted tubs and private balconies.

MOUNTAIN LODGING
Park City Mountain

Park City Mountain Resort owns several accommodations properties at Canyons Village, most of which offer excellent ski access, and are either a short walk from the chairlift or qualify as ski-in/ski-out. All of the resort's lodging can be booked online at https:// parkcitymountain.com/lodging or by phone (866/618-1388, 8am-6pm Mon.-Fri., 9am-5pm Sat.-Sun.).

$100-200

Located right in the heart of Canyons Village, the **Sundial Lodge** (3720 N. Sundial Ct., 866/618-1388, https://parkcitymountain.com/ lodging, starting at $157) is less than a minute walk from the Red Pine Gondola. It has the look and feel you'd expect from a base area lodge owned by the biggest ski resort company in the country (that's Vail), with rustic mountain lodge vibes inside and out. Given the unparalleled ski access, the Sundial is a great affordable option at the Park City base, with around 40 rooms and suites. A little artwork here and a fireplace there elevate the otherwise standard rooms, which come with kitchenettes. Many of the rooms also have mountain views. Amenities include a heated outdoor pool and hot tub and exercise room.

Set back a little farther from skiing, the **Silverado Lodge** (2669 Canyons Resort Dr., 866/618-1388, https://parkcitymountain. com/lodging, starting at $138) is just a five-minute walk from the base area lifts, and also on a shuttle route if you prefer not to walk in

ski boots at all. The feel of the Silverado is a little quieter and more upscale than some of the other Canyons Village lodging options, with high ceilings, spacious decks, and generally elegant rooms. While the smaller studios don't boast as many frills, the lofts and suites manage to strike a balance of colorful modernity and alpine coziness. Amenities include an outdoor heated pool and hot tub, steam room, and exercise room.

Want the next best thing to ski-in/ski-out without dropping close to a grand? Consider **The Miners Club** (4070 Willow Draw, 435/222-0071, https://travelraintree.com/ resorts/the-miners-club, starting at $165), which is a short walk from the Frostwood Gondola that routes to the Canyons Village of Park City Mountain. You can't click into your skis right outside your hotel, but you can eliminate the hassle of parking or transit and go from room to chairlift in mere minutes. The Miners Club also takes cues from Airbnb/ VRBO, offering apartment-style rooms ranging from two to four bedrooms. Every Miners Club suite offers a full kitchen and a private hot tub. Here you're paying for a great location and cozy accommodations, not for amenities that will wow you or extravagance like much of The Miners Club's area lodging brethren. Note that while The Miners Club is close to the base, it's not owned by Park City Mountain, and thus isn't reservable through the resort.

$200-300

With a rustic lodge feel and ski-in/ski-out access, the **Grand Summit Hotel** (4000 Canyons Resort Dr., 866/618-1388, https:// parkcitymountain.com/lodging, starting at $210) is a great option at Canyons Village. In 2017, the property also underwent a major renovation that included updated decor and appliances, as well as a new RockResorts Spa and café. The Grand Summit offers 290 lodging options, including suites with kitchens and fireplaces, as well as luxury penthouses. Amenities include an outdoor pool, fitness area, and child care center.

OVER $500

While the ★ **Waldorf Astoria** (2100 Frostwood Dr., 435/648-5500, www.waldorfastoriaparkcity.com, starting at $1,249) is technically not ski-in/ski-out, it's just a few steps from the Frostwood Gondola that transports riders straight to Canyons Village. As you'd imagine, the price tag comes with a distinctly luxurious feel, white-glove service, and unobstructed mountain views. Ski Butlers also operates within the Waldorf, allowing you to rent gear from the comfort of the lobby. The hotel offers themed specials for everyone from spa-goers to LGBTQ+ travelers, who can enjoy a subscription to *OUT* magazine with their reservation. The Powder restaurant inside is a posh place to get a drink, especially the Pow Day pale ale brewed especially for the hotel by Park City Brewery. Note that while it's just a gondola ride from the base, the Waldorf is not owned by Park City Mountain Resort, and thus cannot be booked through the resort's lodging reservations.

Deer Valley

Like Park City Mountain, Deer Valley offers a number of lodging options at and around its base area, including boutique hotels, condos, and top-tier luxury chalets. There are three primary areas where you'll find lodging around Deer Valley: **Snow Park,** the main base area, which is also closest to Old Town (1-2 mi/1.6-3.2 km away depending on specific location); **Silver Lake Village,** a mid-mountain base area where you'll find ski-in/ski-out options; and the upper-mountain **Empire Pass,** the quietest part of Deer Valley.

Most of the lodging around all three of these areas either enjoys ski-in/ski-out access or lies just a short walk from the lifts—if it's farther than walking distance, most lodges operate free shuttles, or you can use Park City's free public transit system (Routes 4, 6, and 9 serve Deer Valley around 6am-11pm at 30-minute intervals; see www.parkcity.org for details). While some of the lodging around Deer Valley is independently owned, you can

book any of the resort-owned properties at www.deervalley.com/lodging or by phone (800/558-3337).

$200-300

Located in the Snow Park base area, **Silver Baron Lodge** (2880 Deer Valley Dr. E., 435/940-5120, www.deervalley.com/lodging, starting at $210) is one of the most affordable lodging options at Deer Valley. While it may not offer the luxury of some of the other resort-owned accommodations and old-world lodges farther up the hill, it's a fine option that by no means has a "budget" feel. Owned and managed by Deer Valley Resort, the Silver Baron is situated about a third of a mile (0.5 km) from the chairlifts, and only 1.5 miles (2.4 km) from Old Town—a nice compromise for those who plan to spend more time in town. A complimentary shuttle is available for transportation to both. Inside, you'll find a classic mountain lodge feel, with clean, rustic rooms—generally, the bigger the room, the higher end the decor. You can choose from a mix of standard hotel rooms, as well as 1-4-bedroom condos that come with leather sofas, stone fireplaces, and kitchens complete with peninsulas and bar seating. During ski season, enjoy a complimentary breakfast buffet and yoga classes, plus the heated outdoor pool.

$400-500

Located at the Silver Lake Village, the ★ **Goldener Hirsch Inn** (7570 Royal St., 435/649-7770, www.goldenerhirschinn.com, open Dec.-early Apr., starting at $445) is a family-owned luxury lodge with ski-in/ski-out access. Here you'll find old-world ambience at its finest. Each of the 20 rooms, suites, and luxury suites is outfitted with custom decor and features European king beds and luxury furnishings, with fireplaces and private balconies in suites. The mood in the lobby matches, with an antler chandelier and vintage wooden skis mounted to the walls. Amenities include a hot tub and sauna.

OVER $500

Just steps away from the lifts, **St. Regis Deer Valley** (2300 Deer Valley Dr., 435/940-5700, www.marriott.com, starting at $597) is a Marriott hotel located in the Snow Park base area. If you're unfamiliar with the St. Regis line, it's a luxury collection of hotels with roots that stretch back to the first concept built in 1904 in New York. Today, St. Regis properties are owned by Marriott and are known for ornate decor and peerless service. The 181 rooms at St. Regis Deer Valley are no different, with subdued earth tones, fireplaces, marble bathrooms, oversized windows, and private balconies. With beautiful stonework on columns and accent walls and timeless high-end furnishings, the lobby and other common areas set an opulent mood. St. Regis also offers a heated outdoor infinity pool and the Remède Spa. And if you've always yearned for your own butler, you can fulfill that dream here; the century-old St. Regis Butler Service is at the ready to unpack your bags, draw your shades, or just come to your room to personally share the snow report for the day.

In the mid-mountain Silver Lake area: **Stein Eriksen Lodge** (7700 Stein Way, 435/649-3700, www.steinlodge.com, starting at $1,170) might have a reputation for catering to the elite (read: not for kids), but if you're willing to splurge, a 2018 $14 million expansion has added amenities that will keep even the most easily bored child psyched at all hours of the day, from a family-friendly pool and a 56-seat theater to a 3,500-square-foot (325 sq m) entertainment room with Skee-Ball, pinball, and more—and these are just the indoor amenities. The new wine cellar with a private tasting room will keep mom and dad happy, too. Design-wise, the Stein Eriksen feels like the sort of old-world ski lodge you might find in Switzerland, with stunning wood beams, a towering stone fireplace mounted by a deer bust, and vintage ski artwork. The 180 rooms give off a bit of a more modern mountain manor feel. With a five-star spa, the award-winning Glitretind Restaurant, and a ski valet, it's no surprise the Stein continues to sweep "World's Best Ski Hotel" at the World Ski Awards.

Way up a winding road in the Empire Pass area lies the **Montage Deer Valley** (9100 Marsac Ave., 435/604-1300, www.montagehotels.com/deervalley, starting at $1,765), the very picture of luxury. Located in a palatial building nestled in an alpine cirque, the Montage checks all the typical boxes of luxury lodging in the Deer Valley

the Montage Deer Valley

area: impeccable customer service, brilliant views, ski-in/ski-out, awards, etcetera. Inside, the decor is timeless opulence with a dash of alpine—a statue of an early 20th-century skier here, a roaring fireplace there. Rooms all sport the highest-end decor and furnishings, as well as marble bathrooms. Built in 2010, the Montage is one of the newer luxury lodges at Deer Valley, and a few things set it apart. One is its spa, which offers a menu that draws on native Utah ingredients. Also unique to this hotel are Montage Expeditions, which basically consist of the most deluxe national park visitations money can buy. A private plane equipped with a personal tour guide and catering transports guests to the nearby park of their choosing, from Yellowstone up in Wyoming, to Arches down south in Utah. Bubbly fans will also want to check out The Après Lounge, a partnership with Veuve Clicquot Champagne. If you thought a hot toddy and Wagyu sliders was about as fancy as après could get, think again. Montage's exclusive lounge offers caviar, truffle popcorn, and, of course, Champagne.

KIMBALL JUNCTION
$200-300

The immediate surroundings of the **Newpark Resort** (1476 Newpark Blvd., 435/649-3600, www.newparkresort.com, starting at $249) in Kimball Junction are by no means breathtaking. Your adjacent views may indeed be a parking lot or a ski rental shop. But don't let that deter you if you're looking for a more wallet-friendly way to take a ski vacation (especially with kids). There are also upsides to the Newpark's somewhat unglamorous location. You're close to that ski rental shop outside your room's window, as well as numerous dining options and other retail. And the Park City public bus stops right outside the hotel

and will whisk you more or less straight to the Park City Mountain base areas. The convenient location makes this a family-friendly lodging option as well. And despite the immediate surroundings, Newpark has a chic, modern feel inside.

AIRBNBS/VRBOS

Anyone who resides year-round in a tourist town will likely divulge a love/hate relationship with the plethora of **Airbnbs and VRBOs** available to rent. From the perspective of a local who cannot afford to live in the Park City area in part because of the short-term rental phenomenon, Airbnbs/VRBOs are legitimate threats to the livability of resort towns. However, from the perspective of a traveler, they offer a convenient, cozy, and often less expensive alternative to a hotel stay, not to mention a great solution for big families or large groups. Simply search the Park City area on either site to find your abode. However, keep in mind that just because a rental's location is Park City, it doesn't mean you'll be literally steps from Old Town or skiing. You may end up in a condo off the highway, or in an outlying area like Heber. Check the map if location is important to you.

CAMPING

If you want to camp in the Park City area, the best place to do so is along the **Jordanelle Reservoir.** At the **Hailstone** entry point on the reservoir's west side, there is a **campground** (515 UT-319, Heber City, 435/649-9540, https://stateparks.utah.gov/jordanelle, May-Oct., starting at $35 per night) about a 15-minute drive from Old Town. The Hailstone Campground accommodates tents and RVs with nearly 200 campsites, which include restrooms, fire pits, and—at some sites—potable water and electrical hookups.

Information and Services

TOURIST INFORMATION

The **Park City Visitors Office** (1794 Olympic Pkwy., 435/658-9616, www.visitparkcity.com, 9am-6pm daily) is conveniently located right off I-80 from Salt Lake City in the same building as a coffee shop. Caffeinate and get all the maps, brochures, and tips (besides those herein!) that you need for the days ahead. You can also enjoy free Wi-Fi here; take a seat to digest all the information you've received and book some plans and reservations.

If you missed the main visitor hub, you can also get info from the **satellite visitors center** inside the Park City Museum (528 Main St., 435/649-7457, https://parkcityhistory.org, 10am-7pm Mon.-Sat., noon-6pm Sun.). While you get tips, kids will stay entertained by the museum's gift shop inventory surrounding the help desk, from rocks to stuffed animals.

Information-gathering and tips do not have to be reserved for these official offices, however. If you're looking for advice on local recreational opportunities, talk to ski resort guest services, located at the base areas, or chat with the folks at a shop that rents or sells gear for their favorite backcountry skiing spots or bike trails.

Chatting with your server or bartender is also a great way to get local advice on where to play, eat, or drink next. Ask them about their favorite restaurants, trails, and other tips for traveling the area—most of the time, you're bound to encounter unexpected recommendations or smart advice.

EMERGENCY SERVICES

If you become injured while skiing inbounds at a resort, the answer to where to go will be rather straightforward. Likely, you'll flag down a ski patroller, and if the injury's bad enough, they'll transport you down in a sled. If you can ski down on your own, head to the ski patrol clinics or first-aid stations, located at the base areas.

For year-round medical issues ranging from torn ACLs and broken clavicles to altitude sickness, there are many clinics that can help. The closest to the ski resorts is the **Intermountain Park City Mountain Medical Clinic** (1493 Lowell Ave., 435/645-6020, https://intermountainhealthcare.org, 9am-5:30pm daily), an urgent care center. Other options include **Park City InstaCare** (1750 Sidewinder Dr., 435/649-7640, 8am-8pm daily) and **STAT-MD Urgent Care** (1784 Uinta Way E., 435/604-0160, https://statmdurgentcare.com, 8am-8pm Mon.-Fri., 9am-5pm Sat.-Sun.). Note that none of these clinics offer 24-hour care, so for after-hours emergencies or issues, you'll need to call 911 and/or head to Salt Lake, depending on the urgency of the situation.

MAIL AND SHIPPING

If you've got mailing needs, you can use one of three U.S. post offices in the area. There's one right on Main Street for convenience, another is in the strip malls of Kimball Junction, and the biggest is in between the two right on Park Avenue. UPS and FedEx stores and drop-off locations also dot the area.

RECYCLING

Park City has an interesting recycling situation. While curbside recycling accepts most of the usual materials you're used to (from cardboard and cans to plastics), it does not accept glass. So, if you're buying a dozen Champagne bottles for a big celebration or have gone through more than your fair share of bottled six-packs, consider stopping by the Park City Recycling Center on your way out of town. If you're staying in a hotel, the concierge may offer this service complimentarily. If you're at an Airbnb that offers a recycling bin, separate the glass. Located in Prospector, the **Park**

City Recycling Center (1825 Woodbine Way, 435/649-9698, www.recycleutah.org, 10am-5:30pm Mon.-Sat.) offers free recycling of glass, as well as basically any other item you can imagine. Off Kearns Boulevard, there are ample signs pointing you in the right direction to the center, but Google Maps will take you there, too.

LOCAL MEDIA

Tune the radio of your rental car to 91.7 FM. That's **KPCW,** the local community radio station that syndicates NPR shows, spins the tunes of resident DJs, provides local reporting, and implores us all to "listen like a local." This is a great way to get a sense of the town politics, culture, weather, avalanche conditions, and upcoming happenings. If you lose something on your trip, you can also have KPCW post it to the Lost & Found board, which is announced on the radio and posted online as well. You can also listen online wherever you are (www.kpcw.org).

You may also find local publications wherever you're staying, be it a hotel or an Airbnb. *The Park Record* (www.parkrecord.com) is the local newspaper, which offers a sense of what's happening around town. *Park City Magazine* (www.parkcitymag.com) offers a nice take on the local scene, from interviews with local athletes to tips on day hikes and Sundance coverage. To peruse local fluff stories and discover dining options, turn to *Mountain Express Magazine* (https://mountainexpressmagazine.com); you'll find copies inside grocery stories, hotel lobbies, and locations throughout the area.

Getting There and Around

GETTING THERE

Old Town Park City is 32 miles (52 km) southeast of Salt Lake City, about a 45-minute drive via I-80. Kimball Junction is 26 miles (43 km) east of Salt Lake City, about a 30-minute drive via I-80.

From SLC Airport to Park City

The closest major airport to Park City is **Salt Lake City International Airport** (SLC; 776 N. Terminal Dr., 801/575-2400, www.slcairport.com), from which there are several options for traveling to Park City.

CAR

Driving from the airport, it takes about 30 minutes to reach Kimball Junction, and about 45 minutes to get to the ski resorts and Old Town Park City.

You'll find several big-name car rental shops on the ground floor of the airport's parking garage, right across from the three vehicle traffic lanes outside the Arrivals area. If you're traveling in the winter, a vehicle that's AWD/4WD and has snow tires is highly recommended. This can make all the difference between nightmarish drives through blizzards and slow but safe journeys. In the summer, if you're planning on heading out on a lot of dirt-road excursions, you may also consider AWD/4WD, particularly in case you encounter mud.

TAXI/RIDESHARE

You can easily catch a cab, Uber, or Lyft, available in the second lane outside the Arrivals area of the airport ($40-75 depending on day, time, and specific drop-off location). If it's snowing outside, it's not unreasonable to check with your driver to ensure that they have AWD/4WD and snow tires in the interest of your safety.

While you can rely on the availability of Uber/Lyft at the airport to travel to Park City, unfortunately, the return trip to the airport may be a little more complicated. If you're traveling at an odd hour/season or are staying off the beaten path, you may find that no drivers pick up your ride, or that they cancel on you. Try scheduling in advance, or consider booking a taxi ahead of time, which will cost you a little more money.

SHUTTLE

If you're flying in late or prefer the security of a prescheduled ride, there's no shortage of limousine and other fancy cab services you can book ahead of time, such as **Ace Transportation** (435/649-8294, www.649taxi.com, starting at $30) or **Protrans Transportation** (877/255-2631, www.protransparkcity.com, starting at $99).

PUBLIC TRANSIT

There is a public transit option that takes you from the airport to Park City, but it requires a transfer and will likely take about twice as long as driving or a cab. That said, it will save you a lot of cash. Start by following signs for the **TRAX** light rail and hop on the green line (Route 704, www.rideuta.com, $2.50 per one-way ticket) toward West Valley Central Station. The train starts running at 5:38am and comes every 15 minutes until 11:23pm. Nine stops and about 20 minutes later, dismount at the Gallivan Plaza Station. From there, walk just a few minutes to the intersection of 200 S. and Main Street, right across from the restaurant Bambara. Here, wait for the **PC-SLC Connect Bus** (Route 902, www.rideuta.com, operates roughly 5am-7pm, $4.50 per one-way ticket), which comes at uneven intervals that are usually about an hour long. If you arrive well ahead of the next bus, there are many restaurants nearby where you can duck in and grab a coffee while you wait. Once you hop on the 902, it will take you a little under an hour to arrive at the Kimball Junction Transit Center. From there, unless you're staying somewhere in Kimball Junction, you'll likely need to hop on a Park City Transit bus (or cave and call a taxi) to get to Prospector, Old Town, Deer Valley, or other farther destinations. The same public transit trip can be made in reverse, if you're not flying extremely early in the morning. Just budget a solid two hours for the trip.

GETTING AROUND
Local Bus

Park City Transit (www.parkcity.org) offers free buses that cover most of historic downtown, the ski resorts, the shops and outlets in Kimball Junction, and other surrounding areas. While schedules vary by route, most of the routes run approximately 6am-11pm at 20-30-minute intervals. For more information, visit the website and select "Transit Bus" under Departments.

Electric Bike

From spring through fall, you can take advantage of the Millennium Trail, the McLeod Creek Trail, and other recreational paths that connect the dots in the Park City area, which can be traversed using the e-bike share program, **Summit Bike Share** (www.summitbikeshare.com, only available for riders ages 18 and over), with rentals starting at just $2 a trip and located at prominent junctions along the trails. There is no set opening or closing date for this bike share—timing varies depending on snowpack and weather.

Taxi/Rideshare

Ubers and Lyfts are quite active during peak hours and seasons in Park City, and you shouldn't wait much longer than 5 or 10 minutes. You may experience very high surge pricing during busy times, such as the Sundance Film Festival. However, during odd hours (e.g., early morning) or times of year (think spring after the resorts shut down), fewer Ubers/Lyfts are available. If you're staying far from the town center (e.g., in a remote mountain Airbnb somewhere), you may also have some trouble procuring a ride through these apps. The bottom line? Don't rely on them for an odd-hour trip to the airport.

The best bet if you're staying in a more remote area or traveling at off hours is to schedule a ride in advance with a taxi service. If you're going out on Main Street in Park City during peak seasons, you'll likely also see lines of taxis parked waiting for riders. This can sometimes be an easier and more convenient option than ordering an Uber or Lyft, though perhaps a little more expensive. **Park City Direct** (435/655-3010, online booking available at www.parkcitydirectshuttle.com) operates 24 hours a day, seven days a week, though you must book in advance. **Park City Taxi** (800/649-8294, www.parkcitytaxi.com) also covers the Park City area and beyond.

Driving

If you rent a car at the Salt Lake City airport, you'll save a little time shuttling around Park City, but spend a little more money on parking. In the winter, be sure to get a vehicle with AWD/4WD and snow tires, especially if heavy snow is in the forecast. You can also opt to wait until you get to Park City to rent a car—there are a few national chains that operate near hotels in the Prospector area—where you'll find slightly cheaper rental fees. Of course, the cost of securing transportation to and from the airport may outweigh the savings of renting in Park City vs. the airport.

Parking can be a bit of an art form in Park City, depending on how busy a time of year it is, whether there's a major event taking place, and if snow is falling. Ample information about how and where to park is available online (www.parkcity.org/parking). Park City also now charges to park throughout Old Town (up until midnight) to encourage locals and visitors alike to take advantage of public transit options. There's usually free parking at ski area bases, but these can fill up by 9am or 10am, at which point you'll have to park at the Park City High School (1750 Kearns Blvd.) or other satellite lots, then take a shuttle back to the base.

Whether you road-tripped to Park City or are driving a rental car, the hardest times to navigate Park City are during busy events and weekends, when traffic can build up and parking becomes all but impossible. Congestion peaks during Sundance, when many roads close, parking fees skyrocket, and cars come to a standstill at busy intersections. The closer you are to Old Town Park City, the worse the traffic. During Sundance and other big festivals, the town typically sets up designated satellite parking lots with shuttles running to and from these lots and popular destinations like Kimball Junction or Old Town. The best strategy in general during Park City's busiest days is to use public transit, take advantage of available satellite lots, and practice patience.

Big and Little Cottonwood Canyons

An ancient ocean. Volcanoes spewing magma.

Relentless earthquakes. This is the recipe for the Cottonwood Canyons. Over the course of millions of years, these natural forces left behind rock walls, chutes, wide bowls, and other features that make for great skiing, climbing, and other activities beloved by those who call the Wasatch home, and still more who come to visit.

Not only are the Cottonwoods the backyard of Salt Lake, they're also its refuge from bad air. When the inversion strikes the city—usually in the winter—driving up into the Cottonwoods positions you above the smog. This is a good escape plan if you happen to be in Salt Lake City when the air quality deteriorates.

In addition to paralleling one another through the Wasatch Range,

Highlights

Look for ★ to find recommended sights, activities, dining, and lodging.

© MOON.COM

★ **Plunge into a powdery bowl** and enjoy some quiet at uncrowded **Solitude Mountain Resort** (page 161).

★ **Take an easy trek to Donut Falls,** a beautiful waterfall cascading through a doughnut-shaped hole in a shallow cave (page 166).

★ **Soak up history at the Silver Fork Lodge & Restaurant** while you devour

pancakes made with 70-year-old sourdough starter (page 168).

★ **Test your nerve** on a steep rock-climbing route on the **Hellgate Cliffs** in Little Cottonwood Canyon (page 175).

★ **Raise a beer stein** and join the festivities at magical **Oktoberfest,** held every fall at Snowbird Resort (page 178).

the Cottonwoods also share a lot of other common ground. Both are located within the Wasatch-Cache National Forest and offer trails, camping, and rock climbing. Both are home to two ski resorts each—Brighton and Solitude in Big, and Snowbird and Alta in Little. And through each canyon runs a creek sharing the name of the respective canyon.

One of the main differences between the two canyons is size, as their names indicate. Little Cottonwood might be bigger in the "go big or go home" vein, allowing skiers to brave gnarly chutes and huck cliffs. But it doesn't measure up in terms of sheer dimensions. Big Cottonwood is both wider and longer, stretching all the way from Salt Lake City to Park City. In the summer, you can drive through Big Cottonwood Canyon until it turns into Guardsman Pass, and end up on the backside of Deer Valley Resort. In the winter, the pass closes, but snowmobilers continue to traverse the route.

Both Cottonwood Canyons can become rather crowded on weekends in summer and winter. In the summer, you may encounter caravans of slow-moving vehicles, booked campgrounds, and busy trails. Winter is a whole different story, with frequent road closures due to avalanche danger and control, as well as powder day traffic. The best bet, as with most popular tourist destinations, is to visit in the off-season, on weekdays, or at odd hours. Even if you must battle crowds, it's worth it to spend a little time in Salt Lake's beloved canyons.

PLANNING YOUR TIME

A hike, day of skiing, or afternoon climbing session in Big or Little Cottonwood Canyon can easily be worked into a visit to Salt Lake City or Park City. Less than a 40-minute drive from Salt Lake City and under an hour from Park City, both Cottonwood Canyons make for quick getaways. In the summer, when Guardsman Pass opens up, driving into the

eastern end of Big Cottonwood from Park City is even faster. If your activity interests in the Cottonwoods span less than a day or two, stay in Salt Lake City and make your canyon excursions half-day or daylong trips.

If you're planning a ski vacation at one or more of the Cottonwood Canyon resorts, consider staying at one of the ski resort lodges within the canyons to make more efficient use of your time and beat the traffic to the fresh powder. Each canyon has two resorts. Once you commit to a canyon, you can stick to one resort or ski both since the resorts are close together.

Duplicate the same strategy in the summer if your goal is to get to know one or both of the canyons well. Pick a canyon and a resort inn or campground, and make the Cottonwoods your home away from home for however long you please. See all the lakes, climb all the routes on your list, and enjoy the amenities of the two resorts at your fingertips (aka get a massage and a drink after you summit that mountain).

Speaking of drinks, if you're a beer lover, consider visiting Little Cottonwood Canyon in the late summer/fall, when Snowbird Resort hosts two months of Oktoberfest. This might seem an unusual setting for a Bavaria-born celebration of beer, but there is a certain utilitarian, German vibe at Snowbird. Find it in the brutalist lodge, inside the Euro-inspired tram, or amid the big alpine feel evocative of the Alps found around the resort's higher terrain. Oktoberfest aside, the fall is a great time to be in the Cottonwoods to enjoy foliage and trails that are less crowded.

Like most mountainous areas, the Cottonwood Canyons experience off-seasons in the spring and fall. The fall off-season runs from around the time snow begins to fall until the ski resorts open. This varies year by year, but typically late October-late November is not an ideal time to visit, since it may be too cold or snowy to hike, while the ski resorts

---

Previous: alpine lake in Big Cottonwood Canyon; sasquatch at Silver Fork Lodge & Restaurant; The Cliff Lodge at Snowbird.

have yet to open. Early fall, however, is a great time to visit, with generally smaller crowds and beautiful leaves. The spring off-season is shorter in the Cottonwoods than in Park City because the canyons get more snow and the resorts stay open later—sometimes a lot later. While Park City and Deer Valley tend to halt their chairlifts in early April, Snowbird, for example, has been known to keep its ski runs open through early July on good snow years.

Whatever your plans, a helpful place to prepare for your trip to either or both Cottonwood Canyons is the **Salt Lake Ranger District** (6944 S. 3000 E., Salt Lake City, 801/733-2660, www.fs.usda.gov, 8am-4:30pm Mon.-Fri.). The office is located near the mouth of Big Cottonwood Canyon, and helpful resources and maps are available online as well.

Finally, because the Cottonwood Canyons serve as the watershed for the Salt Lake area, no dogs are permitted anywhere in either canyon. For this reason, if you plan to spend a lot of time in the Cottonwoods, it's best to leave your pup at home, or arrange boarding at a facility in Salt Lake City.

Big Cottonwood Canyon

Big Cottonwood Canyon is best known as the home of Solitude and Brighton ski resorts. In the summer, it's where many in Salt Lake City come to play on trails and big granite slabs. Locals and visitors alike spend nights outdoors, perch alongside alpine lakes, and discover what remains of the mining town of Silver Fork—namely, a small community, inn, and restaurant.

This canyon owes its existence to a medley of geologic forces playing out over the course of epochs. A billion years ago, the mouth of Big Cottonwood was the shore of an ancient ocean. This sea deposited sandstone, limestone, and marble along the shore and shallows. Volcanic activity resulted in the granite walls that climbers delight in today. Ice ages put the finishing touches on Big Cottonwood, filling some of the rock cavities with massive glaciers. When the glaciers melted, they left behind a U-shaped canyon, with plenty of rock walls to climb and basins to ski.

With slightly more gentle walls than Little Cottonwood, Big Cottonwood tends to have a reputation for being a less extreme skiing and climbing destination. While the two ski resorts here—Solitude and Brighton—do have plenty of extreme terrain, the steepest of pitches lie in Little Cottonwood. Big Cottonwood is also home to beautiful hiking, from short jaunts to waterfalls, to longer hauls up mountains.

SKIING

Big Cottonwood Canyon is home to two adjacent ski resorts, both with low-key reputations (in a good way), backcountry skiing, and an average of 500 inches (12.7 m) of snow a year. Brighton is known as a well-kept secret with plenty of beginner terrain and high-speed quads. Meanwhile, Solitude stays true to its name with little in the way of lift lines and a lot in the way of quiet untracked powder bowls that require just a little hiking.

★ Solitude Mountain Resort

Some people ski for the scene. Others ski for the snow. Still more ride for some combination of both. Whatever suits you is just fine. But if you count yourself among those seeking snow, not scene, **Solitude** (12000 Big Cottonwood Canyon Rd., Solitude, 801/534-1400, www.solitudemountain.com, tickets starting at $109) is definitely for you. This quieter resort of 82 runs in the Cottonwoods has been around since 1957, when a Moab uranium miner set in motion two chairlifts. Development occurred in fits and starts, and today Solitude has all the amenities one could want at a ski area, without the fuss.

Big and Little Cottonwood Canyons

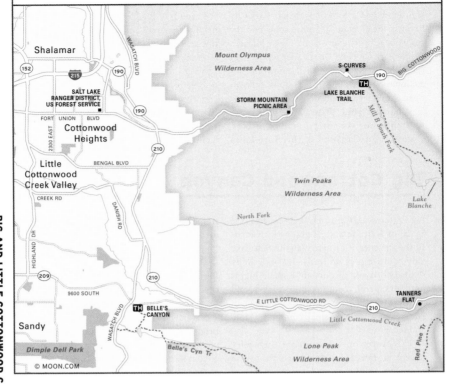

Another thing Solitude has plenty of is lift-accessed backcountry terrain, which makes the resort's name all the more apt. The out-of-bounds goods are accessible by taking the Summit Express lift and hiking along Fantasy Ridge to ski the double black chutes off Black Bess Peak, which top out at 10,479 feet (3,194 m). These chutes give way to powdery bowls that will have you hooting and hollering on good snow days.

While Solitude doesn't edge out Snowbird or Alta over in Little Cottonwood Canyon when it comes to extreme terrain, half of its 1,200 acres is considered advanced or for experts only. Excellent tree skiing can be found in the Headwall Forest. Intermediate skiers

will want to play around the Sunrise Lift area, or take Summit Express up to find flow on the longest run at Solitude, which spans over 2,000 vertical feet (610 m) from Woodlawn to the Honeycomb Return Trail. Beginners will have a great time off the Moonbeam Express lift, and might warm up for the day on Little Dollie, a long green.

Perhaps Solitude's best-kept secret is its **Nordic Center** ($20 per trail user per day) at the base, with 20 kilometers (12.4 mi) of classic and skate-skiing trails, as well as 10 kilometers (6.2 mi) of trails designated for snowshoers. For a couple or family with mixed skiing interests, the co-location of downhill and Nordic skiing is a welcome amenity.

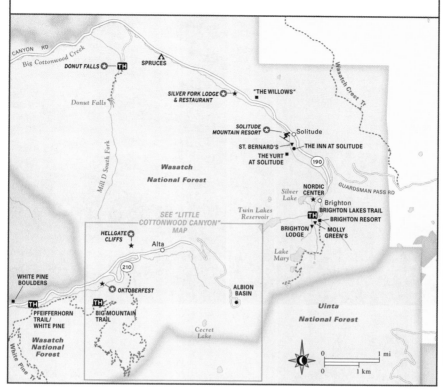

Brighton

If you're the impatient type, **Brighton** (8302 S. Brighton Loop Rd., Brighton, 801/532-4731, https://brightonresort.com, tickets starting at $94) stakes a claim to being the only resort in Utah where you can access all of its 66 runs via high-speed quads. With those uninitiated to ski industry lingo, that means a chairlift that can accommodate four people and gets you to the top of the hill fast. Brighton is also known for being a more locally oriented mountain, with little in the way of advertising. The ski resort takes its name from Scottish immigrant William Stuart Brighton, who arrived in Utah in 1855. Nearly a decade later, he established the Brighton Hotel, which became a place for people to escape the city to explore and relax

in nature. Though the hotel is long gone, it served as the foundation of today's resort.

What else sets Brighton apart? For one, its **terrain parks.** By far, Brighton has the best terrain parks in the Cottonwood Canyons, stretching from just shy of the top of the mountain down to the base area. Another reason to head to Brighton is **night skiing.** Some 200 acres and three lifts—plus the terrain park—stay open until 9pm Monday-Saturday December-April. Brighton even offers lessons at night! That means you could feasibly ski for 12 hours straight with the purchase of one ticket if you're so motivated. Brighton also probably has the healthiest balance in the Cottonwood Canyons of beginner, intermediate, and advanced terrain, as

well as backcountry access via six points on the mountain.

Backcountry Skiing

Like its resorts, Big Cottonwood Canyon has backcountry skiing that's a little more mellow than that found at its sister canyon. Some of the best backcountry terrain lies adjacent to and accessible via Solitude Resort. Brighton also offers six backcountry access points so you can do more turning and less earning. And whether you're skiing the backcountry accessed from a trailhead or via the resort, always remember to bring avalanche rescue gear that you know how to use, travel with a trusted partner, and heed the avalanche forecast (https://utahavalanchecenter.org).

If you'd rather not buy a lift ticket, you can also find excellent backcountry skiing across from Solitude in the Willow Fork area and its surroundings—known locally as "The Willows" (2.5 mi/4 km one-way, 3-4 hours, 1,700 ft/518 m elevation gain, moderate). Here you'll find lower-angle terrain that tends to stay safe when the avalanche risk is high. Park at the Willow Heights trailhead or at the lower Solitude parking lot. Head up the skin track, and when you top out, follow the ridgeline to your descent of choice, which includes tree skiing, mellow pitches, and several dreamy basins like USA Bowl and No Name Bowl.

ROCK CLIMBING

While both Cottonwood Canyons have extensive rock climbing, Big Cottonwood is the less popular of the two. But don't let that fool you. From one end to the other, crags of quartzite beckon, with sport and trad climbs aplenty. Big Cottonwood also has some bouldering as well as a few ice climbs and alpine-style climbs. I asked local climbing enthusiast Jeffrey McCarthy, the author of *Contact: Mountain Climbing and Environmental Thinking,* for some of his

favorite routes in the canyon, and he offered a few recommendations.

S-Curves

In the northern part of Big Cottonwood, the road traces the shape of an "S." Here you'll find four big crags, largely composed of steep sport routes in a variety of grades. This area does tend to draw crowds, due to a short approach and ample protection. But you can elude them if you seek out a hidden gem like **Skyscraper** (5.8+, 170 ft/52 m) on the upper wall. Start by driving 4.25 miles (6.8 km) from the mouth of the canyon, parking in the pullout, and crossing the road to find the Mill B North Fork approach trail. After you pass the third switchback up, head east and follow the trajectory of the Lower Wall. At the end of this wall, you'll find another trail that climbs up a gully toward the Upper Wall. When you reach a boulder, stay right. Skyscraper is a long, exposed climb that requires a 70-meter rope, nine quickdraws, and material to build a tree anchor at the top. Jeff says to expect "spicy route finding" and, once you top out, panoramic views of Big Cottonwood Canyon.

Storm Mountain Picnic Area

The **Storm Mountain Picnic Area** ($5 entrance fee) is the unofficial hub of climbing in Big Cottonwood, with over 70 climbs running the gamut from bouldering and trad to ice come winter. It's also easy to find since—as its name suggests—Storm Mountain doubles as a picnic area with bathrooms. The area can be found 2.85 miles (4.6 km) up the canyon on the left; just look for signs and park in the designated lot. If you park alongside the road, the day-use fee is waived.

One of the absolute classics here is **Goodro's Wall** (5.10c, trad, one pitch), which some say was the first 5.10 climbed in the United States. Local climber and climbing instructor Harold Goodro—also former head of the ski patrol at Alta—bagged the First Ascent in 1949. Find this climb in the subarea dubbed Storm Mountain Island, where you'll also find the first sport route in Big

---

1: Big Cottonwood Canyon in the fall **2:** Donut Falls
3: Lake Blanche

Cottonwood (a mild 5.4). To reach the Island crag, cross the bridge and take one of the obvious short trails until you end up scrambling through a talus field. Bring nuts and cams 2 inches (5 cm) and smaller for protection. Goodro's is one of Jeff's favorite climbs because it flows nicely "so long as you can hang in there to place the gear." Enjoy the hand crack and watch out for the roof!

HIKING

Venture to reach waterfalls, mountain peaks, and alpine lakes—or just hike for the sake of hiking. There are many trails in Big Cottonwood to enjoy, several of which remain accessible by snowshoes in the winter. The spring and late fall, however, can be difficult times to hike since trails will likely be muddy from early or melting snow.

★ Donut Falls

You definitely get your mile's worth at **Donut Falls** (3 mi/4.8 km round-trip, 1.5 hours, 530 ft/162 m elevation gain, easy). A mellow, short hike is rewarded with a beautiful waterfall that cascades through a doughnut-shaped hole in a shallow cave. To get to the trailhead, drive about 9 miles (14.5 km) from the entrance to the canyon and turn right on Forest Road 019 toward the Jordan Pines picnic area. The trailhead is easy to find and follow—stay left at the fork you'll encounter.

Due to its ease and convenience, this trail attracts quite a few hikers in the summer. One way to get around this problem is to hike Donut Falls in the winter, when the waterfall freezes. If fresh snow hasn't fallen recently, the snow usually gets packed down enough to make this trail traversable with sturdy, waterproof hiking boots. But if there's a lot of snow on the ground, consider using snowshoes. During the winter and early spring, the Forest Service road that accesses the trailhead may be fully or partially closed. In this case, you can park on Big Cottonwood Canyon Road and hike the road to the trailhead.

If you want a longer hike, make Donut Falls a stop, not a destination. You can turn a 3-mile

(4.8-km) round-trip hike into a 9-mile (14.5-km) and 2,903-foot (885-m) climb by continuing on the road past the falls to **Kessler Peak Trail** (9 mi/14.5 km round-trip, 6-8 hours depending on pace, 2,903 ft/885 m elevation gain, difficult). To Kessler's 10,403-foot (3,171-m) summit, it's a steep climb without switchbacks that does involve a little scrambling toward the top, so be prepared to take breaks if needed. When you reach the top, enjoy the 360-degree views of both Cottonwoods, Salt Lake City, and even as far as the Uinta Range.

Lake Blanche

You know those nature panoramas that look unreal even with no filter? You can take one of them at **Lake Blanche** (7 mi/11.3 km round-trip, 3-4 hours, 2,700 ft/823 m elevation gain, moderate). The combination of turquoise water, Sundial Peak towering right over the lake, and a bouquet of forest that lights up in autumn make this a very photogenic spot. The trail begins near Brighton Resort starting from the Mill B South Fork Trailhead. Follow signs for Lake Blanche. You'll be hiking through aspen and conifer trees alongside a creek, passing the occasional waterfall. While there are a couple of other lakes at the top of this hike, Lake Blanche is the main attraction, and does require some steep hiking to get there. After you take your #nofilter picture and bask in the views, enjoy a little sunshine on one of the sloping rocks surrounding Lake Blanche. This is a great place to read a book or have a little picnic before embarking on the return trip.

Brighton Lakes Trail

See three lakes in one go in under 5 miles (8 km) on the **Brighton Lakes Trail** (4.5 mi/7.2 km round-trip, 2-3 hours depending on pace, 1,200 ft/366 m. elevation gain, moderate). The trail starts from the east end of the Brighton parking lot behind the Mt. Majestic Lodge. Follow signs for Lake Mary and Lake Catherine. First up, after about 1 mile (1.6 km), is Lake Mary, which is actually a reservoir and the biggest of the three lakes. About a half mile (0.8 km) later, you'll catch views of Lake Martha, the smallest of the three lakes. From here, the trail gets steeper as you head up Catherine's Pass for another half mile (0.8 km) until you reach Lake Catherine. Take in views of the Cottonwoods and the five mountains surrounding Lake Catherine before turning around. In late June and early July, the wildflowers on this trail are stunning.

BIKING

Neither Big nor Little Cottonwood Canyon is known for its phenomenal biking, but you can find a few dozen miles of trails around some of the ski resorts, some of which can be accessed by chairlift.

Solitude Trails

One of the best bets for mountain biking in Big Cottonwood is **Solitude Mountain Resort** (12000 Big Cottonwood Canyon Rd., Solitude, 801/534-1400, www.solitudemountain.com). Lift-serviced biking (10am-6pm daily, $30 day pass, bike rentals start at $60 per day) is open approximately mid-June-September depending on weather and conditions, though trails can also be traversed without a lift for free. Enjoy over 20 miles (32 km) of single-track with a good mix of beginner,

intermediate, and advanced trails. For a fully bike-powered, advanced loop from Solitude Village (8 mi/12.9 km round-trip, 1-2 hours, 1,400 ft/427 m elevation gain, moderate), take Raptor Road to Serenity Trail to Queen Bess. When Queen Bess dead-ends at Roadhouse, hang a right, and after a little less than half a mile (0.8 km), turn right again onto Eagle Ridge—an out-and-back. After you ride Eagle Ridge back down, turn right on Raptor Road to head back to the base.

FOOD

Aside from the litany of dining options at Brighton and Solitude ski resorts (a mixed bag just like all ski resort dining), there's a culinary relic of busier times here in Big Cottonwood that's a must-visit for guests who like a side of history with their breakfast or dinner.

Solitude Mountain Resort

Take a guided snowshoe tour through the woods for an enchanting four-course dinner at **The Solitude Yurt** (12000 Big Cottonwood Canyon Rd., Solitude, 801/536-5765, www.solitudemountain.com/yurt, meet at Powderhorn Adventure Center at 5:30pm Thurs.-Sun. Dec.-early-Apr., $140 pp, alcohol

riding near the summit of Solitude

☆ A Side of History at the Silver Fork

When the **Silver Fork Lodge & Restaurant** (11332 E. Big Cottonwood Canyon Rd., Brighton, 801/533-9977, www.silverforklodge.com, 8am-9pm daily, $19-40, rooms starting at $130 per night) was built in the mid-19th century, things were very different in its surrounding area of the Silver Fork Canyon drainage than they are today. While only around 120 people call Silver Fork home currently, in the 1850s, this was a bustling town of 2,500. Drawn by work in mines and sawmills, people slept in tents and, after long days of physical labor, drank in one of Silver Fork's eight saloons. By the 1880s, after most of the accessible mineral had been extracted, the main livelihood up Big Cottonwood transitioned from mining to ranching.

Nowadays, skiing and hiking are bigger industries than ranching or mining ever were. Yet the Silver Fork, once a general store, still stands in its original spot. Of course, this lodge has been restored and renovated over the years, but you'll still find historical details, like wood beams from one of the mines in the dining room ceiling, old photographs of the lodge's former life, and 1940s-era

sourdough pancakes at the Silver Fork Lodge & Restaurant

tile. Another antique at the Silver Fork is actually edible. The restaurant's sourdough starter has been around for over seven decades and adds historic tang that improves with time to everything from bread to pancakes.

In the summer, the Silver Fork is a great place to stop for lunch or a hearty breakfast after camping—breakfast is also included with every stay at the lodge. Aside from the sourdough specials, you'll find standard breakfast fare, and for lunch and dinner, an American grill menu with some local flavors like trout or Southwestern spicing. A full espresso bar plus a liquor license mean you can pair that miner's breakfast with a cappuccino or Bloody Mary if you please.

If you decide to stay at Silver Fork, book early—it offers just seven rooms, each with a unique array of log cabin-style furnishings. Think wood furniture, wood-burning stoves, quilts, and no TVs. If you're traveling with kids, book the family suite that includes an adjoining room with twin bunk beds. In addition to the complimentary breakfast, the lodge offers a library lounge as well as a sauna.

Just under a mile (1.6 km) west of Solitude Resort and a couple miles down the road from Brighton, Silver Fork is a great place to stay to escape the more crowded resort lodging, or get away for a few sips of Cottonwood history.

extra, ages 13+). This fabulous experience is well suited for a special occasion or splurge meal during a trip. Once inside the toasty yurt, the chefs will prepare an elegant dinner on-site. The menu changes frequently, but leans new American. Expect dishes like shrimp-cucumber gazpacho, apricot ravioli, and caramelized onion tart. Advance reservations are required.

If snowshoeing to your food doesn't sound like your idea of fun, another great option

at Solitude Resort is **St. Bernard's** (12000 Big Cottonwood Canyon Rd., 801/534-1400, www.solitudemountain.com, breakfast 7am-10am daily, dinner 4:30pm-9pm Wed.-Sun., breakfast $18 adults, dinner $42 adults). This base area restaurant is a touch upscale and has a wine list worthy of a recent *Wine Spectator* award. Don't let the fact that St. Bernard's is buffet-style dining make you think twice—this is about as high-end as smorgasbords come, hopping around Europe for inspiration and served alongside a live fire. If you're visiting in the summer, ask to sit on the deck. Adjacent to St. Bernard's is the Library Bar, which serves small plates and a fine drink menu in a bookish space with oversized chairs beholding sunset views.

Brighton

Brighton ski resort is the opposite of hoity-toity, and so is its mountain pub **Molly Green's** (8302 S. Brighton Loop Rd., Brighton, 801/532-4731, https://brightonresort.com, 11am-9pm Mon.-Sat., 11am-5pm Sun., $12-14). You can ski right to this casual restaurant and waltz in with ski boots and all, if you please. Housed inside an A-frame, Molly's gets the mountain feel on-point, with a taxidermy deer mounted on the wall and a central stone wood-fired stove that keeps the inside nice and toasty. The food isn't extraordinary, but it's exactly what you crave after skiing powder or going for a big bike ride in the summer. Cravings for copious amounts of melted cheese can easily be met with the nachos or hand-tossed pizzas.

ACCOMMODATIONS

Your primary lodging options in Big Cottonwood include the historic Silver Fork Lodge & Restaurant and several options at the resorts. If you choose to stay in an Airbnb or condo and cook your own food, plan to stock up on groceries while in Salt Lake City or Park City, since the only grocery options available within Big Cottonwood Canyon are convenience stores.

Solitude Mountain Resort

Solitude Resort owns and manages several different lodging options, ranging from condos and townhomes to The Inn at Solitude (www.solitudemountain.com/lodging, lodging@solitudemountain.com). The resort also offers several ski-lodging packages. Most resort-owned lodging includes amenities like complimentary locker space at the base area and access to Club Solitude, which offers an

outdoor heated pool, saunas, and game rooms for kids.

If you want to go high-end, head to ★ **The Inn at Solitude** (12000 Big Cottonwood Canyon Rd., Solitude, 801/517-7717, www.solitudemountain.com, starting at $175 in summer and $277 in winter). Located right at the base of Solitude, this 46-room lodge melds old-world charm with standard luxury amenities like ski-in/ski-out access and a spa. If you're a package person, there are some great add-ons to wrap into your stay, from early lift access to wine tastings and spa services, including a deep tissue massage that's just what you need after a big ski day. The Solitude Inn also offers a number of free amenities, including outdoor yoga sessions, astronomy talks, and family movie nights.

If you like the familiarity of a hotel yet the space and freedom of a condo, consider the **Powderhorn Lodge** (12000 Big Cottonwood Canyon Rd., Bldg. 3, Ste. A, Solitude, 801/536-5765, www.solitudemountain.com, starting at $250 in summer, $300 in winter). With a mix of one- to three-bedroom condos, Powderhorn is a great option for families or groups. Each condo is equipped with a full kitchen and gas fireplace, and some units also feature private balconies, mountain views, and dining spaces. The condos are simply designed with a country cottage feel. Beyond the convenience of being able to cook your own breakfast before hitting the mountain, you can also buy lift tickets, rent skis, and book adventures from within the lodge—the Powderhorn Adventure Center is located on the first floor, right next to the lodge's bar.

Brighton

In keeping with Brighton Resort's low-key reputation, the 20-room **Brighton Lodge** (8302 S. Brighton Loop Rd., Brighton, 855/201-7669, ext. 120, https://brightonresort.com, starting at $79 per night) is nothing fancy, but a great, affordable place to spend the night if you're skiing Brighton a few days in a row. Enjoy the convenience of ski-in/ski-out access and a complimentary continental breakfast, along with the pleasant atmosphere established by a bright space and Southwestern fabrics.

CAMPING

If you're visiting Big Cottonwood in the summertime, there are a couple of developed campgrounds and many dispersed sites as well. If you're hoping to find a dispersed site or do a little backpacking, make sure you stop at the **Salt Lake Ranger District** (6944 S. 3000 E., Salt Lake City, 801/733-2660, www. fs.usda.gov, 8am-4:30pm Mon.-Fri.), located just before the mouth of the canyon off Fort Union Boulevard, to get maps and recommendations from the Forest Service for areas that permit camping.

★ **Spruces** (435/649-7534, 92 sites, starting at $26 per night, bathrooms and water available) is a large campground with a mix of single, double, and group sites all loaded with amenities, from campfire rings with grill grates to potable water and a volleyball court. You can even buy firewood here from the campground host on-site. Spruces is located 9.7 miles (15.6 km) from the mouth of the canyon. While RVs are permitted at some sites, there are no electric hookups. The campground's springtime opening is dependent on conditions, but it typically opens up in early June, and gets busy soon after. Spruces usually stays open through October, and due to its location in a forest of spruce and aspens, fall is a quiet and gorgeous time to camp here.

GETTING THERE AND AROUND

From downtown **Salt Lake City,** it's about 16 miles (26 km) and a 25-minute drive to the mouth of Big Cottonwood Canyon, accessed by I-215 South, which is the highway that runs closest to the Wasatch Mountains from Salt Lake City. I-215 South is accessible from I-80 as well as several outlying areas southeast of Salt Lake.

The road that runs through Big Cottonwood begins as **Fort Union Boulevard** and turns into **Highway 190.** This state highway runs nearly 20 miles (32 km) until it meets Deer Valley and turns into **Guardsman Pass,** which is only open in the summer. It will take you about 40 minutes to drive the whole length of Highway 190, and longer in winter conditions. The Solitude and Brighton resorts lie toward the far, eastern end of the road close to Deer Valley.

To access Big Cottonwood Canyon from the **Park City** side during summer, head southeast on Main Street and turn left on

Spruces Campground

Hillside Avenue, then take your first right onto Marsac Avenue, which is actually an extension of Highway 224. You'll drive past the Deer Valley base areas and lodging. Shortly after you pass the Montage hotel on your right, the road turns into Guardsman Pass. It's around 5 miles (8 km) and a 15-minute drive from Old Town to the mouth of Big Cottonwood Canyon in the summer.

Because Guardsman Pass is not plowed for snow, it usually closes in late October or early November and reopens in late May or early June, depending on the year. The **Utah Department of Transportation** (https://udottraffic.utah.gov) notifies the public about the pass's opening/closing dates. Due to the pass closure, to reach Big Cottonwood Canyon

from Park City in the wintertime, you'll need to take the long way there via I-80.

In the summer, you need a car to access Big Cottonwood, but if you're coming to ski and staying in Salt Lake, you can ride the **UTA Ski Bus** (801/743-3882, www.rideuta.com, Routes 953, 972, and 994, $4.50 one-way, buses run every 15-30 minutes approx. 6am-8:30pm) from Salt Lake City. The three different Ski Bus routes stop at various Trax light rail stations and prominent points in the city. If you do opt to rent a car to head into Big Cottonwood Canyon during the winter, be sure to get one with AWD/4WD and snow tires. Not only is this important for your own safety, but it's often required by the Utah Department of Transportation when a snowstorm strikes.

Little Cottonwood Canyon

Don't let its name fool you. Little Cottonwood ranks senior to its sister canyon in many ways. It's got a geologically based reputation for being steep and extreme in the goggled eyes of skiers. For the canyon's steep pitches, skiers can thank earthquakes, which slashed precipitous faults into the rock millennia ago. This is actually one of the more recent geologic events in Little Cottonwood's history. Some of the oldest rocks here trace their roots back 1.6 billion years. Like Big Cottonwood Canyon, Little Cottonwood owes its shape to a massive glacier, which, at 12 miles (19.3 km) long, was the biggest and longest in the Wasatch Mountains. And its former location as ancient shore and sea means Little Cottonwood features rock built from prehistoric deposits of clay and sand.

Like Big Cottonwood, Little Cottonwood was home to a thriving population soon after silver was discovered and then staked in 1865. While a few hundred people still call Alta home, it was once the residence of thousands of people, many of whom worked in the mining industry. This population boom led to

severe deforestation that left much of Little Cottonwood tree-less. In the 1930s, a reforestation effort began that is still ongoing today. You can learn a little more about the history of this area at the **Alta Community Center** (10351 E. Hwy. 210, Alta, 801/742-3522, https://townofalta.com, 9am-1pm Mon.-Sat.), which doubles as a library and post office with a historical society exhibit on display. When you live in a town of 400, you co-locate your services!

Today, Little Cottonwood Canyon draws locals and tourists who wish to ski, climb, and explore its trails and wilderness. Little Cottonwood is home to two ski areas, Alta and Snowbird, which are physically connected. There's also steep backcountry skiing to be had here. Come summer, drive through the canyon on the weekend and you're bound to spot climbers working their way up walls of granite.

SKIING

While Utah in general lays claim to "The Greatest Snow on Earth" (a trademarked

Little Cottonwood Canyon

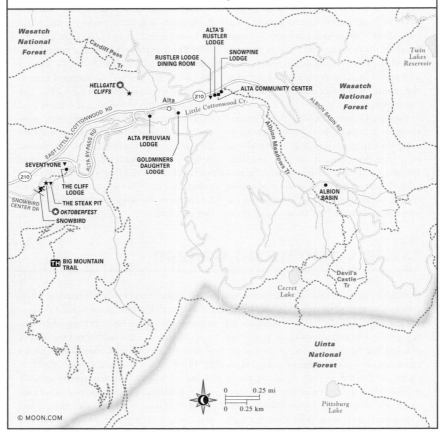

phrase), Alta and Snowbird boast the best snow in the state. While I'm sure there are skiers world- and state-wide who would counter this claim, a perfect storm of conditions does indeed conspire to bless Little Cottonwood with an obscene amount of snow every winter. We're talking some 500 inches (1,270 cm) of snow a season. That's over 40 feet (12 m), or enough to bury your average two-story house twice over.

Utah in general is well positioned because the Wasatch Range consists of the first major mountains that Pacific storms encounter after the Sierras. But by the time these storms arrive, they've lost a lot of their moisture, making for the light, fluffy powder that skiers' dreams are made of. The Cottonwoods specifically also benefit from the lake effect, thanks to the Great Salt Lake, which makes for colder air. Finally, the geometry of the Cottonwood Canyons—Little, in particular—is such that they tend to capture as much snow as possible. Basically, sharp changes in elevation—like those found in canyons—result in more snow. And in the Cottonwoods, there's nowhere for the moisture to escape. The shade afforded by steep canyon walls also helps reduce the harm caused by the melt-freeze cycle on snow quality.

So, who gets more: Alta or Snowbird? It's a toss-up. And if you're that concerned about it, spend a little extra money when you buy your lift ticket and you can ski them both, since they're physically connected with just a little gate in between.

Snowbird

Snowbird (9385 S. Snowbird Center Dr., Snowbird, 801/933-2222, www.snowbird. com, 9am-4:30pm daily, tickets starting at $125) is known for having the most extreme terrain in the Cottonwoods, if not in Utah and the United States at large. Annually, it hosts the Freeride World Tour, where skiers and snowboarders from all over the world navigate big mountain terrain: steep chutes, big cliffs, and big consequences. Yet with 140 runs, there's plenty to ski at Snowbird that doesn't involve any of those things. Snowbird also has a unique futurist European vibe set by avant-garde concrete structures, an aerial tram, and Helvetica font on just about every sign you see.

The **aerial tram** is an efficient way to reach the highest point at Snowbird, but at peak season, it can be a pretty rough ride to the top. The tram is an experience everyone should tick off during a Snowbird ski vacation, but be warned: Once you're done waiting in line, you'll be crammed into a large rectangular space, shoulder to shoulder with your fellow riders.

From the top of the tram, you can access the backside of Snowbird, namely **Mineral Basin,** serviced by two lifts. The sunny bowls back here are the place to be on a powder day, particularly if you're willing to traverse a ways. Mineral Basin is also where you can connect to the Alta ski area. While you can access Mineral Basin from the top of the tram, you can also get there by riding up the Peruvian Lift and entering the very cool Peruvian Tunnel, with historic displays and a moving walkway. Once you're in Mineral Basin, the Baldy and Mineral Basin Lifts let you lap the powder until your quads are burning.

Intermediate skiers will have fun on the playful terrain off the Gadzoom Lift, while beginners will want to stick to the Baby Thunder and Wilbere Lifts. Wherever you ski, if you're not an expert, heed signage carefully so you don't get cliffed out, or find yourself mistakenly on the terrain that the Freeride World Tour athletes launch down.

snowy day at Snowbird

Alta

Adjacent to Snowbird, **Alta** (10010 Little Cottonwood Canyon Rd., Alta, 801/359-1078, www.alta.com, 9:15am-4:30pm daily, tickets starting at $116) is also known for its epic snowfall and fair share of steep terrain and backcountry access. But its roots stretch back much further than Snowbird's. Alta set the second chairlift in the nation in motion back in 1938—runner-up only to what is now known as Sun Valley in Idaho. Back then, Alta was the only ski resort in Utah and a lift ride was just a quarter a pop. Many decades later, the price is about 400 times that.

Aside from history, Alta is also known for its ban on snowboarding, like its compatriot Deer Valley to the east. With a heritage that stretches back decades and a commitment to the original snow sport, Alta does have a "purist" vibe, which may appeal to some and not others. Those who love the history and gumption that define Alta are fully devoted to the ski area, earning the nickname "Altaholics."

Of Alta's 119 runs, over half are considered advanced. Expert skiers will have fun on **Alf's High Rustler,** which allows one to descend the full vertical drop of the canyon's south wall. The pitch starts steep, but mellows out, and ample shade preserves snow quality. Intermediate skiers can get their turns in on the wide **Devil's Elbow** run, with a relatively consistent grade the whole way down.

Among all the resorts in Utah, Alta also holds the distinction of being a leader in sustainability. Alta even has an environmental center, which hosts events like snowshoe tours led by naturalists and sponsors programs like SKE-COLOGY, which allows visitors and especially kids to explore Alta's ecology through self-guided tours, signage, and teacher workshops.

Backcountry Skiing

Opportunities to ski the backcountry in Little Cottonwood Canyon are many. **Snowbird** has two backcountry access gates. One lies off the Gad 2 chairlift and takes you into the **White Pine Touring Area,** where you can ski the **Birthday Chutes.** The other access gate lies just past the Mineral Basin chairlift and takes you into **American Fork Canyon.** However, at Snowbird, the inbound terrain is almost better than whatever you'll find past the access gates, with the added bonuses of less hiking and safer skiing thanks to avalanche control. You can also book a guided backcountry tour at **Snowbird** (801/471-4387, starting at $415 pp). At **Alta,** you can access the backcountry from the top of Supreme Lift in the Catherine's Pass area—though you'll have to skin back up to return to the resort. You can also explore the **Grizzly Gulch** backcountry, adjacent to Alta, via guided out-of-bounds tours through **Utah Mountain Adventures** (801/550-3986, www.utahmountainadventures.com, starting at $395 pp).

If you're an experienced backcountry skier, you can also access Grizzly Gulch via Flagstaff Ridge. And if you're an extremely experienced, skilled backcountry skier, pick up a copy of Andrew McLean's *The Chuting Gallery,* a guide to the backcountry chutes of both Cottonwood Canyons, heavily weighted toward Little. With a foreword from the late mountaineer Alex Lowe, the locally beloved book details over 20 steep chutes in Little Cottonwood to tick off your skiing bucket list. Of course, always "know before you go." Check avalanche conditions prior to heading out and assess snowpack once you're on top of your objective (www.utahavalanchecenter.org).

AERIAL TRAM

The **Snowbird aerial tram** (9am-3:45am daily winter, rides included in winter lift tickets; 11am-6pm daily spring-fall though closing hours may vary according to the sunset, $28 per adult per day spring-fall) is both a very efficient way to get to the top of the mountain and a scenic, breathtaking ride, depending on the season. While the tram closes down for a couple weeks in late spring and toward the end of October for maintenance, it otherwise runs year-round.

The tram takes passengers from the main base area up a 1.6-mile (2.6 km) cable, climbing 2,900 feet (884 m) to the highest point at Snowbird: Hidden Peak, elevation 11,000 feet (3,353 m). The ride takes about 10 minutes and beholds sweeping views of Little Cottonwood Canyon and the mountains rising out of it.

From the top, you can ski Snowbird's front side or drop into Mineral Basin. If it's summertime, you can mountain bike to the bottom or hike the surrounding trails. And if it's just the views you're looking for, you can grab a drink or some food at the Summit dining area.

In the winter, you won't want to ride the tram just to take in the views. It's a utilitarian way to the top, and Snowbird packs in the skiers and riders shoulder-to-shoulder so that you can barely see out the window—let alone breathe! It's not always the most pleasant experience, but it is a memorable one. To avoid crowds in the winter, consider riding on a weekday, at lunchtime, or at the end of the day. In the summer and fall, the ride up the tram offers 360-degree views and a fun, family-friendly activity.

ROCK CLIMBING

Little Cottonwood is known for pearl-white granite walls, slab climbing, and steep cracks that will wear you out in a good way. I turned again to Jeffrey McCarthy, local climbing enthusiast and author of *Contact: Mountain Climbing and Environmental Thinking,* for recommendations.

★ Hellgate Cliffs

Unlike the majority of rock in Little Cottonwood, Hellgate offers hard climbing on limestone cliffs. This area is not very "clean," meaning you'll find a fair amount of loose rock, which makes helmets non-negotiable. Because of this loose rock, strong winds, and the primarily multi-pitch routes, this is not a beginner-friendly or mellow place to climb. If Hellgate still sounds up your alley, find these cliffs 9 miles (14.5 km) up the canyon on the left side of the road across from Alta's

Peruvian Lodge. Jeff's go-to climb here is **Hellraiser** (5.10b, mixed, 500 ft/152 m, five pitches). Emerge victorious above the arete, cracks, and slab, and you'll be on the same level as the local mountain goats, with superb views of the ski resorts across the road.

White Pine Boulders

Boulderers of all stripes can find fun problems in the White Pine Bouldering area. Just under 5 miles (8 km) up the canyon, there's a pullout by a rock wall on the left side of the road. From this pullout, you can access several different subsets of the White Pine Boulders, whether you head north or south. A classic area is the **Party Pit,** which can be found south of the pullout after crossing the logs over Little Cottonwood Creek. Among the southern White Pine Boulders, the Party Pit cluster can be found in the middle. Mom Boulder—distinguishable by hash marks across its surface—has a few classics at various grades. Beginners can boogie up Deserter (V1), while more advanced climbers can test their nerve on the crimpy After Party (V7). Just right of Mom Boulder is the Party Pit Roof Boulder, which offers both a more moderate mantle problem (V4) and a more challenging yet juggy roof (V6-).

HIKING

There's no shortage of trails to explore on foot in Little Cottonwood, from short jaunts to waterfalls and reservoirs, to daylong summit bids. Generally, summer and fall are great times to hike in Little Cottonwood. You can still tackle some hikes in the winter, though you may need snowshoes. Early to mid-spring and late fall are not ideal times to hike, since new and melting snow creates muddy conditions.

Cecret Lake

Only have a couple hours to hike in Little Cottonwood? Make your objective **Cecret Lake** (1.7 mi/2.7 km round-trip, 1.5 hours, 459 ft/140 m elevation gain, easy). This short hike involves only moderate elevation gain

rewarded by gorgeous lakes surrounded by mountains and often frequented by moose. Some of the hike is even paved, making it very accessible for families with young children and less physically fit folks. In late June and early July, the wildflowers here are among the best in the state. Accessibility and beauty conspire to make this hike and Cecret Lake in general rather crowded during peak season and hours, but it's worth the quick jaunt nonetheless.

The lake is accessed via the Albion Basin Trailhead; starting from the mouth of the canyon, follow Highway 210/Little Cottonwood Road for 10 miles (16.1 km) until it turns into the unpaved Albion Basin Road. Continue for another 2.6 miles (4.2 km) and park in the Cecret Lake parking lot on your right.

Devil's Castle Trail

The trail to the sinister-looking peak that is **Devil's Castle** (3.3 mi/5.3 km round-trip, 3-4 hours depending on pace, 1,482 ft/452 m elevation gain, moderate) starts from the same trailhead as Cecret Lake, the Albion Basin Trailhead. Once you reach Cecret Lake about three-quarters of a mile (1.2 km) in, continue along the east side of the lake, ascending the ridge above the lake, to get to the base of Devil's Castle. Once you reach the base, you can perch on a rock and take in the views before turning back, though some climbers opt to scramble along the ridgeline on some mild fifth-class climbing (graded 5.2-5.5) to reach the three summits of the Castle. Another option is to ride Snowbird's aerial tram up and traverse east over the summits of Mount Baldy and Sugarloaf to reach Devil's Castle (4 mi/6.4 km round-trip, 3 hours).

Bells Canyon

If you've got around half a day to spend on a hike, venture into the Lone Peak Wilderness via **Bells Canyon** (4.6 mi/7.4 km round-trip, 2-3 hours, 1,500 ft/457 m elevation gain,

moderate). This trail is easy to access and can be knocked out in a morning or afternoon. Located just past the entrance into Little Cottonwood Canyon on the right side of the road, Bells Canyon Trail is great for those who love being by water. It takes you past a couple of reservoirs, follows a creek for a spell, and leads you to a translucent, ethereal waterfall plunging over granite surrounded by, well, a lot more granite. The reservoirs are nice places to stop for a snack or a little rest. Most of the hiking is moderate, but the final approach to the waterfall is rather steep, so use caution.

Pfeifferhorn Trail

For a tougher adventure in Little Cottonwood, consider bagging **Mount Pfeifferhorn** (11,326 ft/3,452 m), the third-highest peak in the Wasatch Range, runner-up to Mount Timpanogos and Mount Nebo. The hike to its summit (9.6 mi/15.4 km round-trip, 7-9 hours, 3,676 ft/1,120 m elevation gain, difficult) is not technical, but is a physical challenge with some scrambling involved. Start from the White Pine Trailhead, which lies 6.8 miles (10.9 km) up the canyon on the right-hand side of the road. The journey to Pfeifferhorn takes you into the Lone Peak Wilderness and is a colorful one, with Red Pine Lake en route and wildflowers if you're there at the right time (the flowers usually bloom in July and August). The last part of the hike—like most summits—follows the ridgeline to the peak, with a little bit of scrambling involved. But once you reach the top, views of the Cottonwoods, Salt Lake, and Mount Timpanogos await.

BIKING

Due to Little Cottonwood's popularity with hikers and a dearth of bike-only trails, the canyon is not the best place to bike in the Wasatch, particularly during peak crowds. If you do want to mountain bike, the hands-down best place to do so is Snowbird, which offers lift-accessed biking and a few bike-only trails.

1: welcome sign at Alta 2: climbing at Hellgate Cliffs 3: the top of the aerial tram at Snowbird

Snowbird Single-track

Snowbird (9385 S. Snowbird Center Dr., Snowbird, 801/933-2222, www.snowbird.com) is one of the ski resorts in Utah that turns into a mountain biking destination come summer. While this isn't the best riding in the Wasatch, you can string together a scenic and exhilarating loop along the 26 trails here. And if you aren't coming with your own bike, you can rent all the equipment you need right at the 'Bird (bike rentals start at $70 for 3 hours). If you only want to ride single-track and are looking for a shorter loop, stick to the lower-mountain trails, namely, the blue-rated single-track around the base area—but you won't get much in the way of climbing or views. The best approach is just to ride the aerial tram up one or more times and enjoy a fabulous descent on **Big Mountain Trail** (10.7 mi/17.2 km round-trip, 2-3 hours, 2,900 ft/884 m elevation gain, moderate). You can ride up to this trail, but you'll have to grunt it out on a series of dirt roads (Dick Bass Hwy., Rothman Way, and Peruvian Gulch Rd.). However, if you show up before 10am, you can ride the Big Mountain Trail uphill to climb on single-track instead of roads. Whichever way you make it to the top, the descent is a blast involving rock gardens, aspen groves, and scree fields. Keep in mind that the mountain biking season varies dramatically at Snowbird based on snowpack. Some years tram-accessed riding (11am-6pm daily spring-fall though closing hours may vary according to the sunset, $28 per adult per day) may start in June; other years, biking won't really kick off until as late as early August. The season runs through October or early November on late snow years.

FESTIVALS AND EVENTS

★ Oktoberfest at Snowbird

Since 1973—just a couple years after Snowbird's founding—an annual Bavarian celebration of beer has taken over the far end of Little Cottonwood Canyon. For weekends during two months in late summer and early fall, Snowbird hosts **Oktoberfest** (www.snowbird.com/oktoberfest, noon-6pm Sat.-Sun. mid-Aug.-mid-Oct., admission free, $10 parking). The festival takes over Snowbird's entire base area with a *biergarten, marktplatz* of crafts, polka, and a German food tent. Best of all, admission is free and beer and food alike are reasonably priced.

Between the alpine backdrop with glittering foliage and the many festivities, this is a magical time to be at Snowbird. Find crafts and tchotchkes as you stroll through Der Marktplatz, and fill your souvenir stein with local beers from Uinta, Bohemian, and other local breweries. Next, head to the food tent where you can watch traditional polka dancing while eating schnitzel, bratwurst, apple strudel, and other Bavarian favorites. Food tents are also available throughout the base area. And at 3pm every Oktoberfest day, head to the central deck to hear the alphorns bellow into the mountains. Speaking of the mountains, a visit to Oktoberfest pairs well with a ride up the aerial tram, or a hike or bike ride before you imbibe.

FOOD

All of the restaurants in Little Cottonwood Canyon are located at the ski resorts or inside the lodges at the base areas. You'll find a mix of fine dining, ski bum casual spots, and buffet-style dining that may not be write-home-about worthy, but do the trick, especially after a big day skiing.

Snowbird

If you look forward to a fabulous steak dinner on every vacation, add **The Steak Pit** (Snowbird Center Level 1, 801/933-2222, www.snowbird.com, 6pm-9pm daily, $21-60) to your dining destination list. There are no bad cuts on this menu. It's 100 percent USDA prime and Wagyu, all hand-cut. And all steaks come from Snake River Farms in neighboring Idaho. Savor a traditional preparation like the New York strip Oscar, served

---

1: descending the Big Mountain Trail 2: soft pretzels at Oktoberfest, hosted by Snowbird

with roasted asparagus, Alaskan king crab, and béarnaise. The surf options on the menu are also top-notch, with locally sourced trout and indulgences like the lobster tail. Pair it all with a glass of wine from the award-winning list. On your way out, look for a porcupine named Larry who tends to hang out around The Steak Pit in hopes of getting leftovers and loose crumbs from guests.

For a more playful dining experience and throwback to the 1970s, visit ★ **SeventyOne** (9320 Cliff Lodge Dr., Sandy, 801/933-2222, www.snowbird.com/seventyone, 7am-10pm Sun.-Thurs., 7am-11pm Fri.-Sat., $11.95-29.95), which is named for the year Snowbird opened. The restaurant's decor is all 1970s themed, with colorful booths, funky light fixtures, and a gold-plated bar. The open kitchen serves '70s American comfort food updated for modern tastes. While the menu changes seasonally, think an array of flatbreads and burgers mixed with takes on throwback dishes like a crunchy Asian salad, vegan meatloaf, and baked ziti mac and cheese with brisket. Breakfast is served buffet style and includes your standard orders, from Benedicts to baked goods. And don't miss the far-out dessert menu with a mix of sundaes and frozen confections ranging from the classic banana split complete with malted milk balls, to a vegan fruit shake with mango and raspberry.

Alta

Rustler Lodge Dining Room (10380 E. Hwy. 210, Alta, 801/742-4200, www.rustlerlodge.com/dining, 7:15am-9:45am, noon-2pm, and 6pm-9pm daily). If a little old fashioned, the Rustler is a pleasant place to fuel or refuel the skiing experience at Alta. The chef has been here for three decades, so he has his menu dialed and knows that there's nothing better than a bowl of soup on a cold skiing day. You'll find four daily soups on the menu, all accompanied by homemade bread. For a heartier dish, consider one of the sandwiches, like the lentil gyro on garlic pita. The dinner menu is ever changing, but think unpretentious new American cuisine like a game

burger (a mix of Wagyu, elk, and bison), or prosciutto-gruyère-stuffed chicken breasts.

Originally the hospital barracks for the town of Alta, the ★ **Alta Peruvian Lodge** (10000 E. Little Cottonwood Canyon Rd., Alta, 800/453-8488, www.altaperuvian.com, 7:30am-9am, noon-1:30pm, and 6pm-close daily) has been around since 1947 and serves up some mean buffets, as far as buffets go. If you're staying at the Peruvian, you're bound to explore at least one meal here. But if you're not, it's worth heading here for one filling meal in the community-style dining room. The breakfast buffet (7:30am-9am daily) includes an omelet bar capable of fueling the longest ski days with only some trail mix in your pocket for sustenance. Come for dinner and you can indulge in fine American standbys like grilled sirloin with shallot-whiskey demi-glace, or more newfangled dishes such as seared halibut with coconut-cashew-bacon butter. One of Chef Drew Disabatino's personal favorites is the sesame-encrusted, sushi-grade rare tuna over a cold rice salad.

ACCOMMODATIONS

The primary lodging options for the Little Cottonwood overnighter are located at either Snowbird or Alta Resort. Options range from luxury lodges to more affordable accommodations. If you're staying in an Airbnb or condo, buy your groceries for cooking in Salt Lake City or Sandy. Little Cottonwood Canyon has convenience markets, but no grocery stores.

Snowbird

Snowbird owns and operates a range of accommodations, including a hotel and a few condo developments, near its base, all of which you can book through the resort (800/232-9542, www.snowbird.com/lodging). If you're planning to ski, you can also look into their lodging packages that bundle ski tickets with accommodations.

The Cliff Lodge (9320 Cliff Lodge Dr., Snowbird, 801/933-2222, www.snowbird.com/lodging, starting at $114) is an anomaly—in a good way. From the outside, this lodger is sci-fi bunker meets brutalist hall. On the inside, it's pure luxury with a spa that will take the edge off those powder legs. In keeping with the futuristic exterior, the rooms are streamlined and modern—not the usual rustic furnishings you often find in mountain towns. Gazing out the walls of windows from within, you'll feel right in the thick of it—in the mountains, that is. Most importantly, however, The Cliff Lodge is ski-in/ski-out. And after a big day of skiing, when the last thing you want to do is schlep around searching for a meal or someone to fix the coreshot in your ski, the one-stop-shop aspect of The Cliff Lodge is hard to beat. A ski rental and repair shop, a daycare center for the too-young-to-ski set, a champagne lounge, a full-service restaurant—this hotel has it all. Whatever you do, be sure to take a dip in the heated pool or hot tub on the rooftop, surrounded by mountains.

Alta

Alta operates several of its own ski-in/ski-out lodges as well as a collection of condos and unique chalets. You can view and book any of these properties online (www.alta.com/lodging).

One of the oldest still-standing buildings in Alta is now home to the **Snowpine Lodge** (10420 Little Cottonwood Rd., Alta, 801/742-2000, www.snowpine.com, starting at $129). It was built in the mid-19th century as part of one of the many mines in the area. Then it became a general store, and by the 1870s, it was home to the post office. When the Alta ski area opened, it turned into a base area center known as the Rock Shelter for its walls of granite. The Snowpine underwent a dramatic renovation in 2018—a posh facelift that feels a little at odds with Alta's historic, traditional character. But if you're in it for the luxury, stay at the Snowpine, which offers polished rooms with contemporary furnishings in neutral color schemes alongside amenities like a posh spa, oxygen bar, karaoke, and yoga studio.

If you're all about accommodations that evoke the *Cheers*-like vibe of familiarity and a home away from home, consider the award-winning ★ **Rustler Lodge** (10380 E. Hwy. 210, Alta, 801/742-4200, www.rustlerlodge.com, starting at $480), voted best ski hotel in Utah by *USA Today* readers in 2017. This vibe can be partially attributed to the management and staff members who have been with Rustler for decades. Thaw out in the hot tub or eucalyptus steam room, or perch beside one of the lodge's roaring fireplaces.

rooftop pool at The Cliff Lodge

The rooms range from standard kings to deluxe suites and feature modern decor in earth tones. The Rustler also offers a more affordable lodging option for groups of friends on a budget or kids: a dorm room with bunk beds that can sleep six (starting at $195). Several amenities cater to skiers, from spa treatments like a sports massage and ski boot dryers, to a morning stretch class and a complimentary hearty breakfast buffet to fuel big days on the mountain.

If it's a traditional Euro ski chalet feel you're after, spend a night or two at the **Alta Peruvian Lodge** (10000 Little Cottonwood Canyon Rd., Alta, 801/742-3000, www.altaperuvian.com, starting at $400). All 80 rooms have a mountain cottage feel and range from standard queens and spacious suites to gender-specific dorm-style accommodations with bunk beds for skiers and riders on a budget (dorm rooms start at $129 per night and include three meals per day). Amenities include 24-hour coffee, tea, and cookie service, plus a pool, hot tub, and 24-hour sauna. The Alta Peruvian also offers great dining options, from a breakfast buffet to steak dinners—and if you love the convenience therein, you can even book a package deal that includes three meals a day.

One of the most low-key lodging options in Little Cottonwood is in the Alta area at **Goldminer's Daughter Lodge** (10160 E. Hwy. 210, Alta, 801/742-3200, www.goldminersdaughterlodge.com, starting at $292). The lodge takes its name from a saloon that once stood in about the same spot during Little Cottonwood's mining days. The Goldminer's Daughter claims to draw inspiration from the intrepid spirit of skiers and the miners of yore alike. While the actual feel in the lobby is a little more 1970s than 19th-century cabin, you will find rustic touches likes vintage ski posters on the wall and stone fireplaces in the lobby. While the original saloon closed long ago, there is still a saloon inside the lodge, as well as a Top of the Lodge dining room with rock walls and floor-to-ceiling windows framing Alta's ski runs beautifully. All of the lodge's amenities are oriented around skiing. From the spa's ski boot soother treatment with warm mud and reflexology to hearty meals to fuel long days, it's really all about the turns.

CAMPING

There are two primary developed campground options in Little Cottonwood Canyon. **Albion Basin Campground** (Albion Basin Rd., Alta, 801/742-2356, 18 sites, starting at $25 per night, tent camping only, toilets available) has a very short operational window due to its eastern location toward the end of the canyon, where it takes a long time for snow to melt and mud to dry. Opening and closing dates vary depending on how much snow there is in any given year, but it usually doesn't open until early or mid-July and stays open through mid-September. Sitting at 9,500 feet (2,896 m), Albion Basin is a high-elevation, forested campground that enjoys a secluded feel along with wildflowers in July and August.

The other, **Tanner Flats Campground** (7490 Little Cottonwood Canyon Rd., Sandy, 385/273-1100, 31 single sites, 3 double sites, 3 group sites, starting at $26 per night, tent and RV sites available, no electric hookups, toilets and water available) is closer to the mouth of the canyon (just 6 mi/9.7 km) and is usually open early June-October. Tanner Flats has a mix of single, double, and group sites settled in the shade of pine, aspen, oak, and maple trees. Little Cottonwood Creek also flows alongside the campground, adding the pleasant sound of rushing water to the auditory landscape. The campground is near several trails, including the Pfeifferhorn Trail.

Dispersed camping and backpacking are also available throughout Little Cottonwood. If you go this route, stop at the **Salt Lake Ranger District** (6944 S. 3000 E., Salt Lake City, 801/733-2660, www.fs.usda.gov, 8am-4:30pm Mon.-Fri.) near the mouth of Big Cottonwood Canyon to pick up a map and get recommendations from rangers on the best places to camp.

GETTING THERE AND AROUND

From downtown **Salt Lake City,** it's about 35 miles (56 km) (or a one-hour drive) to the mouth of Little Cottonwood Canyon, accessed by I-215 South, which is the highway that runs closest to the Wasatch Mountains from Salt Lake City. I-215 is accessible from I-80 as well as several outlying areas southeast of Salt Lake.

The road that runs through Little Cottonwood begins as **North Little Cottonwood Road** and turns into **Highway 210.** This state highway runs about 10 miles (16.1 km), passing Snowbird and turning into **Albion Basin Road** as it snakes its way into the town of Alta. Here, a few smaller roads fork off to access various campgrounds and hiking trails, such as Cecret Lake Trail. It will take you about 35 minutes to drive from one end of the canyon to the other, and longer if conditions are bad in the winter.

From **Park City,** the entrance to Little Cottonwood is about 47 miles (76 km) away.

This take a little more than an hour, and involves taking Highway 224 to I-80, then hopping on I-215 South just before you reach the foothills of the mountains surrounding Salt Lake City. Unlike Big Cottonwood Canyon, there's no mountain pass connecting Little Cottonwood Canyon and Park City more directly come summertime—the only way in is the long way on I-80 West.

In the summer, you need a car to access Little Cottonwood, but if you're coming to ski and staying in Salt Lake, you can ride the **UTA Ski Bus** (801/743-3882, www.rideuta. com, Routes 953, 972, and 994, $4.50 one-way, buses run every 15-30 minutes approx. 6am-6pm) from Salt Lake City. The three different routes stop at various Trax light rail stations and prominent points in the city. If you do opt to rent a car to head into Little Cottonwood Canyon during the winter, be sure to get one with AWD/4WD and snow tires. Not only is this important for your own safety, but it's often required by the Utah Department of Transportation when a snowstorm strikes.

Ogden

Sandwiched between the Wasatch Range and

the Great Salt Lake, the Ogden area has it all when it comes to land-locked recreation and landscapes. In addition to the city of Ogden, the greater Ogden area includes Ogden Canyon and the Ogden River that runs through it. On the other side of that canyon lies the Ogden Valley, a verdant basin home to great skiing, bucolic landscapes grazed by Scottish Highlander cows, and the towns of Eden and Huntsville. Originally home to the Shoshone people, Huntsville is the only incorporated town in the Ogden Valley, settled by Mormon farmers in 1860. A 10-minute drive from Huntsville, Eden saw its first log cabin go up back in 1857 and is aptly named for its heavenly beauty—a verdant

Highlights

Look for ★ to find recommended sights, activities, dining, and lodging.

★ **Stroll along Ogden's Historic 25th Street** to discover its checkered past and vibrant present (page 188).

★ **Check out the George S. Eccles Dinosaur Park,** Ogden's very own Jurassic Park—complete with animatronic dinosaurs (page 189).

★ **Ski world-class terrain** at the relatively low-key resorts of **Snowbasin** and **Powder Mountain** (page 192).

★ **Take a spirited sip** at the Ogden area's **craft breweries and distilleries** (page 196).

★ **Celebrate train history at The Heritage Festival,** commemorating the anniversary of the Transcontinental Railroad launch with a festival dedicated to train history (page 198).

Powder Mountain ★

158

89

Craft Breweries and Distilleries
15

George S. Eccles Dinosaur Park

39

Ogden ★ 39

★ ★ Historic
★ 25th Street ★

203 Snowbasin

The Heritage Festival

84 89

15 84

0   5 mi
0   5 km

© MOON.COM

rolling valley filled with wildflowers in the summer surrounded by snowcapped peaks.

From city to canyon to valley, throughout Ogden you can discover a rich railroad history, enjoy one of the most charming historic Main Streets in Utah, ski by day or by night, imbibe in Utah's oldest saloon, and observe the stars from an observatory inside a lodge in a Dark Skies-certified town.

This beautiful land served for centuries as a home to the Ute and Shoshone peoples, who hunted the local game and fished the Ogden and Weber Rivers. The first permanent Mormon settlement in the state was founded in this area in 1846 and was originally known as Fort Buenaventura, with the legendary likes of frontiersmen Kit Carson and Jim Bridger making appearances in town. For several decades, Fort Buenaventura was a hub of trapping, homesteading, and timber harvesting. The settlement was later renamed Brownsville, and in 1850 or 1851, was renamed once more for Peter Skene Ogden, a British Canadian fur trader and explorer who came through the area a couple decades earlier.

The next big milestone in Ogden's history came in 1869, when the Golden Spike was driven into the ground in Promontory, about 50 miles (81 km) north of Ogden. This momentous spike officially connected the Union Pacific and Central Pacific rail lines, marking the completion of the Transcontinental Railroad. As the nearest city to this crucial connection point, Ogden enjoyed a boom that lasted several decades. As the local chamber of commerce used to crow, "You can't get anywhere without going through Ogden!" Meaning that if you wanted to ride a train west to California, you were going through not Salt Lake City, but Ogden, then the second-biggest city in the state. The 100-plus trains traveling through on a daily basis brought lodging, shopping, and a relatively rip-roaring nightlife to this little town, and 25th Street was the heart of it all.

Ogden truly epitomized the Wild West days you see depicted in popular media, with saloon shootouts, opium dens, and prostitution. Electric Alley—a narrow path between 24th and 25th Streets that is now a parking lot—was a hot spot of prostitution, organized by the legendary Madame Belle London. With Prohibition came bootleggers, speakeasies, and tunnels built to hustle liquor from maker to drinker. Ogden also saw its fair share of organized crime as its economy collapsed in the post-railroad days and the town slipped into decline, with many of the businesses on 25th becoming shuttered.

After a decline that lasted into the middle of the 20th century, Ogden slowly began to reinvent itself. It has become a college town, home to Weber State University, and has attracted various industries, including outdoor gear and aerospace engineering. Today, it's also a destination for outdoor recreation. The three ski resorts in the Ogden Valley have played no small part in forming that identity. Snowbasin—a self-proclaimed local playground—was the first to the gate in the 1940s, followed a couple decades later by Nordic Valley and Powder Mountain on the other side of the canyon. And as skiing grew more popular as an American pastime in the 1950s and 1960s, so did the Ogden Valley as a destination.

Today, the city is known as a family-friendly town—with a heck of a backyard—that loves a good festival and a hearty brunch.

PLANNING YOUR TIME

While the city of Ogden doesn't have the same quantity of sights, activities, and cultural offerings as Salt Lake City, it does have enough to fill a two- or three-day visit. If you just want to discover the city itself, then budget a day trip or quick overnight. But if you plan to take advantage of the nearby recreational

---

Previous: Snowbasin Resort in the midst of mountains; Ogden's Union Station; a roaring dinosaur at the George S. Eccles Dinosaur Park.

Ogden Area

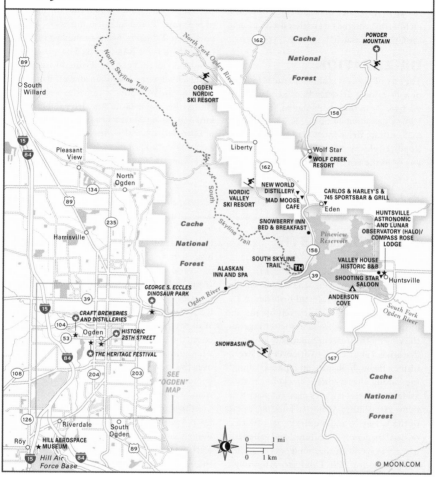

opportunities, then spend a little longer with the city as your base camp. You might spend the morning hiking or biking in the foothills of Ogden, grab lunch in town, then check out a museum or historic site in the afternoon, for example.

If you're coming to the Ogden area to ski or just to explore the Ogden Valley, you can make a worthwhile trip with as little as a day and as long as a week. With three ski resorts, tons of trails, and a reservoir, the Ogden

Valley can keep any active traveler busy for an extended period of time. During your adventurous pursuits in the valley, you can also work in a half-day trip to the city of Ogden, or head there just for lunch or dinner.

Another strategy is to plan a week-long trip that gives town and country equal play, spending a few days in Ogden exploring its cultural and historical offerings, and a few days in the Ogden Valley, skiing, biking, hiking, or however you like to explore the outdoors.

Given its proximity to the Great Salt Lake, Salt Lake City, and the Wasatch Back, a day or two in the Ogden area can easily be tacked on to a trip centered on another destination in the Greater Wasatch.

ORIENTATION

The city of **Ogden** is about 40 miles (64 km) or a 40-minute drive north of Salt Lake City via I-15. From the city of Ogden, the **Ogden Valley** lies about 14 miles (22.5 km) east, or a 25-minute drive away via Ogden Canyon Road (Highway 39). An alternate route, if you're in the northern part of Ogden, is via North Ogden Canyon Road (11 mi/17.7 km, 22 minutes).

In the Ogden Valley, you'll find the towns of **Huntsville** and, about 6 miles (9.7 km) northwest, **Eden.** In between the two towns is the **Pineview Reservoir.** The valley is also home to **ski resorts.** From downtown Ogden, it's about a 30-minute drive (20 mi/32 km) to **Snowbasin,** which lies south of Huntsville, and a 35-minute drive (20 mi/32 km) to **Powder Mountain,** which sits north of Eden. **Nordic Valley** lies 4 miles (6.4 km) east of Eden (an 8-minute drive) and 16 miles (26 km) east of Ogden (a 30-minute drive).

Sights

★ HISTORIC 25TH STREET

Also known as Two-Bit Street, **Historic 25th Street** runs through Ogden's downtown and has one of the most colorful histories of any street in the state. It's survived booms and busts, and borne witness to the outrageous, the violent, the unseemly, and the downtrodden alike. Take a stroll to discover the street's history through plaques on landmark buildings along the avenue. Checkered history aside, 25th Street is a very pleasant place to be in the 21st century. Victorian buildings, views of the Wasatch, and a quirky cast of locally owned businesses, restaurants, and galleries—it's easy to spend an afternoon or even a whole day discovering 25th. This historic thoroughfare also hosts many of Ogden's festivals, including the annual Harvest Moon Celebration and summer farmers markets.

UNION STATION

Aside from 25th Street, one of the other main testaments to Ogden's past is the **Union Station** (2501 Wall Ave., 801/629-8680, www.ogdencity.com/1562/Union-Station, 10am-5pm Mon.-Sat., $5 adults gains admission to all museums), which lies perpendicular to 25th Street, just across Wall Avenue.

Built in 1924, Union Station is a beautiful historic train station worth exploring, home of several small museums, and it serves as a venue for local events, especially in the colder months. One of the more popular museums is the **Utah State Railroad Museum** (2501 Wall Ave., 801/629-8680), where you can discover the history of Black railroad workers who built a community in Ogden, geek out over the model trains, and let the little ones explore kid-friendly exhibits on the railroad. Another highlight is the **Utah State Cowboy and Western Heritage Museum** (2501 Wall Ave., 801/629-8672), which has a name that tells you exactly what to expect: artifacts and displays paying homage to all things Western, from country singers and rodeo queens to artists. You can also explore the Browning-Kimball Classic Car Museum, the John M. Browning Firearms Museum, and several art galleries.

FORT BUENAVENTURA STATE PARK

Before Ogden became a railroad town, a victim of changing times, and then the revitalized community it is today, it was the oldest permanent Mormon settlement in the area, known as Fort Buenaventura, located right on

Ogden

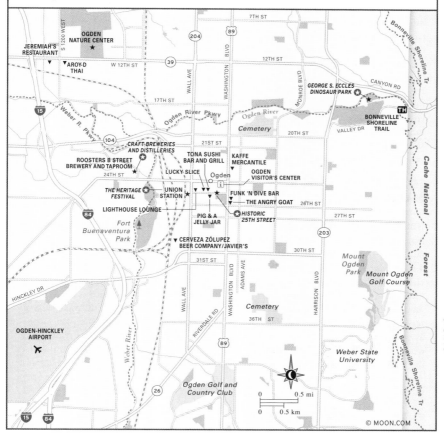

the Weber River. Built in 1846, Buenaventura was a literal fort protecting 32 acres from the Native Americans who were unsurprisingly less than enthused with the Mormon settlement on their long-held territory. Discover this past at the **Fort Buenaventura State Park** (2450 A Ave., 801/399-8099, www.webercountyutah.gov/parks/fortb, $1 pp), where you'll find relics of the trappin' 'n' tradin' days, with replicas of the fort and cabins, a visitors center, and "mountain man" activities throughout spring and summer. Once you're done exploring, take advantage of recreational amenities, like an 18-hole disc golf

course, fishing on the river, and canoeing on a pond. You can even spend the night—the fort has 14 single campsites ($20 per night), two group campsites ($110 per night), tepees ($20 per night), and a free picnic area.

★ GEORGE S. ECCLES DINOSAUR PARK

Strange as it may be, someone decided to create a mini Jurassic Park within Ogden. Located just over 3 miles (4.8 km) east of downtown Ogden at the mouth of Ogden Canyon, the **George S. Eccles Dinosaur Park** (1544 E. Park Blvd., 801/393-3466, www.dinosaurpark.org, 10am-7pm Mon.-Sat., 10am-5pm Sun., $7 adults, $5 children) features an indoor museum with exhibits on dinosaur bones, gems, and rocks, as well as a large outdoor park with to-scale animatronic dinosaurs. What makes this unique is that the dinosaurs are embedded in a naturally forested landscape near the rushing water of the Ogden River. Sometimes you don't notice that allosaurus until it's roaring right behind you! While a dinosaur park is obviously not for all visitors to the Ogden area, it's a great stop for paleontology nerds or families with velociraptor-obsessed kids.

HILL AEROSPACE MUSEUM

Just 7 miles (11.3 km) south of Ogden at the Hill Air Force Base lies the **Hill Aerospace Museum** (7961 Wardleigh, Bldg. 1955, 801/825-5817, www.aerospaceutah.org, 9am-4:30pm Mon.-Sat., free but donations appreciated), which invites visitors to "take a flight through history" with its exhibits and display models. Unsurprisingly, the museum is military focused, and includes education exhibits as well as over 100 aircraft on display, including a 1939 Warhawk. You can also check out the local who's who of pilots in the Utah Aviation Hall of Fame and explore the great gift shop.

OGDEN NATURE CENTER

While you can explore nature all around Ogden, you can learn more about it at the **Ogden Nature Center** (966 W. 12th St.,

801/621-7595, www.ogdennaturecenter.org, 9am-5pm Mon.-Fri., 9am-4pm Sat., $5 adults, $3 children), located just 3 miles (4.8 km) northwest of downtown. On a 152-acre preserve, Utah's very first nature center introduces kids and adults alike to local flora and fauna, including birds of prey, snakes, elk, and foxes. Outside, explore the grasslands and pond of the preserve on a 1.5-mile (2.4-km) walking path, where you can spy birds from a tower, explore a treehouse, and enjoy lunch at the picnic area. The Ogden Nature Center also frequently hosts events, including bird-watching parties and summer concerts. Outings from this museum of nature to nature itself are easy; there's a Bonneville Shoreline trailhead right behind the building.

HUNTSVILLE ASTRONOMIC AND LUNAR OBSERVATORY (HALO)

In Ogden Valley, 15 miles (24 km) east of Ogden, Huntsville is certified as a Dark Skies town. Take a closer look at the night skies at the **Huntsville Astronomic and Lunar Observatory (HALO)** at the **Compass Rose Lodge** (198 S. 7400 E., Huntsville, 385/279-4460, www.compassroselodge.com/observatory), with three behemoth telescopes that peer at planets and stars thanks to a retractable roof. The lodge offers observatory tours and stargazing on most clear evenings after dark ($20 tour, $10 tour for hotel guests, reservations recommended), though overcast skies can interfere.

1: a café paying tribute to Historic 25th Street's former nickname, Two-Bit Street **2:** street art celebrating The Heritage Festival **3:** Union Station

THE CLUB

TWO-BIT STREET Café

THE GIFT HOUSE

CAFÉ

TWO-BIT STREET Café

1

OGDEN RITAGE

2

3

UNION STATION

Recreation

SKIING

The Ogden area is home to three ski resorts. On the south side of Ogden Canyon near Huntsville is Snowbasin, with plenty of extreme terrain to keep expert skiers entertained. To the north lies Powder Mountain, surprisingly home to the most skiable terrain in North America—though much of it is only accessible by hiking or cat. And even closer to Ogden than Powder Mountain is Nordic Valley, perhaps the most affordable and family-friendly downhill ski resort in the state.

★ Snowbasin

Snowbasin (3925 Snow Basin Rd., Huntsville, 801/620-1000, www.snowbasin. com, 9am-4pm daily, tickets starting at $99), located in Ogden Valley about 30 minutes from Ogden, has had more than a few exciting moments in its many decades of operations. As one of the longest-operating ski resorts in the country, Snowbasin has hosted ski races since 1940, became a favorite haunt of World War II veterans of the 10th Mountain Division, and also played host to the 2002 Winter Olympic Games. Snowbasin is a worthy ski destination for all Utah visitors, whether your base camp is Salt Lake, Park City, or Ogden. A little off-the-skied path, Snowbasin offers mellow solitude, crowd-free skiing (read: powder for all), and tasteful luxury woven into the dining and lodging on-site.

This family-owned resort links together four different peaks as well as the bowls of other mountains, topping out at 9,465 feet (2,885 m). Amid its 3,000 skiable acres, there are five terrain parks, gnarly bowls, and a modest amount of beginner and intermediate terrain. Beginners will get their kicks off Becker Lift, while expert skiers can find powder stashes in the Mount Ogden Bowl.

★ Powder Mountain

Powder Mountain (6965 E. Powder Mountain Rd., Eden, 801/745-3772, www. powdermountain.com, 9am-9pm daily, tickets starting at $88, $30 night skiing ticket) is a great resort for families, beginner and intermediate skiers, and those who like to get their turns in after hours. Just over 30 minutes from Ogden, Powder Mountain might have a small-resort feel, but it's actually huge, with 8,464 skiable acres—the most of any resort in the country. However, over 5,000 of these acres are only accessible via cats ($552 pp), unconventional lifts, or with skins and a little sweat, for example, the Lefty's Canyon area. This all makes Powder Mountain a backcountry skier's dream. And the resort's name doesn't lie—Powder Mountain gets over 500 inches (12.7 m) of snow in an average year.

Of the lift-accessed acres at Powder Mountain, 65 percent is designated as beginner or intermediate, which makes this a great mountain for kids and new skiers. Beginners will have a great time on the runs beneath Hidden Lake Lodge—Cobabe Canyon in particular is a nice, long green groomer. Experts may explore the backcountry options at the resort, or play around the Lightning Ridge area, which is said to have first inspired the establishment of Powder Mountain. To get to know the 154 runs and two terrain parks on the mountain a bit better, join one of the free "Pow Mow" tours, which begin daily at 10am and 1pm by the Mountain Adventure Yurt near Timberline Lodge. Powder Mountain also offers night skiing until 9pm, if a little ice and darkness don't scare you.

Nordic Valley Ski Resort

Don't let the name fool you—**Nordic Valley Ski Resort** (3567 Nordic Valley Way, Eden,

1: riding a groomer at Snowbasin **2:** Powder Mountain in spring

801/745-3511, www.nordicvalley.com, 10am-8pm Mon.-Fri., 9am-8pm Sat., 9am-4pm Sun., tickets starting at $45) is actually a downhill ski resort, named in honor of the original owner's Norwegian heritage. Nordic Valley is known for being the most affordable place to ski in Utah. Just a 25-minute drive from downtown Ogden, this small resort spans just 140 acres and has 23 runs accessed by a grand total of three lifts. It also has a very approachable terrain park, perfect for junior skiers looking to get their first taste of air without judgmental onlookers. While this is obviously not a destination for advanced or even intermediate skiers, Nordic Valley is perfect for those learning to ski or skiing with kids. There's plenty of terrain to keep you honing in those turns, and without the steep price tag. The Nordic Valley ski school is also known for being a great place to take a private or group lesson (starting at $39).

NORDIC SKIING
Ogden Nordic Center

If cross-country skiing is more your pace, drive just 30 minutes (17 mi/27 km) northeast of Ogden to the **Ogden Nordic Center** (5950 N. Liberty, 801/648-9020, www.ogdennordic.com, 9am-4pm Fri.-Sun., $6 pp), which hosts Nordic events of the Utah Special Olympics. Here you'll find 20 kilometers (12.4 mi) of skate and classic skiing trails. There is also an indoor center that offers gear rentals, trail maps, and drinks to warm you up from the inside out. The Nordic Center also hosts moonlight glides January-March. If skinny skis aren't your thing, you can also find trails for fat biking and snowshoeing here.

HIKING

Ogden has incredible trail access right from the city. Trail access points pepper the northeastern edge of the city, making it easy to hop on a trail for a quick dose of nature or an efficient workout. Most of these trail access points lead up to the Bonneville Shoreline Trail, which follows the former level of the ancient Lake Bonneville.

Bonneville Shoreline Trail

The **Bonneville-Shoreline Trail** (20-plus mi/32-plus km, easy) follows the original eastern shoreline of Lake Bonneville. The BST is over 100 miles (161 km) in length, stretching in fits and starts from south of Provo to north of Idaho. The greater Ogden area enjoys over 20 miles (32 km) of the BST running along its eastern foothills. Since the trail traverses rather than climbs these foothills, elevation change depends on your entrance and exit points, and which direction you're heading in. In the 3-mile (4.8-km) section traversing the foothills of Mount Ogden, for example, from south to north, you'll climb about 1,000 feet (305 m), while other 3-mile (4.8 km) sections in the Ogden area only hold 250 feet (76 m) of elevation change.

There are a number of different trailheads and access trails to reach the BST for a hike or run. The best resource for this trail is to view the trailhead information under "Pleasant View to I-84" on the official BST website (www.bonnevilleshoretrail.org). One of the closest entry points to downtown Ogden is the 22nd Street Trailhead, which is found at the end of 22nd Street; from here, the **22nd Street Trail** (4 mi/6.4 km round-trip, 1.5 hours, 639 ft/195 m elevation gain, moderate) winds through cliffs, boulders, and brush before meeting up with the BST.

The BST connects with many other trails in the area, runs through fields of wildflowers, traverses creeks and waterfalls, and beholds views of Ogden below and the Wasatch above.

Snowbasin

Come summer, Snowbasin turns into a hiker's paradise, minus the crowds you'll find on peak weekends in Park City and much of northern Utah. With 26 miles (42 km) of trails—and three designated for hikers only—there's no shortage of places to escape into the forest, bask in the wildflowers, and take in staggering views. Pick up a free summer trail map at the Grizzly Center (888/437-5488) at the Snowbasin base area. **Snowbasin Trail** (1.5 mi/2.4 km one-way, 20 minutes, elevation gain negligible, easy) makes for a mellow traverse of the foothills, or you can reach one of Snowbasin's highest points by taking **Needles Trail** to **Cirque Loop** and **Ridge Trail.** The latter route (7.5 mi/12.1 km one-way, 3-4 hours, approx. 2,500 ft/762 m elevation gain, moderate) is more doable if you ride the chairlift up or down, so you don't have to do it as an out-and-back (Needles Gondola runs 10am-6pm Sat.-Sun. mid-late June-early Sept., $16 pp).

MOUNTAIN BIKING

In Ogden, you can mountain bike most of the trails you can hike, with single-track to be found at both Snowbasin and Powder Mountain, close to downtown Ogden, and throughout Ogden Canyon and the Ogden Valley.

South Skyline Trail

The **South Skyline Trail** (18.2 mi/29.3 km round-trip, 3-4 hours, 3,180 ft/969 m elevation gain, difficult) is a beautiful, long stretch of single-track climbing up toward a couple of Ogden's biggest mountains: Lewis Peak (8,031 ft/2,448 m) and Ben Lomond (9,711 ft/2,960 m). Driving on Highway 39 East from Ogden, turn left on Highway 158 North and look for a pullout and the trailhead on the left side of the road after 1.6 miles (2.6 km). This is a multiuse trail, so keep an eye out for hikers, dogs, and even dirt bikers. The trail climbs steadily with sections of switchbacks, and while the grade never grows outlandishly steep, the consistent incline will get to you. As wildflowers pepper your ankles, take in views of Pineview Reservoir and surrounding peaks.

Skyline Trail connects to both Lewis Peak and Ben Lomond Trails (the latter via the North Ogden Divide Trail). You can bike to the top of either peak through connector trails, though these are grueling climbs that will require at least some hike-a-bike for most riders.

Powder Mountain

Many cycling visitors to Utah overlook the mountain biking at **Powder Mountain** (www.powdermountain.com). Come summer at this resort, find over 20 miles (32 km) of single-track spanning beginner and expert terrain alike.

Because of the way that Powder Mountain is laid out, visitors drive to more or less the top of the resort, and then descend. This means that many of the rides start with a little

Pineview Reservoir

downhill before the climb, or err more on the cross-country side of rides.

From Hidden Lake Lodge, intermediate riders can link up a loop by riding **Doctor's Dozen** (4.7 mi/7.6 km one-way, 1 hour, 500 ft/152 m elevation gain, easy) in combination with the **Brim Trail** (6.9 mi/11.1 km round-trip, 1.5 hours, 500 ft/152 m elevation gain, easy). The two trails connect at the southern end of Doctor's Dozen. You can also access the Brim Trailhead off Powder Ridge Road from the upper Hidden Lodge parking lot. Both of these trails navigate through aspen groves and verdant fields of grass with wildflowers during peak season, and include viewpoints of the Wasatch Mountains along the way.

The **Hidden Lake Bike Shop** (6965 E. Powder Mtn. Rd., Eden, www.powdermountain.com, 9am-6pm Sat.-Sun., rentals starting at $50 per day) inside the Hidden Lake Lodge rents mountain bike gear.

WATER SPORTS
Pineview Reservoir
Fed by the Ogden River, **Pineview Reservoir** (6am-10pm daily, day-use fees $7-18 depending on whether you're walking in or using the marina to launch a boat) offers boating, beaching, fishing, and many other water activities. The reservoir lies around 10 miles (16.1 km) east of Ogden at the other end of Ogden Canyon, though you'll have to drive a few miles farther to reach the access points. The reservoir is filled with smallmouth bass, perch, catfish, trout, and even trophy-sized, aggressive tiger muskies, which can reach up to 33 pounds (15 kg) here in Utah. While several of Pineview's marinas charge boaters who enter, admission is free at the Windsurfer, North Arm, and Spring Creek beaches. On the northeastern side of the reservoir, Windsurfer Beach is known for its calm waters and great stand-up paddleboarding. Any and all beaches are equally suited to lounging on the sand and navigating the water by kayak, canoe, Jet Ski, or other watercraft. Boats, Jet Skis, SUP boards, kayaks, and more can be rented from **ClubRec** (3718 N. Wolf Creek Dr., Eden, 801/745-3038, https://clubrecutah.com), located at Cemetery Point along the eastern inlet of the reservoir closest to Huntsville.

Entertainment and Events

NIGHTLIFE
Bars
Funk 'n Dive Bar (2550 Washington Blvd., Ogden, 801/621-3483, 5pm-2am daily) is a favorite local's bar, and about as divey as you can get—except when it comes to the food. Yes, you'll find the usual litany of bar apps, but you can also order off a vegan menu that includes a calzone dubbed the Funk Me Gently. The Funk 'n Dive also hosts events ranging from live music and themed karaoke to open comedy mic nights.

Lighthouse Lounge (130 25th St., Ogden, 801/392-3901, lighthouseogden.com, 11am-1am Mon.-Fri., 10am-1am Sat.-Sun.) is the answer to the question: Where should I go for after-dinner drinks? Dim lighting, a backlit bar, and live music almost nightly set a gritty, cool mood. And if you haven't eaten, there is a nice menu of elevated pub fare.

TOP EXPERIENCE

★ CRAFT BREWERIES AND DISTILLERIES
Ogden is home to two great breweries, while Eden in Ogden Valley has an award-winning distillery worth popping in for some sips and a bottle to take back to the hotel.

Roosters Brewing Co. is a cornerstone of the Ogden community, with a brewery/restaurant on Historic 25th Street, a brewery and taproom in an up-and-coming part of town, and another brewery/restaurant in the nearby town of Layton. While the downtown Ogden location has been brewing and serving since the mid-1990s, the much larger **Roosters B Street Brewery and Taproom** (2325 B Ave., Ogden, 801/689-2879, www.roostersbrewingco.com, 11:30am-10pm Tues.-Thurs., 11:30am-11pm Fri., noon-11pm Sat., noon-8pm Sun.) opened in 2018 and has also established itself as a local favorite. At this bright community gathering spot with a sunny patio, find a dozen beers on tap, including a few showcasing other local breweries and cideries, plus many more brews by the bottle and can. The food stands up to the caliber of the beer, with solid tacos, sandwiches, salads, and indulgences like the Naughty Fries with pepper jack and gorgonzola sauces, spiced up with Louisiana hot sauce.

Cerveza Zólupez Beer Co. (205 W. 29th St., Unit #2, Ogden, 801/917-2319, https://zolupez.com, call in advance for variable and limited hours) specializes in small-batch Mexican beers—like, *really* small batch. Javier Chavez Jr., the brewmaster behind Zólupez, makes just five gallons of each beer at a time. His unfiltered lineup includes brews like pineapple pale ale, mango coconut golden ale, and citrus summer cerveza. Ogden native Chavez started the brewery because

he noticed a dearth of good Mexican beers in the state. While the brewery has limited hours and focuses on production (there's a sales room but no tasting room), you can also try these Mexican beers at his family's restaurant next door, **Javier's Authentic Mexican Food** (205 W. 29th St., 801/393-0955, https://javiersmexicanfood.com, 11am-3pm Mon.-Fri.).

New World Distillery (4795 E. 2600 N., Eden, 385/244-0144, www.newworlddistillery.com, 11am-6pm Tues.-Sat.) describes itself as a destination distillery. But if you're already in the Ogden Valley, there's no reason not to stop by. New World has won awards for its agave-based Oomaw Gin and Oomaw Vodka, and takes pride in distilling, bottling, and serving from one location. In the small, rustic tasting room, sample some of the distillery's more unusual creations, like the Wasatch Blossom Utah Tart Cherry Liqueur. To learn more about New World's unique distilling processes, take a free tour (noon, 2pm, and 5pm Fri.-Sat.).

THEATERS AND CONCERT VENUES

Ogden Amphitheater (343 E. 25th St., Ogden, 801/629-8000, www.ogdencity.

selections from New World Distillery

com/709/amphitheater) is Ogden's only major concert venue and is completely open-air. Drop in for its summer Ogden Twilight concert series (running late May-Sept.), which draws big-name acts, or camp out and picnic during the free Monday Movie Nights, screening family-friendly flicks. The amphitheater, which can accommodate nearly 10,000, also hosts local events like the annual Witchstock Halloween bash and a Christmas village come winter.

Peery's Egyptian Theater (2415 Washington Blvd., Ogden, 801/629-8000, www.egyptiantheaterogden.com) is a relic of the Egyptomania days, built in 1924 to be a grand house of film. Today, this historic, 800-seat theater has been restored to offer a state-of-the-art theater experience, whether you're watching a movie, concert, or live musical. Peery's also serves as a Sundance Film Festival venue.

FESTIVALS AND EVENTS

Ogden loves a good time. For a small city, it frequently hosts events, including local versions of state or national festivities (think Pioneer Day or Pride Festival), and completely unique festivals that are truly Ogden's own.

★ The Heritage Festival

The Heritage Festival (www.ogdencity.com) commemorates the completion of the Transcontinental Railroad, built over a century and a half ago in 1869. For railroad buffs and train-loving kids, this festival is a wonderful way to tap into Ogden's rich rail history. Hosted by the museums of Ogden's Union Station, the celebration takes place during a weekend in early May and includes a healthy mix of celebration and education. The learning side of the festival mostly takes place at Union Station, where trains and exhibits are on display and historians give talks on rail history. Meanwhile, food and art vendors riffing off the rail theme line up on 25th Street while live music plays.

Other Festivals and Events

The **Ogden Farmers Market** (Historic 25th Street, 385/389-1411, https://farmersmarketogden.com, 9am-2pm Sat.) is held throughout a good amount of the year. In the summer, late June-mid-September, the market unites local produce and other vendors along 25th Street, with live music playing at 10:30am and 12:30pm. Late September-October, a fall market takes place at the Ogden Amphitheater. And late January-late February, the market moves inside Union Station, where producers sell preserves, meat, dairy, and limited produce. Amid the food, you'll also find local art and other products.

Since 2002, the **Harvest Moon Celebration** (25th St., www.visitogden.com, late Sept.) has marked the end of summer in Ogden. During a raucous Saturday afternoon and evening, live musicians play, local beer pours, and kids work out their energy with fun activities right up until the moon rises over the Wasatch.

Ogden's answer to Halloween is the family-friendly **Witchstock** (www.visitogden.com, late Oct.). On a Saturday afternoon leading up to Halloween, the town kicks off the spookiest time of year with a costume tea party at the Ogden Amphitheater. A couple hours later, a zombie crawl marches from Union Station down 25th Street. Finally, everyone convenes back at the Ogden Amphitheater for a monster bash with costumes, dancing, and more.

The year-round **First Friday Art Stroll** (www.ogdencity.com/arts, 6pm-9pm Fri.) shows off the art of Ogden, with a tour that runs all the way from Union Station six blocks east. The stops on the stroll are not all galleries—coffee shops, beauty product stores, and more will hang art on their walls for the event, too. Take in new exhibits, probe the minds of artists, pair paintings with live music, and enjoy ever-changing offerings like pop-up events, food trucks, and refreshments.

Food

For a relatively small city, Ogden's got great food. From coffee shops that double as community hubs to some solid ethnic eats, diner-style joints, and pubs, much of the cuisine is concentrated downtown around Historic 25th Street. Over in Ogden Valley, there are fewer dining options. While drinking in Huntsville is a-okay, dining is a little bleak. Meanwhile, over in Eden, there are a few fun places to grab a meal or a cup of internationally inspired coffee. You can also find some dining options at the ski resorts, but none are year-round.

DOWNTOWN OGDEN

Lucky Slice (200 25th St., 801/627-2229, www.theluckyslice.com, 11am-10pm Mon.-Thurs., 11am-2am Fri.-Sat., 11am-9pm Sun., $10.99-23.99) serves "already famous" and "almost famous" pizzas—that's classic pies and house inventions worthy of renown. In the first category, get down with a no-frills New Yorker or a Hawaiian. In the latter, find creations like the Fire Island with garlic cream sauce, capicola ham, jalapeños, pineapple, and

caramelized onions. If you don't trust fame, then build your own. All pies here share the common ground of a NYC-style thin crust. Wings, which come in eight different sauces like chipotle lime and lemon pepper, are the perfect complement to the pie. And vegans will find a menu all their own with plenty of tempting options. In a colorful space with a big chalkboard menu, Lucky Slice has a laid-back pizza joint vibe. You can also find a satellite location at Powder Mountain that operates during the winter only.

★ **Tona Sushi Bar & Grill** (210 25th St., 801/622-8662, http://tonarestaurant.com, lunch 11:30am-2:30pm Mon.-Sat., dinner 5pm-9:30pm Mon.-Thurs., 5pm-10pm Fri.-Sat., $13-15.25) blends traditional Japanese cooking with ingredients and techniques from other cuisines. Owned by Tony, an Ogden native, and his wife Tina, Tona is a combination of their two names. Local and seasonal ingredients, plus sustainable fish, build everything from Asian tapas, sushi, and bento boxes to udon noodle dishes and mochi. Pair it all with a pick from the great sake list. With dim

Kaffe Mercantile

lighting, brick walls, and a sleek sushi bar, Tona makes for a great date night spot, too.

One of Ogden's favorite coffee shops is ★ **Kaffe Mercantile** (1221 26th St., 801/529-0376, www.kaffemercantile.com, 6am-7pm Mon.-Fri., 7am-6pm Sat.-Sun.), which has every coffee drink you could ever want made with ethical Caffe Ibis beans, plus tea, hot cocoa in a variety of flavors, Italian sodas, and more. Aside from strong brew, it's easy to understand why Kaffe Mercantile is a local go-to—it's a welcoming space with cozy furnishings and a giant "COFFEE" sign illuminated in rainbow colors. The small menu includes breakfast sandwiches and quiche, plus pastries and vegan baked goods courtesy of local Lavender Kitchen. Aside from being a stellar coffee shop that now has three locations throughout Ogden, Kaffe Mercantile is also a community hub, hosting weekend backyard yoga (9am), local art on its walls, and locally made goods like notecards and cutting boards you can shop while you sip.

Javier's Authentic Mexican Food (205 W 29th St., 801/393-0955, https:// javiersmexicanfood.com, 11am-3pm Mon.-Fri., $6.99-13.99) is the American dream come alive for Javier Chavez. Originally from Mexico where he was a former track star, Javier opened up shop in Ogden back in 1991. Inside, you'll find a colorful, quaint dining room decorated with Mexican art and flourishes. The menu is massive and the dishes simply prepared in classic Mexican American style, like chiles rellenos with chile verde and enchiladas that warm you from within. The original Javier's was so successful that he opened six more locations along the I-15 corridor. But at this original location in South Ogden, you can sample Mexican-style beers from Cerveza Zólupez Beer Co., a small-batch production brewery next door owned by Javier's son, Javier Jr.

The Angry Goat (2570 Washington Blvd., 801/675-5757, www.theangrygoatpk.com, 11am-11pm Mon.-Thurs., 11am-midnight Fri., 10am-midnight Sat., 10am-8pm Sun., $10-29) is as equally suited for drinking as it is for dining. Pull up a bar stool at the large bar or high-top community table, and order one of 250-plus beers on tap, or a cocktail made with one of the local spirits or a neat pour from the thoughtful Scotch collection. The food menu is scratch-made American cuisine, and a house favorite is the lamb ribs. But you can't leave without trying the Angry Goat Balls, which, thankfully, are not what they sound like (they're fried ricotta balls).

soup and a sandwich at Pig & a Jelly Jar

BEYOND DOWNTOWN OGDEN

Though it was founded by a Canadian, **Jeremiah's Restaurant** (1307 W. 12th St., Marriott-Slaterville, 801/394-3273, www. jeremiahsutah.com, 6am-9pm Mon.-Thurs., 6am-10pm Fri.-Sat., 7am-9pm Sun., $9.99-16.99) has been serving up American favorites in a homey atmosphere since 1979. While it's about 3.5 miles (5.6 km) northwest of downtown, Jeremiah's is a hoot to visit, with a menu that often lacks rhyme or reason. Good barbecue (baby back ribs), Navajo tacos, fajitas, fettuccine alfredo, and other ethnic plates thoroughly acculturated to the American palate all come out of Jeremiah's kitchen. But the restaurant is perhaps best known for its burgers made with a third of a pound of Black Angus beef.

Before owner Raphassa Somcharee (nicknamed "Wan") prepared beautiful rice dishes at ★ **Aroy-D Thai** (1167 W. 12th St., 801/393-2828, www.aroy-d.net, 11am-9pm Tues.-Thurs., 11am-10pm Fri., noon-9:30pm Sat, $11-17), she spent nearly two decades teaching farmers in her home country how to cultivate rice. Aroy-D Thai has won many local awards for its Thai barbecue, curries, and many other dishes, which can be made as tame or fiery as you wish. For the Thai comfort food equivalent to mac and cheese, try the Tom Kha Gai—a thick coconut milk-based soup with chicken and mushrooms served with jasmine rice. Though it's located in a strip mall, Aroy-D is a bright and tranquil place to enjoy a meal, with yellow walls and touches of Thailand—like pink elephant tablecloths—throughout.

After opening in Salt Lake, **Pig & a Jelly Jar** (227 25th St., 801/605-8400, www. pigandajellyjar.com, 7:30am-3:30pm Mon.-Wed., 7:30am-9pm Thurs.-Sun., $6-12.75) spread its Southern breakfast love to Ogden—and be glad it did. In a cheery space defined by yellow and exposed brick walls decorated with colorful murals, you can be as healthy or as indulgent as you want, whether it's for a proper breakfast, lunch, or brunch served all day. Tackle a sandwich stuffed with a triumvirate of Southern cuisine: smoked meat (boneless spare rib), fried green tomatoes, and pimiento cheese on rye. Or stay on the lighter side with a curry chicken salad on a bed of greens. Pig & a Jelly Jar also makes its own unique jams sold by the jar and inspires the best of us to day-drink with its tempting cocktail list.

Out West, you'll notice a lot of places claiming to be the oldest that or the

Shooting Star Saloon

longest-operating this. But the ★ **Shooting Star Saloon** (7350 E. 200 S., Huntsville, 801/745-2002, 11am-9pm Mon.-Sat., 11am-8pm Sun., $4.25-7.25) is the real deal: the oldest saloon in Utah—serving surreptitiously straight through Prohibition—and possibly the oldest west of the Mississippi if you believe the bar's claim. Established in 1879, the Shooting Star Saloon is a tiny little tavern serving nothing fancy and decorated with everything old, from decades-old dollar bills tacked to the walls to antique cash registers. You'll also find animal busts, including one of a St. Bernard named Buck. In addition to a full bar, Shooting Star does serve food, but it's a very simple menu of, as the menu reads, "various burgers . . . all good" (vegetarians and those with special order requests, head elsewhere). This also happens to be the only place in Huntsville to eat dinner.

Carlo's & Harley's & 745 Sportsbar & Grill (5510 E. 2200 N., Eden, 801/745-8226, https://carlosandharleys.com, 11am-10pm daily, $8.99-22.99) serves Tex-Mex that isn't fancy but hits the spot. Carlo's & Harley's is worth visiting alone for a look at the building—an 1890 cabin that's served as a general

store, post office, and dance hall with woodworking techniques allegedly imparted by none other than Brigham Young himself. But today, the historic building sports a decor that's part colorful Mexican, part biker bar, and part Wild West. The restaurant makes four salsas in-house (including one served warm), offers a large menu of all the dishes you could imagine in the Tex-Mex category, and lets guests build their own burger or burrito. While Carlo's & Harley's does have a 21-and-over-only bar, it also has a family-friendly restaurant section and patio seating. Don't miss the spicy, herbaceous Dancing Donkey margarita!

Owned by a former diplomat and colonel who tasted coffee all over the world, **Mad Moose Café** (2429 N. Hwy. 158, Eden, 801/452-7425, http://roughridercoffee.com, 10am-9pm daily, $5.99-7.99) serves its own Rough Rider coffee and creative drinks using it, like the Smilin' Hawai'ian with espresso, white chocolate and macadamia syrup, and steamed milk. In a homey and bright café space, you'll also find a full food menu with incredibly affordable pricing beyond the typical café fare, including burgers, paninis, salads, milkshakes, and more.

Accommodations

As one of the biggest cities in Utah, Ogden has a number of bigger chain hotels, as well as a historic hotel. The farther afield you venture from Ogden, the more charming the lodging. Discover inns and bed-and-breakfasts in Ogden Canyon, Huntsville, and Eden, or camp along the banks of the Pineview Reservoir.

And note that while there are many lodging options close to the Ogden Valley ski areas, the resorts themselves do not have hotels at their base areas. However, Powder Mountain does own and rent out a small collection of townhouses, condos, and cabins nearby (www.powdermountain.com/resort/lodging).

DOWNTOWN OGDEN

Owned and operated by the Hilton, Ogden's **Hampton Inn & Suites** (2401 Washington Blvd., 801/394-9400, www.hilton.com, starting at $96) is set in the historic David Eccles Building, which was originally constructed in 1891, burned down in a 1911 fire, and was rebuilt just a couple years later. Within, the Hampton has a modern feel with 124 rooms sporting colorful, contemporary furnishings. Amenities include a free continental breakfast and fitness center.

BEYOND DOWNTOWN OGDEN

Located in Ogden Canyon, the **Alaskan Inn** (435 Ogden Canyon, Ogden, 801/621-8600, www.alaskaninn.com, starting at $124) has a total of 22 accommodations, including several suites and private cabins. The Alaska theme is tastefully, not excessively, applied with touches like timber beds and exposed log walls. While there isn't a full spa, the Alaskan does offer two massages, and also runs a café with patio seating. If it's a romantic getaway you're in search of, look into one of the inn's nine different romance packages, including everything from couples' massages to sleigh rides. Skiers staying here can even take a complimentary shuttle to the local ski resorts.

★ **Compass Rose Lodge** (198 S. 7400 E., Huntsville, 385/279-4460, www.compassroselodge.com, starting at $229) is a new and welcome addition to the Huntsville area. Its ambience is carefully and expertly predicated upon a strange union of farmhouse, steampunk, the Wild West, skiing, and outer space. The latter makes a lot more sense when you learn that the hotel is crowned by the Huntsville Astronomic and Lunar Observatory (HALO). The lodge offers observatory tours and stargazing on most evenings after dark ($10 tour for hotel guests; schedule when you book), though overcast skies can interfere. Revel in the other smart details at the Compass Rose, from Adirondack chairs on the front lawn and the convenient on-site, ski-themed café, to No. 2 pencils and local Hippie Skin products in the 15 rooms here.

Small, historic, and as charming as the name suggests, the **Valley House Historic B&B** (7318 E. 200 S., Huntsville, 801/745-8259, https://valleyhouseinn.com, starting at $145) feels like staying at an old friend's country manor. Constructed in 1872, the building itself was originally the residence of Huntsville's first mayor. The inn offers three rooms, each unique, and each with a fireplace. A full breakfast is served at your disposal, so no rushing down to the dining room at eight o'clock sharp.

★ **Snowberry Inn B&B** (1315 UT-158, Eden, 801/745-2634, www.snowberryinn.com, starting at $139) is an eight-room log cabin in Eden run by a trained chef, so you can bet the breakfast side of things alone is worth staying here for. That chef also happens to be a local who has made each room a tribute to local history in name and design. You get to schedule your preferred breakfast time between 7am and 9:30am and order off a menu that includes eggs, pancakes, French toast, and many more

the Compass Rose Lodge

breakfast dishes. In the winter, take advantage of the hot tub to soothe sore ski muscles. **Wolf Creek Resort** (3718 N. Wolf Creek Dr., Eden, 801/745-3737, www.wolfcreekresort.com, 2-night minimum, starting at $125 per night) is a planned residential development with resort amenities within Huntsville that also offers a number of Airbnb-style short-term rentals. Billing itself as "more park, less city," Wolf Creek may not charm you with its manufactured vibe, but it does offer a beautiful setting and the convenience of a condo rental with common space and kitchen, well-suited to large groups and families. Amenities include a hot tub, outdoor pool, fitness room, and kids' game room.

CAMPING

Anderson Cove Campground (6702 UT-39, Huntsville, 801/745-3215, mid-May-Sept., starting at $21 per night, RVs permitted, no hookups) sits right on Pineview Reservoir ringed by the mountain scenery of the Ogden Valley. This is a large campground with a mix of nearly 70 single and double sites, plus four group sites that can hold up to 100. Amenities include vault toilets, drinking water, and a general store. Since you're sleeping right on the banks of the reservoir, you can boat, fish, and swim more or less right from your campsite. The campground also has picnic areas, volleyball courts, and horseshoe pits.

Information and Services

TOURIST INFORMATION

If you arrive in Ogden on a weekday, stop by the **Ogden Visitor's Center** (2411 Kiesel Ave. #401, 866/867-8824, www.visitogden.com, 9am-5pm Mon.-Fri.) for more information.

EMERGENCY SERVICES

Ogden is home to the **McKay-Dee Hospital** (4401 Harrison Blvd., Ogden, 801/387-2800), which has 24-hour emergency services. There are also several other urgent care clinics within Ogden, as well as a 24-hour **CVS Pharmacy** (4240 Harrison Blvd., 801/621-2610).

Getting There and Around

GETTING THERE

Most of the information below describes how to reach the city of Ogden from Salt Lake City or Park City. However, if you're traveling directly to the Ogden Valley to reach Snowbasin, Powder Mountain, Huntsville, or the other attractions there from the Wasatch Back, from the Park City area, or from the north, you do not need to travel through the city of Ogden. I-84 connects with I-80 just past the town of Coalville, offering a less trafficked, more scenic route into the Ogden Valley.

Air

The best bet for flying into Ogden is to book your trip into **Salt Lake City International Airport** (SLC; 776 N. Terminal Dr., 801/575-2400, www.slcairport.com), which lies 40 miles (64 km) south of Ogden, a 35-minute drive on I-15. However, Ogden does have a small municipal airport as well. The **Ogden-Hinckley Airport** (OGD; 3909 Airport Rd., 801/629-8262) accommodates commercial flights to and from Arizona, and charters planes to the national parks in southern Utah.

Long-Distance Bus

You can take a **Greyhound** bus (www. greyhound.com) straight to the **Ogden Intermodal Bus Station** (2393 Wall Ave., Ogden, 801/394-5573). From L.A., the trip takes about 17 hours (starting at $134), and from Denver, it's about a 14-hour trip (starting at $111).

The **Utah Transportation Authority** (UTA; www.rideuta.com) runs a bus straight from Salt Lake City into Ogden. Route 470 operates from about 4am until midnight, with buses running every 15-45 minutes depending on the hour at stops throughout both cities and in between ($2.50 one-way). From the southernmost stop in Salt Lake City to the northernmost stop in Ogden, the trip takes a little over two hours.

Train

While you can't roll into town on a grand train like in the late 19th century, you can access Ogden from Salt Lake City and other nearby cities via a light rail line known as the **FrontRunner** (Route 750, www.rideuta.com, $2.50 one-way). The rail line runs frequently, and from the Salt Lake Central Station to Ogden Station, it takes about an hour.

Car

Ogden is located right on the I-15 corridor. From Salt Lake City, take I-15 North for 38 miles (61 km), just over a 40-minute drive. If you're traveling from Park City to the southeast, there are two ways into town with similar drive times. You can take I-80 East to I-84 West (72 mi/116 km, 80 minutes) or take I-80 West through Salt Lake to I-15 North (68 mi/109 km, 90 minutes).

The towns of Huntsville and Eden are located in Ogden Valley. Pineview Reservoir sits in between the two towns (Huntsville on the southeast shore, and Eden to the north). Huntsville is 16 miles (26 km) from Ogden, about a 25-minute drive east through Ogden Canyon on Highway 39 (Ogden Canyon Rd.). Eden is 13 miles (20.9 km) from Ogden via Highways 39 and 158 (at the intersection of the two highways, veer left and north onto Highway 158 instead of continuing on Highway 39); the total drive time is about 25 minutes. Huntsville and Eden are a short 10-minute drive across the valley from each another over 6 miles (9.7 km) of country roads.

GETTING AROUND

Local Bus

Ogden is served by the **Utah Transportation Authority** (UTA; www.rideuta.com). You can spin around on one of the many local routes—including a trolley—that travel around the Ogden area ($2.50 one-way). Ogden is located in Weber County, so select bus routes for Weber County when searching for schedules online. The UTA also operates a ski bus that connects the city of Ogden to Snowbasin and Powder Mountain ($4.50 one-way).

Taxi

Ogden has a couple of taxi services, including **Ogden Taxi Cab & Rideshare Services** (221 25th St. #21, 385/626-9282).

Car Rental

National chains offer a few places to rent a car in Ogden and around the surrounding I-15 corridor. You should check prices online in advance since some car rental companies may be slightly more cost competitive in Ogden than at the airport, but then, of course, you're paying for transportation to and from the airport.

The Great Salt Lake

The Great Salt Lake and its surroundings may

be the most bizarre places you'll ever go. The lake's salinity levels are so high you can float, and its salt flats to the west feel like walking on the moon. Every year, it's the venue for Gullstravaganza, a celebration of seagulls that happen to be stopping by. The lake is home to an island named for antelope and grazed by one of the largest herds of bison in the United States. From its north shore, the country's most famous land art—a spiral that sometimes disappears beneath the water—unfurls in black basalt. And the lake is home to an otherworldly historic concert venue that's been destroyed by fire and flood alike, and has hosted everyone from Bob Dylan to Rob Zombie.

These are the truths about the Great Salt Lake. But there's also

Highlights

Look for ★ to find recommended sights, activities, dining, and lodging.

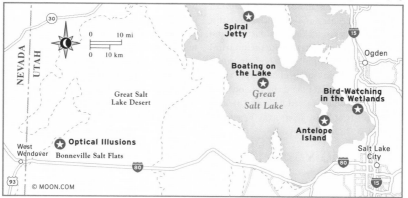

★ **Appreciate land art at Spiral Jetty,** made from spiraling basalt rocks (page 211).

★ **Go boating on the Great Salt Lake,** with salty waters that remain sailable year-round (page 213).

★ **Bust out your binoculars in the wetlands** to catch one of 250 species of birds (page 213).

★ **Take a drive out to Antelope Island,** where **hiking, biking,** and **wildlife** await (page 218).

★ **Capture an optical illusion** with your camera at the **Bonneville Salt Flats** (page 224).

enough lore to fill a night of storytelling around a campfire at an Antelope Island campsite—like the enterprising folks who tried to introduce marine life to the lake, from eels to oysters. Local legend even has it that an entrepreneur released two Australian whales into the Great Salt Lake in 1875. Two years later, several salt workers were exploring the north shore when they spotted a beast with the body of a crocodile and the head of a horse. A couple decades after that, a painter homesteaded Gunnison Island on the Great Salt Lake with fantasies of growing grapes there. That last story is true, but grapes never did take to the island.

Today, the Great Salt Lake remains a strange and fascinating place to visit. You can rent a kayak and paddle across the lake's placid waters. Take a dip in our Dead Sea of the West, and see how much easier it is to float in water saltier than the ocean. Bird lovers can spy pelicans, eagles, and California seagulls, our state bird, from the lake's marshes and wetlands. Art lovers can make the pilgrimage to Spiral Jetty by the late Robert Smithson, or compose mind-bending photographs at the Bonneville Salt Flats. And the curious can camp in the sage-covered hills of Antelope Island, peering up at a pure sky where the Milky Way shines.

PLANNING YOUR TIME

A fulfilling trip to the Great Salt Lake is all about setting your priorities straight. There are attractions for boaters, bird-watchers, hikers, photographers, and artists. If you identify as one or more of the aforementioned, you can safely budget a half or full day to explore the lake. If you're interested in all of the above, you might devote two or three days to your Great Salt Lake experience and consider camping close to the lake, say, at Antelope Island. Do a little route plotting on Google Maps beforehand to ensure you've mapped the most efficient trip. Destinations that might

appear close together on the map might lie a couple hours away by car.

A case in point of attractions bridged by great distances are the big three of the Great Salt Lake. Antelope Island, Spiral Jetty, and the Bonneville Salt Flats are among the most popular, well-known attractions here, but lie hours apart by car. Strike a compromise in your explorations of the lake by picking one of these three to visit, and pairing it with a stop at the Great Salt Lake Marina, which lies en route to these destinations, or a bird-watching trip to the wetlands.

One thing to consider when planning your Great Salt Lake trip is that food and lodging options are quite slim. You can find a few motels or big chain hotels in the small towns surrounding the lake, but if you're looking for something a little nicer, your best bet is to stay in Ogden or Salt Lake City. If you do hope to spend a little longer at the lake, consider camping at Antelope Island or Willard Bay Marina. However, if you're visiting during the summer, these campgrounds may be plagued by biting gnats and mosquitoes. Fall, spring, and even winter are much better times to camp at the lake. Same story for food: You'll find some small restaurants and fast food in some of the towns surrounding the lake, but nothing to write home about. Consider packing in your own food in a cooler if you're planning to explore the lake for a long day or overnight.

If you're visiting the lake to bird-watch, consider timing your trip around when certain birds are present and visible. The University of Utah offers a great resource about which birds are around when (https://learn.genetics.utah.edu/content/gsl/year). Some wetland areas also close down during the late summer and early fall to accommodate breeding and hatching.

Between the heat and the bugs, early spring and fall are generally the best times to visit the Great Salt Lake and Antelope Island. At

Previous: view of the Great Salt Lake from Antelope Island State Park; wild horses grazing by Spiral Jetty; family wading in the Great Salt Lake.

The Great Salt Lake

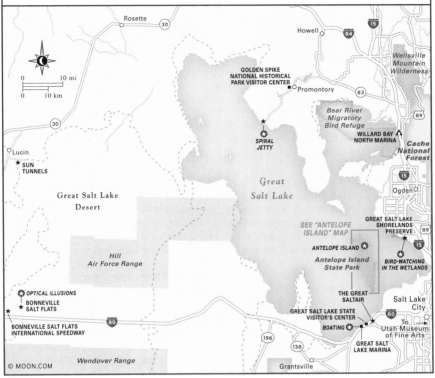

Antelope Island, in particular, bugs can be a big deterrent in the summer. Nicknamed no-see-ums, tiny biting midges usually hatch in early May and stay active through June, swarming visitors. Insect repellent is useless against these tenacious little bugs, so if you do go when they're around, get a head net at the visitors center. Mosquitoes dwell on the island for most of the summer, as well as brine flies, which are harmless if a little unpleasant to be around.

Finally, I include a couple of sights with this region that are not exactly part of the Great Salt Lake and are a long way from Salt Lake City. The first: the Bonneville Salt Flats. The salt flats lie over an hour west of the southern tip of the lake and are not in any way connected to the Wasatch

Mountains. I included them because the salt flats are the relic of what the Great Salt Lake once was thousands of years ago when it was known as Lake Bonneville. When large expanses of the lake dried up, a desert of sodium chloride was left behind. So while it's hardly part of the modern Great Salt Lake, it's an integral part of its history and arguably of its broader salty ecosystem! If you plan on spending a long time at the Bonneville Salt Flats, consider staying in Wendover, or crossing the border to stay in West Wendover, Nevada, which are much closer than Salt Lake City. There is no camping allowed at the Salt Flats.

One other sight that I include with this region, though it lies far from the Great Salt Lake itself, is the Sun Tunnels, a land art installation by Nancy Holt, who was the partner of Spiral Jetty artist Robert Smithson. If you're an art enthusiast—or, even better, a land art enthusiast—it's worth it to make the three-hour drive north from the Bonneville Salt Flats or three-hour drive southwest from Spiral Jetty to see Holt's tunnels, especially if it's the summer or winter solstice, which her artwork is designed around. You can even camp right by the tunnels to catch the early light passing through her sun-oriented tunnels of concrete in the morning.

The Great Salt Lake

As the saltiest lake in the Western Hemisphere and one of the saltiest the world over, the Great Salt Lake is unlike most bodies of inland water you've encountered. You can float on it, sail across it year-round (in spite of Utah's severe winters), and spot millions of birds stopping here on their migratory routes, feeding along the lake's shores. Its history, unique composition, and diverse bird populations make the Great Salt Lake a truly memorable and special place to visit.

An Ancient Lake

The Great Salt Lake is the great-great-grandchild of a massive prehistoric body of water known as Lake Bonneville, where the likes of woolly mammoths and camels roamed. If you think the Great Salt Lake is big, it has nothing on its predecessor, which stretched 325 miles (525 km) long, 135 miles (217 km) wide, and 1,000 feet (305 m) deep, covering most of western Utah and parts of Nevada and Idaho. The lake came into being during the last ice age some 32,000 years ago and persisted until around 14,000 years ago, when a huge, enduring flood transformed the freshwater Lake Bonneville into the smaller, terminal lake we know today.

Saltier than the Sea

How much salt is there in the Great Salt Lake? By percentage, a lot more than there is in the ocean. While the sea is about 3.5 percent saline, the Salt Lake ranges from 5 percent salinity to as much as 27 percent in the shallows. At 75 miles (121 km) long, 35 miles (56 km) wide,

the Great Salt Lake

and up to 33 feet (10 m) deep, that amounts to nearly five billion tons of salt. The reason the Great Salt Lake is so saline is because it's what's called a terminal lake, which means that while four rivers flow in, none flow out. The only escape route for the water is by evaporation, which leaves minerals, like sodium, behind to accrue.

All this mineral buildup allows us to float with ease in the Great Salt Lake compared to other bodies of water. It also may be what catalyzed the formation of a unique type of sand called oolites, which resemble tiny alabaster pearls made from calcium carbonite built up around a core, like a kernel of mineral, or a nugget of brine shrimp feces.

Today, an old railroad causeway bisects the Great Salt Lake. While a train no longer cuts across the lake, the division remains in the form of raised rocks. This partition has altered the ecosystems of the southern and northern sides of the lake, causing different communities of microorganisms (namely, algae) to thrive. As a result, the southern half of the lake appears more bluish, while the northern half is a little reddish—a phenomenon that can only be appreciated from above.

Who Calls the Lake Home

Don't let a sign posted at Antelope Island claiming that the Great Salt Lake is a place no one wanted mislead you. Humans have inhabited the modern Great Salt Lake for thousands of years. The Ute, Paiute, and Shoshone tribes, who lived along the lake's shores seasonally, informed American settlers about the lake as far back as 1776. However, settlers didn't visit the lake until decades later. Among the first colonialist explorations of the Great Salt Lake was one led by explorer John C. Frémont and his mountain man guide Kit Carson in 1843, three years before the Latter-day Saints arrived and stayed for good.

Aside from the humans who now inhabit communities surrounding the lake, a distinctive set of flora and fauna make up the lake's ecosystems. Bacteria and algae thrive, feeding millions of brine flies and brine shrimp, which in turn satiate hundreds of birds—from pelicans and swans to gulls—that pass through on their migration routes. What won't you find at the Great Salt Lake? Fish. The lake is too salty for the usual suspects of freshwater bodies, so cast your line in the nearby rivers and reservoirs instead.

The Truth about the Great Salt Lake

I'll be honest: The biggest lake west of the Mississippi is not exactly a pleasant place to visit. Can it be fun? Of course! Does it have beautiful vistas? You bet. Is it worth visiting? Yes—unless the following unique attributes sound like your worst nightmare. For one, many parts of the Great Salt Lake stink. The unpleasant odor is primarily caused by the decaying corpses of massive amounts of bugs. Which brings me to another unique aspect of the Salt Lake: insect life. The Great Salt Lake ecosystem is one giant "protein factory," as my friend Adam, who monitors birds at the lake for the Utah Department of Wildlife, explains. The birds eat brine shrimp, which eat the brine flies and other abundant insects around the lake—and everybody's happy! Except for bug-averse humans.

For these reasons, the lake isn't really a place where you'd want to spread out a blanket and take dips when the temperature spikes. There are plenty of reservoirs and high alpine lakes in the Wasatch that serve that purpose. The reason to visit the Great Salt Lake lies in its peculiarity, from its core anomalous character, to the various oddities in its wake, from Spiral Jetty to the Saltair.

SIGHTS

TOP EXPERIENCE

★ Spiral Jetty

In the 1960s and 1970s, land art swept the nation. Instead of sourcing materials and mediums from anywhere and everywhere to produce a piece conceived of in the artist's mind, the artist creates a work of art using

the land, inspired by the land, upon the land. Utah holds the distinction of hosting what is arguably the most famous piece of land art ever made: Spiral Jetty, by Robert Smithson.

Spiral Jetty's name says it all: a small constructed extension into a body of water, in the shape of a spiral. Smithson crafted the 1,500-foot-long (457-m) spiral from mud, salt, and black basalt rocks, all of which he found on-site. Spiral Jetty lies along a stretch of the northeastern coast of the lake in an area known as Rozel Point, where the water tends to have a pinkish hue from algae. Aligned with Smithson's interest in erosion, Spiral Jetty never appears the same to the visitor. It might be partially covered by the water or fully submerged depending on lake levels. It could be covered in salt crystals and surrounded by water that appears gray, pea green, or red depending on what the microbial communities are up to.

Smithson, unfortunately, didn't live very long to see how his pièce de résistance would transform with the elements. Three years after completing Spiral Jetty, he died in a plane accident scouting locations for another land artwork in Texas.

If you visit Spiral Jetty, don't just stand there. Smithson hoped his audience would engage with the jetty, walking around it, rather than beholding it from a distance. You should feel different depending on whether you're standing within the spiral, or on its outskirts.

From Salt Lake City, the drive to Spiral Jetty is 2.5 hours and includes unpaved roads. Consider calling the nearby **Golden Spike National Historical Park Visitor Center** (6200 N. 22300 W., Promontory, 435/471-2209) to find out if Spiral Jetty is underwater, so you don't make the trip only to find there's nothing to see.

Before visiting, head to the **Utah Museum of Fine Arts** (410 Campus Center Dr., Salt Lake City, 801/581-7332, https://umfa.utah.edu, 10am-5pm Tues.-Sat., open until 9pm

Wed., $15.95) in person or online to gather some of the excellent resources they offer for the prospective visitor. You can find a practical guide to visiting, with directions and advice on what to bring, and an interpretive guide for exploring the site. Check out the exhibit on Spiral Jetty in the museum, and even rent a free backpack for kids 12 and under to bring along and explore this famous earth art.

RECREATION
★ Boating on the Lake

With a body of water as big as the Great Salt Lake, the most efficient way to explore it is by boat. Head to the **Great Salt Lake Marina** (13312 W. 1075 S., Magna, 801/250-1898, www.gslmarina.com, 9am-5pm daily), where you can set out through this strange waterscape on anything from a single or tandem kayak to a stand-up paddleboard and a pedal boat. While strong winds can create waves on the lake, usually the water is almost eerily calm. Spending a few hours paddling around the lake is a great way to get to know it. Take a tour of some of the lake's many islands, where you can stop for a picnic. Keep your eye—and camera—out for birds. And take a quick dip in the lake to see just how much easier it is to float on salty water. If you'd rather not do the paddling, you can also book a boat tour, allowing you to focus on the scenery.

The marina lies on the southern tip of the lake and is 19 miles (31 km) due west from Salt Lake City, about a 20-minute drive. Boat rentals and tours are available at the marina from **Gonzo Boat Rentals & Tours** (801/989-7281, www.gonzofun.com, kayak rentals starting at $25 for two hours, tours starting at $30 pp). And don't second-guess your plans because of the bugs and odors you may find at the marina! Once you move away from the shore, the insects and the smells they produce will dissipate.

★ Bird-Watching in the Wetlands

Over 250 species of birds call the Great Salt Lake a part-time home. There are a handful

1: Spiral Jetty by artist Robert Smithson 2: The Great Saltair

of species that even live here year-round, like ducks and tundra swans. No matter when you visit the lake, you're bound to find at least a few birds taking advantage of the fact that extremely salty water doesn't freeze. Some of the less saline parts of the lake may freeze over, but the saltiest areas won't.

Perhaps the best time to go bird-watching at the Great Salt Lake is spring, when birds stop over at the lake on their journeys northward. In the wetlands, find pelicans, Canada geese, and herons. May marks the beginning of chick hatching season, so keep an eye out for baby birds in late spring and early summer. Throughout the summer, the Great Salt Lake hosts avian visitors like egrets and ibises. In the fall, find songbirds chirping away along the shores before they head farther south to escape the cold. And come winter, you may find grebes, songbirds, tundra swans, and even bald eagles.

If you've heard a rumor that a lone flamingo inhabits the Great Salt Lake, know that the legends are true, but the solitary Pink Floyd, as he was locally known, hasn't been spotted in years. The Chilean flamingo escaped from the Tracy Aviary in downtown Salt Lake City in the late 1980s and held his own in our inland sea for years. Pink Floyd even inspired a failed movement to import 25 more flamingos from below the equator to keep old Floyd company.

While you're unlikely to catch sight of a flamingo today, you can observe birds here from just about anywhere at the Great Salt Lake—from its shores and wetlands, on one of its islands, or from the thick of things in a boat. But one of the best and most tranquil places to observe birds is the **Great Salt Lake Shorelands Preserve** (3200 W., Layton, 801/531-0999, www.nature.org/greatsaltlake, 6am-9pm daily Mar.-Oct., 7am-6pm daily Nov.-Feb.), which draws as many as six million avian visitors a year. Built and operated by The Nature Conservancy, this 4,400-acre preserve is located on the lake's eastern wetlands. For the hopeful bird-watcher, the site consists of a mile (1.6 km) of boardwalks

traversing the wetlands, linked by several elevated observation structures and exhibits. The best time to go is early morning or twilight. There is no visitors center or staffing here, but restrooms are available, and you can download a free GPS-triggered tour on your phone (www.nature.org/gsltour).

If you want to time your trip around when certain birds are present, the University of Utah offers a helpful resource that indicates which birds are around at what time of year (https://learn.genetics.utah.edu/content/gsl/year). Some areas close in late summer and early fall to accommodate breeding.

ENTERTAINMENT AND EVENTS

Entertainment at the lake? You bet. From a historic concert venue to several celebrations of birds, here are a few ways to pass a day at the lake.

Great Salt Lake Bird Festival

For the bird-watching enthusiasts among us, this annual festival is a can't-miss event. Spanning a long weekend in mid-May, when birds are heading north for the summer, the **Great Salt Lake Bird Festival** (www.daviscountyutah.gov/greatsaltlakebirdfest, tickets vary based on trip) consists of a series of themed field trips and workshops, which can be signed up for separately. Observe everything from owls to raptors everywhere from Willard Bay State Park to ranches surrounding the lake. There's even a workshop on bird photography, and kid-friendly trips suitable for the whole family.

Gullstravaganza

Utah's state bird is the California seagull, which might strike you as a little odd. While these gulls might not bear our state's name, they do bother to visit every winter. One of their most famous sojourns in Salt Lake occurred in 1848, when they swooped in and

1: cairns by the lake 2: Great Salt Lake Shorelands Preserve 3: Great Salt Lake Marina

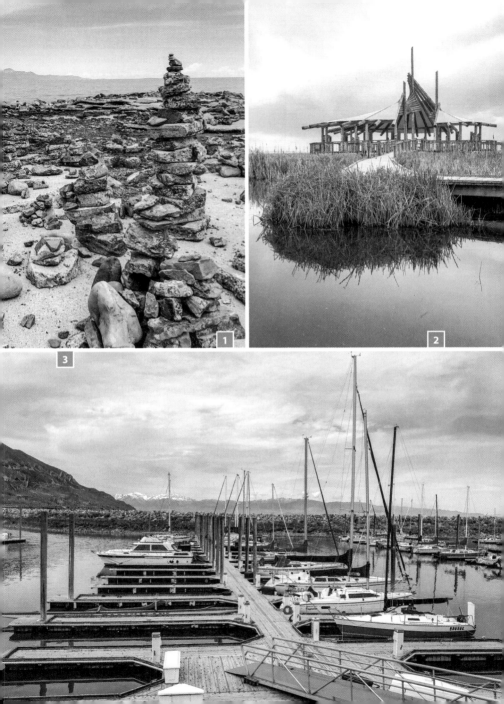

ate a massive cricket hatch that was wreaking havoc on the Latter-day Saints settlers' first farms, saving the crops for the year. All hail the gull! To honor this bird, the Utah Birders, a statewide birding organization, hosts the annual one-day **Gullstravaganza** (http://utahbirders.com, noon-5pm, early Feb., $5 donation to Great Salt Lake Audubon Society) to observe the California gulls and other seabirds descending upon the Great Salt Lake for their breeding season.

The Great Saltair

Drive about 20 minutes (17 mi/27 km) west on I-80 from Salt Lake City and you'll see a building on your right that resembles a cartoonish palace out of *Aladdin*. The first incarnation of the **Saltair** (12408 W. Saltair Dr., Magna, 801/250-6205, https://thesaltair.com), which was built by the Church of Latter-day Saints in 1893, resembled today's version in style, but was much more ornate—think Coney Island meets the domes of Florence somewhere in the Middle East. The Saltair was indeed originally intended to be a Coney Island of sorts: a resort and hub for chaste entertainment. People came to swim, shake a leg on the massive dance floor, ride a Ferris wheel, and partake in a host of other diversions. Around the turn of the 20th century, a community of some 200 people actually lived in "Saltair Village." All of this, until disaster struck—again and again. From 1925 until the late 1980s, the Saltair fell victim to multiple fires, the Great Depression, a receding lake, and flooding. In 1992, a private company rebuilt the resort from a retired Air Force hangar, and the building still stands today, serving primarily as a concert venue that can accommodate a whopping 4,600 people. The Saltair draws a motley mix of indie acts, headliners, and energy festivals. You can stop by this historic venue on your way to the Great Salt Lake Marina, or see a show here if you find an act that coincides with your visit.

FOOD

When it comes to finding a good meal around the Great Salt Lake, there isn't much. There are a string of small rural towns surrounding the eastern shore of the lake, but with Salt Lake City only 20 minutes from the Great Salt Lake Marina, and Ogden close to the northern tip of the lake, you're much better off heading to one of these two cities to eat. And whether you're heading to the Great Salt Lake for a day trip or an overnight camping trip, your best bet is to pack in your own food—pick up sandwiches at a local deli or head to **Harmon's Grocery** (multiple locations, www.harmonsgrocery.com) in Salt Lake City for some excellent prepared foods, snacks, and ingredients for campsite meals.

CAMPING

In keeping with my recommendation that you seek food elsewhere when it comes to a Great Salt Lake trip, I advise you to consider staying in Salt Lake City or Ogden rather than in one of the small towns on the eastern side of the lake. If you're set on sleeping lakeside, camping is the best option, though beware of summer bugs.

Willard Bay North Marina Campground (435/734-9494, 109 sites, including RV campsites with full hookups, $25 per night, water and restrooms available) may not be the most scenic campground you've ever spent the night in, but it will do the trick. The campground is located on the far northeastern tip of Willard Bay, a reservoir connected to the Great Salt Lake on its northeastern side. This is a very developed site, which means amenities are plentiful, for better or worse. Lake activities like boating and fishing are available here as well. (While the reservoir is technically not part of the Great Salt Lake, it's just a few minutes from the lake and its wetlands.)

INFORMATION AND SERVICES

The **Great Salt Lake State Park Visitor Center** (13312 W. 1075 S., Magna, 801/828-0787, https://stateparks.utah.gov/great-salt-lake, 8am-8pm daily) is located at the Great Salt Lake Marina at the southern tip of the lake, just 20 minutes from Salt Lake City. Here you can peruse exhibits about the Great Salt Lake and gather recommendations for your trip.

GETTING THERE

From Salt Lake City, the closest part of the lake is the Great Salt Lake Marina, which is 19 miles (31 km) west of the city, about a 20-minute drive. I-80 West will take you directly there, and you'll pass the Saltair on your right en route to the marina. From Ogden, the closest points of the Great Salt Lake are the wetlands along the eastern shore, including Great Salt Lake Shorelands Preserve (17 mi/27 km south on I-15, 22 minutes).

Antelope Island

How many islands are there in the Great Salt Lake? The answer depends on how high water levels are. But the most visited and largest of these humps of land is without a doubt the 28,000-acre **Antelope Island.**

Part of the reason **Antelope Island State Park** (entrance booth/information 801/773-2941, https://stateparks.utah.gov/antelope-island, 6am-8pm daily, entrance fee $10 per vehicle, $3 per bike) is so special is its bison population—one of the largest in the country. A dozen bison were introduced in 1893 and thrived. Today, they number between 550 and 700 and are protected by the state park, established in 1981. The bison are in good company with many other animals like coyotes, bighorn sheep, and, of course, pronghorn antelope. The land these creatures inhabit and many love to visit is a topographical mélange of beaches, grasslands, desert brush, and even a small mountain called Frary Peak (6,596 ft/2,010 m) that rises well over 2,000 feet (610 m) above the island's shores.

People have been visiting or living on Antelope Island for over 6,000 years, but today many come to Antelope Island for the mere novelty of an island within a salty lake where buffalo roam. Others come to Antelope Island to mountain bike, or to camp beneath a magnificent sky untainted by city lights. Still more come to see the hundreds of bird species that live or visit here. However you explore the island, it's a strange and unique place to discover, and offers a deeper look into the oddity that is the Great Salt Lake.

SIGHTS
Scenic Drive

Take the scenic drive through the island on **Antelope Island Road,** stopping at scenic lookouts and at the historic Fielding Garr Ranch at the island's southern tip. From the entrance to the park on the mainland to the island itself, the causeway is around 6 miles (9.7 km) in length. Once you enter the island, the road continues for a little longer than 10 miles (16.1 km). If you just do the drive without stopping, it will take you about half an hour to drive across the causeway to the end of the road, and much longer if you're stopping to hike and sightsee along the way.

Fielding Garr Ranch

The oldest building in Utah constructed by settlers rather than Indigenous people lies at the **Fielding Garr Ranch** (Antelope Island Rd., 801/773-2941, 9am-5pm daily, free with Antelope Island State Park entrance fee) on the southern half of Antelope Island. In 1848, the Mormon Church asked Fielding Garr to tend to its cattle herd on the island, and Garr never left—nor did several generations of his family to follow. His descendants lived in the modest log cabin he set up on Antelope's eastern shore until 1981, when the state of Utah bought the island, ranch included, and turned the whole thing into a state park. You can still visit the ranch today, wandering the well-preserved site to observe everything from a shearing barn for the thousands of sheep raised here, to the old historic ranch house

Antelope Island

Salt Lake, and the nearby Wasatch Range. While the hike to Buffalo Point may be short, it is fairly steep, so the right footwear and water on a hot midday hike is a must. Once you enter Antelope Island from the causeway, you'll drive about 2.5 miles (4 km) before veering right following signs toward Buffalo Point and the White Rock Bay Campground. If you happen to see buffalo on the trail, remember to observe them at a distance, for your sake and theirs.

FRARY PEAK

If you're willing to put in a half day of hiking, you can make the long trek to the top of **Frary Peak** (7 mi/11.3 km round-trip, 2.5-3.5 hours depending on pace, 2,335 ft/712 m elevation gain, moderate), the island's highest point at 6,596 feet (2,010 m). While it's not exactly a glorious summit—you'll feel more like you've reached the top of a big hill than one of Utah's snowcapped high-octane mountains—you'll be treated to great views of the island and the Great Salt Lake. While the hike can be somewhat popular and packed in the summer, this out-and-back trail is usually passable nearly year-round as long as there hasn't been a big snow recently.

To get to the trailhead, after you exit the causeway onto the island, veer left on Antelope Island Road and continue for just over five miles, then turn right on Frary Peak Trailhead Road.

itself. Some of the buildings are open to the public and staged with artifacts such as original farming equipment and cattle skulls.

★ RECREATION
Hiking

You can explore Antelope Island—and catch sight of the bison herds—by hiking or trail-running around the various scenic stops along Antelope Island Road.

BUFFALO POINT

Shake your legs out during your scenic drive through Antelope Island with a short jaunt to **Buffalo Point** (1 mi/1.6 km round-trip, 30 minutes, 300 ft/91 m elevation gain, easy). This makes for a great sunrise or sunset hike, with panoramic views of the island, the Great

Biking

For an island in the middle of a salty lake, Antelope Island actually has surprisingly good mountain bike riding, concentrated in the more mountainous central areas. Like with everything at Antelope Island, biking is best pursued anytime but summer. In addition to the bug problems that plague the island, the trails can become quite dusty in the punishing aridity. The trails here are also exposed, offering the rider little respite from the sun.

You can also road bike the entirety of **Antelope Island Road,** which is about 45 miles (72 km) round-trip depending on where you start in Syracuse, the mainland town closest to the causeway. The road is mostly flat, so while the mileage to bike the full length of the island may seem high, it will be a cruiser ride. And if you enter Antelope Island State Park on a bike rather than a car, you can even get a discount on your entrance fee ($3 instead of $10). A cross bike with burlier tires is nice if you'd like to take excursions on some of the dirt paths throughout the island.

Bike rentals are not available on the island, so if you don't have your own set of wheels, plan to rent in Salt Lake City.

FIGURE 8 LOOP

The **Figure 8 Loop** (17 mi/27 km, 2-3 hours, 1,700 ft/518 m elevation gain, moderate) strings together several trails navigating the central part of the island. This is more of a series of out-and-backs, loops, and lollipops than a proper loop, but offers a great tour de Antelope. Most of the riding is beginner-friendly, with a few technical sections where riders can easily dismount. Starting from the southeast side of the White Rock Bay Campground, the ride starts on White Rock Loop, which begins as a dirt road that pulls away from the shore into the hills. When you reach a bench, take a quick out-and-back lap on Elephant Head Trail (1.4 mi/2.3 km one-way) for more challenging terrain leading to a view. When you return to the bench, turn right to ride Split Rock Loop (5 mi/8 km) clockwise, which begins with some playful downhill on double-track and ends with a climb up a dirt road. When you climb back up, ride down White Rock Loop, then veer left at the first junction you come to for some flowy single-track back to the trailhead.

Horseback Riding

Between the ranching history and the bison munching on grass by the shores, Antelope Island feels like a place best explored on the back of a horse. This is also a great way to get a read on the island and its myriad landscapes, views, and angles. **R & G Horse and Wagon** (801/726-9514, www.randghorseandwagon. com, 6am-10pm daily) operates right on the island and has experience wrangling horses on movie sets and trail rides alike. The R & G guides can take you for a trot on the beach, a climb into the hills, or on a ride that offers a little bit of both. The rides start from the Fielding Garr Ranch on the southeastern side of the island.

view from Antelope Island, where buffalo roam

The Great Salt Lake's Other Islands

If you're wondering what the Great Salt Lake's other islands are like, it's a strange mix to say the least. Runner-up in size to Antelope Island is **Stansbury Island,** which is technically a peninsula since it's connected to the mainland by a causeway. There you'll find sheep, petroglyphs, and caves to explore. Just northwest of Stansbury Island is another quasi-island called **Carrington,** where brine shrimp aquaculture kicked off in the mid-20th century.

Just north of Antelope Island, **Fremont Island** is named for the explorer John C. Frémont, who "discovered" the lake. But it was originally dubbed "Disappointment Island" by none other than Frémont's alpine escort Kit Carson due to an apparent lack of wildlife. Carson even left his mark here, carving a cross into a rock. Fremont Island is privately owned by Heavy D and Diesel Dave of the *Diesel Brothers* on the Discovery Channel.

Stansbury Island

In the northern part of the lake, **Gunnison Island** once famously hosted a homesteader. In 1895, artist and writer Alfred Lambourne decided to spend a full year on the island and even tried growing grapes, allegedly for wine. However, the grapes never took and he ended up leaving well before a year was up. The end result is his book about the Great Salt Lake titled *Our Inland Sea.*

The Great Salt Lake has several other smaller named islands—Badger, Hat, and Egg in the southern half, and Dolphin, Cub, and Strongs Knob to the north. And there are even smaller unnamed islands that surface when water levels are extraordinarily low, as they will be in the coming years as Utah suffers from drought and climate change.

Bird-Watching

Antelope Island is a birder's Valhalla. From the grassy beaches to the shrubby hills and the Fielding Garr Ranch, there are plenty of places to spy all sorts of feathered friends, from songbirds to birds of prey.

One popular place for bird-watching year-round is actually the causeway into the island itself, which is surrounded by a narrow shore and the lake. Along the causeway, look for the usual waterfowl suspects like California gulls, as well as small wading birds like eared grebes with their beady, fire-engine-red eyes.

Farther inland, look for western meadowlarks and the chubby chukar partridges, which live here in great numbers year-round. Owl lovers can find four sub-species here year-round, from the great horned owl to the barn owl. If you're lucky, you might spy a flock of American white pelicans—they inhabit Gunnison Island to the north—flexing their 100-plus-inch (254 cm) wingspans over nearby waters. In the winter, look for bald eagles perched on the parts of the lake that do ice over.

With hundreds of species and year-round bird populations, Antelope Island is a perennial favorite to look and listen for local birds.

Wildlife Viewing

Antelope Island is one of the best places in the state to peep at large herds of bison. They're easily viewed any time of day right off Antelope Island Road. As you're heading

1: buffalo on Antelope Island 2: antique farming equipment at the Fielding Garr Ranch 3: the causeway into Antelope Island

south toward Fielding Garr Ranch, you're likely to catch them a few hundred feet from the left side of the road, grazing close to the water on the island's eastern shore. Remember that bison are wild animals and they will charge—don't venture too close in pursuit of the perfect photograph. Binoculars will come in handy so you can get a closer look without coming too close. In addition to bison, Antelope Island is home to other mammals including coyotes, mule deer, porcupines, bighorn sheep, and pronghorns. While pronghorns are the island's namesake, technically they are not in the antelope taxonomy. Generally speaking, dawn and dusk are good times to view wildlife on the island.

ENTERTAINMENT AND EVENTS

Antelope Island State Park hosts a variety of events spring-fall. A few highlights are included below; check the Antelope Island State Park website (https://stateparks.utah.gov/antelope-island) for a full listing that includes other events like bike races and documentary screenings.

Bison Roundup

Every year, the Utah Division of Wildlife checks in on the hundreds of bison living at Antelope Island State Park. The annual **Bison Roundup** (late Oct., 9am-2pm) takes place at the Fielding Garr Ranch. Watch horseback riders corral the bison toward the ranch while you learn more about this unique and massive herd and enjoy food and other activities. All in all, it takes about four or five hours to congregate the whole herd at the ranch for a head count. This is also a great chance to photograph bison without putting your life on the line!

Fielding Garr Ranch Ghost Tours

Once a month in the summer, Antelope Island State Park hosts free ghost tours of the old

Fielding Garr Ranch (dates vary, 9pm-11pm, free). Considering the Garr ranch house is the oldest settler-built home in Utah and also the longest inhabited (1848-1981), the potential for ghastly vibes is high. Indeed, ranch manager Carl Aldrich says he collects employee ghost stories, along with his own experiences. One evening, Aldrich returned to the ranch because he forgot to lock a door, and as he was walking through the old ranch house, he heard the sound of people talking even though he was completely alone at the site.

The ranch also hosts more history-focused tours by day if you're not of the supernatural sort (1pm Wed. and Sat. in summer, free).

Star Parties

As a certified Dark Skies Park, Antelope Island is a great place to look up after the sun sets. While you can stargaze solo if you decide to camp for the night, you can also observe stars and planets through telescopes during a **Star Party** (dates vary) hosted by the Astronomical Society (www.ogdenastronomy.com) of the nearby town of Ogden. The viewing takes place at White Rock Bay and the event is free (except for state park fees) and open to the public.

FOOD

Antelope Island is the proud home of one restaurant. Located on the Bridger Bay Beach just a short drive from the causeway into the island, the **Island Buffalo Grill** (4528 W. 1700 S., Syracuse, 801/897-3452, 11am-7pm Mon.-Sat., noon-6pm Sun., $6.50-11.25) is the sort of place that you visit on a whim because you're getting hungry and it's the only thing there. Not only is this grill the only restaurant on Antelope Island, but it's really one of the few places to get a meal on the water in the Great Salt Lake. Enjoy the novelty of its location on the largest island in the Great Salt Lake as you gobble up greasy-spoon fare—burgers, french fries, and all. And if the sight of Antelope Island's roaming herds made you hungry, dig into a buffalo burger!

CAMPING

Antelope Island is one of the best places to camp in the entire Great Salt Lake area—as long as you don't mind bugs or can time your visit around them in the early spring or fall. There are several different campgrounds on the island, all of which are managed by the state park (800/322-3770, https://stateparks. utah.gov/antelope-island).

Right by the entrance to Antelope Island, **Bridger Bay Campground** (26 sites, $20 per night, $18 for second vehicle, no water or electricity, pit toilets) is an excellent place for families and small parties to camp. Bridger Bay is suitable for tents and RVs alike. The campground is located about 1 mile (1.6 km) from Bridger Bay Beach, where potable water is available, as well as flush toilets and showers.

For a quieter place to camp, **Ladyfinger Campground** (5 sites, $20 per night, no water or electricity, pit toilets, tents only) deters crowds with a very short walk in (230 ft/70 m) and a more remote location than the centrally positioned Bridger Bay. Sleep amid the sagebrush and hike to nearby Ladyfinger Point. A downside of the Ladyfinger Campground is that no fires are allowed, so don't camp here if you only sleep outside for the s'mores. While there are limited amenities at this campground, flush toilets, showers, and potable water are available at Bridger Bay Beach, about a mile (1.6 km) down the road.

INFORMATION AND SERVICES

Since the entire island is encompassed within a state park, an entrance fee is required ($10 per vehicle, $3 per bike). The **Antelope Island Visitor Center** (4528 W. 1700 S., Syracuse, 801/773-2941, https://stateparks. utah.gov/antelope-island, 9am-5pm daily) is located in the northern part of the island, just a few minutes from the end of the causeway.

GETTING THERE

Antelope Island lies closest to Ogden; it's about a 20-minute drive southwest on I-15 (15 mi/24 km) to the entrance of the causeway. To get to the island from Ogden, take I-15 South, then take the exit for Antelope Drive and follow signs for the island. From Salt Lake City, the entrance to Antelope Island's causeway is about a 30-minute drive northwest on I-15 (30 mi/48 km).

Before you enter the causeway, you'll stop and pay the park entrance fee and pick up a map. From here, proceed about 6 miles (4.8 km) along the causeway to the island. The paved route through the island—Antelope Island Road—is about 17 miles (27 km) in total, with several diversions to the island's various beaches, campgrounds, and trails.

Bonneville Salt Flats

TOP EXPERIENCE

If you've watched *The World's Fastest Indian, Independence Day,* the series finale of *Mad Men,* or a whole host of other films and shows, then you've seen Utah's legendary salt flats. Ancient Lake Bonneville, from which the Great Salt Lake is descended, gave rise to another legacy: a massive deposit of salt stretching across southwestern Utah known as the **Bonneville Salt Flats.**

This salt desert consists of 30,000 acres of Salvador Dali-level surrealism. Mountains rising out of a white sea. Your mind playing tricks on you as the monotonous backdrop distorts time and space. And cars racing across the 12-mile-long (19.3-km) mass of sodium in pursuit of land speed records.

All this could change, however, because the salt is disappearing. Thirty thousand acres of salt might sound substantial enough to make you thirsty, but a hundred years ago, the salt flats were three times as large, spanning

Sun Tunnels

Utah is actually home to not one, but two of the most famed installations of land art in the country. As the crow flies, 50 miles (81 km) southwest of Spiral Jetty lie the **Sun Tunnels:** four massive concrete tunnels aligned perfectly to frame the sun on summer and winter solstices, located right smack in the middle of nowhere. The artist, Nancy Holt, was married to Robert Smithson, who created Spiral Jetty. Holt purchased the land upon which the tunnels sit in the Great Basin Desert, and lived in Salt Lake City for several years while working on the project, which premiered on the 1976 summer solstice.

What was Holt trying to get across with these tunnels? In short, perspective. In a boundless, barren landscape like the desert, a framing device—like a human-sized tunnel—helps the human mind process what's in front of it. In the same vein, small holes in the walls of the tunnels mimic stars in constellations. The patch of sky and landscape the tunnels frame lies outside the range of the Wasatch, far from any major towns, and about a three-hour drive from Salt Lake City. While the Sun Tunnels are far away from fuel, bathrooms, and potable water, you can camp here for free to witness the sunrise and sunset through these sculptures. Keep the Sun Tunnels on your mind if you visit Spiral Jetty, and make the trek if you're a land art enthusiast.

Sun Tunnels at summer solstice

nearly 100,000 acres. And while much of the salt was once nearly 6 feet (1.8 m) thick, today it's closer to a few inches in most places.

The culprit for the disappearance of the salt is, unsurprisingly, human activity—from the cars racing across the salt and the visitors hiking over it, to the potash mine that operates near the racetrack. In response, the Save the Salt Coalition has begun harvesting brine from the Great Salt Lake and pumping it to the salt flats. But the day may come when this ecologically and culturally historic site may be but a salty memory.

SIGHTS AND RECREATION
★ Optical Illusions

If you've been to salt flats before—in Bolivia or Namibia, for example—then you know this peculiar terrain has a way of messing with your perception. An empty flat landscape of white like the Bonneville Salt Flats doesn't provide your eye with a frame of reference by which to judge distance or size.

This is especially pronounced in photographs, wherein the viewer has even less information to gauge distance and size. Spend some time playing with perception here, staging photographs where one giant subject appears to be pinching or holding a doll-sized subject in the same plane. The optical illusion deepens if you visit after a storm. A layer of water on the salt flats will reflect the sky, so all you see is what's above, doubled and inversed. While you aren't allowed to drive on the Bonneville Salt Flats when they're wet, you can walk on them and straight into a dreamy landscape.

Bonneville Salt Flats International Speedway

An expanse of flat land as immense and

1: illusions coming to life on the Bonneville Salt Flats **2:** campers atop a van at the Bonneville Salt Flats

hard-packed as the Bonneville Salt Flats is a precious commodity when you want to go fast. It didn't take long for people to put two and two together and establish what is now the **Bonneville Salt Flats International Speedway** (Bonneville Speedway Rd., Wendover, 801/977-4300, www.bonnevilleracing.com). People have been speeding across the salt flats since 1896 and setting worldwide land speed records since 1914, when an American race car driver clocked 142.8 miles per hour (229.8 km/h) in a Blitzen Benz. And thus was born "salt fever," as it's referred to today—a fossil-fueled frenzy fed by colorful fast cars careening across a racetrack in white.

In honor of the rich racing history here, the Bonneville International Speedway is entered into the National Register of Historic Places. Historic designation aside, racing is alive and well here with new records set all the time. In 2016, for example, a Venturi set an electric-car speed record of 341 mph (545 km/h). Two years later, a Kawasaki motorcycle smoked the last record in its class, reaching 209 mph (340 km/h). Even old-fashioned yet daring cyclists set records here, drafting at well over 100 mph (161 km/h) behind vehicles.

While you might be lucky enough to catch racers flooring it on the flats during your visit, the Speedway hosts several events, including Speed Week (Aug.) and World of Speed (Sept.). You can also drive out onto the salt flats and test out your own car's horsepower. But do so at your own risk—depending on conditions, the salt crust can act like a layer of mud, which will stick to your tires and leave you stranded. It's also illegal to drive on the salt flats when they're wet, so heed conditions before you floor it.

ENTERTAINMENT AND EVENTS

A grab-bag assortment of events take place at the Bonneville Salt Flats, from ultramarathons to celebrations of rocketry. The most popular events, however, revolve around racing.

Bonneville Speed Week

For six days in mid-August, the fast and the curious come together for **Bonneville Speed Week** (www.scta-bni.org, free to spectate) on the salt flats. Watch a motley mix of antique cars, motorcycles, and speed machines vie for land speed records on the salt. Vendors selling food and souvenirs also congregate near the Speedway. Since this event is in the middle of summer, be sure to bring plenty of sunscreen and a good hat—the salt reflects the sun just like snow, which is a recipe for an awful sunburn.

Bonneville World of Speed

For a long weekend in mid-September, the intrepid and the curious come together at the salt flats to witness history at the other major racing event held here: **World of Speed** (www.saltflats.com, $20 per day for spectators, $50 to watch the whole event). Staged by the Utah Salt Flats Racing Association since the mid-1980s, the event draws racers from all over to set records, all in accordance with the Southern California Timing Association's rules and regulations.

GETTING THERE

The Bonneville Salt Flats lie 90 minutes due west of Salt Lake City on Highway 80 (111 mi/179 km). The closest town is Wendover, which is a little over 10 minutes west of the salt flats (9 mi/14.5 km). For more lodging and dining options, drive a couple miles farther west to cross the border to West Wendover in Nevada.

The Wasatch Back: Heber to Sundance

The Wasatch Back consists of the eastern, less

urban side of the Wasatch Mountains. Topographically, this region lies on the "back" side of the nearly 12,000-foot (3,658-m) mountain range. While Park City is the most prominent place in the region, several other towns, sights, and Wasatch peaks accessible from this region deserve the visitor's attention—this is the Greater Wasatch Back.

The largest of these towns is Heber, which got a tad tempted by the development opportunities that come with being a bedroom community of Park City in a picturesque valley. But look past big box stores and chain restaurants, and you'll find many unique attractions and restaurants. The verdant Heber Valley, which stays a little warmer than Park City, is also a golfer's paradise, with a choice of three scenic

Highlights

Look for ★ to find recommended sights, activities, dining, and lodging.

★ **Take a ride** through history on the **Heber Valley Railroad** (page 231).

★ **Have a soak** in the warm waters of the **Homestead Crater** in Midway (page 237).

★ **Go for a hike** through shimmying aspens and take in majestic fall foliage at **Wasatch Mountain State Park** (page 243).

★ **Tee up at the Wasatch Mountain Golf Course,** set against the backdrop of Mount Timpanogos (page 245).

★ **Escape the crowds and ski** at Robert Redford's authentic **Sundance Mountain Resort** (page 247).

★ **Climb** to the top of **Mount Timpanogos,** home to the only true glacier in Utah (page 255).

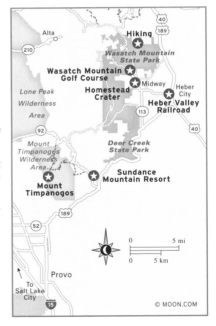

The Wasatch Back: Heber to Sundance

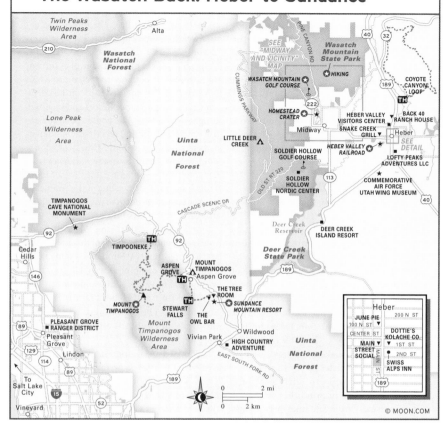

The Heber Valley also includes the town of Midway, just a five-minute drive to the west of Heber. In addition to golf, Midway is also known for its proud Swiss heritage, hot springs, and artistic streak. It's also quieter and quainter than Heber, and is by far the better of the two towns to spend a night or two.

Midway is also the gateway to Wasatch Mountain State Park, which consists of 23,000 acres of state-preserved land. The park offers hiking, mountain biking, golfing, and camping in the summer, and Nordic skiing, tubing, and snowshoeing in the winter. Soldier Hollow Nordic Center, located within the park, even served as a venue for the 2002 Winter Olympics.

Just south of Heber past Deer Creek Reservoir lies Provo Canyon and the town of Sundance, which will take you by surprise in a good way. Dominated by the Sundance Resort—owned by Robert Redford—Sundance is a delightful getaway with skiing,

Previous: riding the Wasatch Over Wasatch Trail; bagpipe players at the Soldier Hollow Sheepdog Championship; Aspen Grove Trail to the summit of Mount Timpanogos.

mountain biking, and some of the best food in the state.

Just a couple miles south of Sundance lies Mount Timpanogos, perhaps the most glorious peak in the Wasatch Range, and the second tallest, too. Visitors flock to Mount Timp, as it's locally referred to, to explore its caves, hike in the mountain's foothills, or put in a full day to reach its 11,750-foot (3,581-m) summit. Running southeast of Mount Timpanogos, with access just minutes from Sundance, the Provo River is a popular spot for tubing and river sports on hot summer days.

PLANNING YOUR TIME

If only one or two of the attractions in the Greater Wasatch Back calls out to you—whether it's golfing in Midway, skiing at Sundance, or summiting Mount Timpanogos—the region can easily be visited as a day trip from Park City or even Salt Lake City. Sundance and Mount Timpanogos lie about an hour from Salt Lake City and 45 minutes from Park City, while Midway is about 50 minutes from Salt Lake and just 30 minutes from Park City. This part of the Wasatch can also make for a great four- or five-day trip in a quieter part of the region.

If you do hope to climb Mount Timpanogos, keep in mind that your time frame is usually from late June or early July through most of September. It's not a technical climb, but it is long and exposed, so you will also need to budget a full day with an early start, and check the forecast to ensure weather will cooperate with your summit bid.

If you're looking for a unique one- or two-night romantic getaway to tack on to a Salt Lake- or Park City-focused trip, consider driving straight to Sundance Resort and spending a night or two here. You could spend the entire time exploring and relaxing at Sundance, or take a half-day trip to Midway or Mount Timpanogos during your stay. Sundance is, in fact, one of the best base camps for a Mount Timpanogos hike, since one of the trailheads lies a couple miles north of the resort, making that early start less painful.

For a longer visit to the Wasatch Back, consider spending a couple nights in Midway and a couple nights at Sundance—and maybe a night or two camping as well. Fill your days with golf, hot springs, hikes, downhill and Nordic skiing, and Heber's family-friendly attractions. The sights and activities of the area can easily fill a four- or five-day vacation.

Summer is peak tourist season here, but winter holds its own, attracting Nordic skiers to Soldier Hollow in Midway's Wasatch Mountain State Park, and downhill skiers to the quieter experience found at Sundance.

Heber

In the shadow of Mount Timpanogos lies the town of Heber. Like many of its neighboring communities, Heber has agricultural roots that still prevail at ranches and farms in the periphery. But as Park City became prohibitively expensive for many locals in the 1960s and 1970s, residents were pushed into communities like Heber. And when developers came knocking, Heber ushered them in with little in the way of discretion. In fact, in 2015, Heber was even the third fastest growing city in the United States.

The upshot is sprawl and a Main Street as loud as the toy aisle at Walmart, filled with big box stores and chains. Yet Heber does retain some of its original charm with unique local businesses and a gorgeous natural setting that still leans pastoral. For excursions in the Greater Wasatch, most routes pass through Heber on U.S. 40, which also makes it a great place to stop for lunch or a ride on the Heber Creeper train.

SIGHTS
★ Heber Valley Railroad

Park City and the Wasatch Back owe at least part of their existence to the railroad. When the Transcontinental Railroad laid its tracks in the late 1860s, many small towns across Utah boomed. Locomotion commotion peaked when the final golden spike connecting the railroad across the Unites States was placed at Promontory Summit north of the Great Salt Lake in 1869.

Today, many miles of track have been removed, and in some cases converted into recreational paths, like the Rail Trail in Park City. Heber, however, is one of the few places where the railroad still chugs its way through the mountains and welcomes the public aboard. The **Historic Heber Valley Railroad** (450 S. 600 W., 435/654-5601, www.hebervalleyrr.org, schedule varies, tickets starting at $8) hosts rides year-round, from short 90-minute jaunts through the scenic Heber Valley, to three-hour explorations of Provo Canyon and themed rides on Christmas, Cinco de Mayo, and other holidays. All rides take place on restored vintage steam engines dating 1907-1922.

Known affectionately as the Heber Creeper, the railroad is located in "Old Town" Heber, an area few would stumble upon because of its location several long blocks west of town. Any ride on the Heber Creeper offers a scenic tour of the area from a different perspective, as well as a glimpse into local history with historical reenactments and presentations aboard. Most rides include a theatrical component, like bandits staging a train robbery or cowboy poetry recited with a guitar. The Deer Creek Express ($20 adults, $15 children) is a great ride if you want a small taste of the railroad and a quick tour of the Deer Creek Reservoir with alpine scenery. Buy your tickets online or at the depot (450 S. 600 W.), which also has a small gift shop of train-themed paraphernalia. The schedule varies from three rides almost daily in the summer to just a few rides weekly in the winter, but it never runs on Sundays. Most rides take place at 11am, 3pm, or 7pm.

Commemorative Air Force Utah Wing Museum

Home to a private airport, Heber often experiences air traffic above. Occasionally, those planes belong to the Utah branch of the American Airpower Heritage Museum here in Heber. For aircraft enthusiasts or

Heber Valley Railroad tracks alongside Deer Creek Reservoir

little kids with big pilot dreams, a visit to the **Commemorative Air Force Utah Wing Museum** (2265 W. Airport Rd., 435/709-7269, www.cafutahwing.org, 10am-4pm Fri.-Sat., noon-4pm Sun. May-Oct. or by appointment, suggested donation of $5 pp) is a great way to pass the afternoon. This Smithsonian-affiliated museum has several vintage, still operational planes, the oldest being a 1942 Boeing Stearman biplane. You'll also find exhibits about local aviators and veterans, as well as air force history focused on World War II. You can even call ahead to schedule a ride on a historic military aircraft (pricing varies).

RECREATION

While the area's greatest outdoor experiences lie closer to Sundance and Midway, there are a few recreational opportunities within or close to Heber.

Biking

Take a tour of the Heber Valley by road bike, or navigate the hills above town. Wherever you ride in Heber, the views of Mount Timpanogos and the Wasatch are wonderfully omnipresent.

In Heber, you can rent mountain bikes at **Uinta Recreation** (1550 S. Hwy. 40 B, 801/613-0288, www.uintarecreation.com, 8am-6pm daily, starting at $45 per day). If you'd like a road bike, rent in Park City.

COYOTE CANYON LOOP

Coyote Canyon Loop (22.7 mi/36.5 km, 3-5 hours depending on pace, 1,700 ft/518 m elevation gain, moderate) traverses exposed terrain over rolling foothills between the Jordanelle Reservoir and Heber. From Heber, head north on U.S. 40 and turn right on Highway 32 toward Kamas. Drive slowly, because after just 1 mile (1.6 km), you'll see a dirt pullout on your right. This is the Riverview Trailhead, and it's not particularly well marked. The trail starts just right of a few small boulders. Start on the single-track and soon you'll find yourself climbing. The trail

is a lollipop, so you'll repeat a short section of trail on the way back. Coyote Canyon is one of the first trails to dry in the Wasatch Back, and it's best ridden in late spring and fall. If you do ride it in the summer, lack of shade means that an early or evening start time is ideal, and sunscreen is a must. This trail can also be fat-biked in the winter.

HEBER VALLEY LOOP

Agricultural countryside, "Little Switzerland" (aka Midway), sublime mountains, and a serene reservoir—these are the backdrops of the **Heber Valley Loop** (10 mi/16.1 km, 1.5 hours, 1,500 ft/457 m elevation gain, moderate). This tour of the Greater Wasatch Back begins on Main Street in Heber. Heading south, turn right on U.S. 189 at the end of town and follow the meandering highway. After about 3 miles (4.8 km), turn right on Highway 113 toward Charleston just as you reach the edge of Deer Creek Reservoir. The views switch from mountain and lake to forest and pasture as you progress on Highway 113 toward Midway. Stay in Midway for lunch or ice cream, then head east on Midway's Main Street, which will turn into Highway 113 again, a quieter country road, and take you all the way back to Heber (3.4 mi/5.5 km, 20 minutes).

Boating

DEER CREEK RESERVOIR

Head south on U.S. 189 and you'll soon discover a body of water hugging the curves of the road. The **Deer Creek Reservoir** (435/654-0171, https://stateparks.utah.gov/deer-creek, 6am-10pm daily in summer, 8am-5pm daily in winter, $10 per vehicle) is one of several reservoirs in the Wasatch Back that draws year-round visitors. People come to boat, swim, fish year-round, and partake in whatever lake sport you can think of. The reservoir is stocked with a couple varieties of trout and bass, as well as walleye. Located at the midway point of the reservoir on its eastern shore, **Deer Creek Island Resort** (5317 US-189, Heber, 435/654-2155, https://deercreekislandresort.com, 11am-7pm

Sun.-Thurs., 9am-7pm Fri.-Sat., $20 SUP, $20 kayak, boats starting at $100) rents a variety of water-sports and safety gear. There's also a restaurant on-site called **Dock of the Bay Grill** (5317 US-189, Heber, 435/671-3367, www.dockofthebayrestaurant.com, 11am-3pm Mon.-Thurs., 11am-9pm Fri.-Sat. Memorial Day-Labor Day, $10-13), which serves American pub fare and stages live music on weekend evenings.

FESTIVALS

Cowboy Poetry Gathering

If you've never heard of cowboy poetry, it's exactly what it sounds like: poetry written by cowboys. You can imagine the themes of the verse: long days on stubborn horses, lost love at the rodeo, and whiskey sipped around a campfire. It can be quite endearing and all the more so when it's read aloud. That's why if you're in town in late October during Heber's annual **Cowboy Poetry Gathering and Buckaroo Fair** (https://hebervalleycowboypoetry.com), you should go! First held in 1995, the event consists of individual performances leading up to a full-on weekend festival celebrating Western culture. Enjoy performances of country music, Western-themed booths with crafts, and a mountain man camp, among other things. General admission is $10 for the weekend (the last two days of the event); individual performance tickets range $5-65.

FOOD

Don't mistake Heber as a hub of only fast food based on a quick drive down Main Street. There are several restaurants that serve delicious, locally sourced food made from scratch, and a number of cute bakeries worth a stop. And if kids are in tow, there are many family-friendly restaurants to choose from as well.

Oh, and what's up with the soda mixers? Wherever there's a strong Mormon presence (like Heber), there are also usually soda mixers, which many Mormons enjoy for breakfast in lieu of coffee, tea, or other hot beverages dubbed illegal in the LDS Church. You'll find soda mixer drive-thrus with long lines in the morning, as well as soda mixers on the menus of cafés. Predicated on the idea that sugar rather than caffeine can put pep in one's step in the morning, these soda mixers typically feature one or two sodas mixed with various syrups.

Big-city chef settles in a small town. It's a story you may have heard before and one that typically goes favorably for the chef and the town alike. The chef gets a slower pace of life, while the town enjoys new talent. In the case of **Main Street Social** (98 S. Main St., 435/657-6534, www.mainstreetsocialutah.com, 11am-4pm and 5pm-9pm Tues.-Sat., $16-28), chefs Ashley and Vanessa Chapman met in London at one of Gordon Ramsay's restaurants, before finding their way to Heber, Utah. They've dug in their Danskos in a restored 19th-century cottage that can accommodate 35, and more in the summer when the blissful, verdant patio opens. Inspired by public houses in England, Main Street Social aims to create a communal vibe, in particular by sourcing locally. The menu keeps things interesting with daily house-made soups, locally inspired cocktails, and dishes like cauliflower risotto or the Pork Tomahawk with maple-chipotle mashed sweet potatoes.

Don't judge a restaurant by its location or facade! For proof, look no further than ★ **Back 40 Ranch House** (1223 US-40, 435/654-3070, www.back40utah.com, 11am-10pm Mon.-Sat., 10am-10pm Sun., $11-30). Given its location off U.S. 40 (hence, the name) in a log cabin, you might pigeonhole the place as serving great greasy burgers, good times, and that's about it. But Back 40, little did you suspect, is a farm-to-table restaurant that sources everything it can from the state of Utah. That organic cheese in your white cheddar bacon mac and cheese? It's from Heber Valley Artisan Cheese a few miles down the road. The grass-fed beef in your steak frites? From a ranch on the Wyoming border. The kombucha on tap? From Ogden. The water in your glass? From Back 40's well. The cabin itself is even something of a local legend, since it

once housed Heber's first bar. If the weather's nice, sit on the patio, which overlooks pasture and the Wasatch Mountains.

If you've been to Texas or Poland, then you know all about kolaches, those delectable circular pastries with a tender dough and a big dab of filling in the middle. **Dottie's Kolache Co.** (1851 95 S. Main St., 435/632-4162, www.dottieskolaches.com, 7am-7pm Mon.-Sat., kolaches $1.75-3) has brought the kolache tradition and other treats to Heber. The kolache options are many and span sweet and savory options for breakfast and lunch. Since the dough errs on the sweet side, I'm a fan of the subtly sweet fillings, like lemon or poppyseed. The sausage, egg, and cheese makes a fine breakfast with one of the espresso drinks available. Here you can also partake in the unique Utah morning soda mixer tradition with a drink like the Mango Tango, made with Mountain Dew, blood orange syrup, and mango syrup.

Pie lovers must make a stop at **June Pie** (133 N. Main St., 435/503-6950, www.junepie. com, 3pm-6pm Tues.-Fri., 11am-2pm Sat., savory pies start at $25, sweet pies start at $20, pie by the slice $5, hand pies $2.50). Owner Tehmi Brimhall is obsessed with pies, and it shows in both quality and the sheer diversity of offerings. You'll find sweet and savory pies alike, with classics (like apple), twists on classics (banana cream with a black bottom), and pies unlike any you've encountered before (grapefruit custard). The savory options also make for a great lunch by the slice, with fillings ranging from chicken curry and quiche to Thanksgiving leftovers. June Pie also sells hand pies that resemble empanadas, but only with sweet fillings—these make great treats to bring along on a hike at Wasatch Mountain State Park.

Situated in Old Town Heber alongside a creek of the same name, ★ **Snake Creek Grill** (650 W. 100 S., 435/654-2133, www. snakecreekgrill.com, 5:30pm-9:30pm Wed.-Sat., 5:30pm-8:30pm Sun., $22.95-27.95)

1: Back 40 Ranch House 2: Main Street Social

serves some of the best food in Heber in a quiet, pastoral setting. Seven blocks west of Main Street, Old Town Heber feels like the set of a Western film, and with a facade that looks straight out of the mid-19th-century Wild West and a quaint country house vibe inside, Snake Creek Grill matches its setting. Chef/owner Dean Hottle has been cooking here since 1999, and his experience shows, with dishes like wild lobster and shrimp corn dogs served with a roasted chili sauce and vegetable slaw, or a cedar-roasted Scottish salmon with Israeli couscous and a lemon-cucumber yogurt sauce. Dishes like these defy genre and convention, and are a pleasant surprise in such a rustic, relaxed setting.

ACCOMMODATIONS
Heber is definitely not the quietest place to stay in the Greater Wasatch Back, but it's certainly convenient and affordable, with lodging adjacent to dining and activities all on Main Street.

It's hard to miss the **Swiss Alps Inn** (167 S. Main St., 435/654-0722, www.swissalpsinn. com, starting at $86) in downtown Heber. This charming, family-friendly lodge offers a taste of Switzerland, inspired by the Swiss presence in the Heber Valley. You'll know it when you see it: The inn resembles a florally decorated Swiss cottage, with two Swiss-costumed statues—straight out of "It's a Small World"—peeking out of a second-story window to *wilkommen* you in. This is a motel, so it's nothing fancy. But it's a fine and affordable place to spend the night, especially with kids, who will enjoy the property's outdoor pool and mini playground, or the larger playground across the street. Adults can unwind in the indoor hot tub.

INFORMATION AND SERVICES
The **Heber Valley Visitor Center** (475 N. Main St., 435/654-3666, www.gohebervalley. com, 9am-5pm Mon.-Fri.) is located at the corner of Main Street and West 500 North, on your right as you pull into town from

Park City or Kamas, or on your left coming from Salt Lake City. The visitors center provides information on Heber, Midway, the Deer Creek Reservoir, and other surrounding areas.

GETTING THERE

Heber is just a 20-minute drive (17 mi/27 km) south from Park City. From downtown Park City, take Deer Valley Drive for a half mile (0.8 km) to Bonanza Drive, turn right, and continue another half mile (0.8 km). Then turn right on Highway 248 East/Kearns Boulevard. After 2.5 miles (4 km), take the exit onto U.S. 40 East. Follow the highway for about 12.5 miles (20.1 km) until it turns into Heber's Main Street.

From downtown Salt Lake City, Heber is about a 45-minute drive southeast (45 mi/72 km). Take I-80 East and after you pass Kimball Junction, take the right exit onto U.S. 40 East toward Heber/Vernal. Drive for about 16 miles (26 km) and U.S. 40 will turn into Heber's Main Street.

Midway and Vicinity

Midway is the "Little Switzerland" of the Wasatch, and a great place to stroll, soak in the natural hot springs, and golf. The town takes its name from its location halfway between two mid-19th-century settlements, where a fort was constructed at the behest of Brigham Young in response to conflict with Native Americans. In the late 19th century, a series of Swiss families began to arrive, who gave the town its Swiss character, which is on full display during the annual Swiss Days Festival in late August.

Originally founded around ranching and homesteading, Midway now counts tourism as one of its primary drivers. Wasatch Mountain State Park, natural hot springs, Swiss-inspired resorts, and a Main Street filled with charming art galleries, restaurants, and boutiques are just a few reasons to while away an afternoon or a few days in Midway.

Summer is the busy season in Midway, when people come to hike and mountain bike at Wasatch Mountain State Park. Those who prefer tee time to trail time flock to Midway to golf at one of the two scenic courses within the park itself. And most enjoy exploring the unique Homestead Crater, a 65-foot-deep (20-m) hole in the wall filled with water heated geothermally by the Earth's mantle.

What does one do in this crater? Soak, yoga on a paddleboard, or even scuba dive to the bottom.

Winter is a quieter time in general in the Greater Wasatch Back, Midway included. But as a former Winter Olympics venue, the Soldier Hollow Nordic Center at Wasatch Mountain State Park attracts cross-country skiers and snowshoers, while the Midway Ice Castles will awe the elementary-aged set. The snowy landscape and peaceful mood make a visit to Midway in the "off-season" worth your time.

SIGHTS AND RECREATION
★ Homestead Crater

The life of Swiss immigrant Simon Schneitter changed forever when, in 1886, he discovered a hole with warm water at the property he'd been homesteading. He soon began entertaining guests, who came to view and soak in the "hot pot." Soon, the Schneitters started serving meals to the growing visitors, and eventually opened a resort. Today, this 10,000-year-old cavity in the earth is known as the **Homestead Crater** (700 N. Homestead Dr., Midway, 435/654-1102, https://homesteadresort.com, 12:30pm-6:30pm Mon.-Thurs., 10:30am-6:30pm Fri.-Sat., 10:30am-4:30pm Sun.,

1: Snake Creek Grill 2: Swiss Alps Inn

Midway and Vicinity

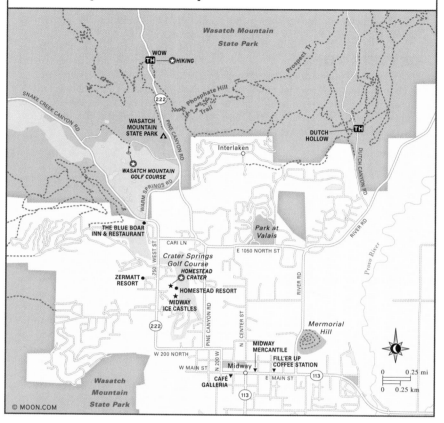

© MOON.COM

swim/soak $13-16 for 40 minutes, snorkeling $18-21 for 40 minutes, scuba dive $22-27 for 1 hour), and you can come to ditch the winter chill, attempt downward dog on a paddleboard, or even scuba dive. Since a resort has been built up around this locally famous crater, you can also stay, dine, and even golf at the Homestead Resort, where the crater is located. If a paddleboard headstand is your goal, yoga classes are offered by **Park City Yoga Adventures** (www.parkcityyogaadventures.com). Regardless of activity type, bring a swimsuit, towel, and flip-flops.

Midway Ice Castles

If you've ever seen—or climbed—a frozen waterfall, you know how enchanting they can be. Well, imagine if someone re-created 20 frozen waterfalls in one spot and blinged them out with thousands of LED lights and instrumental music! That's the **Midway Ice Castles** (700 Homestead Dr., 866/435-2850, https://icecastles.com/midway, 5:30pm-9pm Mon.-Thurs., 5:30pm-10:30pm Fri.-Sat., tickets starting at $10.95 adults, $7.95 children). Are these artificial falls as enchanting as a frozen waterfall in the backcountry? No, but they are a magical sight to behold, in particular for young kids, and much easier to access. So, after the chairlifts stop spinning and the Nordic trails close for the evening, pay a visit to these faux glacial caves, icicles, and features carved by master ice sculptors.

Golf

Crater Springs Golf Course at Homestead Resort (700 N. Homestead Dr., Midway, 435/654-5588, https://homesteadresort.com, open May 1-Oct 31 depending on weather, sunrise-sunset daily, $54 for 18 holes with discounted rates for resort guests) is a great golfing option whether or not you're staying at the resort. You can also pair it with a soak at the Homestead Crater. The par 72 course features pristine landscaping with trees, water features, and mountain views.

FESTIVALS

Swiss Days

Midway leans into its Swiss heritage during its annual **Swiss Days Festival** (Midway Town Hall, 140 W. Main St., http://www.midwayswissdays.com, free), a celebration of the motherland of many a Midway resident through music, crafts, and, of course, cheese. Specific dates vary year to year, but Swiss Days is typically held for two days at the end of August. This celebration has been taking place since the 1940s and brings out locals, nearby residents, and tourists alike. Some 200 vendors line the Midway Town Square, offering Swiss-themed wares, from dirndls and hats to Swiss cheese sandwiches.

Soldier Hollow Sheepdog Championship

Sheepdogs get their 15 minutes of glory and fame during Midway's annual championship event. The competition and festival are held at the Soldier Hollow Nordic Center, which in the summer transforms into a network of trails. At the four-day **Soldier Hollow Sheepdog Championship** (2002 Soldier Hollow Ln., 435/654-2002, https://soldierhollowclassic.com, $11-17 depending on day of event) in late August, sheepdogs go

muzzle-to-muzzle herding a pack of Rocky Mountain ewes on the Olympic Hillside in under 13 minutes. There are also competitions for other breeds, including swimming pups, speedy pups, and rescue dogs. But it's not all about the dogs. There are also food vendors, exotic animals, a raptor show, bagpipe performances, and even a Navajo rug show.

FOOD

Swiss fine dining, thin-crust pizza hand-tossed by a New Yorker, homemade ice cream in a gas station—these are just a few of the great eats to be had in Midway. To discover more Midway eateries, I recommend menu-shopping its Main Street, which is a delight to stroll when the weather's nice.

Crowning the Swiss fine-dining category in Midway is **Blue Boar Restaurant** (1235 Warm Springs Rd., 435/654-1400, https://theblueboarinn.com/dining, 8am-10:30am, 11:30am-2:30pm, and 5:30pm-9pm daily, brunch 9am-2pm Sun, $30-39), located inside a fabulous inn of the same name. If you're the sort of person who entrusts your dining choices to the pros, then you'll want to know that Blue Boar has earned the most Zagat points possible (26), received Best of State in several categories, and enjoyed a *Wine Spectator* Award of Excellence. While you can bet there's raclette on the menu, Blue Boar's other dishes wander around both the Old and New Worlds. The setting, however, is decidedly European, with a formal dining room and verdant outdoor patio. A great reason to visit is Sunday brunch, when you can indulge in a five-course meal, or have at the buffet of pastries, Benedicts, juices, and more.

If you're searching for seafood in the Swiss Alps of the Wasatch, dock at ★ **Midway Mercantile** (99 E. Main St., 435/315-4151, www.midwaymercantile.com, 11:30am-10pm Mon.-Fri., 9am-10pm Sat., 9am-9pm Sun., $17-38), where you can slurp up oysters on the half shell to your heart's content. That and several other seafood-forward dishes on the menu owe their existence to the coastal origins of Midway Mercantile's owners. After

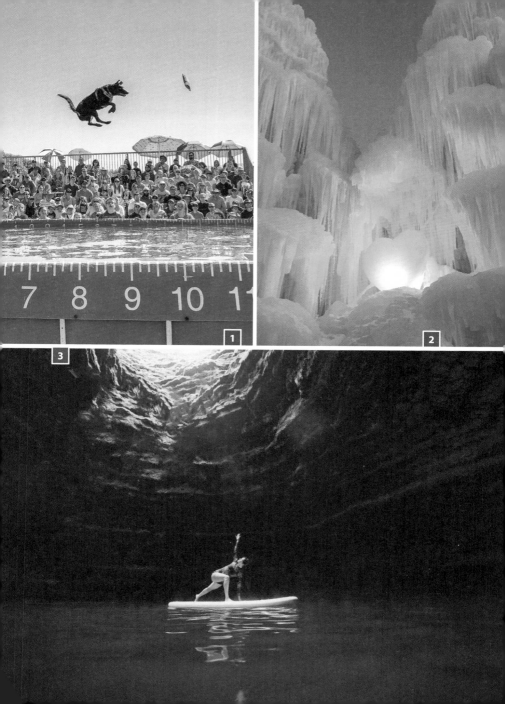

almost two decades in the Seattle restaurant scene, husband-and-wife team John and Sandra decided to seek out a quieter place to do business in Midway. They bought and renovated a historic 1874-built general store, preserving the original floors and brick exterior. You'll also find handmade pastas that change daily, classics like cassoulet, and a pub fare section of the menu that includes more casual dishes such as fish tacos and stone hearth-fired pizza. Don't miss the beverage menu, with morning treats like a $5 Bloody Mary, and inventive cocktails like the Utah's Finest, which features local kombucha and rum with lime, bitters, and agave.

Tom Kha, New York-style wood-fired pizzas and bagels, giant cinnamon buns, Chicago hot dogs, Philly cheesesteaks, homemade fettuccine—this is just a smattering of what you'll find on the many menus at ★ **Café Galleria** (101 W. Main St., 435/657-2002, www.thecafegalleria.com, 7am-9pm Mon. and Wed.-Thurs., 7am-10pm Fri.-Sat., 8am-8pm Sun., $9-15). For that, thank owner and New Yorker Cecil Duvall, who simply wanted to re-create the food of his home in the Wasatch. The restaurant walls here serve as a gallery for Cecil's son's photography of Italy and the ingredients used in the kitchen—hence, the name. The walk-up-only Café Doghouse dishes up the hot dog, sausage, and steak side of the operation.

From a fire truck-red vintage 1930s gas station, **Fill'er Up Coffee Station** (201 E. Main St., 435/657-2700, 6am-6pm Mon.-Fri., 7am-6pm Sat.-Sun.) serves coffee and light breakfast fare, as you'd imagine from the name. But by the time sunny afternoons roll around, Fill'er Up is best known as an ice cream parlor, scooping up its own Bee's Knees Ice Cream. You can enjoy your treats on the go, but there's also café seating inside and on the colorful patio. The ice cream flavors range from standbys like mint chocolate

chip to more unusual varieties like cake batter and horchata.

ACCOMMODATIONS

Midway has plenty of Swiss-themed resorts and quiet getaways to choose from. Many offer their own on-site activities as well as dining, making a relaxed couple of days without ever getting in a car totally feasible.

Named for the popular ski resort in Switzerland, where the iconic Matterhorn Peak angles toward the sky, **Zermatt Resort** (784 Resort Dr., 435/657-0180, https://zermattresort.com, starting at $309) is a large high-end lodge. Swiss architecture defines the character of some 300 guest rooms, ranging from your standard king bed to lavish penthouse suites and chateau villas. As "resort" implies, there are many amenities to enjoy here. Swim from the indoor pool directly into the outdoor pool, or soak in a hot tub beneath a waterfall. There's also a full-service spa, and everything from a pub and a European bakery to fine dining to keep you full without going far.

Home of the Homestead Crater, **Homestead Resort** (700 N. Homestead Dr., 435/654-1102, https://homesteadresort.com, starting at $129) offers Swiss-influenced affordably priced lodging and dining, a peaceful setting, a golf course, and, of course, the main attraction: the crater. The pool and hot tubs are also filled with mineral water from the crater. There are a couple of unique accommodations options, including cottages and condos for larger groups.

If you like to sleep near where you eat and you like to eat well, stay at the ★ **Blue Boar Inn** (1235 Warm Springs Rd., 435/654-1400, https://theblueboarinn.com, starting at $175). The restaurant here is one of the best in Midway, if not in the state, in addition to the French-inspired Truffle Hollow Pub. The inn itself has legit old-world appeal, with wrought-iron balconies, imported antique European furniture, and a name inspired by Howard Pyle's novel *The Merry Adventures of Robin Hood*. The literary inspiration doesn't stop there; each of the dozen rooms is named for

1: dog jumping competition at the Soldier Hollow Sheepdog Championship **2:** Midway Ice Castles **3:** paddleboard yoga at Homestead Crater

and designed in the spirit of an author, from Robert Frost to Jane Austen.

INFORMATION AND SERVICES

The **Heber Valley Visitor Center** (475 N. Main St., Heber, 435/654-3666, www. gohebervalley.com, 9am-5pm Mon.-Fri.) is located at the corner of Main Street and West 500 North on your right as you pull into town from Park City or Kamas, or on your left coming from Salt Lake City. The visitors center provides information on Heber, Midway, the Deer Creek Reservoir, and other surrounding areas.

GETTING THERE

From Heber, it's just a five-minute drive west to Midway. Heading south on Main Street,

turn right on Highway 113 West/West 100 South Street. Follow this for about 3 miles (4.8 km) and it will turn into Midway's Main Street.

From Park City, it's about a 20-minute drive (18 mi/29 km) directly to Midway. Take U.S. 40 East past the Jordanelle Reservoir. After almost 9 miles (14.5 km), you'll come to an intersection with a stoplight at River Road; turn right. After 3 miles (4.8 km), you'll reach a traffic circle. Take the third exit to continue on River Road. Continue for a mile (1.6 km), then turn right on Main Street and drive straight into Midway.

From Salt Lake City, Midway is a 50-minute drive (46 mi/74 km) southeast on I-80 East and U.S. 40.

Wasatch Mountain State Park

In 1961, Utah decided to preserve some 23,000 acres of land in the Wasatch Mountains. Seven years later, this acreage officially became a state park. Today, **Wasatch Mountain State Park** (435/654-1791, https://stateparks.utah.gov/wasatch-mountain, 8am-5pm daily, $7 per vehicle) draws local visitors and tourists from all over to camp, hike, mountain bike, golf, and partake in many more activities in the mountains. At 5,900 feet (1,798 m), the park offers the opportunity to explore trails at a slightly lower elevation than Park City or the nearby Uintas if you wish to acclimate or if you struggle with altitude sickness.

Come winter, Wasatch Mountain State Park offers groomed and ungroomed terrain alike for cross-country skiing and snowshoeing. Stop at the **visitors center** (1281 Warm Spring Dr., Midway, 435/654-1791, https://stateparks.utah.gov, 8am-5pm daily), which lies at the southern edge of the park, for maps, specific recommendations, and directions.

1: Fill'er Up Coffee Station **2:** Café Galleria

★ HIKING

One of the best things about Wasatch Mountain State Park is that it can be hiked year-round. Summer hiking trails in the shade abound. One of the most glorious times to visit for a trek is the fall when the foliage is remarkable and the temperatures pleasant. In the winter, you can still explore the area by foot by strapping snowshoes to your feet. And at a lower elevation and in an area that tends to draw a little more sun, the Wasatch Mountain trails dry more quickly than much of the higher alpine single-track of Park City, for example.

The **Wasatch Over Wasatch (WOW) Trail** (9.4 mi/15.1 km one-way, 5-6 hours depending on pace, 2,400 ft/732 m elevation gain, strenuous) is a newer trail with incredible views and a heart-pumping workout. Ultimately, this trail will extend all the way to Empire Pass in Deer Valley—it's only about a mile (1.6 km) short of this goal as is. To start, turn onto Homestead Drive/Highway 222 from Midway's Main Street, and follow it past the Wasatch Mountain Golf Course.

The road will turn into Pine Canyon Road. About 0.25 mile (0.4 km) past the Oak Hollow Campground, look for a pullout parking area on your right; the trailhead is across the road from this parking area. As an out-and-back trail, you can hike the whole thing (or as far as you want) and then turn around. Or you can set up a shuttle by parking a car at the trailhead and driving up to the end of the trail (about 3.4 mi/5.5 km farther up Hwy. 222—look for the trailhead on the left side of the road and park in one of the large pullouts on the right side of the road). This will allow you the option of turning those 2,400 feet (732 m) of elevation gain into loss if you'd prefer to take in the views without the exertion. No matter how much of the trail you cover or which way you hike, you'll see beautiful views of the Wasatch all along the way. This trail is also popular with mountain bikers.

BIKING
Dutch Hollow Trails
Just a couple miles north of Midway and Heber lie the Dutch Hollow Trails. While these 20 miles (32 km) of trails can be hiked, biked, or navigated by horse, they're becoming increasingly popular with mountain bikers. Grab a map online (look for the "Dutch Hollow Trails brochure" under "Publications" at https://stateparks.utah.gov/wasatch-mountain) or from the Wasatch Mountain State Park Visitor Center and string together a loop that's right for you. One possibility is to start on the **Heber Valley Overlook Trail** (2.3 mi/3.7 km one-way, 30 minutes, 200 ft/61 m elevation gain, easy), which is great for beginners and enjoyable for riders of all abilities. Follow signs to the overlook, where you can take in the whole Heber Valley from Midway to the mouth of the Provo Canyon. You can ride back the way you came, or continue north on the trail past the overlook until it turns into a playful descent. The trailhead for Heber Valley Overlook and the Dutch Hollow Trails is a 10-minute drive northeast from the park visitors center—follow prominent signs off River Road.

Note that bike rentals are not available within the park, so plan to rent in Heber, Midway, or Park City in advance.

GOLF
While it may seem somewhat unusual, there are two golf courses located within the boundaries of Wasatch Mountain State Park. Both are highly rated, but the Wasatch Mountain Golf Course in particular has been deemed

Dutch Hollow Trails at Wasatch Mountain State Park

the best place to tee off in Utah by *Golf Digest* magazine.

★ Wasatch Mountain Golf Course

Poised at 6,000 feet (1,829 m) with inspiring views of the Wasatch Range and the valley below, **Wasatch Mountain Golf Course** (975 Golf Course Dr., 435/654-0532, www. wasatchgolfcourse.com, sunrise-sunset daily, starting at $50 pp) is highly lauded and time-tested, since it first opened in 1967. There are two 18-hole courses to choose from. The Lake Course is a flatter course with water features that have a way of reflecting the sunsets and mountain vistas surrounding you. The Mountain Course gives you and your golfing skills more of a workout, with rolling terrain. As you play across the first nine holes, you'll travel across 2 miles (3.2 km) uphill. Fall is a glorious time to golf here, when you'll be rewarded with a mosaic of red, orange, and yellow leaves sweeping the hills around the course. Take advantage of the hours here, which stay tuned to the sun, so you can find your golf nirvana in the most beautiful light of the day. From the heart of Midway, this golf course is just a seven-minute drive (3 mi/4.8 km) northwest on Pine Canyon Road.

Soldier Hollow Golf Course

Southwest of Midway lies **Soldier Hollow Golf Course** (1370 W. Soldier Hollow Ln., 435/654-7442, www.soldierhollowgolf.com, 6am-9pm daily, starting at $45 pp). The 18-hole Gold Course features more mountainous terrain with elevation changes from hole to hole, as well as native vegetation. For a more straightforward experience, head to the Silver Course, also 18 holes, which beholds mountains—like Timpanogos—rather than traversing them, if that sounds more your pace. Soldier Hollow also offers a pro shop, dining, and a practice area that includes putting areas and a driving range. From downtown Midway, Soldier Hollow is a seven-minute drive (4 mi/6.4 km) southwest on Highway 113 and Stringtown Road.

OFF-ROADING

With access to some 60 miles (97 km) of trail and dirt road available for off-road vehicles, Wasatch Mountain State Park is an ATVer's paradise. Half of this terrain exists within the state park itself, while the remainder is accessible from the park but actually covers Forest Service land. Operating from within the park, **Lofty Peaks** (845 S. Main St., Heber City, 435/654-5810, www.loftypeaks.

golfing at Soldier Hollow

com, 8am-5pm daily, off-road vehicles start-ing at $175 per day) rents out a line of differ-ent ATVs and can also arrange tours. In the winter, much of this terrain becomes acces-sible by snowmobile. Stick to designated roads and trails.

CROSS-COUNTRY SKIING AND SNOWSHOEING

A golfing destination by summer, Soldier Hollow turns into a Nordic skier's paradise in the winter. It even served as a venue for the 2002 Winter Olympics, which means it's equipped with a biathlon range for those who like a little shooting with their skiing. At the **Soldier Hollow Nordic Center** (2002 Soldier Hollow Ln., Midway, 435/654-2002, www.soldierhollow.com, 9am-4:30pm daily in winter, trail pass $10 adults per day, Nordic rentals $20 adults per day), you'll find nearly 20 miles (32 km) of groomed trails that can be used for both cross-country skiing and snow-shoeing. At the on-site **Soldier Hollow Day Lodge,** you can rent ski and snowshoe gear. Right by the trails, there's also a lift-accessed **snow tubing park** (hours vary by day and season, but are generally 10am-8pm daily, starting at $20 for a two-hour session) with descents as long as 1,200 feet (366 m). Light snacks are sold on-site, and there's also a res-taurant across from the lodge.

CAMPING

There are a number of developed sites to choose from within Wasatch Mountain State Park, many with access to showers and RV hookups. There are also four group camp-grounds for larger parties. Many of these sites fill up fast, so book ahead of time. Campsites can be reserved up to 16 weeks

ahead (800/322-3770, https://utahstateparks. reserveamerica.com).

If you're all about the amenities, choose one of the 125 sites at the **Wasatch Mountain State Park Campground** (435/654-3961, open spring-fall depending on weather, $14-30 per night, tents and RVs permitted, full hookups), which is divided into three areas: the Cottonwood, Oak Hollow, and Mahogany loops. All enjoy access to picnic tables, grills, paved parking, potable water, electricity, and bathrooms with hot showers. RV camping tends to dominate in these areas, though tents are permitted as well.

If you're interested in off-roading or searching for a quieter setting to camp at Wasatch Mountain State Park, pick one of the 16 campsites at **Little Deer Creek Campground** (435/654-1791, open mid-spring-mid-fall depending on weather, $14 per night, tents and small trailers only, ame-nities include one restroom and potable water, partial hookups available), which is accessed via a dirt road that can also be explored by ATV. From Midway, Little Deer Creek is a 35-minute drive (10.5 mi/16.9 km) south-west on quiet roads. Much of the drive is on Cascade Springs Drive, which is partially dirt, and Deer Creek Campground Road, which is entirely dirt.

GETTING THERE

Wasatch Mountain State Park surrounds the town of Midway, and lies just a five-minute drive from downtown. From town, head north on Homestead Drive/Highway 222 for about a mile (1.6 km) until you see the visitors cen-ter on your right. You can stop here, or follow directions to the specific trailhead, camp-ground, golf course, or other park attraction you're looking for.

Sundance

Sundance Mountain Resort (8841 N. Alpine Loop Rd., Sundance, 800/892-1600, www.sundanceresort.com) casts a spell over most who visit. It's a spell cast over the course of decades by Robert Redford, conjured up by a commitment to prize the local landscape above all else. Redford has been stubborn in his commitment to, first, the environment and, second, the arts above all else in his stewardship of this beautiful spread of land.

Located in Provo Canyon just a couple miles from Mount Timpanogos, Sundance Resort is not situated within any existing town, but manages to foster the feel of its own community. The successful balance of the outdoors, the arts, history, and fine dining elevate this resort above all in Utah, in my humble opinion. Even if you can't work a night here into your trip, plan to stop at least for a meal, a day of skiing, a hike, or a concert. All activities, lodging, and dining listed for Sundance are at the same address, phone number, and website as the main resort unless otherwise noted.

RECREATION

In the winter, Sundance is a ski resort, with several other wintry activities to choose from. If you're not a skier and visiting in the winter, consider checking out the Nordic Center or testing your nerve on the Winter ZipTour zipline course. When the snow melts and the mud dries, Sundance becomes a new kind of paradise, with one of the toughest road rides in Utah, and beautiful, uncrowded trails snaking around the foothills and mountains surrounding Mount Timpanogos.

★ Skiing

If you hate the scene that is skiing these days, you'll love Sundance (9am-9pm Mon., Wed., Fri., and Sat., 9am-4:30pm Tues., Thurs., and Sun. early Dec.-early Apr., tickets $85). It has the vibe of a small family-owned resort without the crowds and Disneyworld feel of a corporate ski area. A lift ticket is also less expensive here than it is at the Cottonwood or Park City resorts.

Runs are a well-balanced mix of beginner, intermediate, and advanced. Plenty of

THE WASATCH BACK: HEBER TO SUNDANCE

SUNDANCE

Sundance Mountain Resort

beginner terrain exists off Ray's Lift from the base. Expert skiers can get their kicks off Red's Lift, which takes you to the top of Red's Mountain—test your nerve on Vertigo. If you ride up Red's, stop at **Bearclaw Cabin** (801/223-4157, 11am-3pm daily) to take in 360-degree views of the Wasatch Mountains, including Mount Timpanogos, up close and personal. The restaurant serves beer, wine, and a simple menu that includes nachos and chili.

Sundance Resort is also one of the few in the Wasatch to offer **night skiing** four days a week (Mon., Wed., Fri., and Sat.). In fact, most of the front side of the mountain remains open these evenings until 9pm.

Gear for rental and demo—as well as lessons—are available on-site, and complimentary tours of the mountain are also available to newcomers.

Nordic Center

If you prefer horizontal over vertical skiing, check out the **Sundance Nordic Center** (9049 Timphaven Rd., Sundance, 801/223-4170, 9am-5pm daily, $18 full-day pass, classic ski rentals $20 per day, skate-ski rentals $23 per day). Here you'll find 15 kilometers (9.3 mi) of groomed trails for both classic and skate skiers that take you through aspen groves with alpine views. In addition to cross-country gear, you can also rent snowshoes ($13 per day) or a tow-behind sled to pull along kiddos too little for skis ($15 per day). The Nordic Center also offers lessons and clinics (starting at $35 pp).

Ziplining

The **Winter ZipTour** (844/947-8687, $59 pp) course includes over 2,100 feet (640 m) of elevation loss, sometimes at speeds cresting 65 miles per hour (105 km/h). Cold air in your face and views of Mount Timpanogos for 3,870 feet (1,180 m) of zipline—talk about an invigorating ride! Be sure to bundle up before you hit the zip—a balaclava or buff might come in handy on those really chilly days.

If a winter zipline ride sounds a little too chilly for you, the **Sundance ZipTour** (844/947-8687, starting at $79 pp) is also available in the summer. Choose from two different tour lengths, depending on how much ziplining you can handle.

Scenic Lift Rides

Ray's Lift offers **scenic lift rides** (10am-6pm daily mid-May-early Sept., 10am-5pm daily early Sept.-early Oct.); tickets are $20 for adults, $28 for an all-day pass. There are panoramic views of Sundance below and the surrounding mountains. There's also **Bearclaw Cabin** (801/223-4157, 11am-3pm daily), where you can get snacks, lunch, and drinks. You can also go for hikes or bike rides from the top of the lift.

Mountain Biking

Sundance offers over 25 miles (40 km) of single-track traversing hillsides over valleys and through forests. The biggest downside to mountain biking here is that the resort requires you to pay to play. This makes sense if you're riding Sundance's chairlifts up to enjoy descent-only biking, which is the norm at many ski resorts that offer biking in the summer. In this case, you purchase a chairlift day pass ($28) or single ride ($15). But even if you don't wish to ride the lift, you need a trails-only day pass ($7). Rentals are available on-site at Sundance Mountain Outfitters ($60 per day).

Sundance offers free trail maps that can help you piece together the perfect ride. You can also stop in the bike shop or flag down a bike patroller to get trail recommendations suitable for your ability level and time constraints. Be sure to hit **Archie's Loop** (2.2 mi/3.5 km, 30 min, 1,300 ft/396 m elevation gain, moderate), which offers some of the best panoramic views in this trail system. And heed the warnings for downhill experts-only biking routes—some feature mandatory rock drops and steep pitches, where even dismounting and hiking your bike would be impossible.

Road Biking

If you're in it for the climbs and the views, the **Alpine Loop** (30 mi/48 km, 3-5 hours, approx. 2,700 ft/823 m elevation gain, difficult) is a ride for the bucket list. Whether you're staying at Sundance or just parking there for the day, the main resort parking lot is your starting point. From here, continue west past the resort on Highway 92 for about 15 miles (24 km), past Mount Timpanogos all the way into American Fork Canyon. The name "loop" is misleading here; most ride this as an out-and-back, because to forge a loop would involve a whole lot of miles and cycling on less than ideal highways. You can turn around at an earlier point within American Fork Canyon for a shorter ride; just pedal back the way you came and enjoy the views from a different perspective.

If you do want to ride the true loop (40 mi/64 km, 6-8 hours, 4,200 ft/1,280 m elevation gain, difficult), start from downtown Midway and prepare to ride unpaved and rougher roads. Once you reach Heber, hop on the Deer Creek Trail, which is a part of the Provo-Jordan River Parkway, either off U.S. 189 where it meets the Deer Creek Reservoir, or from Soldier Hollow in Midway. Ride the trail until it connects with U.S. 189. Turn right on Highway 92, and a couple miles past Sundance, hang a right on Forest Road 114 toward Cascade Springs and take Cascade Springs Drive back into Midway.

Horseback Riding

Between the Western vibes of the resort and the beautiful scenery, Sundance is a great place to go for a horseback ride. Less than a mile (1.6 km) up Highway 92 from the main resort area, the Sundance Stables offer small-group and private Western-style guided rides (1-2 hours, starting at $75 pp). There are beginner-friendly options for families and those without riding experience, as well as more extensive excursions that venture toward Stewart Falls or are staged at sunset. You can even take a ride that brings you to a scenic spot where you'll dismount and practice 40 minutes of yoga before returning to the stables.

Fishing, Rafting, and Tubing

The **Provo River** runs alongside U.S. 189 with access just minutes from Sundance and is a popular spot for anglers and river rats. After just a mile (1.6 km) from Sundance heading south on U.S. 189, turn left on South Fork Road and you'll immediately see a popular put-in spot for the Provo. If you have your own equipment, you can just show up here, park, and fly-fish, kayak, raft, or tube. But if you need a little gear and guidance, Sundance Resort offers guided fly-fishing. You can also rent equipment or book a guide through **High Country Adventure** (3702 E. Provo Canyon Rd., Provo, 801/224-2500, https://highcountryadventure.com, 9:30am-6:30pm daily, tubing starts at $19, guided rafting starts at $36), which is located right at this put-in spot.

Hiking

While there are 10 miles (16.1 km) of trails to choose from at Sundance, the hike to **Stewart Falls** (3 mi/4.8 km one-way, 2-3 hours, 650 ft/198 m elevation gain, moderate) is by far the best, offering a big reward for only a little work. Named for a Scottish family who homesteaded the Aspen Grove area in the early 20th century, Stewart Falls is a three-tier waterfall and a place as peaceful as it is majestic. There are multiple starting points for this popular hike, but the easiest to access and find is Aspen Grove, 2 miles (3.2 km) up Highway 92 from Sundance Resort. There is a small fee ($6) to use this trailhead, and there are a few trails that start here, as well as diversions on the trail itself, but follow the well-marked signage to Stewart Falls. Along the way, you're mostly in the forest, with a couple of creek crossings. The trail takes you to the top of this waterfall, but if you're a confident scrambler, you can work your way down to the base of the falls and cool off in the creek it descends into. If you're staying at Sundance, there's a shorter trail that begins in one of the parking lots of

the Mandan cottages, part of Sundance's lodging array. There are also trails to Stewart Falls from the base of Sundance Mountain, as well as a path from the top of Ray's Lift.

ENTERTAINMENT

While many of Utah's attractions revolve around the state's natural beauty, Sundance is one unique case that is also squarely rooted in the arts. Most have heard the name "Sundance" before and recognize it as the large independent film festival. However, this resort predates the film festival. Of course, it all ties back to actor Robert Redford and his role in *Butch Cassidy and the Sundance Kid* and many more films.

Fine Arts

A fun fact about Robert Redford is that before he made it as an actor, he used to paint. He even studied painting in Florence. This explains the strong presence of the fine arts at the resort. Between art workshops and open studios, there are many ways to get inspired and tap in to the right side of your brain at Sundance.

ART CLASSES

In Sundance's Art Studio, choose from one of the three daily art workshops, which range in topic from pottery and painting to jewelry and journal making. The two-hour classes are held at 10am, 1pm, and 3pm, but reservations must be made 24 hours in advance (801/223-4535). There are also additional classes held from time to time on other mediums, such as printmaking, oil painting, or wheel-thrown pottery.

OPEN ART STUDIOS WITH ARTISTS-IN-RESIDENCE

Sundance also hosts artists-in-residence who come to Sundance to work in relative solitude in an inspiring natural setting. The artists

tend to play with themes relevant to the area, such as Western landscapes or Indigenous art. Every Saturday, noon-5pm, these artists open their studios to share their finished products and works in progress with guests. During this time, the artists are on-site to discuss their work with visitors and answer questions, and their art remains on display for a fortnight after these presentations.

Music

Sundance hosts free outdoor concerts, concert series, and occasionally bigger names. You'll also find free live music on most Friday and Saturday nights at the Owl Bar.

BLUEBIRD CAFÉ CONCERT SERIES

Sundance partners with Nashville's musically oriented Bluebird Café to bring Nashville musicians to Utah. If you haven't heard of the café, it's reputed to have hosted just about every successful name in country music on its stage. The Bluebird Café Concert Series brings this talent to its outdoor amphitheater, the Eccles Stage, on select weekends in July and August (doors open 7pm, show starts 8pm). Seating is available on the lawn ($45) or on reserved bench seating ($50), and a barbecue dinner is also available ($20).

SOUNDS OF SUMMER CONCERT SERIES

On Sundays early July-early September, Sundance hosts free outdoor concerts in the green space right by Ray's Lift at the base area (5pm-7:30pm). Seating on the green is first-come, first-served—bring a blanket! No packaged food or outside alcohol is allowed, but food and beverages are available on-site. If you're lucky enough to be staying at Sundance during this event, attending is a no-brainer. If you're not lodging here, a Sounds of Summer Concert is a great way to discover Sundance at the affordable price of $0.

Performing Arts

Discover some of the **film history** at Sundance by taking a walk from the Foundry

---

1: mountain biking at Sundance Mountain Resort
2: Belle & Sebastian playing at the Sound of Summer Concert Series

Grill to the Tree Room. In the hallway between these two restaurants, you'll find old photographs with captions that forge a clearer picture of Sundance's history, Redford's vision for the area, and the many stars who've visited over the years.

In late January/early February, the annual Sundance Film Festival hosts screenings in the Sundance Screening Room. Sundance also partners with Utah Valley University to host live theater (lawn tickets $22, bench tickets $34-38), which usually includes a play or musical that runs for several weeks during the summer. These performances take place at the scenic outdoor stage of the Eccles amphitheater, about 500 feet (152 m) up the hill from the base area.

FOOD

Food manages to unite the triumvirate of Sundance's identity: history, nature, arts. You'll dine in buildings that hark back to the area's history, as well as more broadly to Western heritage. You'll find menus that change frequently to feature seasonal ingredients, as well as local meats like bison. And you'll find food presented as art. Particularly at the Tree Room, the dishes are composed with a dose of creative genius. In addition to

the two concepts outlined below, Sundance offers a more casual grill and a deli with tempting baked goods.

Whether you want to enjoy the open, outdoor creekside seating or grab a sandwich or smoothie to take on a hike or to a concert at the resort's Eccles Stage, Sundance Deli (801/223-4211, 7am-9pm Sun.-Thurs., 7am-10pm Fri.-Sat., $9-15) is your place. It actually has some of my favorite food at Sundance, with sandwiches on homemade bread and colossal cookies. Try a breakfast burrito or smoothie bowl in the morning, and the mushroom banh mi or smoked pork sandwich for lunch, and don't miss one of those cookies or a pastry on the side. The deli also serves smoothies, espresso drinks, and milkshakes.

Believe it or not, The Owl Bar (801/223-4222, 4pm-11pm Mon.-Thurs., 4pm-1am Fri., noon-1am Sat., noon-11pm Sun., ages 21+ only, $12-22) was originally built in the late 19th century in Thermopolis, Wyoming. Then and there, it was known as the Rosewood Bar, and none other than Butch Cassidy used to knock back drinks on its stools. Now it's housed in the log cabin complex where most of Sundance's dining concepts are located. The Owl Bar has a rough and ready atmosphere, the saddle Redford rode in *Butch*

pastries from the Sundance Deli

Cassidy and the Sundance Kid, a healthy collection of whiskeys, and live music just about every Friday and Saturday night. This is also the most affordable place to grab dinner at Sundance, with a menu of elevated bar food like poutine and a duck confit quesadilla. Check current hours before you head there; hours fluctuate and the bar may close during a few weeks in the off-season.

The Tree Room (866/627-8313, 5pm-9pm Tues.-Thurs., 5pm-10pm Fri.-Sat., ages 12+ only, $32-50) is named for a native pine tree that Redford refused to chop down to build the restaurant. Instead, the restaurant was constructed around this large tree, and named for it, too. Soon after, the tree died, but it was preserved and remains in the dining room today. While the Tree Room is pricey, it serves the best food at Sundance and is a joy to experience. You'll dine among Native American artworks from Redford's own collection in a log cabin room with subdued lighting. Take it from the Forbes Four-Star rating, Best of State awards, and a *Wine Spectator* Award of Excellence, or take it from me, but the Tree Room is indeed one of the finest places to eat in Utah. You'll find artful appetizers—if you find octopus on the menu, order it—and entrées that run the usual gamut of fine dining, with seafood, poultry, steak, and a thoughtful vegetarian option. I've enjoyed one of the best steaks I've ever had in the Tree Room, and always manage to polish off a dessert, styled to play off the woodsy setting.

A more laid-back alternative to The Tree Room, the Foundry Grill (801/223-4220, 7am-10:30am and 11:30am-4pm daily, dinner 5pm-9:30pm Sun.-Thurs., 5pm-10pm Fri.-Sat., brunch 9am-2pm Sun., $19-46 for dinner entrées) has a naturally lit dining room with antique farming equipment decorating the walls. In the summer, you can also sit on a pleasant patio with the sound of a creek rushing by. The food is New American with standards (think eggs Benedict and a burger for lunch or dinner) and more inventive dishes like a breakfast cauliflower hash or braised short ribs served with crepes and arugula. The Foundry also offers vegan and kids' menus, as well as some memorable desserts, like a gingerbread mousse cake or sweet potato-chocolate cheesecake pie.

ACCOMMODATIONS

The standard accommodation option at Sundance (starting at $218) feels premium. A concierge will escort you to a cottage with Southwestern flair, wood touches, and amenities like a kitchenette and a patio. There are four other room types that get bigger and more stocked with amenities. Rates vary dramatically depending on time of year, day of the week, and whether the resort is hosting an event. Sundance's online booking makes it very easy to find a time to stay that accommodates your budget. If you have a bigger party, look into one of the 15 mountain homes, which range 2-7 bedrooms. Each of these properties is completely unique and features amenities like hot tubs and fireplaces. Every stay at Sundance comes with two lift passes, whether it's to ski in the winter or for a scenic ride in the summer. Other lodging amenities include free yoga and meditation daily, as well as a spa with unique offerings like reflexology or treatments for kids.

INFORMATION AND SERVICES

You can plot a trip to Sundance—activities, lodging, events, and all—by visiting its website (www.sundanceresort.com) or calling the main line for the resort (801/224-4107). When you arrive, park in the lot and enter the main building, which is navigated through an open-air hallway. To your immediate right is the lobby, where you can check in if you're staying here, or find out who to talk to or where to go to plan your desired experience during your stay. The main building also contains a bike/ski shop and bathrooms.

GETTING THERE

Sundance lies about a 25-minute drive (about 18 mi/29 km) southwest from Heber.

Robert Redford, the Sundance Kid

The real Sundance Kid, Harry Alonzo Longabaugh, was stubborn. By the time he was around 20, he had joined forces with outlaw Butch Cassidy to rob trains and banks at gunpoint. His stubbornness ultimately killed him; he fled from the law to South America and died in a shootout. Perhaps when Robert Redford played the Sundance Kid in the 1969 movie *Butch Cassidy and the Sundance Kid,* a little bit of that stubbornness rubbed off on him. If he's been one thing in his stewardship of this iconic resort, it's headstrong, yet in a good way.

Before Robert Redford came into the picture, Sundance was a small ski resort run by the Stewart family, who emigrated from Scotland. Since the 1890s, they'd been homesteading this scenic corner of the Provo Canyon. In 1944, the Stewarts opened the Timp Haven ski resort, named for the mountain that casts its shadows over the whole area: Timpanogos. While the ski resort was small with just a single T-bar lift, local families loved skiing these scenic lands for over two decades. When the Stewarts put the resort up for sale in 1969, Robert Redford swooped in, wanting to protect this special place from the hands of developers. What was Redford doing in Utah, anyway? He had long ago fallen in love with the Rockies, and also already owned a home in the area, because his former wife, Lola Van Wagenen, was born in Provo and married Redford in the same town in the late 1950s.

While a lot has changed here, far more hasn't. Redford made an early commitment to limit development and protect the open lands of aspen groves, mountains, and forest surrounding that first solitary ski lift. After all, that's why he bought the resort: to save these lands from unchecked growth. And Redford has kept his word. This is where his stubborn streak comes in. He could easily develop more guest cottages to meet peak demand, but he hasn't. He could expand the parking lot, which often fills up, but he even demanded that his staff reduce the parking lot size because he felt it infringed on the peaceful vibe of the property. When he built the Tree Room restaurant, he refused to cut down a pine tree, instead choosing to build the dining room around it (the tree died soon after, but that's beside the point).

For those confused about the Sundance Kid, the resort of the same name, and the now internationally renowned film festival, let's set the record straight. Though he played the Sundance Kid prior to buying the resort, Redford claims he didn't name the property for his role, but for the way sun dances across the mountains. The resort predated the film festival, which didn't get its start until the late 1970s and began under a different name. Then, in 1981, Redford founded the Sundance Institute at the resort as a way to support and share the arts. A few years later, the Sundance Institute took over the film festival and lent the event its name. Today, the festival primarily takes place in Park City, but also hosts screenings in other locations like Salt Lake City and Sundance Resort. In case you're not confused enough, Redford also owns the Sundance Catalog, which sells clothing, furniture, and other goods inspired by the American Southwest.

During the first decade of the Sundance Resort's life under Redford's watch, little happened. But after the film festival got its start, the resort saw more traffic, and more, albeit modest, development. Now, Sundance Resort stretches across 50 acres and includes cottages, a dining complex, a small collection of mountain homes, an art studio, and a screening room. Yet 450 acres of the property remain undeveloped, some accessible by chairlifts or trails, and some tenaciously preserved for the sake of preservation.

At the end of Heber's Main Street, turn right on U.S. 189 and drive south for 14.6 miles (23.5 km). Turn right on Highway 92—this turn can be easy to miss since it comes up around a bend while you're driving at high speeds. Continue for 2.5 miles (4 km) on a winding road uphill and you'll see Sundance on your left.

From the Wasatch Front and Salt Lake area, it's about an hour southeast to Sundance (51 mi/82 km), taking I-15 South to U.S. 189 North to Highway 92 West.

Mount Timpanogos Wilderness

Mount Timpanogos is the undisputed glory of the Wasatch. It's the second-highest peak in the range—runner-up to Mount Nebo to the south by some 200 feet (61 m). Yet its unique silhouette, mythology, and breathtaking path to its summit make it by far the most popular mountain in Utah. Encompassing the mountain and its foothills is a 10,518-acre designated wilderness area—one of nine in Utah—which lies southwest of Heber and Midway and closely neighbors Sundance. The foothills are where the Wasatch Back rises to become the actual range before descending back into the American Fork area of the Wasatch Front.

While the mountain Timpanogos consists of several peaks, the highest stands at 11,750 feet (3,581 m). Mount Timp takes its name from the Timpanogos Nation (https://timpanogostribe.com), who have resided in the area since around AD 1400. Often mistakenly referred to as members of the Ute Tribe, the Timpanogos are actually Shoshone. In the mid-19th century, after a series of wars with and massacres at the hands of incoming Mormons, the Timpanogos moved their home to the Uinta Valley Reservation over 100 miles (161 km) away from the mountain they consider sacred.

The name of the tribe itself translates to "rock canyon of water": *tumpi* (rock) + *panogos* (canyon or mouth of water). The etymology of the tribe's name and the mountain is befitting of Mount Timpanogos, with its waterfalls, lakes, and spring snowmelt forging streams down the mountain. People from all over Utah come to the Timpanogos Wilderness to witness these waterfalls, sleep in the foothills, explore the mountain's caves, and crown its tallest peak.

Nothing quite gets at the sublimity of this mountain like the myth surrounding it. There are many versions, but most go something like this: During a severe drought—which really did occur in Utah as well as across the greater American Southwest—the tribe called upon Princess Utahna to sacrifice herself in hopes of bringing rain. As she was about to jump off the mountain to her death, a warrior named Red Eagle implored her to stop. Perhaps caught up in the wild emotions of the moment, Utahna mistook Red Eagle for the great god of Mount Timpanogos. Together, they decamped to the caves, where they fell in love.

One day soon after, an animal—perhaps one of the native moose or mountain lions—attacked Red Eagle. Seeing his wounds, Utahna realized her mistake—that Red Eagle was no god at all—and sealed her fate as a sacrifice. Red Eagle retrieved her body and carried her back to the caves, where their hearts become entwined in a massive, 4,000-pound (1,814-kg) stalactite: the Great Heart of Timpanogos, which you can see at the Timpanogos Caves National Monument today. Viewed from afar, the profile of Mount Timpanogos itself shows Utahna, lying on her back in the Wasatch for all eternity.

SIGHTS AND RECREATION

TOP EXPERIENCE

★ Summiting Mount Timpanogos

Climbing 11,750-foot (3,581-m) Mount Timpanogos is on many a local's and tourist's summer summit list. Part of its allure stems from the fact that it is home to the only true glacier in Utah, and the geology that comes with this distinction. Marked by glacial cirques, vast basins, waterfalls, turquoise lakes, and plenty of terrain above tree line, Mount Timpanogos feels alpine and epic, but doesn't require alpine climbing to summit. Of course, all this water means that the mountain erupts in wildflowers come summer—columbines, alpine buttercups, and forget-me-nots, among them. The mountain's forests are built from aspens, fir, maple, and other trees that do well in harsh environments. All of this terrain is home to mountain goats, elk, moose, marmots, and other wildlife characteristic of the Rocky Mountains.

Atop Mount Timpanogos, you can behold both the Wasatch Front, the Wasatch Back, and many neighboring peaks, including the Wasatch's largest, Mount Nebo. There are two primary ways to summit Mount Timpanogos, neither technical, but both relatively long. One starts from the Wasatch Front in American Fork Canyon: **Timpooneke Trail** (14 mi/22.5 km round-trip, 6-9 hours depending on pace, approx. 4,500 ft/1,372 m elevation gain, strenuous). The other begins from Provo Canyon: **Aspen Grove Trail** (15 mi/24 km round-trip, 7-10 hours, approx. 5,500 ft/1,676 m elevation gain, strenuous). Within a couple miles of the summit, the trails merge into one path to the peak. Aspen Grove is generally considered the more strenuous of the two trails, with steeper grades.

It's worth noting that there are a couple miles of discrepancy in accounts of total mileage from trailhead to summit, as well as variation in elevation gain, reported by different guidebooks, maps, and online resources. This is perhaps due to changes in trail maintenance over the years as well as different possible paths to the summit when the trail gives way to a scree field scramble. The trail stats above represent the more commonly cited, average figures found.

Both trailheads are accessed off Highway 92 (the Alpine Scenic Loop). Aspen Grove Trail starts off Highway 92 just a couple miles up the road from Sundance; Timpooneke Trail is about 4 miles (6.4 km) up Highway 92 from Aspen Grove Trail, though note that this is a section of the road passable only in the summer. To use either of these trailheads requires a modest day-use fee ($6 pp). Another option is to park a shuttle car at one trailhead and start from the other; then you can cover one trail on the ascent and the other on the descent to see as much of Mount Timpanogos as possible.

A few words of caution: Don't plan on climbing Mount Timpanogos in the late fall, winter, or early spring unless you're an experienced mountaineer well-versed in avalanche rescue gear and practices, and be sure to heed the danger that the significant snowfall poses. Many climbers have died on Mount Timpanogos, by cold, clumsiness, or

the trail from Aspen Grove to Mount Timpanogos

ignorance. A friend of a friend once turned back from the summit early due to weather conditions and spied a man seated on a rock. He approached him and put his hand on his shoulder to notify him of the incoming storm only to discover that the seated man was long dead and frozen. Unless you're an experienced alpine climber, the easiest time to summit is late June or early July through September. You can learn the latest conditions by visiting or calling the nearest Forest Service office: **Pleasant Grove Ranger District** (390 N. 100 E., Pleasant Grove, 801/785-3563, 8am-4:30pm Mon.-Fri.).

The biggest obstacle you may encounter in your plans to climb Mount Timpanogos is parking. If you're planning to climb on a Sunday or holiday weekend July-mid-September, you'll need an alternative plan. You could arrive extraordinarily early (well before sunrise), secure a camping spot nearby, or stay at Sundance and find a ride for the 2 miles (3.2 km) to the Aspen Grove Trailhead. You might also consider backpacking in and breaking up your hike over two days. If these all sound like inconveniences, consider coming early or late season, or hiking on a weekday.

As you climb past cirques and scramble up the final scree field toward the summit on tired legs, keep in mind local Ben Woolsey, a retired postal worker who in 2018, at age 76, climbed Mount Timpanogos for the 1,000th time in some 50 years of getting to know this storied mountain.

Other Hiking

If you hope to explore the Mount Timpanogos Wilderness area but aren't in it for a summit, the best hiking is on the same trails used to access the peak of Mount Timpanogos, without actually following the whole trail to the peak. You can easily turn back at any point to get in the mileage and experience you're looking for. **Timpooneke Trail** (7 mi/11.3 km one-way, 3-5 hours, approx. 4,400 ft/1,341 m elevation gain, strenuous), on the American Fork side, or **Aspen Grove Trail** (7.5 mi/12.1 km

one-way, 3-6 hours, approx. 4,900 ft/1,494 m elevation gain, strenuous), on the Provo Canyon side, are both great out-and-back opportunities to see waterfalls, lakes, and wildflowers, and get a sense of the area. On Timpooneke, it's just under 2 miles (3.2 km) to hike to Scout Falls and another 5 to get to Emerald Lake. Following Aspen Grove, it's around 6 miles (9.7 km) to the Hidden Lakes, and another mile (1.6 km) to reach Emerald Lake. The same parking problems that plague those attempting to reach Mount Timpanogos's summit strike all hikers; plan to visit on weekdays or in early summer or mid-fall, as long as you heed the snowpack or turn around before you get into the snowier terrain toward the summit.

Timpanogos Cave National Monument

The caves where Red Eagle and Princess Utahna of yore fell in love—and where their love is memorialized in the Great Heart of Timpanogos—lie on Highway 92 about 7 miles (11.3 km) west of the Timpooneke Trailhead. For cave lovers, a visit to the **Timpanogos Cave National Monument** (2038 Alpine Loop Rd., American Fork, 801/756-5239, www.nps.gov/tica, 7am-7pm daily May-Nov., $12 pp) is a must. Formed around 200 millennia ago, this cave system may not compare to others in the nation in terms of size. But what it lacks in quantity, it makes up for in mythology and a less common feature of caves known as helictites. These deposits form in limestone caves and, unlike their bulbous descending cousins, are narrow, twisting formations that appear at once delicate and sinister, like the fingers of a beckoning goblin. You can visit the caves from around May through November, and they are only accessible by a steep 1.5-mile one-way hike gaining over 1,000 feet (305 m) of elevation. A tour is required to explore inside the caves themselves. Within the cave, the path is dimly lit and paved, and involves some stair-climbing. Together, budget about three hours for the hike and tour. The tour itself lasts about an hour and can accommodate 16 people. Purchase your tickets in advance online to avoid long wait times or sold-out tours. If you would like to try your hand at some more-technical spelunking skills, consider the Intro to Caving Tour, which lasts 4.5 hours and covers 3 miles (4.8 km) ($22 pp).

CAMPING

As far as developed campgrounds go, **Mount Timpanogos Campground** (801/785-3563, www.recreation.gov, open mid-May-Oct., 27 sites, $24 per night, tents and RVs permitted with a 30-foot (9.1-m) vehicle limit, no hookups available, drinking water and restrooms available) is among the best. Located right off Highway 92, the campground sits in the shade of aspen, maple, and pine trees right in the thick of the Wasatch Mountains. This alpine location means high elevation, so if 7,600 feet (2,316 m) sounds high to you, consider acclimating nearby before committing to a night spent at this altitude. If you're camping with a big group, there's also a large group site nearby called Theater in the Pines.

If you're interested in camping in the Mount Timpanogos Wilderness area because you hope to summit the mountain, you might consider **backpacking** instead. There are many places to hike in with camping gear along both the Aspen Grove and Timpooneke Trails leading to Mount Timpanogos's summit. On Aspen Grove Trail, start looking for camping about 5 miles (8 km) in, just a couple miles shy of Emerald Lake. Backpacking here is a nice way to outsmart the crowds and break up your summit bid.

GETTING THERE

From Sundance, the first trailhead to access Mount Timpanogos, Aspen Grove, lies just 2 miles (3.2 km) farther west on Highway 92.

Aspen Grove Trail is about a 30-minute drive (30 mi/48 km) southwest from Heber. At the end of Heber's Main Street, turn right on U.S. 189 and drive south for about 15 miles (24 km). Turn right on Highway 92. Continue for a little over 4 miles (6.4 km) on a winding road uphill and you'll see Sundance on your left. Continue west on Highway 92 to reach the trailhead.

From Salt Lake City, it's about an hour (53 mi/85 km) southeast to the Aspen Grove Trailhead, taking I-15 South to U.S. 189 North to Highway 92 West. In summer (when Highway 92 is passable), you can just continue on Highway 92 for about 4 miles (6.4 km) to reach the Timpooneke Trailhead. For the rest of the year, getting from Salt Lake to the Timpooneke Trailhead will take you just under two hours (64 mi/103 km), heading southeast either via I-80 through Park City, or on I-15 South.

Kamas, Oakley, and the Uintas

The Uintas are where you go to get lost. Of course, people do get legitimately lost here from time to time, and you may see a couple of missing person flyers hung at informational kiosks, or even search parties. But there's also the more innocuous opportunity to lose oneself in the Uintas, with over 450,000 acres of remote wilderness without the slightest inclination of cell service.

What are the Uintas? The Uinta National Forest is technically part of the Wasatch-Cache National Forest. It spans close to a million acres in northern Utah, stretching toward the southwestern edge of Wyoming. Nearly half of that acreage is designated wilderness: the High Uintas Wilderness, filled with perennially snowcapped peaks and high alpine

Highlights

Look for ★ to find recommended sights, activities, dining, and lodging.

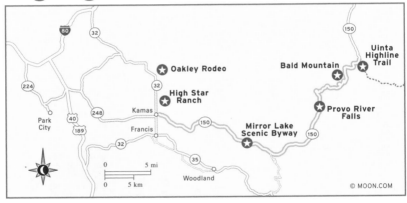

© MOON.COM

★ **Test your mountain biking skills** on the rock gardens at **High Star Ranch** (page 265).

★ **Whoop it up** watching bull riding and bucking broncos at the **Oakley Rodeo** (page 273).

★ **Drive the Mirror Lake Scenic Byway,** one of the highest roads in Utah, leading all the way to Wyoming (page 276).

★ **Take in the views** at this series of **falls on the Provo River,** plunging over cliff after cliff (page 276).

★ **Hike** to the summit of **Bald Mountain,** where you can catch sweeping views and even spy a mountain goat (page 277).

★ **Traverse the Uintas,** the only mountain range in the United States that runs east-west, on the **Uinta Highline Trail** (page 279).

lakes. Speaking of mountains, the highest in Utah is located here: Kings Peak, which towers at 13,527 feet (4,123 m).

There are multiple entry points to the groves of pine, spruce, fir, aspen, and other trees and shrubs of the Uintas. One of the most popular lies at the north end of the town of Kamas. Here, one of the main streets in town turns into the Mirror Lake Scenic Byway—also referred to as Mirror Lake Highway or Highway 150—which bisects the Uintas; 60 miles (97 km) on this road and you'll end up in Evanston, Wyoming!

In the summer, people flock to the Uintas to hike, car camp, backpack, climb, and fish, and that's just the beginning. Come fall, the Uintas is a popular hunting destination. In the winter, snowmobilers, cross-country skiers, and backcountry skiers come here to escape the crowds of Park City. Spring is a quieter time in the Uintas, as locals and tourists abide the time line of snowmelt and mud that must dry. It can be a nice time of year to visit for a short hike or just a scenic drive if you're not averse to imperfect conditions.

Kamas may not be a town in and of itself worth visiting, but coming from Park City and Salt Lake City alike, it's the unofficial gateway to the Uintas (the sign you pass as you enter town says as much). It also happens to be where I live, though I still wouldn't recommend you spend much more time than a stop for a meal in town. There are a couple of good places to go for ice cream or lunch on your way in or out of the Uintas.

The country road on which Kamas lies (Hwy. 32) also hosts several other sleepy ranching towns, all a little smaller than Kamas. To the south is Woodland, where you'll find amazing biscuit sandwiches; to the north lie tiny Peoa and Oakley, home of a longstanding summer rodeo and a diner with a story.

PLANNING YOUR TIME

One could spend a lifetime attempting to learn the Uintas, and still only know the half of it. Indeed, the Uinta mountains, forest, and wilderness are so vast, you could spend your whole vacation exploring them.

If you want to spend a few days or as much as a week or more in the Uintas, the best game plan is to sleep in the Uintas, too. There are not a lot of great lodging options in the area— a tiny B&B here, an Airbnb there. And if you stay closer to Park City, you've got at least an hour drive to a trailhead, or far more depending on where you want to go.

Camping options in the Uintas abound. There are a few spots to RV camp, ample car camping, and endless backpacking options. That said, during the summer, campsites are reserved very quickly. If you can book in advance, do. Otherwise, you may need to dedicate a little more time to finding a dispersed camping spot, or be willing to part with your car and carry your camping supplies to a more distant campsite. Once you commit to backpacking—even if you're only hiking a couple miles from your car—camping options abound across these public lands.

If you're spending a long time in the Uintas, you can plan multiple hikes, summits, or other adventures, from fishing to rock climbing. Plot an adventure a day and bring the gear you'll need for each, or hire a local guide. You can easily work in a few rest days during an extended stay in the Uintas, planning scenic drives, lighter hikes, and days spent picnicking beside sparkling lakes.

Another option is to visit the Uintas as a day trip from Park City or Salt Lake. Leave as early as you can to maximize your day. You might pick one big hike or mountain to climb, or decide on more of a tour of the area, driving to various points of interest and weaving together shorter trails. On your way out of town, stop in Kamas for a milkshake.

Previous: rocky crags at Cliff Lake; Provo River Falls; Mirror Lake.

Kamas, Oakley, and the Uintas

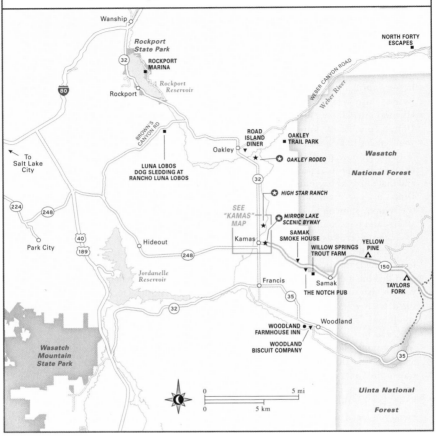

If you're more interested in the towns of Kamas and Oakley, and less so in the Uintas, you can definitely make half-day or day trips to these towns. One reason to do so is if you're a mountain biker. Ride the single-track at High Star Ranch or the Oakley Trail Park, and stay for lunch. Road bikers might come to bike Mirror Lake Scenic Byway for a few miles, or to summit Bald Mountain Pass—a grueling climb!

If you're looking more for a quaint rural town experience, visit Kamas and Oakley any day but Sunday, when these towns really hit the snooze button.

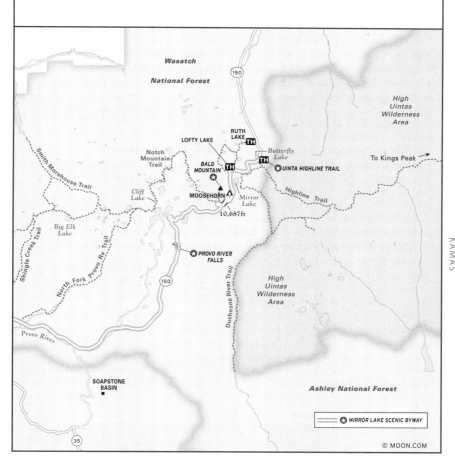

Kamas

The identity of the town of Kamas (CAM-iss) is strongly Mormon, compared to Park City, yet it's in the throes of transitioning into a more heterogeneous community as people are driven farther from Park City and its high cost of living. Originally known as the Rhoades Valley in tribute to Thomas Rhoades, one of the original settlers, Kamas takes its modern name from *Camassia quamash,* a flowering herb eaten by some of the Native Americans who once called the area home. The Kamas area long served as the hunting grounds and sometimes home of the Northern Shoshone and Ute, as well as the Uintah tribe, a band of the Utes. As you'll see, the name "Uintah" (also spelled "Uinta" and pronounced YOU-in-tah) has proliferated across Utah, with a forest, mountain range, wilderness area, county, brewery, northeastern Utah Indian reservation, and many more entities bearing the moniker.

When the Mormon settlers arrived in Kamas in 1859—nearly a decade prior to Park City's establishment—there was some hostility between them and the Indigenous people who had long used these lands as hunting grounds. These tensions eventually led the Mormons to build a 16-foot-high (4.9 m) log fort, in which they constructed homes, a schoolhouse, and other buildings. Conflict peaked when a Native American boy was captured, chained up inside the fort, then killed during a Native American raid on the settlers. While the fort no longer stands, a cabin built alongside it does. Today, this building serves as a **Daughters of Utah Pioneers Museum** (52 W. 2200 S., 435/783-4479, by appointment only, free admission) with pioneer artifacts on display within. Ultimately, as the story goes in many sites of colonialism, the settlers prevailed and the tribes lost their hunting grounds.

In addition to a prominent LDS community, Kamas is also defined by its historical and present industries, including logging, ranching, and serving as the gateway to the High Uintas. On the eastern end of town, the **High Star Ranch** development feels like a totally different place, emblematic of the gentrification taking place as people are financially pushed farther from Park City but may have different budgets and tastes than those who grew up in Kamas. Here you'll find a large concert venue and event center (the DeJoria Center), a tavern, mountain biking trails, and houses that look more Park City than Kamas.

RECREATION

Calling Kamas a "gateway" is accurate. There is a lot to do near Kamas—mostly in the Uintas—and not a whole lot within Kamas itself. The main highlight is a new single-track trail system located in the hills behind High Star Ranch about a mile (1.6 km) east of town. Some of the lower trails also allow foot traffic, but others are biking only. In other words, it can be a fine place to get in a short trail run or take the dog for a walk, but isn't great for a long, scenic hike.

Biking

The main draw for bikers in Kamas is the single-track trail system built and located by High Star Ranch. There is also a road ride that loops together Park City and Kamas, but

State Road Tavern at High Star Ranch

Kamas

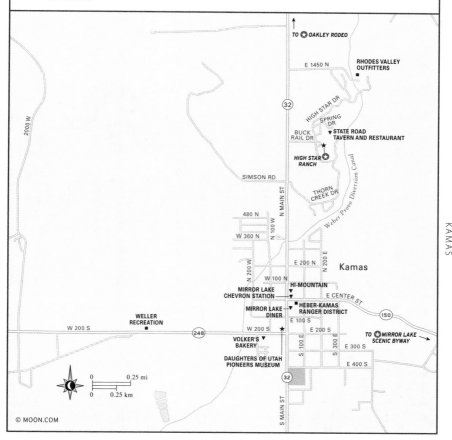

there's no reason to travel to Kamas to begin this ride if you're staying in Park City. If you want to use Kamas as your starting point, begin the **Brown's Canyon Loop** (approx. 30-mi/48-km loop, 3-5 hours depending on pace, approx. 2,100 ft/640 m elevation gain, strenuous) by heading north on Main Street, which turns into Highway 32; at Peoa, turn left on Browns Canyon Road and follow it until it intersects with Highway 248; turn right onto Highway 248 and follow it into Park City. Complete the loop by taking Highway 248 all the way back to Kamas. The ride offers both pastoral and alpine scenery,

including views of Mount Timpanogos and the Jordanelle Reservoir.

Note that there are no bike rental shops in Kamas, so you'll need to gear up in Park City if you're not bringing your own bike.

★ HIGH STAR RANCH SINGLE-TRACK

The recently built 20-mile (32-km) **High Star Ranch Trails** (www.highstarranch.com) offers some of the best riding in the Park City area, and also the least crowded. Beginner and advanced riders alike will have a blast here. You can loop together mellow single-track

meandering through sagebrush with gentle switchbacks. Or, you can head to the very top of the trails at nearly 8,000 feet (2,438 m) in elevation and crush gnarly rock gardens and optional jumps on the descent. Keep in mind that while these trails are multiuse, some stretches are designated uphill bikers only or downhill bikers only, and in some cases, are built for hikers as well. Heed the signage to avoid a collision. The trails are mostly well marked with difficulty ratings and use restrictions.

Start by parking in the huge dirt lot beside the DeJoria Center (970 UT-32, Kamas). From here, hop on the single-track in the corner of the lot farthest from the buildings. Follow this trail until you see a little gate on your left where you must dismount over a cattleguard. For an **easier loop** (3 mi/4.8 km, 1 hour, approx. 250 ft/76 m elevation gain, easy), hang a right at the first junction onto Lazy Dazz. Stay right to get on Tombstone, then turn right back onto Lazy Dazz for a final switchback climb before descending on Graveyard, which will intersect again with Lazy Dazz and take you back to the trailhead.

For a **more challenging loop** (6 mi/9.7 km, 1.5 hours, 570 ft/174 m elevation gain, strenuous), stay left at the first trail junction and start your climb up Escalador. After about 20 minutes, you'll reach a junction with a rock bench and trees—a popular spot to stop and rest. From here, make a sharp right to stay on Escalador, which will eventually turn into Saddle Loop. At this point, descend Bad Hombre and Whip It trails. To make the ride longer, keep climbing on **The Chase** (2 mi/3.2 km, approx. 400 ft/122 m elevation gain) for another 20 minutes until it turns into a romp of a descent over fun berms and rock gardens you'll want to try twice. There are many add-ons and alternatives to make this ride even longer or more challenging if you're so inclined. Get a map online before you head to the trails (www.highstarranch.com). Reward

your ride with a beer at the State Road Tavern when you're done.

Guide Services

If you want to go horseback riding, hunting, or mountain biking and lack the equipment and know-how necessary to do so, **Rhodes Valley Outfitters** (970 N. State Rd. 32, 435/731-0560, www.rhodesvalleyoutfitters.com, 9am-5pm Mon.-Fri., starting at $85 per hour) offers guiding services for all of the above. This is really just a small sampling of the activities Rhodes Valley can take you on, with a whole range of other possibilities like archery and fly-fishing. Partnered with and based out of High Star Ranch, Rhodes Valley specializes in horse trips, and can even arrange custom pack trips so you can get out into the backcountry without hauling all the weight.

FOOD

Kamas is by no means known for its food, but there are some fun places to dine as well as treats in unexpected places. I like eating out in Kamas best in the summer during the days of patio dining and ice cream cones.

★ **Mirror Lake Diner** (35 S. Main St., 435/783-0110, www.mirrorlakediner.com, 7am-4pm Sun.-Wed., 7am-9pm Thurs.-Sat., $8.25-13.50) is great for breakfast and lunch alike. This bright, friendly diner also serves dinner Thursday-Saturday, though its menu and ambience feel better suited to daytime eating. All the servers are chipper, but in a small-town, not cloying way. My favorite order is the huevos rancheros for breakfast, and the Duchesne Tunnel B.L.A.S.T. with sweet potato fries for lunch. You can also get beer by the can or bottle and wine. One oddity on the menu: The fish-and-chips come with potato chips, not fries. (I'm going to give Mirror Lake the benefit of the doubt and assume this is a tongue-and-cheek menu decision.)

What won't you find inside the catchall **Hi-Mountain** (40 N. Main St., 435/783-4466, 8am-9pm Mon.-Sat., $4.95-7.50) on Main Street? Anything spirited, for one. Look no further than the display of action figures

---

1: the DeJoria Center at High Star Ranch 2: riding the single-track at High Star Ranch

from the Book of Mormon for the answer to why. This little general store is a joy to peruse as an impromptu exhibit on rural Mormon culture in America, a great place to stock up on obscure candy, and an even better spot to get a burger or milkshake (or malt, sundae, etc.). With 85 shake flavors—and the ability to customize one if you've thought of something Hi-Mountain hasn't—surely you'll find something that suits you. Straightforward breakfast sandwiches also hit the spot without hitting the wallet, and burgers are everything you'd want in a greasy spoon order. Try the Gonburger topped with cheddar, bacon, barbecue and fry sauces, and not one but two onion rings on top.

While **Volker's Bakery** (https:// volkersbakery.com) used to have a brick-and-mortar shop in Kamas, the building was demolished to make way for a parking lot. Today, it serves out of a permanent wood-sided trailer parked at the corner of W. 200 S. and S. Main Street on the right side of the road on your way into town. While hours vary, you can usually count on the Volker's outpost being open on summer weekends. Specialties include European pastries and breads, including a jalapeño-asiago bread that you'll have to restrain yourself from eating in one sitting. The bakery sells its wares to local restaurants and at area farmers markets as well.

There are two restaurants inside High Star Ranch: the **State Road Tavern** and its sister downstairs, the **State Road Restaurant** (both restaurants: 970 UT-32, 435/783-3530, www.stateroadtavern.com, 5pm-10pm Thurs.-Fri., 10am-2pm Sun., $12-27). The difference boils down to liquor laws, which should come as no surprise since you're in Utah. The State Road Restaurant doesn't have a bar area—though they do serve alcohol—and is thus more of a family-friendly spot. While Sunday brunch on the patio is nice, dinnertime ambience at the downstairs restaurant is a little lacking, with overly bright lights creating a

cafeteria feel. Meanwhile, upstairs, you'll find a bar and stage that often hosts live music, a fun faux honky-tonk vibe, and a gorgeous balcony overlooking the landscaped lawn and creek below—but no kids allowed. The menus at both the tavern and restaurant are the same, specializing in smoke, which you can savor in barbecue dishes or even smoked pork ramen. A highlight of this eclectic menu is smoked chicken wings, which pair well with the smoked old-fashioned. It's a little over-priced, but the State Road Tavern is a great option for those who want a more upscale dining option in the Kamas area—or who want a spirited cocktail, rather than just beer or wine.

As many food-obsessed individuals will attest, great food can occasionally be found in a rather unlikely place: the gas station. This holds true in Kamas, where the **Mirror Lake Chevron Station** (2 N. Main St., 435/783-4375, 5:45am-9pm daily) also operates a seriously impressive bakery. Doughnuts, apple fritters, chocolate croissants, and more irresistible pastries line plastic cafeteria trays in a lit display to the right of the cash register. It's just about impossible to get gas here before noon without buckling to the tempting scent of mace, yeast, and sugar counteracting the smell of, well, gasoline. While the offerings change from time to time, there's generally a mix of glazed, filled, frosted, and powdered doughnuts—and they're insanely affordable, starting at a buck a pop. My favorite is the old-fashioned blueberry cake doughnut. If you're in it for the fritters, they usually make an appearance in the display at around 10am.

Located in Woodland 6 miles (9.7 km) southeast of Kamas, the ★ **Woodland Biscuit Co.** (2734 E. State Hwy. 35, 435/783-4202, www.woodlandbiscuitcompany.com, 8am-2pm Fri.-Sun., 11am-2pm Mon.-Tues., $9.50-14.50) is a popular breakfast and lunch spot year-round. The café appears suddenly on a quiet country road where you'd never expect to find something to eat, let alone something delicious. Housed inside a historic general store building, Woodland Biscuit Co. serves biscuit-centric breakfast plates and

1: Woodland Biscuit Co. 2: a cheeseburger at Hi-Mountain

---

sandwiches like The Woodland, with sausage, gravy, and a drizzle of honey on a biscuit. You can also order biscuits à la carte with jam and butter. In spite of its out-of-the-way location, the Woodland Biscuit Co. is almost always busy. Expect a wait and somewhat slow service in the summer, in particular, when you can take a seat on the patio chairs with a cup of coffee and soak in the pastoral setting. The interior here is pastoral, too, with a simple, one-room layout and large bags of flour on display.

ACCOMMODATIONS

Kamas—and its neighboring communities along Highway 32—are light on lodging. There are a couple of small inns, a few offerings on Airbnb/VRBO, and that's about it. Of course, there is also plenty of camping in the Uintas to be had. One thing to note for the Airbnbers out there, is that if you do a search, you may see a number of properties—most likely condos or townhomes—pop up with Kamas addresses that are not actually in Kamas, as most know it. Kamas's municipal limits extend along much of Highway 248. At some of these properties, you will actually be closer to Park City than you will be to the town of Kamas. That's just fine, unless you wanted more of a country town vibe than condo village vibe, or were hoping for closer proximity to the Uintas.

One of the best accommodations in the Kamas area is in Woodland, just a few miles down the road from Kamas. The ★ **Woodland Farmhouse Inn** (2602 E. State Rd. 35, 435/783-2903, https://woodlandfarmhouseinn.com, starting at $119) is exactly what it sounds like. The charm level is high with quaint furnishings, a riverside location, a friendly owner, and farm animals out back—two pigs, a couple cats, a tribe of Nubian goats, Steve the Lonely Turkey, and a team of ducks bobbing about the pond. The building itself was constructed in 1897, and also boasts a front porch with rocking chairs that will sway you back to simpler times.

GETTING THERE

From Park City, Kamas is a 20-minute drive east (15 mi/24 km)—take Highway 248 east, which takes you right into Kamas. To drive into the downtown, turn left on Main Street/Highway 32. There are a few alternative routes that include ducking off Highway 248 on Brown's Canyon Road, which takes you to Peoa near Oakley.

From Salt Lake City, it's a 45-minute drive east to Kamas (44 mi/71 km), following I-80 to U.S. 40 East and Highway 248 East.

Park City Transit (www.parkcity.org) runs a free public bus between Park City and Kamas (Route 11). Its schedule is designed to work for commuters who work in Park City and live in Kamas, with buses running every hour 5:45am-7:30am and 3:30pm-5:30pm daily. The bus picks up right across from Kamas Food Town, and it takes a little over 30 minutes to get to Park City's Main Street. If you're headed to Kimball Junction or Salt Lake City, you'll need to catch a transfer from Old Town Park City.

Oakley

Oakley is a blink-and-you'll-miss-it town just 5.5 miles (8.9 km) north on Highway 32 from Kamas. There's no Main Street and not much of a town center to dawdle around. For this reason, don't drive over with an "anything goes" attitude. Select trails and book guided adventures in advance—or come for an ice cream sundae at the itinerant Road Island Diner.

RECREATION AND ACTIVITIES
Hiking

In 2018, a volunteer trail organization built a modest network of multiuse trails dubbed the **Oakley Trail Park** (www.southsummittrails. org). The park features a mix of short multi-use and biker-only trails, and it's just a few minutes from downtown Oakley. Heading south on Highway 32, hang a left on E. 4200 N., which will turn sharply left after about a mile (1.6 km) and turn into 1000 East Road. Keep following the road north as it turns into N. Boulderville Road and Pinion Lane. Right after you pass the Oakley Artesian Water

Company on your left, the park will be on your right.

For hiking, **Lower Lariat** and **Upper Lariat** (1.5 mi/2.4 km round-trip, 45 minutes, approx. 150 ft/46 m elevation gain, easy) comprise a pleasant loop in the foothills, starting directly across the road from the Oakley Artesian Water bottling facility. For more of a workout, head up **Seymour Canyon Trail** (3 mi/4.8 km one-way, 3-4 hours, approx. 1,600 ft/488 m elevation gain, moderate), which reaches the highest elevations of all the options in this trail system. It starts at the south end of the park's dirt parking loop. Maps of the park are available online.

Mountain Biking

The **Oakley Trail Park** (www. southsummittrails.org) also includes a pump track as well as several uphill- and downhill-designated trails for bikers, including Lower/Upper Rodeo and Barrel Racer. For a fun **quick loop** (2.5 mi/4 km, 45 minutes, approx. 200 ft/61 m elevation gain, easy), climb Lower and Upper Lariat Trails. Continue onto

Oakley Rodeo Grounds

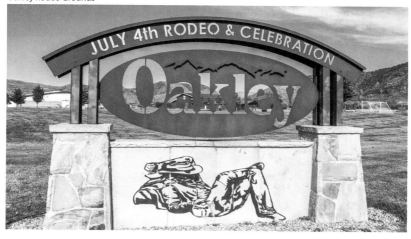

a dirt road, pass Upper Rodeo (which is downhill only), stay right at the first fork, left at the second fork, then look for Oakley Trail immediately on your right. Hop on Oakley Trail for about 100 yards to get to Upper Rodeo, which you can descend to Lower Rodeo. Maps of these trails are available online.

Note that there are no bike rentals available in Oakley, so you'll need to get your equipment in Park City.

Boating and Fishing

Originating in the Uintas, the Weber River runs 125 miles (201 km) all the way to the Great Salt Lake, and is great for fishing. For more fishing and lake sports, head northwest toward Wanship, and within a few minutes, you'll arrive at the Rockport Reservoir, where you can boat, swim, or just enjoy a day at the "beach," as we call lounging alongside a reservoir in Utah.

ROCKPORT RESERVOIR

Just a few miles northwest of Oakley lies the **Rockport Reservoir** (435/336-2241, https://stateparks.utah.gov/rockport, 6am-11pm daily, $12 day-use fee), which is good for swimming, boating, fishing, and any other lake sport you can think of. To get there from Oakley, travel north on Highway 32 for 6 miles (9.7 km) to the southern tip of the reservoir; from there, you can stay on Highway 32, which hugs the western and quieter shore, or turn right on Highway 302 to access the eastern, more developed side.

A designated state park, Rockport opened in 1966 about a decade after the dam that created the reservoir was constructed. At the bottom of the reservoir lie the remnants of an old town dating back to 1860 called Rock Fort, named for the fort the settlers inhabited. Eventually, they renamed the town Rockport, most people left, and then the state bought the land to build the Wanship Dam. So there you have it: a lake with a ghost town at the bottom. On the east side of the reservoir sits the **Rockport Marina** (9040 N. State Hwy. 302, Peoa, 435/336-7368,

www.marina-at-rockport.com, 10am-6pm Mon.-Thurs., 9am-7pm Fri.-Sun., Jet Skis starting at $85 per day, boats starting at $79 per day, kayaks and paddleboards starting at $25 per day), which offers rentals and also operates a barbecue and deli. The marina rents out a couple of on-site cabins and yurts; public campgrounds are also available. Come winter, like most of Utah's easily accessible reservoirs and lakes, Rockport becomes a popular ice fishing and snowmobiling spot.

WEBER RIVER

Fly-fishing is fantastic in the **Weber River,** including where it runs through Oakley. This stretch of the river, from its headwaters in the Uintas to Rockport Reservoir, is known as the Upper Weber River. You'll find an abundance of brown trout and Rocky Mountain whitefish, as well as some rainbow and cutthroat trout. Look out for private property because the river traverses some privately held land.

Horseback Riding

Most of the trails in Oakley that can be hiked can also be enjoyed on horseback. And in this rodeo town, a trail ride feels just right. The Lower and Upper Lariat Trails in the **Oakley Trail Park** (www.southsummittrails.org) are both multiuse trails that allow foot, bike, and hoof traffic alike. If you didn't bring your own horse, the local outfitter **North Forty Escapes** (Stillman Ranch Rd., Oakley, 435/631-4011, http://northfortyescapes.com) can get you in the saddle.

Dogsledding

One mode of exploring winter landscapes that doesn't immediately come to mind to many visitors is dogsledding. Imagine the joy of cruising through a snowy landscape with a dozen huskies gallivanting through the snow ahead. For dog lovers, dogsledding should be a bucket list activity. It's a sport that also tends to put kids into a state of pure ecstasy and uncontrollable laughter. As you shout "whoa" to go faster, remember to take in the winter scenery from this new perspective, lower to the ground, traveling at high speeds, and just one of the pack.

Guide Services

If **horseback riding** or **dogsledding** appeal to you but you didn't happen to bring your own horse or team of huskies, you'll be in the market for an outfitter. Luckily, there's a great guiding service that operates out of the private Stillman Ranch right in Oakley. In the winter, **North Forty Escapes** (Stillman Ranch Rd., Oakley, 435/631-4011, http://northfortyescapes. com, adventures starting at $69 pp) offers guided dogsledding adventures, snowmobile romps, and sleigh dinners. Across its sprawling 9,000 acres lies a mix of meadow, mountains, rivers, and aspen groves frequented by elk, eagles, and other wildlife. In the summertime, North Forty switches gear from snow to dirt. Take a horseback ride through an aspen grove, romp around open pasture or dirt roads in a Razor, or go fly-fishing in the Weber. If you're celebrating a special occasion with family or a group of friends, the sleigh/wagon ride dinners are a year-round worth-it splurge: Following a sleigh ride in

the snowy season or a wagon ride after the melt is a four-course barbecue dinner inside the Stillman Ranch lodge ($99 pp).

Just a couple minutes down the road from Oakley in Peoa, another dogsledding outfitter is ready to take you on a tour of the Wasatch Back. **Luna Lobos** (4733 Browns Canyon Rd., Peoa, 435/783-3473, www.lunalobos.com, $140 pp) is a family-owned operation with the distinction of being year-round. In the winter, the Luna Lobos dogs will tour you around the ranch. When the snow melts, the dogs pull you in an off-road vehicle in a unique experience dubbed the Dog Safari.

ENTERTAINMENT AND EVENTS

The Oakley Rodeo is the event of the year in this sleepy town. You may find occasional other minor events such as outdoor concerts or South Summit Trail Foundation fundraisers.

★ Oakley Rodeo

Since 1935, the **Oakley Rodeo** (4300 UT-32, 435/783-5753, www.oakleycity.com, four days in early July at 8pm, tickets start at $15) has been staged in Oakley. This annual summer event spans several days and sells out

the well-traveled Road Island Diner

relatively fast, so consider buying tickets in advance. The rodeo is an opportunity to watch classic competitions like barrel racing and bull riding, and is also a glimpse into small-town southwestern America. If you're uncomfortable watching the involvement of animals in these sorts of events, you may want to avoid the experience altogether. Each night of the rodeo starts with a prayer, features the rodeo clown, and offers a different lineup of competitions, so you may only see cattle roping, for example, on one night. All seating is outside and under the sun, so bring a hat and layers depending on the forecast. While you can buy and also bring your own food, alcohol is strictly prohibited.

FOOD

Oakley's only restaurant, the ★ Road Island Diner (981 W. Weber Canyon Rd., 435/783-3467, https://roadislanddiner.com, 8am-8pm Thurs.-Sun., $8.50-18.95) has been on its fair share of road trips. Its story begins in New Jersey, where a run of the Jerry O'Mahony Diner Company's prefabricated #1107 diners were designed and built with marble countertops, Tiffany glass-stained windows, and other art deco stylings. This specific diner first opened up shop in 1939 in Massachusetts,

before being purchased by a Greek restaurant owner who moved the whole thing to Rhode Island, where it operated for decades. Part III of the diner's life story dawned in 2007, when it was transported across the country to Oakley and enjoyed a rehab. If you're a fan of diners, this one is a must-visit. Though the food can be a little uneven, some of it is excellent, including from-scratch soups, bread, ice cream, cake, and pie. It's hard not to cave to dessert, which is displayed all across the counter. The diner also bakes up several gluten-free desserts and breads so everyone can partake. Another good bet? The Silver Dollar Crab Cakes, which trace their origins back to Maryland, where a couple of the owners are from.

GETTING THERE

Oakley is a 25-minute drive (16.5 mi/26.5 km) from Park City. Take Highway 248 east, which takes you right into Kamas. Turn left on Main Street/Highway 32 and head north for 5.5 miles (8.9 km) to reach Oakley.

From Salt Lake City, it's a 50-minute drive east to Oakley (49 mi/79 km), following I-80 to U.S. 40 East, Highway 248 East, and Highway 32 North.

There is no public transit direct to Oakley.

Uinta Mountains

The term "Uintas" describes a vast tract of mountain, forest, and remote wilderness in northeastern Utah. It takes its name from the Uintah band of the Ute Tribe; the name itself is derived from a Ute word pronounced "Yoov-we-teuh," which translates to "pine tree" or "pine forest." While the Uintas may have been used as hunting grounds as long as 12,000 years ago, we know that over 700 years ago, an Indigenous people called the Numic lived in the midst of what is now the Uinta National Forest. About a century later, Utes moved into the area, too, and lived off the land in the form of hunting and gathering until the

Mormons arrived in the mid-19th century. As the Mormons settled the valleys and basins nearby, the Uintas became an even more important place for the Utes to retreat to when conflict arose.

Today, the Uintas beckon thousands of visitors with trails, camping, and scenic driving. People from Kamas, Park City, and all over the state, country, and world come here to fish, hike, hunt, climb, snowmobile, ski, and get lost in the best and worst of ways. Among precipitous drops, thousands of acres of remote wilderness, and the bears, moose, and cougars that live here, there are plenty of reasons to visit the Uintas with caution and respect.

Herein, I cover only the portion of the Uintas accessed via Kamas—an area that's part of what's known as the High Uintas. You can also access the High Uintas from other entry points, including Duchesne via Heber, Vernal, and Evanston, Wyoming, to the north.

The High Uintas exist within the larger Wasatch-Cache-Uinta National Forest, comprised of spruce, fir, pine, and aspen stands blanketing a hefty chunk of northeastern Utah. Over 450,000 acres of this forest are officially designated as wilderness, which means no motorized vehicles or mountain bikes allowed. To venture into the wilderness, therefore, you'll need to be human- or horse-powered. The backbone of the High Uintas is the Uinta Range, the only major mountains in the United States that run east-west, rather than north-south. Sculpted by Precambrian glaciers, the Uinta Mountains also include the highest point in Utah: Kings Peak, which is also a relatively easy summit. The High Uintas are lands of not only trees and mountains, but water and lots of it. Here you'll find over 1,000 natural lakes and the headwaters of four rivers that the entire state depends on for water.

This section includes a mere smattering of highlights and activities in this slice of the High Uintas. For every trail or sight described here, there are hundreds of others to explore. To seek out other options suited to your interests, the best place to call or visit is the **Heber-Kamas Ranger District** (50 E. Center St., Kamas, 435/783-4338, www. fs.usda.gov, 8am-4:30pm Mon.-Fri. year-round, also open 8am-4:30pm Sat. Memorial Day-Labor Day), located en route to the High Uintas. You can also reach out to local guides and outfitters, explore state-managed websites and maps, and pick up entire guides devoted to hiking, skiing, climbing, or fishing in the vast Uintas.

While driving through the Uintas is free, if you plan to park anywhere to access trails or picnic grounds, you must purchase a **recreation pass** ($6 for 1-3 days, $12 per week, additional fees apply for camping and vary by campground). You can purchase passes in Kamas at the Heber-Kamas Ranger District, Chevron Gas Station, or Kamas Foodtown or in nearby Samak at the Samak Smoke House. You can also use self-service pay stations along the Mirror Lake Byway, or purchase a pass at the recreation fee station, which you'll find 6.3 miles (10.1 km) up the Byway on your right; it includes a self-service

KAMAS, OAKLEY, AND THE UINTAS
UINTA MOUNTAINS

Bald Mountain rising above Mirror Lake

station if you're traveling through at odd hours. All the revenue from these fees goes toward improving the Mirror Lake Byway area.

PLANNING YOUR TRIP

If you're coming to the Uintas to pursue a sport that requires specialized equipment, know that there are few rental options within Kamas. There is one shop—**Weller Recreation** (936 W. SR 248, Kamas, 435/783-4718, www.wellerrec.com, 8:30am-6pm Mon.-Fri., 8:30am-3pm Sat.)—on the way into town that rents motorized equipment (snowmobiles, ATVs, etc.), but there are no rental shops for Nordic or downhill skis, bikes, camping equipment, or any other gear in Kamas or its neighboring towns. Your best bet is to rent in Park City, which is only about 20-25 minutes from the start of Mirror Lake Scenic Byway.

SCENIC DRIVES AND STOPS

Whether you only have a little time to spend in the Uintas, or you'd like to make some stops on the way to or from your hike, there are many places to pull over and have your breath quickly robbed by the majestic mountain views. The entire drive through the High Uintas on Mirror Lake Scenic Byway is a worthy experience in and of itself.

★ Mirror Lake Scenic Byway

Completed in 1942, the **Mirror Lake Scenic Byway** traverses the Uinta Mountains, originating in Kamas and emerging just south of Evanston, Wyoming. To hop on the Byway from Kamas, drive north on Main Street and turn right on Center Street. Once you turn on Center Street, the Heber-Kamas Ranger District is immediately on your right. After about three blocks, just past the high school, the road turns into Mirror Lake Scenic Byway. Also known as Highway 150, Mirror Lake Scenic Byway runs for 65 miles (105 km), and is Utah's highest paved road, reaching 10,715 feet (3,266 m) at the top of Bald Mountain Pass.

The top of Bald Mountain Pass, located just under 30 miles (48 km) from Kamas, is a great place to stop for panoramic views, hiking, and photo opportunities your friends won't believe. This pass summit is also where the trailhead to hike Bald Mountain is located.

The Byway usually closes for the winter in November around 15 miles (24 km) from Kamas, just past the Soapstone Basin Road turnoff, and reopens around Memorial Day.

★ Provo River Falls

In this popular spot, the Provo River plunges over cliff after cliff for about a mile (1.6 km). To get here from Kamas, travel on Mirror Lake Byway for about 24 miles (39 km) and look for signs on your left. None of the waterfalls are enormous, but the combination of so many of them is enchanting, which is why they've been featured in several movies. If you're a believer in the power of negative ions, you'll experience the calming effect of plenty of them here. The soothing sound of rushing water makes this a place where you could while away hours—except for the crowds. Visit early in the morning or at an odd time of year if you want to escape them. While you can literally see the falls from the parking lot, walking for even just 5 or 10 minutes up or down along the falls is rewarded by more waterfalls and greater solitude. With moderate scrambling and no shortage of rocks to overturn, this is also a fun place for kids—and dogs—to explore.

HIKING

With hundreds of thousands of acres and hundreds of miles of trails, hiking in the High Uintas is just about limitless. Best of all, since many of the trails exist partially or fully within wilderness, you won't be competing with many other users for trail real estate. On stretches of trail in designated wilderness, you'll never hear the *braaaap* of a dirt bike, or be dislodged by a mountain biker. If your primary goal is views and pleasant tours of the forest, there are many easily accessible hikes to choose from. If you're seeking solitude, the more miles you hike on a trail, the fewer people you'll see. Even after the first mile (1.6 km) of what may seem a busy trail originating from a full parking lot, the crowds will begin to dissipate.

Mirror Lake

The namesake for the byway that gets you anywhere in the Uintas from Kamas, Mirror Lake is often considered one of the most beautiful natural water bodies in the Uintas, if not in the entire state of Utah. For that reason, it is heavily trafficked. The **Mirror Lake Shoreline Trail** (1.5 mi/2.4 km, 1 hour, negligible elevation gain, easy) loops around the perimeter of the lake and is outfitted with kiosks and signs that allow adults and kids to discover more about the ecology and history of the area. At Mirror Lake, you'll also find several picnic areas, as well as a large campground. Mirror Lake is 32 miles (52 km) from Kamas following Mirror Lake Byway, about a 45-minute drive. After 31.3 miles (50.4 km), turn right on Forest Road 104 and follow signs for Mirror Lake. Park in the main lake parking lot. The Shoreline Trail is the obvious dirt path encircling the lake—some sections over wetter areas have a wood boardwalk.

While the Shoreline Trail is a nice meander, the **Mirror Lake Trail** (4 mi/6.4 km round-trip, 2 hours, 380 ft/116 m elevation gain, easy) will take you into the High Uintas Wilderness. When you turn right from Mirror Lake Byway onto Forest Road 104, veer right at the second offshoot from the road to find this trailhead, which starts at 10,000 feet (3,048 m). A 1-mile (1.6-km) hike will be rewarded with another body of water: Bonnie Lake. And 2 miles (3.2 km) in, you'll reach the Uinta Highline Trail, which you can continue on for as long as you please (it's nearly 100 mi/161 km), or consider your turnaround point.

Lofty Lake Loop Trail

All high alpine lakes have a certain allure to them, but some truly spectacular ones are found on this trail, which comes highly recommended from Lee Maness, a customer service representative with the Heber-Kamas Ranger District. The trail begins at mile marker 32 on the left side of Mirror Lake Scenic Byway at the Pass Lake Trailhead. From here, **Lofty Lake Loop Trail** (4.4 mi/7.1 km round-trip, 2-3 hours, 930 ft/283 m elevation gain, moderate) takes you on a tour of views and lakes, with a workout of a climb to start. Kamas Lake in particular is an unusual, gorgeous body of water; its near rectangular shape framed by mountains makes it look like a teal swimming pool in the middle of the alpine. Continue on to Loft Lake and finally Scout Lake, before the trail loops back toward Mirror Lake Scenic Byway. There are also campgrounds at the lakes if you wish to turn this into a short backpacking trip.

★ Bald Mountain

Sitting at the highest point of Mirror Lake Byway, **Bald Mountain** (4 mi/6.4 km round-trip, 3 hours, 1,200 ft/366 m elevation gain, moderate) is an easy win—a short hike with no technical climbing required and a trailhead that's easy to find. Park at the top of Bald Mountain Pass, 29.2 miles (47 km) from Kamas. The hike to the summit (about 2 mi/3.2 km) is steep, so be conscious of signs of altitude sickness and take it slow if necessary. To reach the very top at 11,943 feet (3,640 m), you'll need to hike along a narrow ridge with lethal drop-offs on both sides. For that reason, don't hike this trail if you're nervous about heights or aren't surefooted. Due to the ease of access, this is a popular trail, especially during summer weekends, so expect to be rewarded with sweeping views, not solitude. At the top, take in the headwaters of the Uinta's four rivers, sparkling lakes, and maybe even a mountain goat.

The top of Bald Mountain is a terrible spot to be in a thunderstorm, so keep your eyes on the skies and descend if any threatening clouds materialize.

Kings Peak

While Mount Timpanogos to the west usually steals Kings Peak's thunder, there's no denying that Kings is the highest in Utah at 13,527

feet (4,123 m) above sea level. **Kings Peak** (28.8 mi/46.3 km round-trip, 2 days, approx. 4,100 ft/1,250 m elevation gain, strenuous), however, is actually a more moderate summit to achieve than Mount Timp. Theoretically, it's possible to climb Kings Peak in a day, but it would be a very long day requiring an early start. Unfortunately, the most viable route to summit Kings Peak starts in Wyoming, not Kamas, but I still include it here because it can be done as a two-day backpacking trip from Kamas.

Starting from Kamas, it's a little under three hours to the trailhead (138 mi/222 km). Drive north on I-80 for a little over 92 miles (148 km), then head south on Highway 410 to Road 017, which you'll stay on for about 12 miles (19.3 km). At the fork, go east on Road 077 for about 5 miles (8 km) until you reach Henrys Fork Trailhead. From here, hike moderate terrain dotted with lakes. At the Elk Horn Crossing trail junction, head south. In a couple miles (3 km), you'll pass Dollar Lake, a popular dispersed camping area and stopping point. You could camp here for the night or continue a few more miles. But if you're doing Kings Peak as a two-day trip, find a campsite before the trail starts to climb up Gunsight Pass. A good dispersed camping option is alongside Henrys Fork Lake.

When you're ready to hike to the peak, leave any unnecessary weight you've carried at the campsite to pick up on the way back. From Henrys Fork Basin, the trail climbs sharply with only one small descent ahead in the path to the summit. Be sure not to confuse the smaller South Kings Peak with the true Kings Peak, which is less than a mile (1.6 km) north of its southern counterpart and remains the higher of the two by a mere 9 feet (2.7 m). Of course, you could bag both peaks in one easy swoop. Like most thirteeners and fourteeners, the last few miles toward the peak navigate scree and boulder fields, so expect some non-technical scrambling.

1: biking the rugged trails of the Uintas 2: view from Lofty Lake Loop Trail

★ Uinta Highline Trail

If you've got around a week to spend in the Uintas, the **Uinta Highline Trail** (95.7 miles/154 km, at least a week, 16,700 ft/5,090 m elevation gain, extremely strenuous) is an epic traverse across the biggest mountains in Utah. The trail holds steady around 10,000 feet (3,048 m), and several 12,000- and 13,000-foot (3,658- and 3,962-m) mountains can be climbed via detours from the Highline Trail. Much of the trail lies above tree line, which makes for expansive views of the Uinta mountains, forest, lakes, and wildflower meadows. Given the remoteness of the trail and high vantage points, this is also an excellent place to spot wildlife, from bear and moose to birds of prey.

While the Highline Trail can be hiked from one end to the other, with a ride back or shuttle arranged at the finishing point, it can also be hiked in sections as out-and-backs from numerous different access points. If you only have a day, you can get a taste of the trail that will surely motivate return trips. For day hikes or one-night backpacking trips, use the trailhead closest to Kamas (directions below) to make the most of your time. You can hike out anywhere from 4 to 9 miles (6.4 to 14.5 km) before turning around for a solid day's experience on the Highline Trail.

The Uinta Highline Trail can be approached from either Kamas or Vernal; to start from Kamas, drive 34 miles (55 km) on Mirror Lake Scenic Byway (about 50 minutes) until you see a sign on your right for the Highline Trail.

Be extra conscientious of wildlife, strong winds, and lightning.

CLIMBING

Too hot to climb in Salt Lake or the Utah desert? Escape to the Uintas where the temperatures stay cooler at higher elevations. The rock here is mostly high-quality quartzite, and the routes are a well-rounded mix of sport (about 40 percent of climbs) and trad (30 percent of climbs), with a few top-roping areas and a little bit of bouldering. There is also a mix of single-pitch and multi-pitch climbs; approach time ranges from about 10 minutes to an hour.

Ruth's Lake Climbing Area

One of the most popular climbing areas in the Uintas, **Ruth's Lake** offers several different walls of single-pitch sport routes from 5.6 to 5.12. There are also a few trad routes and a handful of places to set up top-ropes. The Ruth's Lake area doesn't get a lot of sun, so it's perfect for hot day cragging, but not so great for cooler weather.

From Kamas, drive 35 miles (56 km) on Mirror Lake Byway, just a few miles past the Bald Mountain Pass summit. At mile marker 35, look for a parking area on your left, then hike along the mellow trail for just under a mile (1.6 km) to the lake and crags. When you reach a junction with a cairn (a stack of rocks designed to mark trails), hang a left toward the cliffs. Most of the climbs are found at the **Chief Wall** and the **Good Medicine Area,** and are just a 20-minute approach from the car. The latter is the first wall you'll discover from the trail. There are also a few mostly unnamed bouldering problems in the area if you want to bring your pad. One of the favorite routes at Good Medicine is **Black Elk,** a 5.10a sport climb with an arête, a chimney, an off-width—a little bit of everything. To reach Chief Wall, continue on the trail for a few more minutes, staying left at all junctions until you reach the cliff. This area features a well-rounded mix of mostly sport climbs that lean easy, making it a great place for beginners and new leaders alike. Ruth's Lake is also an excellent spot for hikers, anglers, and non-climbers tagging along in search of gorgeous views.

Cliff Lake Climbing Area

Cliff Lake is exactly what it sounds like: a south-facing cliff standing tall above a glimmering alpine lake. It tends to draw fewer crowds than Ruth's Lake, and offers single-pitch beginner to moderate sport and trad climbs from 5.5 to 5.10c, and is a great place for beginner trad leaders. The apron of the cliff is a large talus field, which provides a real sense of exposure on the routes, even if you're just 10 feet (3 m) off the ground. This sense of vulnerability is rewarded with sweeping Uinta views—take a picture from the top of the climb!

To get here from Kamas, drive 27 miles (43 km) on Mirror Lake Byway until you see signs for Trial Lake/Crystal Lake on your left. Turn left onto this paved road and follow signs to the Washington Lake Campground. The road will turn to dirt. Park at the Crystal Lake Trailhead. (If the lot is full, there are some impromptu spots along the road, or you can park in another lot and walk a little farther.) From here, it's about a 25-minute approach. Start on the Crystal Lake Trail and watch for a small, popular trail on your right accompanied by a low-to-the-ground rusted sign that reads "To Cliff Lake." At Lilly Lake, hang a left and continue on a steep trail up a ridge. Hike past Cliff Lake toward the cliff. There are a few campsites here, so you could do this as an overnight trip. **Squanto** (5.10) is a fun challenge with a tricky beginning, while **The Vulgarian** (5.8) is great for a newer trad leader, offering excellent protection. At 5.6, **Glory** makes for a superb warm-up in a spot that gets plenty of sun.

BIKING

There are two possibilities for bicycling through the Uintas. The first is to road bike part or all of the Mirror Lake Scenic Byway from Kamas—a challenging but rewarding ride. The other option is to take a mountain bike to the many dirt roads around the Uintas. Of course, there are also many trails that lie outside the bounds of wilderness that could be mountain biked, but they are not built for mountain biking and are infrequently traveled by bikers. The single-track and double-track trails in the Uintas are often steep, rocky, and in general not ideal for mountain bikes. Furthermore, many of the trails outside the wilderness area are heavily trafficked by hikers and horseback riders, who bikers must yield to. The Forest Service recommends instead that mountain bikers ride the network of 4WD and ATV trails, or the mellow Scenic Byway Trail.

Mirror Lake Scenic Byway

On weekends in the summer, you're likely to see at least a few cyclists parking by the South Summit High School (45 S. 300 E., Kamas) and lubing up their road bikes for a big ride. What are they riding? Chances are, it's **Mirror Lake Scenic Byway,** which starts just past the school. Do like the pros and park in the many empty spaces on 300 E. If it's a weekday in the spring or fall, you can easily find parking on other side streets in Kamas. From here, the classic ride is to bike to the top of Bald Mountain Pass and back again (60 mi/97 km round-trip, 5-7 hours, approx. 4,000 ft/1,219 m elevation gain, strenuous). Another option is to ride all the way to Evanston, Wyoming, which lies just under 80 miles (129 km) from Kamas, and figure out a shuttle back. Or you could ride for as long as you desire from Kamas and turn around at any point. The countless campsites riders will pass on Mirror Lake Byway make for numerous options to do this as an overnight. On the way back into Kamas, consider stopping for a celebratory beer at The Notch—from here, it's just a couple miles of mostly flat and downhill riding before you finish your more than half century of a ride!

Keep in mind that about 15 miles (24 km) out from Kamas, the Byway closes for the winter in November and doesn't officially reopen until close to Memorial Day, depending on weather.

Scenic Byway Trail

The mellow **Scenic Byway Trail** (8.5 mi/13.7 km one-way, 3-4 hours depending on pace, 1,600 ft/488 m elevation gain, easy) runs parallel to the Mirror Lake Byway. It also features a 3-mile (4.8-km) interpretive stretch, including a giant bird's nest children can climb inside and informational kiosks. While many hike this trail in the summer, it can also easily be biked. The trail starts 6.2 miles (10 km)

from Kamas on the right side of the road. Park across the road at the Yellow Pine Trailhead.

MOTORIZED SPORTS

There's no shortage of dirt road and snowy landscapes to explore in the non-wilderness-designated portion of the Uintas via off-road vehicles. When it comes to off-roading as a visitor, it's unlikely that you've road-tripped here, towing your snowmobile or ATV on a trailer, but if you have, all you need is a map. If you're experienced with the off-road vehicle you intend to use, you can rent one on your way into Kamas. If you're inexperienced, you can go with a local outfitter offering equipment and guidance alike.

The closest rental shop for equipment is **Weller Recreation** (936 W. SR 248, Kamas, 435/783-4718, www.wellerrec.com, 8:30am-6pm Mon.-Fri., 8:30am-3pm Sat., ATVs start at $100 for four hours, snowmobiles start at $150 for four hours), which is on your left as you pull into Kamas on Highway 248 from Park City. Weller specializes in sales and trade-ins, but it does offer rentals as well. In addition to the vehicles themselves, Weller also rents trailers to tow the vehicles (though your car will need a hitch) and helmets. Rentals are available in four- and eight-hour increments. Keep in mind that you need to be fully capable of operating this equipment independently. Weller does not provide training on the equipment or test you to make sure you can safely operate it.

You can find motorized winter outfitting services with a rental shop and guide out of Heber: **Uinta Recreation** (1550 S. Hwy. 40 B, Heber, 801/613-0288, www.uintarecreation. com, 8am-6pm daily, $200 pp not including rentals, two-person minimum) offers guided snowmobile tours in the winter.

New or veteran, equipment owner or not, everyone needs a **Motorized Vehicle Use Map** to legally and safely navigate the Uintas by off-road vehicle. Furthermore, the map will help you find the best destinations and views on your off-roading experience. You can pick one up at the ranger district office in Kamas or Heber, and you can also find a download-able version online (www.fs.usda.gov/uwcnf).

Off-Roading

Whether you've got a dirt bike, an ATV, an RZR, or any other sort of off-road vehicle, the **Taylor Fork/Cedar Hollow** area caters to all-terrain vehicles, with more than 22 miles (35 km) of dirt trails navigating some 1,400 feet (427 m) of elevation change. While there are some beginner trails in this area, most are moderate or difficult. To get to Taylor Fork, approximately 9 miles (14.5 km) from Kamas on Mirror Lake Byway, look for signage on your right. Have a wild romp through aspen and conifer trees, then ride to the ridgeline to take in the famous views of the Uintas.

Snowmobiling

Soapstone Basin makes for great winter excursions on snowmobile. From Kamas, drive 14.6 miles (23.5 km) on Mirror Lake Byway until you see Soapstone Basin Road on your right. This is right before the point at which the road closes from around November through most of May. From here, drive up the road, which contains some switchbacks. There are several miles of groomed road here to sled around, all in the basin below Soapstone Mountain. Bear in mind that there is some private property here, including mostly summer homes, a YMCA camp, and Forest Service employee housing, so be cognizant of trespassing. It's also recommended to stick to the groomed roads, rather than head into a powder field where you may get stuck depending on the snowpack. Another option is to just park where Mirror Lake Byway closes to cars, and continue on Mirror Lake Byway for a scenic wintry tour of the High Uintas.

SKIING

Like hiking, skiable terrain in the Uintas is practically endless—but much of it is difficult to access. While there is no chairlift-accessed skiing, there is no shortage of backcountry bowls and Nordic trails to discover. There are a few Nordic trails that lie just a few miles

from Kamas and have become quite popular on nice winter weekend days. As for back-country skiing, a system of seven yurts, both on the Utah and Wyoming side, lures in winter adventurers every winter for overnight missions. There are also mellow day outings into the Uintas as well as serious ski mountaineering missions waiting to be achieved.

Nordic Skiing

While there are several trails popular with Nordic skiers in the winter, the only one that's groomed is **Beaver Creek Trail**—also known as the **Scenic Byway Trail** (5.5 mi/8.9 km one-way, 2-3 hours depending on pace, 600 ft/183 m elevation gain, easy). The trail is accessed 6.2 miles (10 km) from Kamas and is on the right side of the Byway. Park on the left side at the Yellow Pine Trail lot. The trail travels through forested terrain as well as alongside a creek where beavers live. The trail is groomed from time to time, and since dogs, showshoers, and snowmobiles are prohibited, tracks stay in good condition.

Backcountry Skiing

The **Castle Peak** area offers plenty of easy and moderate terrain, plus two peaks and a yurt for more intensive adventures. To get here from Kamas, drive 8.7 miles (14 km) on Mirror Lake Byway and park where the Byway meets Upper Setting Road (Forest Road 035). From where you parked, follow an old logging road for about 2 miles (3.2 km) into Coop Canyon alongside Coop Creek. After another 1.5-mile (2.4-km) climb, you'll see Castle Peak to the northwest. There is plenty of skiable terrain in the vicinity, or you can choose to summit and ski Castle Peak (10,234 ft/3,119 m) or Duke Peak (10,605 ft/3,232 m), which offers a steeper, more dynamic descent. Another option is to ski about 6 miles (9.7 km) to **Castle Peak Yurt** (435/649-8710, https://whitepinetouring.com, starting at $175 per night), which can accommodate up to eight

---

1: autumn in the Uintas 2: a climber at Cliff Lake 3: early-season climbing at Ruth's Lake

people. This is just one of several yurts in the Uintas, most of which have a woodstove, firewood, bunk beds, and lighting—bring your own food and sleeping bags.

FISHING

With over 1,000 natural lakes, many seldom visited, several reservoirs, and the headwaters of four rivers, it's safe to say that the Uintas are an angler's paradise. However, it wasn't always this way. Many of these lakes have no natural fish population. Since 1927, the Kamas Fish Hatchery has been stocking many of the lakes and reservoirs in the Uintas, some by plane. Nowadays, you can cast in just about any lake on the map, though conditions do vary from year to year. Many of the lakes do require an approach, which might be as short as 10 minutes or as long as a day or more depending on your objective. Great fly-fishing also exists in the **Provo River,** which runs parallel to the Mirror Lake Byway from miles 12-25, with numerous access points for anglers along the way. The vast majority of the fish found in the Uintas are different varieties of trout, which make for excellent campfire meals.

If you have minimal fishing experience, consider hiring a local guide to show you around and recommend the right bait. **Jans** (1600 Park Ave., Park City, 435/649-4949, www.jans.com, 8am-7pm daily, $400 pp, $500 per couple, includes equipment, transportation from Park City, and food), an outfitter based in Park City, guides full-day fly-fishing trips in the Uinta Wilderness.

Big Elk Lake

Big Elk Lake is one of the closest lakes to Kamas, just over 10 miles (16.1 km) down Mirror Lake Byway, but it does require another 6 miles (9.7 km) on a four-wheel-drive-only road that can become impassable in muddy conditions. At mile marker 10.6 on Mirror Lake Byway, turn left on Norway Flats Road and travel about 7 miles (11.3 km), staying on the main road. A 4WD vehicle with high clearance—and a driver comfortable navigating rough roads—is a must. Once you

reach the end of the road, Little Elk Lake lies just a short 0.3-mile (0.5 km) hike to the west, while Big Elk Lake is just 0.8 mile (1.3 km) farther. Big Elk Lake is one of the largest in the Uintas, and deepest, too, with a depth of 110 feet (33.5 m). Due to its location at the end of a rough road, with a hike to boot, Big Elk doesn't usually see big crowds. The fish are primarily brook and cutthroat trout, can be caught from the shore or a boat, and are most likely to bite in the morning and evening.

Mirror Lake

Mirror Lake draws hikers looking for a quieter trail, picnicking families, and anglers seeking a beautiful high alpine lake in which to try their luck. Part of the Duchesne River drainage, Mirror Lake is 36 feet (11 m) deep, over 53 acres across, and filled with rainbow, albino rainbow, and fingerling brook trout. Fish from the shore or a boat. Mirror Lake is 32 miles (52 km) from Kamas following Mirror Lake Byway, about a 45-minute drive. After 31.3 miles (50.4 km), turn right on Forest Road 104 and follow signs for Mirror Lake.

Butterfly Lake

Shaped somewhat like a butterfly and occasionally covered in lily pads, serene **Butterfly Lake** is a great spot to catch rainbow and albino rainbow trout. Find it by driving 34.1 miles (54.9 km) from Kamas on Mirror Lake Byway, and look for signs for Butterfly Lake Campground on your left. The lake is co-located with a small campground and right across the road from an access point to the Highline Trail, so you can easily follow a morning of fishing with a hike and then spend the night.

Willow Springs Trout Farm

If you're looking for a fishing experience accessible to kids and true beginners—or just don't want to bother getting a Utah fishing license—stop at this small trout farm in Samak off Mirror Lake Byway just 3.5 miles (5.6 km) from Kamas. Run by the same family for several decades, **Willow Springs Trout Farm** (153 Samak Country Estates, 435/783-4608, hours vary) is generally open every day except Tuesday during the summer, though specific hours, days, and season varies; call or check the Facebook page for updated hours. Willow Springs rents out poles to catch the farm-raised rainbow trout on-site, and will even clean your fish for you for a small sum to make dinner that much easier.

Cliff Lake

Cliff Lake is a peaceful fishing spot to catch cutthroat trout. The 20-foot-deep (6.1 m) lake also sits below a popular climbing cliff so you can watch daring climbers scale the rock as you wait for the fish to bite. If the fish aren't biting, continue on the trail and you'll come upon more lakes. Clyde Lake lies about a mile (1.6 km) farther north and usually has good fishing as well. There are several dispersed areas to camp around Cliff Lake if you don't mind hauling in your camping supplies a little over a mile (1.6 km).

Cliff Lake lies about a 40-minute drive (27 mi/43 km) from Kamas. After 25 miles (40 km) on Mirror Lake Byway, turn left on Forest Road 041 toward Washington, Crystal, and Trial Lake Campgrounds. Take the second right onto Forest Road 038 toward Washington Campground and Crystal Lake Trailhead, and follow the road until it ends in a parking lot. From here, it's about a 25-minute approach. Start on the Crystal Lake Trail and watch for a small trail on your right accompanied by a low-to-the-ground rusted sign that reads "To Cliff Lake." At Lilly Lake, hang a left and continue on a steep trail up a ridge until you reach the lake.

CAMPING AND BACKPACKING

Diverse camping options exist in the Uintas. There are several massive group sites that can accommodate hundreds of people; over a dozen developed campgrounds off the Mirror Lake Scenic Byway, many with potable water and bathrooms; two spots for horse camping

equipped with stables; approximately 300 dispersed campsites across national forest; and endless national forest and wilderness acreage to backpack into.

The best place to search for available campgrounds is on the **Uinta-Wasatch-Cache Forest Service** website (www.fs.usda.gov/uwcnf). From there, navigate to "Recreation" and then "Camping." Here, you can view the rules for dispersed camping, or navigate to "Campground Camping" to view developed campgrounds. To see campgrounds close to Kamas, look at those listed for the Heber-Kamas Ranger District. About half on this list are off Mirror Lake Byway, while the others are in the same ranger district, but accessed via Heber or other nearby towns.

Planning Tips

The key to success for camping in the Uintas is to prepare well in advance. If you have your eyes set on an established campground during the summer, reserve online as far in advance as you can (six months is ideal). Dates that campgrounds open vary, with some opening as early as late May and others opening as late as early July. Most campgrounds stay open until early or mid-September. The **National Recreation Reservation Service** (877/444-6777, www.recreation.gov) usually opens up most campground reservations 240 days in advance. You may be shocked to find that many of the campgrounds fill up on summer weekends months in advance. For developed sites, fees usually range $16-21 per single site. Even if you pay to camp, if you park at a trailhead anywhere besides your campground, you still need to purchase a recreation pass, which starts at $6.

If you plan to camp outside of established campgrounds, advance planning should take the form of scoping out a spot, determining how you'll get there, and bringing all necessary equipment to get by without services. You'll also need to think about season; while you may not be restricted like you would with campground opening/closing dates, the road does close November-Memorial Day weekend, and snow might interfere with your camping plans beyond those dates.

Dispersed camping or backpacking in the Uintas requires that you plan for your own water (research freshwater nearby and bring the appropriate filtration/treatment systems), pack in food, and bring bear safety equipment as well. Dispersed camping is allowed on any national forest or wilderness land outside established campgrounds and in areas that do not block roads or entry/exit points. It's allowed for up to 14 days in a 30-day period, and all waste must be packed out. For more rules regarding dispersed camping, stop by the Heber-Kamas Ranger District, or visit www.fs.usda.gov.

As for fires, no matter where you camp, any fire restrictions in the county apply. If we continue to be in the midst of a drought with hot, dry summers, there's a very good chance fire restrictions will indeed be in place during the summer months. These will be posted at the Heber-Kamas Ranger District, available online, and generally noted at developed campsites throughout the area. If there's no fire ban, always remember to heed Smokey the Bear's campfire rules. That fire goes to sleep when you do.

Campgrounds

The closest campground to Kamas, **Yellow Pine Campground** (33 sites, toilets, no water or hookups, tents and RVs permitted, open early May-early Sept., no advance reservations, starting at $18 per night) is 6 miles (9.7 km) up Mirror Lake Byway and offers well-sheltered camping amid stands of ponderosa and lodgepole pine. It's also one of the first campgrounds to open for the year, and the last to close. While no potable water is available, a creek runs through the area if you have a treatment system, or you can pack in your own water. The campground is also located right by the Yellow Pine Trailhead and across the road from the Scenic Byway Trail, which can be traversed by foot, horse, or bike.

Tucked just below Bald Mountain and Hayden Peak just past Mirror Lake Byway's summit, ★ **Moosehorn Campground** (33 sites, drinking water, toilets, no hookups, tents and RVs permitted, open early July-mid-Sept., online reservations available, starting at $23 per night) is a serene and gorgeous camping spot right off the road about 45 minutes (30 mi/48 km) from Kamas. Park at the Moosehorn Campground lot, then hike down a small trail to the lake and campsites. You can also fish in the lake, or bring a canoe to paddle around the waters.

Another spot to camp that's close to the water is **Mirror Lake Campground** (78 sites, drinking water, toilets, no hookups, tents and RVs permitted, open early July-Sept., online reservations available, starting at $23 per night), located just under 40 minutes (26 mi/42 km) from Kamas. With access to fishing, picnic areas, and mellow and more challenging trails, Mirror Lake is a popular place to camp with great views of Bald Mountain. As one of the biggest campgrounds in this part of the Uintas, Mirror Lake does tend to feel less intimate or "away from it all" compared to some of the smaller campgrounds.

About 25 miles (40 km) up Mirror Lake Byway from Kamas, a trio of lakes—Washington, Trial, and Crystal Lakes—is co-located with two sizable campgrounds (Washington Lake Campground and Trial Lake Campground) as well as several trailheads. **Washington Lake Campground** (49 sites, toilets, no drinking water or hookups, tents and RVs permitted, open early July-Sept., online reservations available, starting at $23 per night) is right by its namesake lake. The campground is located about 40 minutes (26.5 mi/42.6 km) from Kamas; after 25 miles (40 km) on the Byway, look for a turnoff for Washington, Trial, and Crystal Lakes on your left and follow signs toward Washington Lake Campground. The campground is also just a little over a mile (1.6 km) farther down the Byway from Provo River Falls, so it's easy to make a stop at this scenic waterfall during your camping trip. Trial

1: Samak Smoke House 2: The Notch pub

Lake Campground is similar to Washington Lake Campground but is paved; of the two, unpaved Washington Lake Campground feels slightly less developed.

FOOD

Four miles (6.4 km) down Mirror Lake Scenic Byway from Kamas lies the town of Samak, which bears a name that is indeed the inverse of "Kamas," and yes, that's on purpose. The town is mostly a collection of cabins, trailers, and mountain homes dispersed across about 2 miles (3.2 km) of Mirror Lake Scenic Byway before the road starts to climb in elevation. Here you'll find two dining options. Neither is a traditional restaurant, but both are interesting windows into the area, and worth stopping at briefly on your way to or from the deeper Uintas.

Formerly the canteen for a mine in the Deer Valley area, the cabin in which the **Samak Smoke House** (1937 UT-150, 435/783-4880, https://samaksmokehouse.com, 9am-5pm Mon.-Thurs., 9am-8pm Fri.-Sun. Memorial Day-Labor Day, 9am-5pm daily Labor Day-Memorial Day) is located now calls the Uintas home. There are a few reasons to make a stop at the Smoke House. The first is that it's literally open every day, year-round—an impressive feat considering how sleepy Mirror Lake Scenic Byway is from November through April. The second is the smoker, which imparts big flavor to beef jerky and smoked trout alike. The smoked meats and cheeses on offer make for great souvenirs or gifts. The Samak Smoke House operates a café with coffee drinks, hot chocolate, soups, and sandwiches—great for picking up a picnic lunch to enjoy in the Uintas—as well as an outdoor barbecue on Sunday evenings in the summer (5pm-8pm). The Smoke House also sells a variety of maps, souvenirs, packaged goods, and other random general store inventory.

Formerly known as the Beaver Creek Inn, ★ **The Notch** (2392 E. Mirror Lake Hwy., 435/783-6244, www.thenotchpub.com, noon-11pm Mon.-Thurs., noon-1am Fri., 11am-1am Sat., 11am-11pm Sun., $10-15) is the best bar in the Uintas, in part because it's also the only bar. The Notch also serves pub fare, including good barbecue and a solid burger. The vibe is middle-of-nowhere-in-the-mountains, and the company varies depending on the time of day and year, from timeworn locals of the town of Samak and hunters looking to warm up, to bikers passing through. On weekend evenings, you can find live music here, and in the summer, the patio's a fine place to sit. The Notch is a great place to stop for a beer after a long hike to soak in the *Walker Texas Ranger* vibes.

GETTING THERE

There are several entry points to the Uintas, including Duchesne and Roosevelt in Utah and Evanston in southwestern Wyoming. I describe most of the activities here in reference to Kamas via the Mirror Lake Byway, a popular entry point and the closest to Park City and Salt Lake City. There is no public transportation to the Uintas, and with little to no phone service/Wi-Fi there, you may be able to get an Uber/Lyft in, but you won't be able to get one out.

Background

The Landscape

GEOGRAPHY

The Rockies arc through the northern part of Utah, defining its geography, economy, and identity. In this landscape of basins and peaks are several ranges: the Wasatch, the Uintas, and the Oquirrhs. All three of these mountains take their names from Indigenous vocabulary. Wasatch means a low place in the high mountains. Uinta is a Ute term for a pine forest. And Oquirrh is a Goshute word loosely translating to wooded mountain.

Most well-known among locals and visitors alike is the Wasatch,

home to the vast majority of the state's ski resorts, which become networks of summer trails when the snow melts. Along the range's 250-mile (405-km) run, Mount Timpanogos (11,750 ft/3,581 m) is perhaps the most well-known and frequently summited.

Two of the main populated regions in northern Utah are named according to their location in relation to the range: the Wasatch Front (the Salt Lake area) and the Wasatch Back (the Park City area). The Great Salt Lake sits in the basin of the Wasatch and is a mere relic of a massive ancient lake called Bonneville that once lapped at the foothills of the Wasatch.

While the Wasatch are perhaps Utah's most eminent range, the Uintas are the biggest—Kings Peak towers at 13,527 feet (4,123 m). Stretching from Kamas up to Wyoming, the Uintas are also one of the only ranges in the United States that run north-south rather than east-west. Here lie endless acres to hike, camp, backcountry ski, and explore. The eastern part of the range consists of smaller peaks, while the western part is often referred to as the High Uintas, for obvious reasons.

The forgotten range of northern Utah is the Oquirrhs, which sit on the southern side of Salt Lake City across from the Wasatch. You won't hear many locals or guidebooks talking about recreating in this range, though trails do exist. This is in part due to the fact that the Oquirrhs are smaller, topping out at 10,676 feet (3,254 m) (Lewiston Peak), as well as to the long history of mining here, the scars of which are more than evident as you drive past the range on the way to the Great Salt Lake.

CLIMATE

Utah enjoys four distinct seasons, which are more extreme in some areas of the Wasatch than others. For example, summer is hotter in Salt Lake City and Heber than it is in Park City and Sundance, while the inverse is true

in the winter. In the summer, temperatures top out in the low 90s F (32°C) in the Wasatch Back, but soar into the low 100s F (38°C) in the Salt Lake area. Generally, the higher you are in elevation, the cooler it is. This typically amounts to about a 3°F (1.7°C) temperature decrease per 1,000-foot (305-m) altitude increase. While the stray thunderstorm or rainy morning can strike the Wasatch in the summer, it's much drier than other Rocky Mountain states like Colorado. As the second-driest state in the nation after Nevada, Utah may get a lot of snow, but it's fairly arid the rest of the year.

In the winter in the Wasatch Back and the Cottonwood Canyons, daytime lows rarely get into single digits, and even more rarely dip below 0°F (-18°C). January is often the coldest month, with spring skiing conditions beginning to appear in early March. Winter in Salt Lake is more moderate, with daytime temps often reaching the 40s F (5-9°C) and higher. Winter storms primarily come from the Gulf of Mexico and the Pacific Ocean. Though these storms pepper the Sierra Nevadas with powder first, this area gets its fair share. The mountains can see nearly 700 inches (1,778 cm) of snowfall on good snow years—that's almost 60 feet (18 m)!

Fall and spring in the Wasatch—particularly the Wasatch Back—are anyone's bet. Often referred to as the off-season or, in spring's case, the mud season, these months could be extensions of the previous season, with snow lasting well into June and a temperate fall that feels like summer. Or, they could be early harbingers of the next season, with snow falling in September and dry trails and 70°F (21°C) temps in April. While these seasons are a great time to visit to escape the crowds, weather and trail conditions are a gamble.

Utah also basks in sunlight, with Salt Lake City receiving an average of 222 sunny days a year (compare that to 205 for the national

Previous: view from the top of Mirror Lake Scenic Byway.

average). And at high altitude, that sun sure can feel strong, so be extra vigilant about sun protection, even in winter.

ENVIRONMENTAL ISSUES

Among the litany of environmental issues facing just about any place on the map, three stand out in Utah: air quality, climate change (and its implications for the snowpack and water supply), and public lands. The latter plays out more dramatically in southern Utah, but the politics that determine the fate of our beloved red rock to the south are staged in the capital, and yank at the heartstrings of most who call Utah home.

The Inversion

Salt Lake City and parts of the Wasatch suffer from very poor air quality, in part due to a phenomenon known as "The Inversion"—a reference to the geographic position in a low bowl that traps cold air and pollutants. The result is air that has alarmed and mobilized everyone from local moms to local doctors, but the government has not taken significant enough action to address this problem.

Climate Change

Many places are on the "climate vulnerable" list, and the Wasatch is among them for many reasons. The potential downfall of the ski industry, pivotal to the local economy, is one of them. It should come as no surprise that the ski industry depends on snow. During bad snow years, opening dates may get delayed. Closing dates move up. More snow must be manufactured (read: $$$). And fewer skiers and snowboarders are motivated to hit the slopes, deterred by poor conditions and exposed rocks bound to result in damage to skis and boards.

More gravely, as the second-driest state in the nation, Utah has much to worry about in a hotter, drier world. Planners are already raising red flags about the conflict inherent in projected population growth and the reality of the current and future water supplies.

Lack of water not only has implications for drinking water supplies, agriculture, and the resources to produce fake snow for the slopes, but also for how long and devastating wildfire season is each year.

PLANTS

Trees, scrub, wildflowers, and other plants abound across the Wasatch. Generally, the flora you'll find depends on your altitude. In the foothills (4,500-7,800 ft/1,372-2,377 m), which include most of the cities and towns like Salt Lake City and Ogden, you'll find shrubs, juniper, chokecherry, stinging nettle, and elderberry, which Mormons famously pick and turn into syrups and teas.

Stretching across the hills are also vast seas of sagebrush, where deer and elk graze during the winter. While the abundant sagebrush may not take your breath away, it's long been used to create medicines and in ceremonies, like burning a bundle of it to spiritually cleanse a new home. Around the foothills are also taller trees like maple, willow, oak, and cottonwoods, which rain white fluff in the summertime.

In towns like Park City and the surrounding open space, the montane zone (6,000-9,500 ft/1,829-2,896 m) presides, with taller trees like ponderosa pine and quaking aspen, where birds sing and nest. Travel a couple thousand feet (610 m) higher into the subalpine zone (8,100-11,000 ft/2,469-3,353 m), and forests thrive everywhere development doesn't. Alongside roads and trails, find Engelmann spruce, Douglas fir, lodgepole pine, and more coniferous trees.

The subalpine zone is also where wildflowers bloom in the summer. Some local favorites include red Indian paintbrush, pink elk thistle, purple columbine, and blue camas lily, for which the town of Kamas is named.

The higher you climb out of the subalpine zone, the more tenacious life must become. Trees grow shorter to withstand harsh winds, and are more dispersed across the landscape. Above 10,800 feet (3,292 m), you officially enter the alpine zone, where trees no longer

The Utah Public Land Controversy

On December 28, 2016, in the final days of his presidency, President Barack Obama established **Bears Ears National Monument.** This designation of 1.35 million acres of public lands didn't come out of the blue. It was the hard-won victory of the Inter-Tribal Bears Ears Coalition, composed of the Navajo, the Hopi, the Uintah and Ouray Reservation, the Ute Mountain Ute, and the Zuni, all working together for years with local conservation nonprofits and citizens.

The land known as Bears Ears is sacred to the tribes who fought for it. Yesterday, it was the home of their ancestors, with over 100,000 archaeological sites like cliff dwellings and rock art stretching back 3,500 years. Today, it's a site of ceremonies and a tangible portal to the past. And in the future, the tribes who fought for it hope it will continue to be a culturally, historically, and environmentally rich place for generations to come.

But these acres are not only valued by the tribes. Locals and visitors alike go to Bears Ears to climb, camp, hunt, fish, hike, and otherwise explore these breathtaking acres. Of course, Bears Ears is also home to flora and fauna, from hanging gardens and bighorn sheep to great horned owls.

In short, Bears Ears has scientific, historical, cultural, biological, and recreational value. Few put it better than the voices of the Inter-Tribal Coalition. Explains Regina Lopez-Whiteskunk, a member of the Ute Mountain Ute Council, "It's very important that we take every step in protecting our heritage. We are of the land, we don't quite own it but we're here as caretakers. If we can help protect that and justify where our native cultures and customs come from we can protect it in the face of new challenges."

A little less than a year after Bears Ears was officially protected, President Donald Trump announced on December 4, 2017, that he would shrink the size of the monument by 85 percent to just 228,784 acres. At the same time, he also reduced the size of nearby Grand Staircase-Escalante National Monument by about half. Just a few months later, the federal government officially began the process of opening up the redacted acreage of Bears Ears to oil and gas exploration.

Today, the fate of this sacred land remains unknown. Since the monument was reduced, five tribes and environmental groups have sued the Trump administration over the changes to Bears Ears. In Utah, while members of the Coalition tribes, many outdoor enthusiasts, environmentalists, and others continue to voice their support for the reinstatement of the original Bears Ears designation, others, including the state government, celebrate Trump's action.

Some suspect that Utah's aversion toward federal public lands stretches back to the late 19th century, when Mormons felt shunned by the nation and sought safety and autonomy in the Wasatch. From the territory's struggle for statehood as a result of its polygamous ways, to its ideological clash with many a left-wing administration, Utah tends to prefer that the federal government stay out of its affairs. Meanwhile, the fate of much of Bears Ears remains in jeopardy.

grow. Here in the tundra above tree line, vegetation is scarce.

ANIMALS

Unlike flora—which can migrate, but very slowly—fauna is not confined to one zone or another. They move and disappear depending on the season. Small mammals range from the prolific chipmunk scampering across the trail, to weasels, beavers, porcupines, and marmots, which you might catch sunning themselves on rocks during quiet mornings.

The most common fish in lakes, reservoirs, and rivers are Pacific salmon and several varieties of trout—cutthroat, rainbow, and brook included—though many of the fish are raised in hatcheries and deposited into these water bodies.

Utah is also home to 465-some species of bird. Spy them everywhere from the Great Salt Lake to the Swaner Preserve wetlands to the Uinta National Forest. Some common and noteworthy local birds include waterfowl, grouse, grebes, songbirds, migratory hummingbirds, large cranes, and fierce birds of prey.

Just as easy to spot as a Uinta chipmunk is the mule deer that often falls victim to cars when dashing across the highway. While a wildlife bridge over I-80 is designed to protect the lives of deer and other mammals whose habitat has been bifurcated by development, many more roadways are hazards for drivers and wildlife alike. Scarcer large mammals include elk, cougars, bobcats, black bears, and moose.

At the far reaches of the subalpine zone and above tree line, you may find pikas *feeee*-ing across scree fields, mountain goats braving jagged cliffs, and the occasional hungry bear searching for insects.

While Utah was once home to grizzly bears, the last—an 1,100-pound (500 kg) behemoth known as Old Ephraim—was slain on August 22, 1923. And the jury is still out on whether any wolverines or lynx still roam the forests of the Wasatch.

History

INDIGENOUS ROOTS

While the animals and plants detailed above have long called the Wasatch home—not to mention a few other ancient wild cards like camels and mastodons—the first humans arrived during the last ice age. About 20,000 years ago, humans crossed the Bering Strait. The earliest evidence of humans in Utah stretches back 12,000-some years.

By around AD 400, the Fremont and Ancestral Pueblo cultures emerged and began to leave behind more tangible evidence, from structures to artwork, like the petroglyphs prevalent in the southwestern part of the state. Around AD 1200, Numic hunter-gatherers began to migrate into Utah, eventually forming the Ute, Paiute, Goshute, and Shoshone people, who still call Utah home today. By the time the Great Salt Lake—which the Western Goshute referred to as *ti'ts-pa* ("bad water")—had been "discovered" by 19th-century explorer John C. Frémont, these Indigenous tribes had been in the area for centuries.

Sometime between AD 300 and 1300, the way of life for Indigenous people in the Utah area began to change dramatically, as it did for those inhabiting much of the West. In addition to hunting and gathering for sustenance, the people we now refer to as the Fremont began to grow beans, corn, and other vegetables. They also constructed sturdier shelters and started storing grain.

Changes also came about as a result of the weather—or, more accurately, the climate.

Severe megadroughts plagued much of the Southwest around AD 800-1300. This severely impacted life for the people living in the area, causing fighting and outmigration to wetter climates.

Compared to your run-of-the-mill colonizer, Mormons held a different view of the Indigenous people they vied with for land and resources. If you know a thing or two about Mormonism, then you may recall that the Book of Mormon tells of two branches of the Israelite family—the Nephites and the Lamanites—who migrated to the Americas 2,500 years ago. As religious legend goes, the Lamanites killed off the Nephites, who have been awaiting redemption ever since. Mormons believe that the Indigenous people of North America are the descendants of the Nephite people, cursed with dark skin.

Unfortunately, Israelite blood did not stop the Mormon settlers from attacking Indigenous people, but it did lead them to undertake programs like the Indian Student Placement Program. From 1947 to 2000, the church took some 50,000 Indigenous children from reservations, relocated them to Mormon families for nine months of the year, and converted them to Mormonism.

THE MORMON MIGRATION

The short answer to why the Mormons went west to Utah is persecution. Previously, the church had been headquartered in Nauvoo,

Illinois, where they were the victims of mob violence culminating in the assassination of their leader, Joseph Smith, in 1844.

That was the final straw for Brigham Young, who decided that it was high time to find a new home. They packed up the wagons and handcarts, and headed west, wintering in Nebraska. Cold, illness, and death marked the journey, and Young was even famously afflicted with Rocky Mountain fever toward the end.

On July 24, 1847, after 111 days on the go, Young and his caravan arrived in the Salt Lake Valley. When Young emerged from Emigration Canyon and gazed out upon the valley from what we now call the Foothills, he declared, "It is enough. This is the right place." Today, July 24 is celebrated as Pioneer Day, an official state holiday.

Young and others briefly questioned that certainty in the year that followed as difficulties arose. A particularly memorable one involved a cricket infestation of the Mormon crops. But seagulls swooped in at the last viable moment, devouring the pests and saving the crops in an event now known as the Miracle of the Gulls.

Ever since, Mormons have flocked to Utah to live and visit. In the two decades following Young's arrival, over 60,000 Mormons relocated to the Utah Territory. Members of the Church of Jesus Christ of Latter-day Saints continue to dominate the population, accounting for over 60 percent of its total residents. And every year, as many as five million people make the pilgrimage to the LDS headquarters at Temple Square.

MODERN TIMES

Rooted in Indigenous cultures and carved by Mormon pioneers, the story of Utah is also plotted around the industries that have boomed, busted, and in some cases persisted. One of the oldest professions in the modern economy is that of the miner. Many relocated to Utah to work in mines, some of which still operate today. The railroad industry—its construction, its operation, and the people it brought to and through the area—also significantly influenced the development and culture of Utah for about a century beginning in the early 1860s. In addition to mining, religion, and trains, the military and aerospace industries have also shaped the state, along with higher education.

For the first couple decades of the railroad's heyday, Utah was not even an official state, mostly due to clashes between the federal government and the church-controlled state government led by Brigham Young. President James Buchanan even declared a short-lived Mormon War in response to Young ruling the state as a theocracy that embraced polygamy. But shortly after the state government banned polygamy and made some other concessions, Utah became the 45th state on January 4, 1896.

While mineral extraction persists today, recreation has risen out of the ashes of the gold and silver mines of yore, particularly in Park City and the Cottonwood Canyons. The 20th-century dawn of ski resorts, the 1919 establishment of its first national park (Zion), the 2002 Winter Olympics—these phenomena and more have shaped Utah into a destination for skiers, hikers, bikers, climbers, and many more outdoor enthusiasts.

There's no doubt that the Church of Jesus Christ of Latter-day Saints continues to play a dominating role in everything from politics to bars to downtown culture—the church actually purchased parts of Salt Lake City's Main Street in 1999 for over eight million dollars. But over time, the church's growth has been slowing and Utah and the Wasatch have become less homogenous, with more immigrants arriving, Utah liquor laws becoming slowly but surely laxer, and more "gentiles" joining governing bodies.

Local Culture

DIVERSITY

It's hard to argue with the statistics, which are whiter than a powder day at Snowbird. Over 87 percent of Salt Lake County is white, and that percentage edges 3 percent higher when you look at state demographics. Yet year by year, Utah and its cities grow less homogenous.

To the surprise of some, Utah also welcomes immigrants, even through periods of xenophobia—particularly Muslim xenophobia. Most chalk this up to the fact that many Mormons view themselves as refugees, historically driven out of various homes by religious persecution. This lies in contradiction to the fact that the church has a long history of racism and prejudice based on sexuality. Furthermore, in the early 20th century, businesses owned by non-Mormons often suffered at the hands of boycotts by those who followed the "local religion."

In *Hidden History of Utah,* former *Salt Lake Tribune* columnist Eileen Hallet Stone chronicles the minority reports of Utah. Greek towns sprouting up in the early 20th century. A long history of Latino communities. Basque immigrants and Black miners who settled in Ogden. Thousands of Chinese immigrants that built the railroad and Italians mining for coal. Women who dared to stake land solo and homestead. A Russian Jewish immigrant who launched Salt Lake's "Wall Street of the West." And the 1916 election of Utah's first and only Jewish governor: Simon Bamberger. Eighty-some years later, and Utah had its first LGBTQ+ state legislator: Jackie Biskupsi, who later become Salt Lake's first openly gay mayor and second female mayor.

INDIGENOUS CULTURES

Today, Utah is home to eight tribal governments. The Indigenous people of the Wasatch and Utah view themselves not as owners of the land, but as caretakers. This perception has allowed them to live sustainably across generations and in harmony with their environment. Obviously, this way of life was disrupted by colonization.

Some of Utah's tribes share common ancestry and are even just bands within a larger tribe. For example, the Shoshone, Paiute, and Ute are part of a larger group known as the Newe, translating to "the people." Over time, they divided into more formal groups of extended families, in part due to the stress wrought by colonization and development.

One of the only tribes still officially based near the Wasatch is the Northwestern Band of the Shoshone Nation, located north of Ogden near the Idaho border. While the arrival of settlers spelled trouble for all the Indigenous inhabitants of Utah, the 1869 completion of the Transcontinental Railroad exacerbated the situation for the Shoshone, attracting ever-greater numbers of people to compete for land and resources.

The other nearest tribe is the Skull Valley Band of the Goshute, located about 45 miles (72 km) southwest of Salt Lake City. Utah is also home to the Paiute Indian Tribe, the San Juan Southern Paiute Tribe, the Confederated Tribes of Goshute, the Navajo Nation, the Ute Indian Tribe, and the White Mesa Community of the Ute Mountain Ute Tribe.

To discover more about Utah's Indigenous nations, check out individual tribal government websites for upcoming events such as powwows, look up celebrations during Indigenous Peoples Day (formerly Columbus Day, 2nd Mon. of Oct.), visit a reservation, and see the Native Voices permanent exhibit at the Natural History Museum of Utah in Salt Lake City.

THE LDS CHURCH

With over 16 million worldwide members, the "local religion," as the Church of Jesus Christ of Latter-day Saints is often referred to, continues to thrive and dominate the affairs of Utah. While the church is still expanding and has often been named the fastest-growing religion, that growth has started to slow.

Within the Wasatch especially, the religious dynamic is changing. As of 2018, Mormonism is no longer the religion held by the majority of citizens in Salt Lake County. Indeed, in many parts of Salt Lake City, not to mention Ogden and Park City, the presence of Mormonism is scarcely felt.

Over the years, the church has also inched toward a more progressive identity. Several decades ago, it allowed Black men to aspire to priesthood. And as of 2019, same-sex couples are no longer considered heretics. The church attributes such changes to what it describes as missives from God.

In addition to changing its policies, the church has rebranded itself over the years. It's changed its name to Reorganized Church of Jesus Christ of Latter-day Saints, to Saints of Community of Christ, and back again. It's asked not to be referred to as "Mormon" or "LDS," then changed its mind again.

The best way to learn about Utah's local religion is to head to Temple Square or This Is The Place Park in Salt Lake City.

LITERATURE

Literature of the Wasatch specializes in religion, nature, and the American West. Relevant reading in the Latter-day Saints category include *The Rise of Modern Mormonism* penned by a church leader, or cut to the chase and read *The Book of Mormon* itself. For a more lighthearted rendition of that text, read *The Book of Mormon Script Book* or see it on the stage, ideally at the Eccles Theater in Salt Lake. If you want to peer into the darker side of the religion, consider Jon Krakauer's *Under the Banner of Heaven.*

Celebrated nature writers who are from or who lived in the state include Wallace Stegner, Rick Bass, and nationally renowned poet and nonfiction writer Terry Tempest Williams. All of these authors have grappled with the environmental issues unique to the American West, as well as paid homage to its unique landscapes.

A wild card local author is sci-fi writer Orson Scott Card, who grew up in Utah and attended both Brigham Young University and the University of Utah. For a fictional take on the history of 19th-century Utah, read his novel *Saints.*

You can discover these and more local authors and regional literature at independent bookstores throughout the Wasatch. Ask for shelves dedicated to local authors, the West, and nature.

VISUAL ARTS

Utah is best known for land art, nature-based art, and Indigenous art. The vast majority of art galleries around the state specialize in these genres. You'll also find exhibits at art museums in Salt Lake City covering these subjects.

That first category emerged in the 1960s and is epitomized by the late Robert Smithson's Spiral Jetty on the Great Salt Lake, as well as his partner Nancy Holt's Sun Tunnels in the Utah desert. Nature-based art is exactly what it sounds like—photography and paintings depicting wildlife, mountains, and quaking aspen trees. Indigenous art is created by members of the tribes established in Utah. Navajo rugs are a particularly well-known entry in this category, and are often sold during annual sales across Salt Lake City and Park City.

MUSIC AND DANCE

Utah loves a good outdoor concert. On a near daily basis throughout summer, you can find recurring concerts staged in outdoor amphitheaters, many of them free. One of the favorite venues in the Wasatch, Salt Lake City's Red Butte Garden, is also outdoors. Come winter, the outdoor music persists, but is usually held on weekend afternoons at ski resort base areas, where outerwear, beer, and a little dancing keep the audience warm.

Salt Lake City, Park City, and Ogden all attract big-name acts, especially to their bigger venues, but also host local bands and locally loved genres like bluegrass and country music.

The Utah Symphony has been a major U.S. orchestra since 1940, playing both locally and across the country with some 175 concerts a season. Their official home is Abravanel Hall in Salt Lake City, but in the summer, they take up residence at the Deer Valley Music Festival. Utah also has an opera, founded in 1878.

In dance, Ballet West is a celebrated local institution, established in 1963 and based out of Salt Lake City's Capitol Theatre. The company tours and also performs locally. Salt Lake City is also home to a contemporary dance company and repertory dance company.

FOOD

A medium-rare bison burger, a saucy gyro, a slice of cake. Utah is a great place to enjoy these and many more dishes. Those three examples represent some of Utah's culinary strong suits: cuisine of the Rocky Mountain West, ethnic food, and sweets.

Cuisine of the West is technically unde-fined, but is traditionally heavy on the red meat and locally caught or raised animals. You'll find buffalo burgers, elk steak, and trout on many menus. Sometimes—espe-cially at ski resort dining establishments—this Rocky Mountain West cuisine takes cues from the other skiing communities of the world, from Norway to the Alps.

Thanks to the many immigrants and refu-gees in northern Utah, there's also a surpris-ingly great array of global cuisines. Some of this is thanks to Spice Kitchen, a Salt Lake nonprofit that helps immigrants, refugees, and low-income individuals become culinary entrepreneurs. From Lebanese and Jamaican to Sudanese and Korean, there are some fan-tastic local food carts, trucks, and hidden gems across Salt Lake City, with a few pep-pered in around Park City and Ogden as well.

Finally, the state's sweet tooth suppos-edly stems from the fact that members of the Church of Jesus Christ of Latter-day Saints are not permitted to indulge in alcohol or warm beverages, leading them to sin in the form of sweets. Confectioners, creameries, gelaterias, froyogurterias, soda mixer drive-thrus, ko-lache drive-thrus, cookie shops, doughnut shops, French patisseries, Latin *panaderias,* and more wherever you turn to fuel your ex-plorations in the Wasatch.

Essentials

Transportation

GETTING THERE
Air

The main airport serving Salt Lake City and the greater Wasatch area is **Salt Lake City International Airport** (SLC; 776 N. Terminal Dr., 801/575-2400, www.slcairport.com), which is about 15 minutes from downtown Salt Lake and no more than an hour from any of the other areas included in this guide. The Salt Lake airport is a major hub for Delta Air Lines, with nine other airlines stopping in Salt Lake, including Alaska Airlines, Frontier, JetBlue, and Southwest.

The airport has plenty of dining, shopping, and services, and is serviced by the TRAX light rail (www.rideuta.com), several car rental services, public buses, taxis, and rideshares.

Ogden also has a small commercial airport connecting the dots between the Wasatch and parts of Arizona as well as the national parks in southern Utah. Heber is home to a small private airport.

Train

For long-distance train travel, **Amtrak** (800/872-724, www.amtrak.com) makes stops in the area in Salt Lake City, Ogden, and Provo.

Bus

Greyhound (800/231-2222, www.greyhound.com) serves the Wasatch area, offering stops in Salt Lake City, Park City, Heber, and Ogden.

Car

The main highways connecting northern Utah to its border states of Idaho, Wyoming, Colorado, Arizona, and Nevada are **I-80** east-west, and **I-15** south-north. However, there are many smaller scenic routes that might take a little longer, but experience less traffic and more beautiful views. Examples of such routes include **U.S. 40** to Colorado and **Highway 150** (Mirror Lake Scenic Byway) to Wyoming.

CAR RENTAL

Car rentals are available at the Salt Lake City International Airport, as well as in downtown Salt Lake City, Park City, Heber, and Ogden. If driving in the winter, it's worth spending a little extra to get a 4WD/AWD vehicle with snow tires. If you're visiting during other seasons but planning to travel on dirt roads, get a 4WD/AWD vehicle with high clearance.

GETTING AROUND

Light Rail

Operated by the **Utah Transportation Authority** (UTA; www.rideuta.com), the **TRAX light rail** services most of Salt Lake City, including the airport. The UTA **FrontRunner** train (Route 750) connects Salt Lake City with bedroom communities and outlying areas, including Ogden, Provo, and Orem.

Bus

The **Utah Transportation Authority** (UTA; www.rideuta.com) operates over 100 bus routes throughout Salt Lake that cover gaps in the TRAX light rail service. This same bus system also services inner-city travel in Ogden. The UTA also operates ski buses that connect the ski resorts in the Cottonwood Canyons with Salt Lake City, as well as Snowbasin with the city of Ogden.

The **Town of Park City** (www.parkcity.org) offers a free public bus service that connects Old Town, ski resorts, Kimball Junction, and other outlying areas.

Car

The same highways that get you into the Wasatch from surrounding states—**I-80** and **I-15**—also connect the communities therein. **I-215** connects Salt Lake City to Sandy, Cottonwood Heights, and the Cottonwood Canyons. **I-84** connects Ogden and the Great Salt Lake with Salt Lake City and the Wasatch Back. **U.S. 40** connects Heber, Sundance, and Park City, while **Highway 248** bridges Kamas and Park City.

In general, traffic throughout the Wasatch is limited compared to other metropolitan areas. You'll experience the worst traffic at rush hour on I-15, I-215, in the Foothills neighborhood of Salt Lake City, and in downtown Salt Lake City, as well as on Friday afternoons and Sunday afternoons as people head

ESSENTIALS
TRANSPORTATION

out on and return from weekend road trips. It's also easy to get stuck on the area's one-lane roads behind a big semi or slow driver, so exercise patience and pass with care.

Taxi/Rideshare

Taxis and car services are available throughout the established cities and towns of the Wasatch; however, with the exception of the downtown areas of Salt Lake City, Park City, and Ogden, you're better off scheduling these rides in advance. Rideshares are widely available at the Salt Lake City International Airport, in downtown Salt Lake City, downtown Park City, and downtown Ogden. However, if you're in an outlying area or traveling at an odd hour, expect a long wait and have a backup plan. You may get lucky in the smaller towns of the Wasatch (like Kamas and Heber), but generally rideshare availability here is limited and unpredictable. Do not rely on rideshares or hailing a taxi to get to and from trailheads and public lands, like wilderness areas.

Bicycle

In general, most of the areas of the Wasatch are bicycle-friendly and very popular with road cyclists. In 2018, *Bicycling Magazine* rated Salt Lake City the 16th-best city in the United States for biking with scores of 33/40 for safety, 22/30 for friendliness from other road users, and 7/10 for culture. The **Salt Lake City Transportation Division** runs a helpful online resource (www.bikeslc.com) with routes, maps, bike parking areas, and other information. You can also pick up a bike throughout the downtown area through **Green Bike SLC Bikeshare** (https://greenbikeslc.org).

If you're planning to bike between the downtown areas and the Foothills or Avenues of Salt Lake City, plan to power through some pretty big hills that, combined with the altitude, may knock the wind out of you.

In Park City, though there aren't many designated bike lanes, there is a paved recreational path that connects Kimball Junction, Old Town Park City, and other neighborhoods like Willow Creek. The city offers e-bike rentals at junctions throughout this path through **Summit Bike Share** (www.summitbikeshare.com).

In the smaller towns of the area, traffic is limited and it's generally very easy to vie with other vehicles for real estate on the road.

Travel Tips

WHAT TO PACK

The contents of your suitcase should be totally dictated by the time of year you visit and activities you have planned. Year-round, some necessities include layers (including during the summer, when nights become chilly or thunderstorms strike the mountains), sun protection (sunscreen, a hat, and sunglasses), and sturdy footwear for excursions on trails or icy streets.

In terms of clothes, mountain towns and cities generally lean casual. Even if you're planning to go to a nice dinner in Salt Lake or Park City, you can usually get away with jeans and a nice top. Versatile clothes that can transition from an activity like light hiking to après drinks to dinner are popular out West as well.

From spring through fall, it's usually best practice to bring a raincoat into the mountains. However, Utah is much less rainy than many of its neighboring Rocky Mountain West states, like Colorado and Montana.

In terms of outdoor activities, most rental shops rent out equipment (including bikes, skis, poles, helmets, boots, and more), but not the clothing suitable for these activities. It's worth buying your own ski/snowboard outerwear, bike clothes, etc., even if it's just secondhand.

TOURIST INFORMATION

Many of the tourist centers for cities in the Wasatch hold limited hours, so consider calling in advance.

The **Salt Lake City Visitors Center** (90 S. West Temple, 801/534-4900, www. visitsaltlake.com, 9am-5pm daily) is located downtown near the Salt Palace Convention Center.

The **Park City Visitors Office** (1794 Olympic Pkwy., 435/658-9616, www. visitparkcity.com, 9am-6pm daily) is located in an office building in Kimball Junction.

The **Heber Valley Visitor Center** (475 N. Main St., Heber, 435/654-3666, www. gohebervalley.com, 9am-5pm Mon.-Fri.) is located in downtown Heber.

The **Ogden Visitor's Center** (2411 Kiesel Ave. #401, 866/867-8824, www.visitogden. com, 9am-5pm Mon.-Fri.) is located in downtown Ogden.

For public lands, stop by the nearest U.S. Forest Service ranger district office or state park office for complimentary maps and advice, as well as guides and other resources available for purchase.

COMMUNICATIONS

Nearly all hotels and most coffee shops offer free Wi-Fi. There are a few public areas as well where you can connect to Wi-Fi, such as public libraries and the airport.

Cell phone signals are strong within city and town limits, but often diminish or drop altogether on the roads in between—plan accordingly. You'll find spotty or no service the farther into nature you venture. For example, there is limited service in the Cottonwood Canyons, and very little cell service throughout the Uintas.

STATE LAWS
Alcohol

Utah is saddled with strict and convoluted liquor laws (https://abc.utah.gov/laws). If you want to get a drink at an establishment licensed as a restaurant, for example, you'll be required to order food (even if only an

appetizer). Conversely, if you want to get a drink at an establishment licensed as a bar (including most of the state's breweries), everyone in your party must be 21 and over—no babies or kids allowed.

Happy hour is banned in the state, and so are beverages on draught with an alcohol content exceeding 3.2 percent; the solution is to order by can or bottle. There are also restrictions regarding how much liquor can be poured into a cocktail and what time alcoholic beverages can be served and sold. Alcohol laws have become progressively laxer over time, and some anticipate that laws will continue to loosen in the future.

Tobacco

In the state of Utah, smoking is prohibited inside all publicly accessible indoor spaces and public buildings. Smokers must stay 25 feet (7.6 m) from building entrances, exits, and windows.

Marijuana

While medical marijuana was legalized by voters in 2018, the state has a long way to go in terms of instituting a functional system. A medical marijuana card is also extremely difficult to obtain.

INTERNATIONAL TRAVELERS
Entering the United States

To enter the United States, a tourist is required to have a passport and visa, except for Canada, Bermuda, and countries eligible for the Visa Waiver Program (https://travel.state.gov). To obtain a visa, usually you'll need to visit the U.S. embassy in your home country at least a few weeks prior. You can check the estimated wait time for a visa for a citizen of your country online.

Customs

Individuals 21 and over can import one liter of duty-free alcohol and up to $100 in gifts tax-free. If the value of the gifts—whether for yourself or others—exceeds $100, you'll have to pay duty on the items. Anything that you purchased, inherited, bought in a duty-free shop, or intend to sell should also be declared. You also cannot import meat, produce, or invasive species for obvious reasons. International travelers have to declare cash amounting to over $10,000.

Money

Most businesses in Utah accept major credit and debit cards. In fact, some businesses are increasingly moving to credit card only. You can change currency at major banks, which usually keep standard office hours on weekdays, with limited hours on Saturdays. Banks are typically closed on Sundays and national holidays. However, you can find 24-hour ATMs in bank lobbies, grocery stores, and often hotels, with cash withdrawals available for a small convenience fee.

Driving

Except for residents of Canada, visitors to the United States must bring a driving permit or license from their home country, and most states require foreigners to also obtain an International Driving Permit in their home country prior to departure (https://usa.gov/visitors-driving). In the United States, most rental cars have automatic transmission. The driver sits on the left side of the car and drives on the right side of the road.

ACCESS FOR TRAVELERS WITH DISABILITIES

From Salt Lake City International Airport, you can rent an accessible van through **Wheelchair Getaways** (888/433-1891, www.accessiblevans.com). The Utah Transportation Authority (UTA; www.rideuta.com) TRAX light rail and bus systems also accommodate people with disabilities, including a Paratransit Service for those who cannot be accommodated by standard service.

A great local resource for people with disabilities is the Park City-based **National Ability Center** (435/649-3991, https://

discovernac.org), which helps people of all abilities participate in sports and the outdoors through adaptive adventures, including skiing, rock climbing, horseback riding, biking, and water sports.

While national forests and wilderness areas are often difficult to access for some people with disabilities, Utah has many scenic drives with overlooks as well as state parks with accessible features, such as wheelchair-accessible campgrounds, bathrooms, and boating access; see the **state parks** website (https://stateparks.utah.gov/accessibility) for more information.

TRAVELING WITH CHILDREN

Utah is generally a very family-friendly state. When exploring outdoors, always keep a close eye on kids, since wildlife, cliffs with steep drops, or other hazards could lie just around the corner. Be especially wary of dehydration, altitude sickness, and sunburns with kids—all three of these conditions are much more likely to occur in a high-altitude, dry state like Utah. And as mentioned above, establishments licensed as bars (including breweries) do not allow anyone under the age of 21 to enter the premises.

WOMEN TRAVELING ALONE

In general, there are no issues for solo female travelers unique to Utah or the Wasatch. I have walked the city alone at night, camped solo, and hiked or biked alone on long trails many times and never felt threatened. Utah and Salt Lake City crime rates are generally low and on the decline. If you do head out into the backcountry or wilderness alone, bringing along a dog or the means to protect yourself may at least provide more peace of mind.

SENIOR TRAVELERS

If you're over 60 years of age, keep an ID on you to take advantage of discounts at most national and state-owned public lands with fees and at many businesses. **EngAGE Utah** (www.engageutah.org) is a nonprofit that runs programs, events, and resources for the senior population in the state.

LGBTQ+ TRAVELERS

In spite of the Church of Jesus Christ of Latter-day Saints' stance on homosexuality and its notorious gay conversion therapy, Salt Lake City was once named Gayest City in America and is known for having a strong LGBTQ+ community. Throughout June, you'll see rainbow flags hanging in many business windows downtown, in the 9th and 9th district, in the Avenues, and throughout the city. LGBTQ+ travelers should have no trouble traveling through the Wasatch, but if you feel less than welcome anywhere, it might be in the more rural areas of the state.

The **Utah Pride Center** (1380 Main St., Salt Lake City, 801/539-8800, www. utahpridecenter.org) maintains a calendar of LGBTQ+ community events—some of which it hosts, including **Pride Fest** in June—and lists local resources and support services. **Q Pages** (www.qpages.com) offers a directory of Utah businesses (including accommodations and dining options) that serve as allies to the LGBTQ+ community. *Q Salt Lake* Magazine (www.qsaltlake.com) covers LGBTQ+ news and stories in Utah.

Utah Gay Ski Week (www.utahgay skiweek.com) invites LGBTQ+ skiers and riders to hit the slopes of Park City Mountain Resort for a week in late February or early March, with special ski ticket deals and accommodation rates.

TRAVELERS OF COLOR

The primary fact to be aware of if you're a traveler of color is that Utah is very homogenous. Salt Lake County is the most diverse in the state, yet still dominated by white people (over 87 percent). While demographics are changing, it's impossible not to be struck by the lack of diversity in Salt Lake City and beyond, especially if you're coming from a major U.S. city. That said, Utahns of all backgrounds tend to be welcoming and friendly to all, in spite of any differences.

The **NAACP Salt Lake Branch** (www. naacp-saltlakebranch.org) provides resources and hosts occasional events that promote equality for minorities and fight prejudice. **Black Lives Matter Utah** (www. blacklivesmatterutah.com), the local chapter of the global civil rights movement, and the **Utah Black Chamber** (www.blackchamber. com), an organization that works to enhance the economic development of the state's minority population, both maintain directories of Black-owned businesses in Utah.

Recreation

PUBLIC LANDS

Over 75 percent of Utah's land is publicly owned, which positions it third in the United States in terms of public land composition, right on the tails of Nevada and Alaska. However, large chunks of this public land are found in the southern half of the state, where mountains and forests give way to desert filled with red rock. Still, the Wasatch area in the upper half of the state enjoys significant public land access, from a vast national forest filled with wilderness areas to several state parks.

Whenever you head into public lands, remember to follow the seven **Leave No Trace** principles (www.lnt.org) to minimize your impact on the outdoors: (1) Plan ahead; (2) stay on trails and camp on durable surfaces at least 200 feet from water bodies; (3) pack out your waste and deal with human waste responsibly; (4) leave nature alone (e.g., don't pick the flowers); (5) only have a fire in a ring/pit and always put it out; (6) respect wildlife; and (7) respect your fellow explorers.

National Forest

The Wasatch is home to one sprawling national forest that began as three separate yet
contiguous forests. Over time, the government merged these forests to create one: the
Uinta-Wasatch-Cache National Forest
(www.fs.usda.gov/uwcnf), over two million
glorious acres of Douglas fir, Engelmann
spruce, Rocky Mountain juniper, families of
aspen, and many more species of tree. Since
ecosystems tend to ignore political borders,
this forest spills into Idaho and Wyoming,
though over 80 percent of it stretches across
northern Utah, encompassing the Uinta and
Wasatch Mountains.

The Uinta-Wasatch-Cache National Forest
is managed through seven ranger districts; for
the region covered herein, the relevant offices
include Salt Lake, Heber-Kamas, and Ogden.
The national forest is filled with trails and developed and dispersed campsites. Dispersed
camping possibilities are numerous, and
backpacking opportunities are near limitless.
The developed campsites and some parking
areas charge fees—get the details in each individual chapter or check with the relevant
ranger district.

Wilderness

Within the Uinta-Wasatch-Cache National
Forest are seven wilderness areas that represent about a quarter of the total forest (or over
300,000 acres), including the **High Uintas
Wilderness,** accessible via the Mirror Lake
Scenic Byway from Kamas, as well as the
Twin Peaks and **Lone Peak Wilderness
areas** found down Big and Little Cottonwood
Canyons. These are some of the favorite backpacking destinations for locals and tourists
alike.

BLM

Most of Utah's ample Bureau of Land
Management acreage lies to the south. There
are only very small parcels of BLM land in the
Wasatch region, not covered in this guide.

State Parks

Utah has over 40 state parks, about a quarter of
which are located in the Wasatch. Many of these
state parks exist to manage the recreational opportunities surrounding the state's **reservoirs,**
including **Jordanelle, Rockport,** and **Deer
Creek.** The Great Salt Lake is also largely managed by the state via its Department of Natural
Resources at the **Great Salt Lake State Park**
and **Antelope Island State Park.** Most
state parks charge fees that vary depending on
whether you're camping or just visiting for the
day, and what type of vehicle you arrive in; see
the **state parks** website (https://stateparks.
utah.gov) for more information.

National Parks

There are no national parks in the Wasatch.
Utah's "Mighty Five," as they've been branded,
are located in southern Utah (Zion, Bryce,
Capitol Reef, Canyonlands, and Arches).

SKIING AND SNOWBOARDING

Utah is known as one of the best ski destinations in the country, with 10 diverse resorts and an average of 500 inches (12.7 m)
of snowfall a year. Park City is home to the
most expensive skiing, including the largest
resort in Utah and North America—**Park City
Mountain**—as well as **Deer Valley,** the posh-
est by reputation. Up Big Cottonwood Canyon
lie **Brighton** and **Solitude,** and over in Little
Cottonwood Canyon are the connected resorts
of **Snowbird** and **Alta.** The southernmost ski
resort in the region is **Sundance** at Robert
Redford's resort in the Wasatch Back. And in
the northern part of the Wasatch lies some of
the most affordable skiing in the region just
outside Ogden: **Snowbasin, Nordic Valley,**
and **Powder Mountain.** Both Deer Valley
and Alta do not permit snowboarders.

HIKING

The Wasatch is a paradise for hikers and backpackers, with dozens of mountains to summit

and endless miles of trails to explore. With a little grit—and perhaps a pair of snowshoes—hiking is possible year-round in the region, though most popular in summer, when the wildflowers are abloom, or in early fall, when the temperatures are delightful and the foliage even more so. With plenty of days of sunshine, there are more beautiful days for hiking than not.

BIKING

Northern Utah is a mountain and road biking mecca, with the first mountain bike trail system rated gold by the International Mountain Bike Association, and no shortage of scenic rural highways and country roads to pedal over. **Park City** in particular is reputed to be a hub of Olympians and competitive athletes in training, so don't be surprised to be consistently outclassed by a spandex-wearing, trail-crushing local. Just consider yourself inspired!

CLIMBING

While most of the state's best climbing lies farther south in Moab and Indian Creek, there is great rock climbing in the Wasatch, most of which is found in the **Cottonwood Canyons.** Little Cottonwood Canyon in particular is a destination for local climbers. There is also some ice climbing to be found in the Cottonwoods, and a few frozen waterfalls in the Uintas, though the approach to the base of these climbs is a journey in and of itself.

BOATING AND FISHING

The Wasatch is home to several different reservoirs where boating, fishing, and other water sports are popular. Most of the major **reservoirs—Jordanelle, Rockport, Deer Creek**—have marinas that rent equipment. In Utah, individuals 18 years of age and older can operate a personal watercraft without any sort of education, supervision, or certification requirements. **Educational course requirements** apply to boat operators younger than 18 years old; see www.boat-ed.com/utah for more information.

In these bodies of water, some of the most common local fish include Pacific salmon, as well as various species of trout, including cutthroat and rainbow. **Licenses** for fishing—as well as hunting—are available for purchase over the phone, online, and in various stores like grocery stores, Walmarts, and sporting goods stores; see the **Utah Division of Wildlife Resources** website (https://wildlife.utah.gov) for more information. A fishing license is required for individuals ages 18 years and older, and costs $75 for a year. Hunting licenses are usually obtained via seasonal lottery.

GOLF

The Wasatch is a great place to golf, with moderate summertime temperatures at many courses, and a long golfing season for others. Many of the courses are quite hilly and offer gorgeous backdrops to your 18 holes. Public and private golf resorts exist throughout Salt Lake City, Park City, Heber, Midway, and Ogden. Some courses are country clubs and accessible only via membership or a relationship with a member, but there are plenty of options for the unconnected visitor.

CAMPING

With hundreds of developed national and state campgrounds, numerous dispersed camping options in the Uinta-Wasatch-Cache National Forest, and plenty of backpacking in the hundreds of thousands of acres of wilderness, the Wasatch area is a camping mecca. From camping along the shores of a reservoir, to sites that allow you to wake to the sound of the rushing Provo River, the nights under the stars here are also beautiful. Developed campgrounds typically have amenities and charge fees, while dispersed overland camping and backpacking is usually free.

About half the campgrounds in the area begin to open in mid-May, with the remainder at higher elevations opening by early July. The majority of campgrounds in the area stay open through September. During the summer, if you can make reservations in advance, you should do so, or plan on getting to your destination early. Reservations for most federally and state managed campgrounds can be made through the **National**

Recreation Reservation Service (877/444-6777, www.recreation.gov); it usually opens up most campground reservations 240 days in advance.

Health and Safety

For emergencies, dial 911 or go to the nearest 24-hour hospital emergency room. Always carry your insurance card and ID on you, no matter where you're traveling in the region.

AIR QUALITY

Many new residents and visitors are surprised to discover that such a beautiful state suffers from such poor air quality. Salt Lake City ranks 14th for ozone pollution in the United States and eighth for seasonal particle pollution. While Salt Lake City is generally worst in the state, a dozen counties in northern Utah suffer from dangerous levels of particle pollution and ground-level ozone pollution, due to vehicles, industries like power plants, and wood- and coal-burning stoves.

Here in Utah, we like to refer to the problem as "The Inversion," as if it's our topography, not our habits, that are to blame for our bad air. What the locals are referring to is Salt Lake City's position in a valley surrounded by the Wasatch and Oquirrh Mountains. In the winter, this topographic bowl traps cold air and pollutants. During inversions, for days or even weeks on end, the skies turn a smoggy gray, you can barely see the sun, and inhaling the air is equivalent to smoking a pack of cigarettes a day. While we can't control our geography, we can control the pollutants we send into the air, which is something that the state government is reticent to do in a meaningful way.

Luckily for the visitor, if an inversion strikes during your visit, all you have to do is seek higher ground. Drive up into the Cottonwoods or to Park City to rise above the smog. The same is true in the summer, which doesn't see inversions, but does see air quality

days bad enough that the experts recommend you stay inside. Simply seek higher elevation or stay inside.

To find out what the air is doing in the Salt Lake City area before or during your visit, you can check the air forecast on the **Utah Air Quality** website (https://air.utah.gov), which documents both particle and ground-level ozone pollution and makes recommendations accordingly. Most local TV and radio stations also report the forecast. Usually, voluntary action is instituted, but occasionally the government imposes mandatory measures (e.g., carpooling and refraining from burning wood indoors or out).

ALTITUDE SICKNESS

Altitude sickness is a common and usually mild affliction that strikes visitors to high-altitude regions. Usually, symptoms only manifest in high altitude, which is defined as over 8,000 feet (2,438 m). Symptoms usually strike within 12-24 hours of arriving at high altitude, and include dizziness, fatigue, loss of appetite, trouble sleeping, and lethargy. The best remedy is usually to seek lower ground. If symptoms become severe—like affected motor functions, severe headache, nausea, or confusion—reduce altitude immediately and seek medical help.

In the Wasatch, most of the cities and towns sit low enough that you're unlikely to experience altitude sickness in an urban environment. The trouble begins when you head into the mountains, whether it's the Uintas or the Wasatch. Therefore, give yourself a few days to acclimate in town before scrambling up a 12,000-foot (3,658-m) peak. And if you do experience altitude sickness while hiking up a mountain, always favor your own health over your summit bid by turning back for lower ground.

HYPOTHERMIA

Hypothermia is a year-round threat in the mountains that occurs when someone loses heat more quickly than they can generate it. The initial signs of shivering and slurred speech can give way to unconsciousness and death. Worst of all, the sufferer is not usually aware that they're hypothermic, because symptoms emerge slowly. To prevent hypothermia, use synthetic insulation and fabrics, and always pack rainwear and layers appropriate for the forecast and adventure at hand. If hypothermia is suspected, change out of wet clothes, layer up, and seek medical attention immediately.

HEAT EXHAUSTION

Heat exhaustion manifests with profuse sweating and a quickened heartbeat from a body overheating. Other symptoms include heat cramps, dizziness, nausea, and cool moist skin. In the Wasatch, it often results from setting out on an exposed trail in the heat of the day (e.g., high noon) and often without the necessary sun protection and water resources. If you think you're suffering from heat exhaustion, rest in the shade to cool down and drink cold water.

WILDERNESS TRAVEL

Aldo Leopold got it right: "In wildness is the salvation of the world." But it also holds the potential termination of your own life if you're not careful. Every summer in the Uintas, missing person flyers hang at parking lot trailheads. With hundreds of thousands of acres, it's easy to become lost, or for a simple sleight of step to become lethal.

If possible, always travel with someone else in the wilderness, and always bring a first-aid kit, basic survival kit, and navigation system. And that fresh creek water might look refreshing, but it may carry diseases or parasites like *Giardia lamblia*. Always pack in your own water or water treatment system. For bigger backcountry excursions, a satellite messaging device can save your life, since much of the Wasatch backcountry lacks cell phone reception. And if you do travel alone, always tell someone exactly where you're going and when you expect to return, so that if you don't, they can alert local search and rescue crews.

In wintry conditions, don't go into the backcountry unless you're educated about snow safety and rescue. Before heading out, check avalanche conditions at the **Utah Avalanche Center** (https://utahavalanchecenter.org), and always carry a shovel, beacon, and probe. If you're not knowledgeable about avalanche safety, the best bet is to go with a guided service.

WILDLIFE

Before the Wasatch was home to any settlers or humans, it was home to wildlife, and still is. Respect the local animal populations both for their sake and yours. The primary animals you should be concerned about in the area for your own safety include moose, rattlesnakes, bears, and mountain lions (also called cougars), and more or less in that order.

Generally speaking, keep your distance, staying at least 300 feet from wildlife. Stay on trails, which wildlife tend to avoid. Make noise as you travel (even if you're alone) to alert wildlife that you're there, so you don't surprise, say, a mama bear and her cubs. Never try to approach wildlife to take a selfie, and never ever try to feed wildlife of any kind. Finally, avoid running away from wildlife—you'll never outrun a bear, mountain lion, or moose, and running can trigger an attack response.

While **moose** look sort of friendly in an aloof way, they're actually the most aggressive animal you can encounter in the area. You're most likely to encounter a moose in forested areas or near water at higher elevations. If you see a moose, speak softly and begin backing away slowly. If the moose looks like it might attack—raised hair, grunting, kicking feet—seek cover behind a tree, boulder, car, or anything you can use to separate you and the moose. If it attacks, play dead and protect your internal organs.

Rattlesnakes are not an issue once you're as high as Park City, but if you're hiking in the foothills of Salt Lake, they're a real concern. If you see or hear a rattlesnake, stop moving immediately. If you can't see it, try to determine where it is. Slowly back away from the snake, holding a trekking pole or other object in front of you. Never try to remove a snake from the trail or throw rocks at a snake. If you're bit, you'll need to seek medical help immediately for antivenin.

The Wasatch has no grizzly bears left, but plenty of **black bears,** which are often reputed to be cowards! But these cowards can still take your life. Avoid encounters in the first place by always properly storing your food at a campsite, hung high in a tree or sequestered in a bear-safe container. If you do encounter a bear, face it and try to look and sound as big as possible, holding up whatever you can to appear even larger. If you have bear spray, use it if the bear starts to approach. If you don't have bear spray, and the bear is charging, fight back, using whatever you can.

As the saying goes with **mountain lions,** they usually know where you are, but you almost never know where they are. Sightings are rare and cougars do not want to attack you. But if you do come across one, stand your ground and hold eye contact. Slowly back away while speaking loudly and firmly. If you suspect the cougar is going to attack, make yourself look as big as possible and clap your hands. If the cougar attacks, try to fight back however you can.

In any of these cases, if you have small children with you, slowly pick them up. And dogs—especially if unleashed—can also be endangered. Prevent your dog from attempting to fight any of the above predators by keeping it leashed. Rattlesnakes are perhaps the biggest threat to a dog, which will often be curious about the snake. In rattlesnake terrain, always keep your dog leashed and on-trail.

Finally, remembering what to do when encountering which type of animal can be difficult. If you're planning to travel into the backcountry, consider creating a cheat sheet for yourself so you recall how to respond.

SPORTING ACCIDENTS

If you're going out into national forest areas during hunting season, wear Day-Glo orange to be easily visible to others. Big game season in Utah runs mid-August-early November, while small game season stretches through February. Hunters are usually most active in the pre-dawn and early morning hours of the day.

THEFT

Crime is generally low in Utah. For the purposes of the Wasatch traveler, bikes are often stolen within the city and should always be locked up. Trailheads are also a common site of theft. Don't leave valuables in your car at the trailhead; if you must leave things in the car, try to obscure them from view.

Resources

Suggested Reading

Cuch, Forrest. *History of Utah's American Indians*. Salt Lake City: Utah State Division of Indian Affairs, 2003. A look into the tribes of Utah, including their history, politics, religion, and culture by an Indigenous author writing for the Utah Division of Indian Affairs and the Utah State Historical Society.

Gessner, David. *All the Wild That Remains*. New York City: W.W. Norton & Company, 2016. American essayist David Gessner takes a tour through Utah to learn more about his literary heroes who called the state home—Edward Abbey and Wallace Stegner—and the issues they wrote about, from environmental justice to wilderness.

Krakauer, Jon. *Under the Banner of Heaven*. London: Anchor, 2004. Taking a break from his usual topic of the mountains, celebrated writer Jon Krakauer investigates fundamentalist and polygamist Mormon communities, and the darker incidents that lie in their past.

McLean, Andrew. *The Chuting Gallery: A Guide to Steep Skiing in the Wasatch Mountains*. Paradise: Paw Prints Press, 1998. With a foreword by the late climber Alex Lowe, this is the essential guide to ski mountaineering in the Wasatch, with the beta on 90 chutes, primarily in the Cottonwood Canyons.

Parker, Trey, Robert Lopez, and Matt Stone. *The Book of Mormon Script Book: The Complete Book and Lyrics of the Broadway Musical*. New York City: Newmarket Press, 2011. If you have yet to see the Broadway musical (or just love it to pieces), devour the full script of *The Book of Mormon* for a more comical take on the local religion.

Prince, Gregory, and Robert Wright. *David O. McKay and the Rise of Modern Mormonism*. Salt Lake City: University of Utah Press, 2005. This work by Mormon scholars examines how former church president David O. McKay tripled membership during his tenure in the mid-20th century, catapulting the religion into a dominant one globally. The book uses many of McKay's own writings to develop its account.

Stegner, Wallace. *Mormon Country*. Lincoln: University of Nebraska Press, 2003. Environmental writer and historian Wallace Stegner documents how the Mormons settled what was considered by most (aside from the Indigenous people already there) to be inhospitable lands.

Stone, Eileen Hallet. *Hidden History of Utah*. Mount Pleasant: Hidden History Press, 2013. A former *Salt Lake Tribune* columnist delivers minority reports from Utah's past, examining how non-Mormon and often immigrant communities and individuals shaped the state's past and future.

The Utah Society for Environmental Education. *A Guide to the Mirror Lake Scenic*

Byway. Salt Lake City. If you plan to spend time in the Uintas via Kamas, this pivotal guide will alert you to the scenic stops, trails, campgrounds, and more to the precise mile marker along the Mirror Lake Scenic Byway. This guide is available for purchase with cash or check only at the Heber-Kamas Ranger District (50 E. Center St., Kamas, 435/783-4338, 8am-4:30pm Mon.-Fri. year-round, also open 8am-4:30pm Sat. Memorial Day-Labor Day).

Twain, Mark. *Roughing It.* Chicago: Sun-Times Media Group, 1872. This semi-autobiographical travelogue includes Twain's journey through Utah, including observations about the Great Salt Lake, encounters with Brigham Young, and sips of "the Mormon refresher" known as valley tan, which modern distillery High West has since revived.

Williams, Terry Tempest. *Refuge: An Unnatural History of Family and Place.* New York City: Pantheon, 1992. Award-winning local Utah and Mormon writer Terry Tempest Williams poetically compares the health effects on her family of nearby nuclear testing in Nevada to the struggles faced by bird communities inhabiting the Great Salt Lake.

Internet Resources

Federal Campsite Reservations
www.recreation.gov
Where you can search for and make reservations for campgrounds inside national forests.

Mountain Bike Project
www.mtbproject.com
Online wiki with beta on mountain biking trails and popular routes. Most of the trails here are under "Northern Utah" and "Salt Lake City and Wasatch Front."

Mountain Project
www.mountainproject.com
Online wiki with beta on climbing areas and routes. Navigate to "Wasatch Range" or "Uinta Mountains" under "Utah" for crags and boulders in the northern Utah region.

Mountain Trails
www.mountaintrails.org
Park City-based foundation with trail maps, current conditions, and event info.

National Forests
www.fs.usda.gov/uwcnf
U.S. Forest Service site for the Uinta-Wasatch-Cache National Forest with recreation guidelines and maps.

Park City Visitors Center
www.visitparkcity.com
Detailed online resource to the Park City area, including dining, lodging, and an event calendar.

Ride UTA
www.rideuta.com
Routes, schedules, and fare info for the Trax light rail and buses serving the airport, Salt Lake City, Ogden, and travel between Salt Lake City and Park City.

Salt Lake City Visitors Center
www.visitsaltlake.com
Tourist information focused on the capital, including event calendar, lodging and dining, and activities.

Ski Utah
www.skiutah.com
Plot your ski vacation with info on every ski resort in Utah, snow reports, and special deals.

South Summit Trails Foundation
www.southsummittrails.org
Info and maps for trails in Oakley, Kamas, and surrounding areas.

State Parks
https://stateparks.utah.gov
Information about Utah state parks, including many of the Wasatch's reservoirs. This is also where you can make campsite reservations for campgrounds within state parks.

Sundance Film Festival
www.sundance.org
Programs, schedules, and passes for the annual Sundance Film Festival.

Temple Square
www.templesquare.com
Tourist information on the Temple Square attractions, from dining and tours to the Tabernacle Choir performance schedule.

Utah Office of Tourism
www.visitutah.com
A trip planner, activities, and relevant articles for the entire state.

Utah.com
www.utah.com
Statewide travel site with destinations, local outfitters and guides, and deals.

RESOURCES
INTERNET RESOURCES

Index

List of Maps

Photo Credits

All photos by Maya Silver, except:
Title page photo: Kenny Tong, Dreamstime.com; page 3 © Legacyimagesinc, Dreamstime.com; page 6 © (bottom) Charles Knowles, Dreamstime.com; page 7 © (top) Iainhamer, Dreamstime.com; (bottom right) Junko Barker, Dreamstime.com; page 8 © (top) Asterixvs, Dreamstime.com; page 10 © Snowbasin Resort; page 12 © Visit Park City; page 15 © (top) Valentin Armianu, Dreamstime.com; (bottom) Valentin Armianu, Dreamstime.com; page 16 © (top) Michael Gordon, Dreamstime.com; page 17 © Johnny Adolphson, Dreamstime.com; page 20 © (top) Eric Broder Van Dyke, Dreamstime.com; page 22 © (bottom) Spvvkr, Dreamstime.com; page 32 © (bottom) Snowbasin Resort; page 39 © (top) Rick Boland; page 41 © F11photo, Dreamstime.com; page 46 © Bcpix, Dreamstime.com; page 53 © (top left) Eoakden94, Dreamstime.com; (top right) Jeremy Christensen, Dreamstime.com; (bottom) Helena Bilkova, Dreamstime.com; page 56 © (top right) Milosk50, Dreamstime.com; page 65 © (top left) Saltcityphotography, Dreamstime.com; (bottom) Kobby Dagan, Dreamstime.com; page 78 © Christy Rossi Photography/IRC; page 93 © (bottom) Michael Gordon, Dreamstime.com; page 106 © Michael Gordon, Dreamstime.com; page 111 © (bottom) Roman Tiraspolsky, Dreamstime.com; page 116 © (bottom) Visit Park City; page 118 © Deepfrog17, Dreamstime.com; page 121 © Visit Park City; page 122 © Sierra Prothers; page 125 © Victoria Wickline; page 133 © Wasatch Brew Pub; page 135 © (top right) Visit Park City; (bottom) Visit Park City; page 137 © (top) Visit Park City; (bottom) Ritu Jethani, Dreamstime.com; page 143 © (top left) Visit Park City; page 146 © (top left) Visit Park City; page 159 © (top left) Matt Crawley; page 164 © (top left) Alex Moliski; page 176 © (top right) Alex Moliski; page 179 © (bottom) Chris Segal; page 181 © Matt Crawley; page 184 © Snowbasin Resort; page 194 © (top) Snowbasin Resort; page 206 © Aquamarine4, Dreamstime.com; page 207 © (top left) Bruce Jenkins, Dreamstime.com; page 210 © Wilco Speksnijder, Dreamstime.com; page 212 © (top) Sherylp3, Dreamstime.com; page 220 © Johnny Adolphson, Dreamstime.com; page 221 © (top left) Delstudio, Dreamstime.com; (bottom) Bevanward, Dreamstime.com; page 224 © Aaron Hinckley, Dreamstime.com; page 225 © (top) Mkopka, Dreamstime.com; (bottom) Alex Moliski; page 240 © (top right) Nicholas Benson, Dreamstime.com; (bottom) Visit Park City; page 278 © (bottom) Victoria Wickline

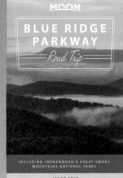

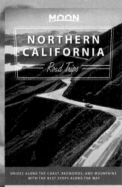

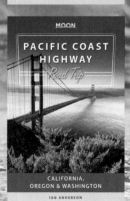

MOON

PACIFIC NORTHWEST
Road Trip

SEATTLE, VANCOUVER, VICTORIA,
THE OLYMPIC PENINSULA, PORTLAND,
THE OREGON COAST & MOUNT RAINIER

ALLISON WILLIAMS

MOON

ROUTE 66
Road Trip

JESSICA DUNHAM

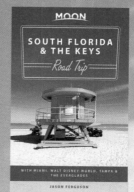

MOON

SOUTH FLORIDA
& THE KEYS
Road Trip

WITH MIAMI, WALT DISNEY WORLD, TAMPA &
THE EVERGLADES

JASON FERGUSON

MOON

SOUTHERN
CALIFORNIA
Road Trips

DRIVES ALONG THE BEACHES, MOUNTAINS, AND DESERTS
WITH THE BEST STOPS ALONG THE WAY

IAN ANDERSON

MOON

SOUTHWEST
Road Trip

LAS VEGAS, ZION & BRYCE, MONUMENT VALLEY,
SANTA FE & TAOS, AND THE GRAND CANYON

TIM HULL

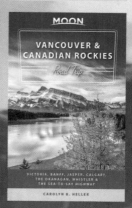

MOON

VANCOUVER &
CANADIAN ROCKIES
Road Trip

VICTORIA, BANFF, JASPER, CALGARY,
THE OKANAGAN, WHISTLER &
THE SEA-TO-SKY HIGHWAY

CAROLYN B. HELLER

MOON

YELLOWSTONE TO
GLACIER NATIONAL
PARK
Road Trip

JACKSON HOLE, CODY, THE GRAND TETONS
& THE ROCKY MOUNTAIN FRONT

CARTER G. WALKER

MOON

the
OPEN
ROAD

50 BEST
ROAD TRIPS
in the USA

From Weekend Getaways
to Cross-Country Adventures

JESSICA DUNHAM

MOON

Road Trip
USA

25TH ANNIVERSARY EDITION

CROSS-COUNTRY ADVENTURES ON
AMERICA'S TWO-LANE HIGHWAYS

Jamie Jensen

FIND YOUR ADVENTURE

MOON

ACADIA
NATIONAL PARK

HILARY NANGLE

MOON

ARCHES &
CANYONLANDS
NATIONAL PARKS

W. C. McRAE & JUDY JEWELL

MOON

BANFF
NATIONAL
PARK

HIKE·CAMP
SEE WILDLIFE

ANDREW HEMPSTEAD

MOON

DEATH VALLEY
NATIONAL PARK

JENNA BLOUGH

MOON

GLACIER
NATIONAL PARK

HIKING · CAMPING
LAKES & PEAKS

BECKY LOMAX

MOON

GRAND
CANYON

HIKE·CAMP
RAFT THE
COLORADO RIVER

TIM HULL

MOON

GREAT SMOKY
MOUNTAINS
NATIONAL PARK

HIKING · CAMPING
SCENIC DRIVES

JASON FRYE

MOON

JOSHUA TREE
& PALM SPRINGS

JENNA BLOUGH

MOON

MOUNT RUSHMORE
& THE BLACK HILLS

LAURAL A. BIDWELL

MOON

ROCKY
MOUNTAIN
NATIONAL PARK

HIKE·CAMP
SEE WILDLIFE

ERIK ENGLISH

MOON

SEQUOIA &
KINGS CANYON

HIKE·CAMP
SEE REDWOODS

LEIGH BERNACCHI

MOON

YELLOWSTONE
& GRAND TETON

HIKE, CAMP
SEE WILDLIFE

BECKY LOMAX

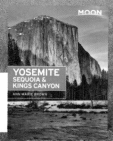

MOON

YOSEMITE
SEQUOIA &
KINGS CANYON

ANN MARIE BROWN

MOON

ZION &
BRYCE

W. C. McRAE & JUDY JEWELL

In these books:

- Full coverage of gateway cities and towns
- Itineraries from one day to multiple weeks
- Advice on where to stay (or camp) in and around the parks

Trips to Remember

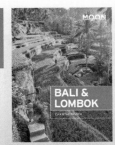

BALI & LOMBOK
CHANTAE REDEN

ECUADOR
& THE GALÁPAGOS ISLANDS
BETHANY PITTS

GREEK ISLANDS & ATHENS
SARAH SOULI

ICELAND
JENNA GOTTLIEB

TRIP OF A LIFETIME
MACHU PICCHU
MACHU PICCHU, CUSCO & THE INCA TRAIL
RYAN DUBÉ

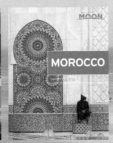

MOROCCO
LUCAS PETERS

NEW ZEALAND
JAMIE CHRISTIAN DESPLACES

OAXACA
ERIN COPELAND

TRIP OF A LIFETIME
PATAGONIA
INCLUDING THE FALKLAND ISLANDS
WAYNE BERNHARDSON

PRAGUE, VIENNA & BUDAPEST
JENNIFER D. WALKER
& AUDREY SCALLON

ROME, FLORENCE & VENICE
ALEXEI J. COHEN

Epic Adventure

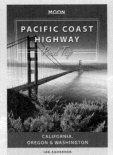

PACIFIC COAST HIGHWAY
Road Trip
CALIFORNIA, OREGON & WASHINGTON
IAN ANDERSON

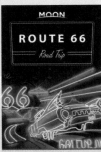

ROUTE 66
Road Trip
JESSICA DUNHAM

YELLOWSTONE TO GLACIER NATIONAL PARK
Road Trip
JACKSON HOLE, CODY, THE GRAND TETONS
& THE ROCKY MOUNTAIN FRONT
CARTER G. WALKER

MOON

AMALFI COAST

With Capri, Naples & Pompeii

LAURA THAYER

MOON

ARUBA

MOON

BAHAMAS

MARIAN CARINE NOYLE

Beachy Getaways

MOON.COM
@MOONGUIDES

MOON

BAJA

JENNIFER KRAMER

MOON

BELIZE

LEBAWIT LILY GIRMA

MOON

BERMUDA

ROSEMARY JONES

MOON

COSTA RICA

MOON

DOMINICAN REPUBLIC

LEBAWIT LILY GIRMA

MOON

FIJI

MOON

FLORIDA KEYS

With Miami & The Everglades

JOSHUA LAWRENCE KINSER

MOON

FRENCH RIVIERA:
NICE, CANNES, MONACO & ST-TROPEZ

JON BRYANT

MOON

JAMAICA

MOON

MAUI

With Molokai & Lanai

GREG ARCHILA

MOON

PUERTO RICO

SUZANNE VAN ATTEN

MOON

PUERTO VALLARTA

With Sayulita, the Riviera Nayarit & Tlaquepaque

MADELINE MILNE

Get inspired for your next adventure

Follow @**moonguides** on Instagram or subscribe to our newsletter at **moon.com**

#TravelWithMoon

MAP SYMBOLS

▤	Expressway	○	City/Town	✕	Airport	⚓	Golf Course
	Primary Road	◉	State Capital	✕	Airfield	Ⓟ	Parking Area
	Secondary Road	✹	National Capital	▲	Mountain	▰	Archaeological Site
	Unpaved Road	✪	Highlight	✦	Unique Natural Feature	▮	Church
	Trail	★	Point of Interest			▣	Gas Station
	Ferry	•	Accommodation	⟅	Waterfall	⬭	Glacier
	Railroad	▼	Restaurant/Bar	▲	Park	▨	Mangrove
	Pedestrian Walkway	▪	Other Location	TH	Trailhead	◿	Reef
	Stairs	∧	Campground	⛷	Skiing Area	⬓	Swamp

CONVERSION TABLES

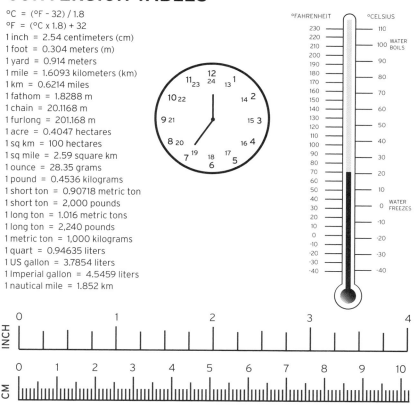

°C = (°F - 32) / 1.8
°F = (°C x 1.8) + 32
1 inch = 2.54 centimeters (cm)
1 foot = 0.304 meters (m)
1 yard = 0.914 meters
1 mile = 1.6093 kilometers (km)
1 km = 0.6214 miles
1 fathom = 1.8288 m
1 chain = 20.1168 m
1 furlong = 201.168 m
1 acre = 0.4047 hectares
1 sq km = 100 hectares
1 sq mile = 2.59 square km
1 ounce = 28.35 grams
1 pound = 0.4536 kilograms
1 short ton = 0.90718 metric ton
1 short ton = 2,000 pounds
1 long ton = 1.016 metric tons
1 long ton = 2,240 pounds
1 metric ton = 1,000 kilograms
1 quart = 0.94635 liters
1 US gallon = 3.7854 liters
1 Imperial gallon = 4.5459 liters
1 nautical mile = 1.852 km

MOON SALT LAKE, PARK CITY & THE WASATCH RANGE
Avalon Travel
Hachette Book Group
1700 Fourth Street
Berkeley, CA 94710, USA
www.moon.com

Editor and Series Manager: Kathryn Ettinger
Acquiring Editor: Nikki Ioakimedes
Copy Editor: Ann Seifert
Graphics Coordinator: Scott Kimball
Production Coordinators: Scott Kimball, Darren Alessi
Cover Design: Faceout Studios, Charles Brock
Moon Logo: Tim McGrath
Map Editor: Kat Bennett
Cartographers: Erin Greb Cartography, Kat Bennett
Indexer: Greg Jewett

ISBN-13: 978-1-64049-835-8

Printing History
1st Edition — January 2021
5 4 3 2 1

Front cover photo: Devil's Castle © Bill Crnkovich, Alamy Stock Photo
Back cover photo: Salt Lake Temple © Gino Rigucci, Dreamstime.com

Printed in China by RR Donnelley

Avalon Travel is a division of Hachette Book Group, Inc. Moon and the Moon logo are trademarks of Hachette Book Group, Inc. All other marks and logos depicted are the property of the original owners.